FROM RESOURCE ALLOCATION TO STRATEGY

From Resource Allocation to Strategy

EDITED BY
Joseph L. Bower
Clark G. Gilbert

OXFORD
UNIVERSITY PRESS

OXFORD

UNIVERSITY PRESS

Great Clarendon Street, Oxford OX2 6DP

Oxford University Press is a department of the University of Oxford.
It furthers the University's objective of excellence in research, scholarship,
and education by publishing worldwide in

Oxford New York

Auckland Cape Town Dar es Salaam Hong Kong Karachi
Kuala Lumpur Madrid Melbourne Mexico City Nairobi
New Delhi Shanghai Taipei Toronto

With offices in

Argentina Austria Brazil Chile Czech Republic France Greece
Guatemala Hungary Italy Japan Poland Portugal Singapore
South Korea Switzerland Thailand Turkey Ukraine Vietnam

Oxford is a registered trade mark of Oxford University Press
in the UK and in certain other countries

Published in the United States
by Oxford University Press Inc., New York

British Library Cataloguing in Publication Data

Data available

Library of Congress Cataloging in Publication Data

Data available

Typeset by SPI Publisher Services, Pondicherry, India
Printed in Great Britain
on acid-free paper by
Antony Rowe Ltd., Chippenham, Wiltshire

ISBN 0-19-927744-3   978-0-19-927744-5

1 3 5 7 9 10 8 6 4 2

To our wives, Nancy and Christine, who remind us with grace that our allocation of time to our families is the surest manifestation of our personal strategies

Preface

It is now commonplace that the work of economists deals with organizations whose behavior is deeply embedded in social phenomena. It is also true, though not nearly as well accepted, that social organization is significantly impacted by economic forces. These ideas were the opening thoughts in a preface to the 1970 book, *Managing the Resource Allocation Process,* and continue to serve as the cornerstone of the work reported here. But from a perspective 35 years later, we believe there has not been enough progress in business research explaining the interaction between organizational and economic forces. Sometimes it seems that researchers in economics and sociology, while acknowledging the importance of the other's subject area, seem committed to see how far one of the disciplines can be stretched to explain phenomena that seem to be the subject of the other, without compromising core assumptions of the initial discipline.

This is particularly odd because professional managers have been building organizations that draw on research from both fields. Even financiers talk about the 'social' dimensions of a merger. The best human relations officers now sit close to top corporate management and help develop leaders who can craft and deliver profitable economic strategies in brutally competitive times. And while there has been some progress in theory—we now have organizational economics and behavioral finance—there is less progress than one would expect given how much we have learned about the way economic enterprise actually works.

In fact, the idea for this book grew out of a frustration with this slow progress. We thought that researchers might be helped if we could bring together a series of studies beginning in 1970 and ending just this year that describe how economic enterprise actually works in dealing with strategic resources and issues. These studies have in common a multidisciplinary approach to the theory that helps explain and provide a basis for improving management behavior. They share methodology as well: all involve careful field observation in multiple settings. The studies from the 1990s have been increasingly complemented by empirical work that confirms both the significance of the exogenous variables considered (such as changes in environmental turbulence, or the existence of discontinuous technology) and the generality of the findings.

These studies point to a clear picture of how large organizations organize to manage their resources. Without exception, these activities are distributed more widely across the organization than is usually imagined. More challenging for both descriptive and normative theories of decision making, activities whose consequences are interdependent will typically proceed independently and simultaneously, posing huge problems where coherence is a central requisite for efficiency and effectiveness.

While it would seem that such complexity would defy the ability to use the research, it has provided the basis for numerous tools. Portfolio strategy systems were developed by consulting companies soon after weaknesses in conventional capital budgeting systems were identified. Incentive systems based on individual and team objectives (MBO systems) were built to deal with the limitations of systems built on structural symmetry. Project finance tools were developed to serve strategies whose financial demands exceeded the capabilities of resource allocation systems built to commit internal cash flow.

But again, with exceptions, management researchers have lagged in recognizing and explaining the progress being made in the field. Somewhat like medicine before modern biochemistry began to provide a fine-grained picture of human functions, scientists raced to catch up and explain what great clinicians could accomplish—in this case, great managers. We feel sure that management researchers can do a better job of catching up with great management practitioners if they take advantage of some of the work reported here. To test that hypothesis, we asked four distinguished discipline-based researchers to consider the implications of the body of the book for their own fields. In their responses, all have developed intriguing questions for future research.

Our hope is that all readers have the same experience. We present a straightforward way of looking at an organization in terms of two processes: one considering the substance of options brought forward, the other involving the choice among options. That distinction is evident in each chapter. We also consider how those choices are made. The first chapters offer a model of the process. The second group of chapters considers how that process breaks down. The third section considers different approaches to fixing those breakdowns, and the fourth section examines the role top management plays in dealing with these issues in very demanding environments, ranging from high technology to globalization.

If our hope is fulfilled, you will become intrigued and find ways of probing deeper into the dilemmas reported.

J.L.B.
C.G.G.

Acknowledgements

The research stream that has led to *From Resource Allocation to Strategy* commenced at Harvard Business School under the late Dean George P. Baker. He supported a young assistant professor who wanted to spend two years studying one company long before 'ethnographic studies' acquired a certain cachet. Professors Kenneth Andrews and Roland Christensen were what this book calls the 'integrating level managers', investing their credibility as supervisors in backing the idea. Since then, Deans John McArthur and Kim Clark have continued to support faculty engaged in what has come to be called process research. We begin this acknowledgement with sincere thanks for their support.

More recently, this process has played out for another young assistant professor who felt that this research was still not well understood by many of our colleagues in the field of strategy. Thus, we extend thanks to Harvard Business School research director V. Kasturi Rangan, who heard passion from a young scholar, saw the potential, and lent his credibility in backing this project when many others felt it was too risky and suggested time be invested elsewhere. We also appreciate Teresa Amabile, head of the Entrepreneurial Management Unit at HBS, for her willingness to support this project by providing Clark Gilbert a teaching sabbatical that allowed the focus needed to complete this project—a resource allocation decision that most certainly reflected a strategy of commitment to junior faculty development.

The work of this book was conducted in two forums: thesis and faculty research by individual authors and a series of seminars and workshops conducted during the mid and late 1990s at Harvard Business School. We are indebted to all the faculty who have provided advice and counsel, as well as the many that attended the seminars and workshops. In particular, we want to thank Chris Bartlett, Robert Burgelman, Andrew Campbell, Richard Caves, Clayton Christensen, Yves Doz, Kathleen Eisenhardt, Tom Eisenmann, Richard Foster, Charles Galunic, David Garvin, Michael Goold, the late Sumantra Goshal, Boris Groysberg, Philippe Haspeslagh, Robert Hayes, Rebecca Henderson, Walter Kuemmerle, Daniel Levinthal, Ashish Nanda, Tomoyoshi Noda, Margaret Peteraf, Joel Podolny, Michael Raynor, Michael Roberto, Gabriel Suzlanski, Don Sull, Alva Taylor, Quy Tran, and Andrew van de Ven. We are particularly indebted to the Harvard Business School's Division of Research for its continued support of our research, seminars, and workshops.

In developing *From Research Allocation to Strategy*, we were buoyed by the help and enthusiasm of the chapter authors, in particular those who contributed chapters commenting on the research from the perspective of their discipline. This was true scholarly courtesy, and we want to thank Dan Levinthal, Marjorie Peteraf, Joel Podolny, and John Roberts. We were also helped by numerous faculty who read chapter drafts and made many helpful suggestions. In addition to those listed above, we are grateful to Ben Esty and Jan Rivkin. We appreciate, as well, the cooperation of the *Strategic Management Journal* and *Organization Science* for their permission to reprint Chs. 6, 10, and 13.

Finally, our heartfelt thanks go to Debra Kendall and Tom Cameron for their help in improving the book. Tom provided expert editorial assistance in refining successive drafts of the manuscript. Debra's ongoing devotion to the project and review of the final manuscript made our task easier and the final product clearly better.

Contents

List of Figures

List of Tables

List of Contributors and Affiliations

Joseph L. Bower, Harvard Business School, Harvard University

Clark G. Gilbert, Harvard Business School, Harvard University

Yves Doz, INSEAD

Robert Burgelman, Graduate School of Business, Stanford University

Clayton M. Christensen, Harvard Business School, Harvard University

Donald N. Sull, London Business School

Walter Kuemmerle, Harvard Business School, Harvard University

Tomo Noda, INSEAD

Thomas R. Eisenmann, Harvard Business School, Harvard University

Michael E. Raynor, Deloitte Consulting

John Roberts, Graduate School of Business, Stanford University

Daniel A. Levinthal, Wharton School of Business, University of Pennsylvania

Margaret A. Peteraf, Tuck School of Business, Dartmouth

Joel Podolny, Yale School of Management, Yale University

Part I

Introduction to the Resource Allocation Process

1

Linking Resource Allocation to Strategy

Joseph L. Bower, Yves L. Doz, and Clark G. Gilbert

*Introduction: How the Allocation of Resources at Opel
Determined Strategic Outcomes*

The fall of the Berlin Wall on 9 November 1989 was a watershed
event. Although 400,000 Soviet troops remained in East Germany,
and the economy was completely cut off from the West by separate
laws and a non-convertible currency, it was clear that the economic
tectonic plates were going to shift. The East German market would
open. How should a major multinational manufacturer of consumer
goods respond to events that clearly affected their business in Europe? Conventional thinking about corporate strategy would lead one
to imagine the process of making strategy to begin with the assembly
of a corporate-level task force to study the demand and competitive
conditions in the market that would soon be opening. Some assessment of strengths and weaknesses and opportunities and threats
(SWOT) would follow. This analysis would provide the foundation
for plans to enter the market in a way consistent with the corporation's strategic thinking about the global competitive situation. On
the basis of that analysis, the parts of the organization responsible for
business in Europe or more specifically, West Germany, might be
asked for proposals. To the extent that these proposals would involve
commitment of significant amounts of capital, their projected profitability would be assessed by financial staff and compared with corporate targets or hurdle rates. Strategic choices would be the result of
a managed process of analysis. But consider what actually happened
at Opel, the division of General Motors responsible for auto production and sales in Germany.

Louis R. Hughes, a 40-year-old native of Ohio who did not speak German, had been appointed chairman of the Opel Vorstand (executive board) in April 1989. His previous assignments had been in the finance organization working for his mentor Jack Smith who was now serving as GM's vice-chairman heading up all overseas activities. Hughes's charge was to reduce the bureaucracy at Opel, introduce lean manufacturing, and cope with the German national champion, Volkswagen, which had 22 per cent of the market to Opel's 16 per cent and Ford's 10 per cent. A few days after the Berlin Wall came down, Smith called Hughes and asked him what he was planning to do since he was head of the logical unit of GM to respond. Less than a month after that call, Volkswagen announced a joint venture involving investments of $3–4 billion with East Germany's automobile Kombinat that controlled all automotive production and the major distribution outlets in East Germany. New cars would roll out in four years.

At Opel, East Germany was terra incognita. Before the end of November, a proposal to conduct a market survey of recent émigrés was approved. As well, a decision was taken to build a distribution network based on independent dealers rather than any parts of the existing state-owned sales and service system. The Opel sales organization went to work recruiting and acquiring dealerships. At the same time, Hughes began high-level enquiries that might lead to manufacturing opportunities. Their focus came to rest on the Kombinat's assembly facility at Eisenach, which was something of a stepchild in the system and looked to fare even worse under Volkswagen.

As he pushed ahead, Hughes found his colleagues and the Opel organization locked into a view of the future competitive situation that had Opel the eternal 'Number Two' to Volkswagen. As a step in changing that situation, Hughes rejected plans based on those forecasts and requested new ones that had Opel's target as Number 1 in East Germany. Keeping his bosses at GM Europe (Zurich) and Corporate (Detroit and New York) informed, and ignoring directives to stay away from the East German authorities, Hughes moved aggressively to negotiate an agreement with the local management at Eisenach in March. By April, the first television advertisements for Opel were aired in East Germany, emphasizing the advanced technology and environmentally friendly characteristics of Opel cars. In October, three days after reunification was announced, German Chancellor Helmut Kohl drove the first Opel car off the line at Eisenach. The next day, the car was exhibited at the Berlin auto show.

Finally, Hughes moved to plan and seek Detroit corporate staff approval for a major manufacturing facility at Eisenach. Although he was eventually successful, he had to overcome considerable questions about the wisdom of putting a new plant in what would soon be a high-wage country. GM's global strategy was to locate new focused factories in low-wage countries such as Spain. It appeared to corporate staff as if Eisenach represented a commitment to what might well become a high-wage country. To overcome that perception, he made heavy use of the political and emotional arguments associated with the end of Soviet hegemony to complement the economic analysis provided to the corporate staff. (This description paraphrases portions of the case study Adam Opel AG (A), Harvard Business School 9-392-100, revised 25 April 2000, © 1992 by the President and Fellows of Harvard College.)

What a contrast to the conventional view. Instead of corporate taking the lead based on careful new analysis, corporate is preempted by a division acting in what some staff believed was a clear contradiction of well-established corporate strategy. In turn, Hughes responded effectively to an early move by Volkswagen that looked as if it would tie up most of the long-term East German market. Although he kept his superiors informed, Hughes moved quickly to create options at Eisenach that were news to both East German authorities and Volkswagen—not to mention US-based corporate staff. To enable these things to happen, he used the emotions of this historic event to mobilize what had been called a bureaucratic organization to move with lightning speed to build distribution and a marketing program, and then to modernize an ancient assembly facility. His days were filled with meetings, some with Opel colleagues, but also with government figures such as Kohl, and with East German officials, labor leaders, and the US ambassador.

What we can see is that GM's strategic response to the opening of the Berlin Wall was a result of some initial impetus provided by Jack Smith's question and Volkswagen's preemptive move, of some rough-and-ready studies made by Opel's marketing group, of an extensive series of probings and negotiations with East German figures in the government and at the Eisenach plant, of Hughes's ambitions for Opel in Germany, of Hughes's development of a series of arguments that demonstrated the importance to local sales of local manufacture, all in the context of Hughes original mandate to improve the operations of Opel in West Germany.[1] Both GM's European headquarters and corporate appear to have been swept up by the momentum created by Hughes's actions. When *resources* were committed to support Hughes's plans, *de facto*, the *strategy* of General Motors adjusted to incorporate the idea that local manufacturing might be a desirable approach to increasing local market share. The intellectual framework held by corporate staff may not have changed, the words on paper may not have changed, but the strategy of GM did. (The eventual significance of the change would turn on subsequent commitments. Was this an overture or an aberration?)

We call the processes that led to this change strategic because what this example makes clear is that if an executive were trying to control the evolution of GM's strategy, he or she would have to manage the processes that led to the outcome at Eisenach. Those processes and not the documents labeled strategy at corporate headquarters would determine the direction of GM's fortunes in Europe. More generally, the strategic process is the evolution of explicit strategy, in response partly to changes in strategic intent, in the capabilities of the organization, in the market, and also in response to competitive moves.[2]

The story of Eisenach's development has the elements of stirring entrepreneurship by a business unit manager facing dramatic change in his environment. The fall of the Berlin Wall was a 'hundred year storm'. There are also elements here of a division management out of control. But we are not relating the story to exemplify good or bad management. The strategic process—the way strategy was made by a commitment of capital resources to plans shaped by an extensive mix of forces, only a portion of which were elements of corporate policy—is the reality of strategy making in large organizations.

Studying Resource Allocation

The story at Opel, then, is unique only in that the events were so dramatic. The more general observation that strategy is made by a series of resource commitments that are themselves the outcome of organizational processes was reported in 1970.[3] This book, which reports a body of subsequent research extending over three decades, describes how resource allocation drives strategy. The initial study of resource allocation in the context of strategy was conducted in the late 1960s in National Products, a large multibusiness firm. Today, we would call it a 24-month ethnographic study.[4] National Product's management was frustrated. Although they presided over a treasure trove of businesses and technology and used sophisticated systems for planning and capital budgeting, their performance was average at best. The research revealed that what was actually driving strategy was the pattern of resource allocation, and this in turn was driven by the way businesses were organized and managers were measured and rewarded (just like Opel).

The front line and middle managers who made the plans for new products, new plants, and new markets thought that the way they were being evaluated, promoted, and paid was a clear indication of what top management wanted them to do. Performance was evaluated and pay and promotions were determined by a 'Hay' system that used the size of businesses (sales and assets), the number of employees, profitability, and other measures to assign points to jobs for determination of salary and incentives.[5] So while top management sought growth and profitability from business where the company had a strategic advantage, all the business unit managers (such as Lou Hughes) competed for resources with other units so they could use those resources to grow the importance and success of their own business units. In the way National's capital budgeting system actually worked, resources were allocated on the basis of the attractiveness of plans, adjusted for the credibility of the plan's authors. Given the degree of prior screening, by the time they reached the corporate finance committee, all plans looked pretty good. But top management had too limited an understanding of their detail to make a critical, substantive assessment of their likely validity. The credibility of the manager who took responsibility for the proposal, not words and numbers in the proposal *per se*, was the determining factor in allocation. Middle-level general managers running divisions or groups put their reputation for good judgment at stake, and in so doing often their career, by selecting and sponsoring strategic initiatives and resource allocation requests from among all those put forward by subordinate operating managers.

Observing this process, three levels of general managers could be seen making decisions: those on the line running profit centers, those at the top leading the corporation, and general managers in the middle running divisions or groups responsible for the oversight of profit centers, their budgets, their plans for growth, and their requests for capital resources. First-level general managers worked with functional managers (running sales, engineering, and manufacturing) to develop business-unit budgets, long-term plans, and capital budget requests. Mid-level general managers functioned somewhat as brokers, sponsoring the business unit plans they favored and cutting or holding back those about which they had reservations. Corporate-level managers were responsible for approving requests. Although formal responsibility for allocating capital was at the corporate level, division and group managers (such as Lou Hughes!) made the most critical decisions. The following comment captures the work of general managers in the middle:

What it really comes down to is your batting average. Obviously, anything cooked up [by a profit-center business unit] I have to sell and approve. My contribution is more in the area of deciding how much confidence we have in things. The whole thing—the size, the sales estimate, the return—is based on judgment. I decide the degree of optimism incorporated in the estimates. . . . The key question is: 'How much confidence has management built up over the years in my judgment?"[6] (The key at Opel was that Jack Smith trusted Lou Hughes.)

Managers learn about that level of confidence from two primary sources: the first is whether their requests for resources are typically granted, and the second is the way they are measured and compensated. Above-average raises, promotions, and approved requests signal confidence. Unwillingness to provide resources signals disapproval of performance or intentions and hence a lack of confidence in one's judgment. General managers in the middle know this and only 'send up' proposals they think will be funded. Indeed, they use informal channels to pretest their thinking and lobby influential decision makers. Top managers know this and count on the process. Consequently, when requests finally get to formal meetings for approval at which many projects may be on the agenda, it is unusual when one is turned down.

Rather than pathology, this reflects a reasonable use of management time. If proposals are debated by the best talent of the company, and if they are backed by the senior managers with responsibility for overseeing the businesses, then final approval is likely to be a formality. Otherwise, a great deal of the most valuable management effort has been wasted. A model of the resource allocation process (the RAP model) along with these findings was published in Bower's 1970 book. A series of corroborative and comparative studies followed that used the model with considerable success to examine resource allocation in a wide variety of situations ranging from vertically integrated, to high technology, to start up, to appointed and elected public sector managers.[7] All these studies focused on physical and financial resources.[8] The next chapter presents the original model and discusses the break from traditional capital budgeting theory. The remainder of this book is devoted to how the work that followed extended and deepened our understanding of strategic processes.

General Characteristics of the Resource Allocation Process

Before moving to the body of the book, it is worth noting that the perspective developed in this first chapter is not a conventional view of strategy. It is fundamentally inconsistent with any model or tool for decision making that presumes a unitary decision maker or the comparability of quantitative analyses produced by subunits of the firm, or even the stability of understanding about what events and

Table 1.1 *General characteristics of resource allocation*

Structure	Process
Knowledge is dispersed across levels and units	Processes are dispersed across levels and units
Power to make commitments is dispersed across levels and units	Activities of all sorts proceed simultaneously
Roles are narrowly defined and inevitably in conflict	Processes are iterative

decisions are strategic. By looking inside the black box of resource allocation, we are introducing a new set of characteristics that must be considered when thinking about crafting strategy. In other words, the behavior observed at Opel and National Products is not idiosyncratic. Both structural and procedural characteristics of the resource allocation process are stable across time and industry (see Table 1.1). We list them here and discuss them briefly, but return to them throughout the book.

The Structure of Resource Allocation: Multiple Participants and Multiple Influences

• *The knowledge required for strategic decisions is dispersed among levels and across the organization.* For example, at Opel the understanding of the emerging East German market was in the hands of the sales and marketing group who grasped how the new East German consumer behavior would affect the choice of advertising message and choice of car model. The skills necessary to build a world class 'lean' assembly facility resided in GM's Canadian operation (CAMI) and a GM joint venture with Toyota (NUMMI) based in California. Knowledge of the overall GM overseas operations was in Detroit, while the financial staff focused on the need for long-term economic performance. Such dispersion of knowledge means that managers with deeply different perspectives are contributing to the same decision-making process. Marketing and sales managers were very sensitive to the effect of local production on the image of Opel among new consumers. Conversely, corporate planning staff, more attuned to the benefits of cross-border integration and the search for low labor cost locations that underpinned GM's manufacturing strategy, was quite disturbed by the conclusions Hughes had reached about the importance of local manufacturing to local sales. The relative attractiveness of his East German proposal depended on this relationship, which they deemed spurious. As in the Opel Eisenach case, much of this kind of knowledge is subtle and complex enough not to be exchanged and analyzed easily, nor to be verified or second-guessed easily, making reconciliation of contested knowledge a social exercise, based on trust and mutual understanding.

• *The power to make commitments is distributed over the organization.* The clearest example of this proposition could be seen in the relationship of Lou Hughes to Helmut Kohl. Apparently, Kohl developed a real affection for this young American who insisted on speaking his imperfect German and was committed to investing in ways that would support the unification process. Managers in Detroit had to be wary of overriding their local manager in a way that might undermine the position of the head of their largest foreign subsidiary. They also had to be sensitive to the need to foster Lou Hughes's personal commitment to whatever choices were made about Germany, to make sure he felt that the decisions for which he was responsible were his, beyond the call of duty and the rewards metered by performance evaluation systems.[9] Therefore, even if power to allocate resources is formally centralized, a careful top management might not choose to contravene positions taken by key executives closer to the ground.

• *Organization roles are narrowly defined and inevitably in conflict.* Hughes was responsible for Germany; someone else was responsible for all of Europe; still others were responsible for all of GM. Each had a different perspective of how corporate objectives could be best moved forward. And from their individual perspectives, despite the conflicts, each might be right. Before one gets to questions of politics or self-interest, the dispersal of knowledge means that managers engaged in the strategic process, who believe opposite propositions, might all be correct when the question is viewed from the perspective of their organization. This is the source of the famous Myles' Law: 'Where you stand is a function of where you sit.' Each manager considers a different set of facts, usually those most pertinent to success in his or her operating role.

The Process of Resource Allocation: Simultaneous across Levels and Iterative over Time

• Most crucially, *the activities impinging on resource allocation commitments are dispersed across levels and proceed simultaneously.* The notion of a centrally managed strategic process depends upon central control of sequence that rarely exists. Hughes's conversations with Kohl may have made the subsequent reservations of corporate staff irrelevant. Conversely, corporate management might have approved major capacity expansion decisions elsewhere in Europe when Hughes was discussing with Kohl, undermining the whole situation. Country managers often have the ability to commit their companies before all corporate voices have a chance to weigh in. Indeed, facts are always being created at operating levels that enhance or undermine corporate initiatives.

The opportunity to pursue Eisenach was developed by one of the leaders of Opel's union organization in a conversation with a relative in East Germany. Conversely, corporate initiatives, once launched, often gain a momentum that makes their implementers oblivious to new developments and changing conditions. Managers in the middle are constantly challenged with how to respond to misalignments between initiatives that have been delegated to them and corporate policies, having to balance the need for consistency over time so that momentum can cumulate with the fact that well-informed discrepant initiatives may be a lead indicator of a need to change course, or at least to adjust strategic direction.

• This leads to two final propositions that are at the heart of our definition of strategic process: *Decision making evolves over time as events play out, and options develop in an iterative process.* When Jack Smith called Lou Hughes, there was no Eisenach option. Until the contact was provided through the union, Volkswagen's preemptive move was a complete success. Until market research had been done, the importance of a manufacturing location in East Germany was unclear. Once new options or critical inputs emerge, the situation needs to be revisited, making the crafting of strategy an endless real time iterative process. Commitments must be made. Otherwise there can be paralysis, a constant debate where no strategy is actually implemented with commitment and continuity, and where operating managers cynically wait for the next 'flavor of the month' and deflect one strategic initiative after another. A successfully managed strategic process provides real guiding purpose at the same time that it permits flexibility and learning. There is room for strategic priorities to evolve and reshape in light of the success or failure of strategic initiatives, thus enacting, as argued by Burgelman, a new strategic context.

Again, we use a brief case example to illustrate these ideas. Timken Corporation is a bearings and alloyed steel provider that faced a situation somewhat parallel to GM's in Eastern Europe. A simple resource allocation commitment led to a significant shift in corporate strategy.

In 1995, Timken acquired a plant in Poland that made tapered roller bearings. The acquisition was partly to prevent SKF, its main European competitor, from acquiring it. This was because it needed capacity and this was a cheap addition, and also because it hoped to enter Eastern European markets. Although trivial in its amount, that investment led over the next several years to a complete change of strategy. In short, Timken shifted from a strategy of product differentiation through technology leadership to a very different approach. Several steps led to the change. First, the plant used a different process to make bearings that were adequate for most applications but not quite as good as Timken's. Nonetheless, and against corporate instructions, European managers, measured on the performance of Poland, and desperate to use its capacity, sold bearings to Peugeot for gearbox applications.

This *fait accompli* led Timken to accept ISO 9000 products and to introduce a second brand aimed at European and American mid-market carmakers, not BMW and Mercedes. The fact that the plant in Poland also was very focused, designed to be part of an integrated East European supply network, led Timken to reconsider its own supply system and to shift from a strategy of local responsiveness, where each plant served its own local markets, to one of global integration, like GM. These two evolutions in turn triggered a reinterpretation of strategic priorities toward cost competitiveness with standard products in mass markets, rather than quality differentiation in niche markets, and paved the way for subsequent alliances with NSK, a major Japanese competitor, and other companies, a deep break for a traditionally very insular company. In sum, a seemingly unimportant investment, made for superficial reasons, led to a complete redirection of strategy and a redefinition of the strategic context. (The Timken Company (A) (A1) (B), INSEAD Case Studies, 2003)

The Structure and Process of Resource Allocation have Important Implications for Strategy

• *The allocation of resources shapes strategic outcomes.* How resources are actually allocated and used determines strategic outcomes—not the words on paper or policies. Bower's 1970 study reports an incident where a corporate comptroller discovered that a factory had been built by a division without approval by the corporation. Division management believed that the business required the facility and that corporate would not approve it. They used hundreds of small work orders to circumvent the capital budgeting process. Graham Allison's account of the Cuban missile crisis provides a more dramatic example of the same phenomenon. During the embargo, the Navy forced a Russian submarine to the surface against orders from the Secretary of Defense because that was what naval commanders (the operating level) believed was the right thing to do.[10] In both the Opel and Timken cases, resource commitments actually moved critical policies of the company in a different direction from the announced strategy at the time of the actual commitment. In the case of Opel, this opened up a manufacturing strategy that was different than GM's previous strategy for Europe. In the case of Timken, the seemingly peripheral acquisition of a low-cost plant in Poland led to a complete product market repositioning for the company. The point is not that resource allocation leads to unintended strategic outcomes, but that managers wishing to manage strategic outcomes need to manage the resource allocation process and the forces that shape it. Early commitments can lock in strategic outcomes and result in both intended and unintended changes in strategy.

• *Operating managers can play a significant role in shaping strategic outcomes.* Because resource allocation shapes strategic outcomes, all those involved in resource allocation will have an effect on the revealed strategy. Unlike models that assume a single decision maker, or only senior decision makers, a resource allocation perspective of strategy making is decidedly multilevel and multiperson. Louis Hughes's ability as a division manager to change corporate-level strategy at GM reveals the importance of a multilevel perspective. A seemingly local decision to acquire low-cost manufacturing capacity through a small acquisition resulted in important strategic changes at Timken. In Ch. 3, Burgelman describes how resource commitments by the managers of Intel's fabrication facilities shifted the focus of Intel's corporate strategy from DRAMs to microprocessors. In Ch. 6, Christensen and Bower show how the desire of business unit managers to satisfy the needs of major customers resulted in strategic outcomes not considered at corporate. The importance of operating commitments at lower levels in the organization is a theme repeatedly revealed throughout the research presented in this volume.

• *The structure of resource allocation shapes strategy.* When Lou Hughes requested a plan for East Germany, he got back a plan that looked like West Germany. Absent his intervention, plans were likely to perpetuate the past. From Bower's original research at National Products, we learned that the charters of a business unit determined the focus of managers, and the systems for compensation and promotion determined new business direction. We called the organization, the measures and information, and the incentives, the 'structural context' of the company. Because the reality of strategy is the result of resource allocation, and because resource allocation is substantially influenced by structural context, we learned that 'structure drives strategy' just as Chandler taught us that strategy should shape structure.[11] Throughout the book, we will see how the structure of previous internal commitments (to reporting structures, to strategy statements, etc.) and external commitments (to customers and capital markets) constrain changes in resource allocation and consequent changes in strategy.

- As a consequence of the multilevel, distributed, and simultaneous aspects of operating and strategic process, *ex ante there is almost always true uncertainty about which decisions will have strategic consequences*. It is often not obvious which decisions will have long-term effects on the direction, character, and prosperity of the organization.[12] At Opel, in the instance of the union leader, earlier actions of Hughes when he arrived must have created a crack in what had been historically a hostile relationship between the union and company management. Whatever it was that Hughes did to create better human relationships turned out to be strategic when the time came. Specific actions may turn, in retrospect, to have been strategic, but no one knew at the time, as with Timken's acquisition in Poland. This relative unpredictability of what will turn out to be strategic means that for top managers, the judgment of specific managers counts more than the detailed logic of proposals. Assuming managers stay in the company, judgment is honed over time in the course of a career. The logic shifts constantly and is always, legitimately, open to reinterpretation. In that sense, a corporate emphasis on selecting, developing, and managing people over time in a very disciplined process appears particularly justified. Recurring management participation in a stream of decisions over time not only builds skills, commitment, and stewardship responsibilities, but also provides multiple opportunities to calibrate judgment and build, test, and deepen trust.

In summary, the structure and process characteristics of resource allocation outlined previously have important implications for strategy. These characteristics are summarized in Table 1.2.

It may seem that an implication of this work is that there is a lack of direction in the form of strategic content coming from the top. Whereas the importance of the bottom-up process is a critical contribution of this line of research, the role of corporate management remains vital, if different. To begin, even in the Opel example, the phone call from Jack Smith was a critical initiating and empowering event. But more fundamentally, the research discussed in this

Table 1.2 *Implications for strategy*

The allocation of resources and execution of process determines strategic outcomes
Operating managers can play a significant role in shaping strategic outcomes
Structure influences operations and shapes resource allocation. Hence, structure shapes strategy
Over time, small decisions can trigger a sequence of increasingly important ones, so it is not clear *ex ante* what is strategic

book is concerned with how corporate thinking concerning strategic content affects resource allocation, and how that process can be improved.

Research presented later in this volume indicates that there are other forces that shape the resource allocation process (RAP). These include the formal statement of strategy from the top, powerful existing customers, and capital markets. How these forces interact with RAP has important implications for the strategy realized. The reader will have to be patient, however, for much of that research is discussed in Parts II–IV of this book.

How Do Other Literatures Deal with These Conditions?

We have already noted that these basic propositions are not a conventional view of the world. Nor are they a neutral view. They lead to major implications for how we consider strategic process. Although this represented a real break from most previous research on the topic in 1970, today some of these issues are being addressed in other literatures. We note briefly some of the recent work in the section that follows so that readers familiar with these disciplines can be aware of the connections. In the same spirit, we have asked four distinguished scholars from disciplines concerned with strategy to reflect on the implications of this body of research for their fields, presented in Part V of this book.

Many researchers write about topics that would appear to be germane to the process. Our goal in this section is to indicate briefly those areas of the literature in economics and organization theory that deal with aspects of RAP. We do this, however, with caution. Note that the differences between the findings in this book and the assumptions underlying discipline-based theory can be considerable. If one forgets that theorists are seeking *power* in their models, it is easy to interpret the major discrepancies between what RAP researchers report and the assumptions supporting theory as criticism where none is intended. Our brief survey touches on financial economics, transaction cost economics, agency theory, competitive strategy, resource dependence theory, behavioral decision theory, and evolutionary theory.

Financial Economics

The place to begin any such survey is with the theory of the firm. The basic question for most economists has been whether the way firms are managed has created value. A natural reaction to the complexity we have described is to imagine that it cannot be managed as well as a market might do it, hence financial economists hypothesized and found that diversified firms, particularly conglomerates, traded at a discount. Recent articles have called that finding into question, arguing that poor performers diversify.[13] In Ch. 16, John Roberts examines the ways financial economists have begun to address other issues related to firm performance and organization systems. The result seems to highlight the uncertainty about the effects of the internal capital market that we call the resource allocation process on the performance of the firm.

Transaction Cost Economics

Developed by Oliver Williamson, transaction cost economics asks the economists' question in a different way: Why is so much economic activity conducted inside firms rather than in an open market?[14] In particular, why are there multibusiness firms? The issues we have discussed are examined from the perspective of the cost effectiveness of governance. For activity to be organized inside a single firm and coordinated through some form of hierarchy rather than in an open market, it must be because it is more efficient to do it that way. Where the business units of the firm are related, various efficiencies from operating and strategic coordination are the answer. In a multibusiness firm, the allocation of strategic resources ought to be at least as efficient as the capital markets to justify the existence of the firm. (Again the market provides the standard.) Efficiencies would be expected to be found in the improved information available to resource allocators in the corporate office and not available to outside investors.

Williamson argues strongly that because knowledge is specialized and distributed and roles narrowly defined, the only role of corporate management is to allocate capital among units—the management of the internal capital market. Corporate management knows more about the potential profitability of business units, but not the details of running those units. This idea has been the focus of important work by David Teece. In effect, he has argued that skill at the transfer of knowledge justifies extending the scope of the firm.[15]

One finds some attempts to deal with the dispersal of knowledge and group decision making in game theory, but attempts to incorporate the kind of complex information and incentive structures break down quickly.[16] The problem, modeled as a nested game, is quite intractable. Much more progress has been made in organizational economics where the unit of analysis includes people and organizational units.[17] We discuss agency theory as a precursor to the field.

Agency Theory

Developed by Jensen and Mechling, agency theory comes close to a RAP perspective. Accepting that there may be economic benefits in a large hierarchy, Jensen and Mechling focus on the conflicts in perspective that develop between owners (the principals) and managers (their agents) and on how principals can best make their agents serve their interests.[18] Their basic proposition is that if managers are given the appropriate decision rights (if the problems facing a company are appropriately subdivided and the responsibility and authority for solving each properly assigned) and if they are compensated properly, then managers' perspectives and interests will be aligned with that of the owners and appropriate decisions will be made. In the language used in the 1970 RAP model, Jensen and Mechling argue that the structural context can be used to align the interest of agents with principals. Jensen and Mechling are particularly concerned that professional managers often have an incentive to act in ways that destroy value for shareowners. For example, if managers at National Products were rewarded for making their business large rather than profitable, they would continue to invest in businesses that rewarded them, even if profitability deteriorated over time.

There is significant evidence that this argument characterizes accurately an important problem. Indeed, research on the economics of organization that has developed from the foundation of agency theory is congruent in spirit with much of the work reported here on strategic process. Still, agency theory addresses only some of the organizational conditions listed above. Although the theory posits that knowledge, power, and activity are distributed, it assumes that it is feasible to define decision rights and incentives so that interests are aligned and therefore decision making can be designed to be coherent. In contrast, we report that around strategic issues, decision rights are almost inevitably in conflict because issues cannot be neatly decomposed into modules nor fully anticipated, and thus coherence in the strategy process can result only from active real-time management. Myles' law (where you stand is a function of where you sit), in a relatively unstructured situation like strategy development, also makes individual interventions somewhat idiosyncratic. Simultaneity, the dynamics of strategic events, and ex-ante uncertainty play havoc with the design of decision rights and incentives. The more strategic the questions under consideration, the more likely the systems of decision rights and incentives in place at a point in time *interfere* with a coherent approach, because those systems were designed with a different set of circumstances in mind. Contemporary work on the economics of organization is beginning to address these problems, and in that sense it comes closer to the work discussed in this book.

Organizational economists who have examined the fact that knowledge is distributed in organizations are Luis Garicano, Milton Harris, and Arthur Raviv.[19] A common characteristic of all this work is that knowledge is treated as stable. You have it or you do not. The idea that how a manager interprets facts is likely to differ depending on role (as opposed to incentives) is not yet part of the problem under examination. As we will see in Part IV of this book, this has important implications for thinking about different roles in the firm's hierarchy.

Competitive Strategy

From the perspective of strategic process, the most important contribution of the work in competitive strategy has been the revelation of how substantively complex are the strategic challenges facing contemporary business units as they compete over time in rapidly changing global markets. Choices among the units of a multibusiness corporation cannot be reduced to simple comparisons of projected future financial performance nor simplified to the ex-ante allocation of decision rights and design of proper incentives. Instead, as initially developed by Michael Porter, an extensive consideration of competitive and industry dynamics needs to be considered.[20] An entire field of research and consulting, incorporating a wide range of ideas from value analysis to game theory, has substantially elaborated Porter's analysis.

Of particular interest here is the work of the Boston Consulting Group. Their empirical work revealed that because of experience effects, businesses need to invest strategically in order to achieve leading market share.[21] Other research showed that business profitability was often associated with relative market share.[22] For multibusiness firms, this meant that investment programs of several business units, each trying to build competitive advantage, would tax available cash flows. Choices had to be made based on prospective strategic conditions both to anticipate the funding needs of individual businesses and to assess the viability of each element in the portfolio of businesses, not on historic rate of return.[23]

These ideas had major implications for the problem of strategic resource allocation. In particular—and entirely congruent with the normative implication of RAP that companies had to allocate funds among businesses as opposed to projects—company managements sought to be sure that the proposals emanating from their business units met the tests of competitive strategic analysis. But perhaps more important, managers could see that the resources needed to capture dominant market shares could not possibly be available for all the businesses. Multibusiness company managers were more aware of the necessity of choice, and even the possibility that exit from a business could be a necessity.

The Resource-Based View (RBV) of strategy has offered an alternative view of the management problem we are considering.[24] As Peteraf expresses the point in Ch. 18, the Resource-Based View of the firm directs attention to how a firm's resources affect external competitive processes and outcomes. The pattern of resource accumulation is the basis for predictions about competitive success and firm performance. To date, the potential for linkage to work on resource allocation process has not been exploited.

Although of continuing importance to the strategic management of companies, the primary effect of the economic and organizational research on strategy described above was to be found in the improved *content* of strategic plans. The dilemmas of organizational process we have described were not resolved. Indeed, in some instances they were exacerbated as extensive strategic planning staffs at division and corporate levels engaged in protracted battles around the resource allocation process. Careers still depended upon business performance, and performance was helped by appropriate investments. Those depended on access to funds. So, division managers in roles like that of Lou Hughes developed more elaborate strategic plans to help them in the internal competition for funds.[25]

Nonetheless, like financial economics, the work on strategy content provides a normative standard for managers of strategic process. If a firm's processes do not resolve the problem of focusing resources so that plans meet the tests of strategic analysis, then resources almost certainly will be wasted and the fortunes of the involved business units placed in jeopardy.

Resource Dependence Theory

From the field of sociological research, resource dependence theorists brought a different perspective to the discussion of strategy. Most prominently led by Jeffrey Pfeffer and Gerald Salancik, they argued that a business was primarily dependent on customers and investors for its success.[26] They would support the firm as long as its products and services were most attuned to their needs. In calling attention to the importance of competing externally for customers and investors rather than internally with other divisions, the perspective makes an important contribution. From the perspective of the management of strategic processes, the challenge implied is to manage resource allocation so that the evolving needs of customers are served, and their voice in the process is heard.

One important problem that has been uncovered in more recent research is that the mechanisms of resource dependence can lead customers to capture the resource allocation process. As developed in Ch. 6, Clayton Christensen has shown that the consequence is the virtual inability of the resource allocation process to deal with strategic opportunities of no interest to current customers.[27]

The resource dependence perspective may be extended to relationships among managers, where each tries to escape dependence on others in decision making and resource allocation, and to preserve discretion and autonomy while imposing dependence on others.[28] External alliances, such as Hughes's relationship with Chancellor Kohl, become sources of power internally. By pointing out such interactions between external relationships and internal power and dependency patterns, resource dependence models shed useful light on the politics of strategic decisions and allow a richer understanding of managerial self-interest than simpler economic models such as agency theory.

Behavioral Decision Theory

Behavioral decision theory was developed by Simon, Cyert, and March[29] who were dissatisfied with the assumptions about behavior that support the conventional theory of the firm that underlies subsequent developments such as agency, transaction, and financial theory. In a sense, the set of organizational conditions laid out above in Table 1.1 is an empirical version of the behavioral theorists' assertion that managers do not behave as rational economic maximizers of business profit and loss. But whereas we have observed managers trying to do their very best for themselves, their business, and their company over time in very complicated circumstances of collective decision making,[30] the school of behavioral theorists constructed a model in which individuals are represented by levels of aspiration on relevant dimensions. Instead of maximizing, they solve problems by seeking solutions that satisfy their aspiration. Group activity is explained in terms of coalitions of individuals. Interdependence is specifically ruled out through powerful 'quasi-resolution of conflict' and 'sequential attention to goals' axioms that effectively isolate individual decision makers.[31] Nonetheless, the problem-solving behavior of individual managers provides a critical building block in the model of resource allocation described in Ch. 2.

Evolutionary Economics

Using behavioral theory to model firms, evolutionary economics posits that corporations are bundles of action routines to which new routines are added through (often trial and error) learning, and from which old and unused routines are discarded.[32] Firms adjust to changing environmental demands by this evolution in their routines. Although descriptively representative of the evolution of many industries, the kind of adaptive incremental 'one routine at a time' learning posited by the original evolutionary economics models is not fully consistent with major strategic changes and watershed points. Later treatment, which introduced punctuated equilibrium, dealt more successfully with this problem.[33] Yet, the implicit view of strategy processes as changes in relatively disjointed, or loosely coupled systems, where multiple participants contribute to streams of actions that are often reconciled only ex-post in the articulation of a new strategic context points toward an accurate model of the process, and thus provides a useful conceptualization. In other words, actions and experimentation precede strategy, the latter being the explicated learning and the retained lessons from the former.[34]

Conclusion

We conclude this introductory chapter with a reminder of our purpose and our approach. Our intent in writing this book is threefold: First, we hope to communicate the unique character of the resource allocation process and its link to strategy through the development of a formal model. Second, we hope to show how this model has evolved over 30 years of research development. Finally, we hope to better connect the research on resource allocation to the field of strategy as a whole.

Part I of this book provides the context for how the model of resource allocation has evolved over the last thirty-five years. In the next chapter, we begin the process of introducing the original model. Joseph Bower introduces the model in its original form. Then, in Ch. 3, Burgelman discusses his efforts to work with the Bower model and expand it. Gilbert and Christensen conclude the introductory part by articulating a research approach for developing theory through the discovery of anomalies—observations not predicted by previous theory. They argue that the approach was employed by both Bower and Burgelman and then followed by subsequent RAP scholars to develop the model. Parts II, III, and IV are organized around key themes—the breakdown in bottom-up process, the restoration of the bottom-up process, and the role of direct corporate intervention. Part IV presents a group of essays from discipline-based researchers who consider the implications of resource allocation research on their own fields. We conclude the book by presenting a formally revised model of the resource allocation process. That is what lies ahead, but it is to Bower's and Burgelman's models that we now turn.

Endnotes

1. Henry Mintzberg speaks of *emergent strategy*. See H. Mintzberg and J. Waters (1985). 'Of Strategies, Deliberate and Emergent'. *Strategic Management Journal*, 6: 257–72.
2. This definition was first framed in 1974 by Eoin Travelyen, 'The Strategic Process in Large Complex Organizations', Harvard Business School doctoral thesis.

3. J. L. Bower (1970). *Managing the Resource Allocation Process*. Boston, Mass.: Harvard Business School Press.

4. National Products is a disguised name. See ibid.

5. The Hay system was an approach to management performance assessment and compensation marketed by the consulting firm Hay Associates. It was used by many large companies during the 1970s.

6. Bower, *Managing the Resource Allocation Process*.

7. Many of these studies are discussed in Joseph L. Bower and Yves Doz (1978). 'Resource Allocation: A Social and Political Process', in Charles Hofer and Daniel Schendel, *Strategic Management*. Englewood Cliffs, NJ: Prentice Hall.

8. In Ch. 20, we suggest that whether the allocation of human and intangible resources might pose different problems is an important area for further study.

9. 'Ours is not to reason why, ours is just to do and die,' may sometimes be a military necessity, but today it is not regarded as preferred practice in any organization.

10. G. J. Allison (1971). *Essence of Decision: Explaining the Cuban Missile Crisis*. Boston, Mass.: Little Brown.

11. A. D. Chandler (1964). *Strategy and Structure*. Boston, Mass.: MIT.

12. The phrasing intentionally paraphrases the definition of strategic in Kenneth Andrews (1965). *A Concept of Corporate Strategy*. Homewood, Ill.: Irwin.

13. J. M. Campa and S. Kedia (2002). 'Explaining the Diversification Discount'. *Journal of Finance* 57: 1731–62. Belen Villalonga (2004). 'Does Diversification Cause the "Diversification Discount"?' *Financial Management* 33: 5–27. Belen Villalonga (2004). 'Diversification Discount or Premium? New Evidence from the Business Information Tracking Series'. *Journal of Finance* 59: 479–506. J. Martin and A. Sayrak (2003). 'Corporation Diversification and Shareholder Value: A Survey of Recent Literature'. *Journal of Corporate Finance* 9: 37–57.

14. O. E. Williamson (1981). 'The Economics of Organization: The Transaction Cost Approach'. *American Journal of Sociology* 87/3: 548–77.

15. David J. Teece (1980). 'Economies of Scope and the Scope of the Enterprise'. *Journal of Economic Behavior and Organization* 1: 223–47. Id. (1982). 'Towards an Economic Theory of the Multiproduct Firm'. *Journal of Economic Behavior and Organization* 3: 39–63.

16. Jean Tirole's text (1988), *The Theory of Industrial Organization*, Cambridge, Mass., MIT, is the classic application of game theory to the analysis of firm behavior. In one classic attempt to use decision theory to examine formally one of the case studies in Bower (1970), the HBS Decision Theory Seminar abandoned its effort when the attempt to construct the relevant decision tree failed after two hours of work.

17. John Roberts discusses this literature in Ch. 16.

18. M. Jensen and W. Meckling (1976). 'The Theory of the Firm: Managerial Behavior, Agency Costs, and Ownership Structure'. *Journal of Financial Economics* 3: 305–60.

19. Luis Gariocano (2000). 'Hierarchies and the Organization of Production'. *Journal of Political Economy* 5:108. M. Harris and Artur Raviv (Feb. 2000). 'Organizational Design'. CRSP working paper No. 499, EFA 0271.

20. Building on the work of Business Policy Research at Harvard Business School (e.g. K. Kenneth Andrews (1965). *A Concept of Corporate Strategy*. Englewood Cliffs, NJ: Irwin) and the body of industrial organization economics, Michael Porter provided the foundation for an extensive field of strategy research. M. Porter (1980). *Competitive Strategy: Techniques for Analyzing Industries and Competitors*, and (1985) *Competitive Advantage: Creating and Sustaining Superior Performance*. New York: Free Press.

21. BCG's work established that average total unit costs declined at a logarithmic rate as a function of cumulative volume. Because earlier studies of direct factory cost revealed a similar 'learning curve', the name 'experience curve' was felicitous.

22. Sidney E. Schoeffler, Robert D. Buzzell, and Donald F. Heany (Mar./Apr. 1974). 'Impact of Strategic Planning on Profit Performance'. *Harvard Business Review*, 139–40. For a more detailed review of the literature on competitive strategy, see: Pankaj Ghemawat, (Spring 2002). 'Competition and Business Strategy in Historical Perspective'. *Business History Review*, 37–74.

23. William Fruhan's research illuminated the dilemma. GE, for example, could not afford to fund its profitable computer business in the face of IBM's formidable cash flow. To do so would force it to underfund dozens of profitable businesses where its position was stronger.

24. B. Wernerfelt (1984). 'A Resource-Based View of the Firm'. *Strategic Management Journal* 5: 171–80. J. B. Barney, (Oct. 1986). 'Strategic Factor Markets: Expectations, Luck, and Business Strategy'. *Management Science* 32: 1231–41. I. Dierickx and K. Cool (Dec. 1989). 'Asset Stock Accumulation and Sustainability of Competitive Advantage'. *Management Science* 35/12: 1504–11. J. B. Barney, (Dec. 1989). 'Asset Stock Accumulation and Sustainability of Competitive Advantage: A Comment'. *Management Science* 35/12: 1511–13. Id. (1991). 'Firm Resources and Sustained Competitive Advantage'. *Journal of Management* 17: 99–120. M. Peteraf (1993). 'The Cornerstones of Competitive Advantage: A Resource-Based View'. *Strategic Management Journal* 14: 179–91.

25. Things got so bad at one company famous for its strategic planning activities that divisions were allegedly graded by corporate staff on the covers of their strategic planning books!

26. J. Pfeffer and G. R. Salancik (1978). *The External Control of Organizations*. New York: Harper & Row.

27. C. M. Christensen and J. L. Bower (1996). 'Customer Power, Strategic Investment, and the Failure of Leading Firms'. *Strategic Management Journal* 17: 197–218.

28. This behavior was first described and conceptualized by Michel Crozier (1967). *The Bureaucratic Phenomenon*. Chicago: University of Chicago Press.

29. J. G. March and H. A. Simon (1958). *Organizations*. New York: John Wiley & Sons. R. M. Cyert and J. G. March (1963). *A Behavioral Theory of the Firm*. New York: Prentice Hall.

30. In the resource allocation model developed in Ch. 2, such managers are described as intendedly rational.

31. There is also a tendency to describe as satisficing rational behavior that includes sequential decision making (the step-by-step approach often looks like a compromise), and rational decision making under conditions of high uncertainty.

32. R. Nelson and S. Winter (1982). *An Evolutionary Theory of Economic Change*. Cambridge, Mass.: Harvard University Press.

33. C. J. G. Gersick (1991). 'Revolutionary Change Theories: A Multilevel Exploration of the Punctuated Equilibrium Paradigm'. *Academy of Management Review* 16/1: 10–36. M. L. Tushman and E. Romanelli (1985). 'Organizational Evolution: A Metamorphosis Model of Convergence and Reorientation', in L. L. Cummings and B. M. Staw (eds.), *Research in Organizational Behavior*, vii. 122–71. Greenwich, Conn.: JAI.

34. Henry Mintzberg speaks of *emergent strategy*. See H. Mintzberg and J. Waters (1985). 'Of Strategies, Deliberate and Emergent'. *Strategic Management Journal* 6: 257–72. C. E. Lindblom (1959). 'The Science of "Muddling Through"'. *Public Administration Review*, 79–88.

2

Modeling the Resource Allocation Process

Joseph L. Bower

Introduction

The very complexity that limited the ability of the disciplines to capture the essential elements of strategic processes would seem to limit the possibility of building a model of the process itself. In fact, a series of questions first asked in Bower's 1970 study of resource allocation made it possible to present the phenomenon as a set of three basic processes acting over three generic levels of organization influenced by an identified set of forces.[1] Subsequent researchers have used the same conceptual ingredients, and literally dozens of clinical studies have demonstrated the explanatory value of the model.[2]

When dealing with complex phenomena such as strategic processes, it is difficult to provide conventional statistical corroboration of a model. The questions are whether a model is complete and informative enough to use as a basis for normative analysis or action and whether there is a better model. Bower's resource allocation model remains in use after thirty-five years. Although the model has been revised over that time, the underlying premises summarized in Ch. 1 still hold. The resource allocation process is a complex, multilevel phenomenon that fundamentally shapes a firm's strategy. As noted below and described in Ch. 3, Robert Burgelman extended the model, to distinguish between strategic activity that falls within the bounds of institutionalized corporate strategy and that which emerges from subunit activity in a way that makes the model congruent with an evolutionary perspective. Subsequent scholars strengthened the model by examining and applying it to other critical aspects of the strategic process. In Ch. 4, Clark Gilbert and Clay Christensen address the way these scholars used observed anomaly to expand our understanding of the model. In the final chapter of the book, we revisit the model and revise it to take account of the strategic process research of the last thirty-five years. Because it provides the foundation for later work, we start with the original model.

The RAP Model: Three Processes and Three Levels

The best way to think about a resource allocation model is to answer the questions one might ask if one were observing a corporate finance committee discussing a series of capital projects presented for review and approval. Why is this particular set of economic and technical characteristics being specified? Who developed those characteristics? Who sponsored this project? Why? What considerations influence whether this project is approved? What explains the way this meeting functions in relationship to the project?

Then, keeping in mind that most companies believe that innovation is vital for success, one can contemplate the implications of the analysis in Table 2.1 for the managers sitting around that finance committee table. Although the data came from Bower's 1970 book, managers of contemporary industrial companies would not find the data surprising. It was not that new products were not profitable for National Products. It was just difficult to predict which products would be profitable. Projections of cost reductions were reliable, but one did not want to make profitable investments on an incremental basis in a fundamentally weak business. For managers several levels removed from the operations, these were difficult judgments to make. There were many projects to review each month. At General Motors, one project from among a dozen might be Lou Hughes's proposal for a plant at Eisenach.

Table 2.1 *Discounted Actual Results Compared With Discounted Forecast: 60 Projects at National Products*

Type of project	Mean	PV actual results / PV forecasted results
Cost Reduction		1:1
Sales Expansion		0:6
New Products		0:1

Source: J. L. Bower (1970). *Managing the Resource Allocation Process*. Boston, Mass.: Harvard Business School Press, 13.

What became apparent after two years of observation throughout many offices and locations of National Products is that a minimum of three resource allocation processes were under way. RAP activities were distributed over the operating units and the divisions and group general managers responsible for those units. One process shaped the economic and technical specifics of the project. Another process determined which projects eventually made it to the finance committee. A third process involved the set of forces that turned out to be the primary influences on how the first two worked. The first process was called *definition*, the second *impetus*, and the third *structural context*.

Definition is the process by which the basic technical and economic characteristics of a proposed investment are determined.[3] Questions to ask about a proposal for using strategic resources include: Where did the idea come from? Who decided we should build a plant this big in this place using this technology? Who decided we should acquire this company?

The conceptual answer to these questions is grounded in the behavioral theory of Simon, Cyert, and March.[4] Clinical research has made it clear that the concrete specifics of a strategic commitment are defined by functional managers in response to discrepancies between what they are currently achieving and what they have been asked to achieve or believe they can achieve. In turn, the way their jobs are defined, the way the business is measured, and how they themselves are measured and rewarded determines their concept of achievement.

Usually, the response is to a problem or opportunity perceived by operational managers who have both a specialized operating role and access to the required knowledge. In their role, operational managers interact with functional subordinates, customers, suppliers, government figures, and union leaders. They also know what really works on the shop floor or in the lab. How their roles are defined and measured determines which knowledge is salient and when there is a need to act. A plant general manager, for example, may recognize that new technology permits substantially lower costs and faster cycle times. A product manager compares sales forecasts to capacity and sees a gap emerging in the future. That knowledge of the gap triggers planning for expansion. A competitor announces new capacity or demand accelerates. The discrepancy between what the manager expects will happen without action and what is expected of his business provides the justification for action. The anticipated gap provides confidence that the results forecasted in a proposal will be realized.

Think of Lou Hughes at Opel. He cannot ignore the opening in East Germany, cannot let Volkswagen take too strong a lead there, knows he needs a lower-cost manufacturing site, and perhaps believes he has a good sense for the importance of local production to the morale of potential customers. General managers in the middle, however, are unlikely to have a corporate strategic perspective on project definition, because of three features of their situation:

- Their knowledge is likely to be local, specialized, and context-dependent.
- Roles and measurements reinforce this specialization.
- Perceptions of self-interest may get in the way.

Indeed, their job is designed to give them a product or geographic or functional perspective. In retrospect, if a broader view turns out to have been more appropriate, we often say the manager was 'parochial'. What is clear from the clinical data is that these managers were asked and paid to be parochial. Indeed, this is the problem with agency and contingency theory. Ex ante, jobs are defined so that interests of subunits and corporate are aligned. But ex post, they almost always turn out to be different from what is required.

The behavior of managers at the corporate level is no different. What they can do reflects the substance of what they know. Information at their disposal is usually much more aggregate than that of the functional, product, and geographic specialists who lead operating units. Their sources are different, their networks are broader, but their inputs are less detailed, except by accident of previous experience. Specific proposals for mergers and acquisitions often have their origins at corporate levels because the perspective of managers at that level comprehends other companies rather than just operating detail. They also receive proposals from investment bankers.

Central to the process perspective is that thinking at specialist/ business units, intermediate, and corporate levels proceeds *at the same time*. In deciding when and how to deal with a shortage of capacity, plant managers do not immediately consult headquarters leadership. If they are any good, plant managers understand what is expected of them and the significant power delegated to them. They will keep headquarters informed, but first will do a lot of work with their team. Meanwhile, headquarters will continue with its resource planning. The simultaneity of action at multiple levels of an organization is critical to understanding why intended strategy does not necessarily match the result of cumulative strategic commitments.

Ideally, the thinking and actions of managers at operating levels reflects a corporate perspective. Corporate objectives and corporate strategy often are transmitted in mission statements and similar 'white papers'. Beyond that, contemporary managements often invest in extensive processes of education and communication to help operational managements understand the strategic intentions of top management. The goal is to have the intellectual context of operating managers' thought shaped by corporate intent—to have everyone 'on the same page'. But that rarely happens. Research reveals that in order to encourage better operations, companies design organization, information, and incentives so that operating managers focus tightly on specific responsibilities.

The Opel story is a good example of the risk of disconnect between corporate and operating management. GM corporate had concluded that at the end of the day it would be vital to have overseas production capacity in low-wage countries. New capacity in East Germany was not obviously consistent with this objective. Hughes was able to build a plant in Eisenach because he successfully devised arguments that were approved despite objections from corporate staff.

Many companies apply some concrete version of agency theory to overcome communication problems between corporate and operating management. The measurement system for businesses and managers is specified in some detail so all objectives are aligned. Inevitably, the language of these systems is financial. Net Present Value and Economic Value Added analyses are examples.[5] The problem is that complexities of a multiyear strategy map poorly into a financial plan tied to annual rewards. Currently, the prevailing expression of the theory 'pay for performance' is to pay for this year's performance. Operating managers understand this imperative very well.

The distinction between projects that fit well with corporate thinking and those like Eisenach that emerge and effectively modify corporate thinking was the focus of subsequent work on strategic process by Robert Burgelman. He argues that the way projects such as Eisenach are managed has much to do with the ability of companies to innovate.

Impetus, the force that moves a project toward funding, is the willingness of a general manager in the middle to sponsor a project in the counsel of corporate officers.[6] The obvious question that follows from the preceding discussion is 'which proposals get approved and funded?' It is here that observed practice departs most dramatically from dominant prescriptive theory. More intriguing, much practice departs from the premises underlying almost all strategic resource allocation systems.

As noted in Ch. 1, the theory underlying the systems most companies use for capital budgeting posits a portfolio of opportunities

defined by the operating divisions. These opportunities can be characterized by the pattern of future cash outflows and inflows associated
with each proposed use of funds. All proposals should be funded
whose present value was positive, using the company's cost of
capital to discount those flows. In fact, almost all financial budgeting
systems operate in this fashion, in the sense that operating units
describe their proposals in the form of financial flows and make the
calculation prescribed.

What we see repeatedly, however, is that the decision about which
project to back is not made primarily on the basis of the relative
attractiveness of the proposals ranked by projected return. The attractiveness of the proposals is important, but actual selection is not made
on the basis of a ranking. The process of review and discussion of the
projects as they move from draft studies to documents going to the
finance committee or the board of directors involves testing and probing assumptions and projections. The critical aspect of such proposals
is that they are about the future. Whether the numbers will turn out to
be realistic projections turns on the quality of the detailed inputs on
which they are based (as the table earlier in this chapter makes clear).

For example, when Opel requested GM's support for a new plant at
Eisenach, a critical question was about projected sales in East Germany
if a plant were built, as opposed to projected sales if cars were supplied
from Russelsheim or another GM plant in Europe. Russelsheim was
out of capacity, and Hughes argued strongly that local supply would
improve local market share. Corporate staff thought that idea was
unsupportable. From the perspective of the executives making the
final decision, the attractiveness of the project depended on whom
you trusted more—the staff or Lou Hughes. Also important was that
Hughes was the manager responsible for the results of Opel, not the
corporate staff. For that matter, various details of Hughes's proposal
reflected his acceptance of technical and economic arguments made by
his engineers and marketing people.

In the end, from a corporate perspective, it is the track record of the
general manager in the middle who signs the proposal that determines
the way the projections and calculations it contains are regarded. In
fact, when they pick up a proposal, top managers usually look first for
the name on the signature line before reading anything else. The name
says much about what you need to know. Particularly in multibusiness
or high-technology companies, some or all of top management may
have little basis for making an independent assessment of the detailed
foundations of the proposal. But when the sponsor of a proposal has a
record of always producing results that are as good or better than

promised, it is easy to approve that project even if the venture appears risky.[7] The reverse is also true when the sponsor has a record of being overly optimistic. Even if the project sounds like a 'slam dunk', something probably was overlooked or some positive projection was exaggerated.

In effect, top corporate officers behave like bankers who provide funds based on the reliability of the borrowers. In turn, as the quote in Ch. 1 makes clear, general managers in the middle sponsor only projects that strike them as providing an acceptable risk/reward trade-off. In fact, since the reputational effects of unfulfilled promises are so costly, general managers in the middle tend to sponsor only projects that appear, ex ante, to have negligible risk of turning out worse than proposed. Indeed, from a corporate perspective, analyzing a project's risk/reward trade-off is a principal role of general managers. Often, they are both the last level of executive in the hierarchy—looking downward—to understand what the corporation's strategic objectives are about, and the last level—looking upward—to understand the key details of the particular operating business.

Structural Context

This analysis leads directly to the final question. What is it that determines the content developed by specialists and the decision to provide impetus for projects by general managers in the middle? In both cases, research reveals that it is the formal organization, the way businesses are measured, and the way functional and general managers are measured and rewarded. We call these structures and systems the structural context of the organization.

In this framework, structural context is defined as the set of forces that influence the processes of definition and impetus. It is worth emphasizing the obvious elements of this observation. We have noted in Ch. 1 that information is distributed across the several levels and multiple units of a company's organization. The reason is precisely because specialists have been hired to bring their talents to bear on the particular needs of the company, subject to the integrating efforts of their general managers. How they use this information depends not only on the responsibilities that they have been given but also on how their performance is measured and rewarded. If the costs of excess capacity are severe for a plant manager, but costs for running out of capacity are negligible, that manager will be slow to propose new capacity. Indeed, since the situation we hypothesize is often the case, managers often wait to propose new capacity until they are so pushed to meet current demand that returns on new capacity appear sure.

In that same situation, we can imagine that the sales manager will take a very different view. The general manager of that unit will work to resolve the disagreement. How that balance is struck will determine the strategic posture of the company. If the announced corporate strategy is to build ahead of demand, but general managers are rewarded primarily for having high return on assets, we can imagine that very little capacity will in fact be put in place before demand is clear.

It is the remarkable sensitivity of management behavior to the structural context of the company that leads to a very important paradox. Although proponents of contingency theory, and particularly Alfred Chandler, argue that structure should be aligned to serve strategy, researchers continually report that it is the structural context that shapes the pattern of a company's resource commitments that in turn add up ex post to be company strategy. *Structure shapes strategy*.

The Model

We can summarize the preceding discussion by noting that three processes represent the answers to the three questions: the way content is defined, the way impetus for commitment is developed, and the way structural context shapes the first two. The participants in those processes function at the level of operating specialists and corporate top managers. Sitting between the corporate forest and the operating trees are the general managers in the middle who integrate the functional activity below them, as well as integrate the business thinking of those units with the corporate perspective above them.

General managers in the middle normally have such titles as division manager, country manager, or group manager. They are easy to pick out because, although they have responsibility for profit and loss, they report to higher-level general managers. (In very large companies, general managers may report to them.) Because they function as translators between the language of corporate objectives and policies and the language of business unit specifics, they must be bilingual—fully understanding corporate- and business-unit interaction. And as we have noted, their judgments are key.

The patterns of operations and analysis and commitment discussed were originally represented in a simple 3×3 model (Table 2.2). The corporate definition involves the mission, goals, and portfolio thinking of a company's top management. Strategy scholars call this 'corporate

Table 2.2 *The original RAP model*

	Definition of Content	*Impetus* for Commitment	Structural Context
Corporate	Corporate mission, financial goals and objectives, aggregate policies; may include technical and economic strategy	Commitment of funds and other resources	Designs formal organization, measures of business and managerial performance, incentives, and the work environment
General Manager in the Middle	Integrates corporate and business unit thinking, translates	Sponsors projects and plans that fit, slows or rejects those that don't; competes for resources	Interprets and adopts to business-unit needs
Operating	Business-unit/functional activity and policies. Proposes business-unit strategy, new investments	Champions proposals for new business, new capability, new capacity	The rules of the game

strategy'. For Opel, it included GM's decision to achieve global competitiveness through focused factories based in low-wage countries. As a general manager in the middle, Hughes knew this but responded to the opportunity facing his business unit in a way that challenged corporate thinking. Within his organization were functional leaders, particularly in manufacturing and engineering who *championed* building a new plant at Eisenach. Hughes actively sponsored this proposal, and commitment was forthcoming from Detroit. The rules governing these processes of planning and funding were governed by corporate capital budgeting procedure.

Subsequent Developments in Resource Allocation Theory

Much of the work reported in this book discusses how subsequent scholars have improved our understanding of strategic process and expanded and refined the RAP model to incorporate their findings. In part I, we continue to use the model as a way of tracking the development of knowledge and understanding since 1970. In Ch. 3, Robert Burgelman explores the difference between a response induced by top management and an autonomous response, in the sense that the response is devised by an operating unit and then funded by general managers in the middle in a way that comes to change corporate thinking. As noted in Ch. 1, this is what happened at Timken as opposed to GM where corporate strategy remained unchanged. Using the 3×3 model, we note that the success of the Polish initiative resulted in a change in corporate definition of Timken strategy. Using Burgelman's model, we track the autonomous (bottom-up) change in strategic context. In Ch. 4, we close part I with Gilbert and Christensen's articulation of a model of theory development based on anomaly, recategorization, and theory revision. They use the model as a road map to show how subsequent scholars of resource allocation have been able to use this process to generate more insight into the RAP model.

The research described in subsequent chapters deals with other aspects of the top management question. Part II, introduced by Don Sull, explores the problems that develop when the bottom-up process of resource allocation breaks down, in the sense that resource commitments fail to deal adequately with shifts in strategic circumstances. In the studies reported here, problems such as response to disruptive technologies or business divestment pose severe difficulties for even well-run firms. Christensen and Bower explore the particular difficulties posed by disruptive changes in technology. Sull describes the challenge of withdrawal from a business when the environment shifts but the structural context does not change. And Kuemmerle examines how political and personal conflict among middle managers can distort the bottom-up process of resource allocation.

Part III, introduced by Clark Gilbert, reports on the way top management can restore the bottom-up process by managing the context that shapes definition and selection. Noda and Bower show how early differences in structural, strategic, and capital market context can cause firms with otherwise similar capabilities facing similar opportunities to realize very different strategies. Then, Gilbert shows how senior management can actively reframe the way operating managers interpret external events, allowing them to shape strategic outcomes by reframing the forces that shape the bottom-up process of the firm.

Part IV, introduced by Thomas Eisenmann, focuses on when corporate intervention requires more than just managing context, but also involves direct intervention in definition and impetus processes, changing the substantive content of business unit strategy. Eisenmann and Bower consider ways in which entrepreneurial action of top management can overcome limitations of RAP. Michael Raynor introduces real options as a way to conceive of strategic management of RAP. Finally, examining strategic process in the context of multinational companies, Yves Doz describes an approach to organization in which widespread distribution of information as well as the activity of strategic integration is more explicitly recognized. This leads him to consider the central role that top management plays in managing strategic process.

In Part V, a series of essays by a group of academics whose interests include strategic process, but whose research is grounded in a discipline, provides perspective on the process research laid out in the main body of the book. John Roberts considers the implication of the resource allocation process for the approach to corporate finance taken by financial economists. He notes that even though some economists have begun to incorporate a more complex view of a firm into their models, standard finance texts still treat capital budgeting as if projects should be ranked by projected financial return. Daniel Levinthal considers the implications of the resource allocation process for strategic adaptation to environmental change. Margaret Peteraf highlights connections to the resource-based view of the firm, emphasizing potential collaborations between the two perspectives. Finally, Joel Podolny uses network theory to propose a novel view of the role of corporate management. The closing essay by Joseph Bower and Clark Gilbert reviews the line of development over thirty-five years of research, discusses how the model has developed, and examines a series of fundamental questions that remain to be answered.

Endnotes

1. The model was developed to describe the allocation of capital. It quickly became clear that the model could be used to analyze the allocation of other critical resources, including operating funds, human resources, key people, and information—any strategic process. Because we are examining how the process of resource allocation significantly influences what strategy will be, we shift in later chapters and discuss the strategic process.
2. For a survey of the early studies, see J. L. Bower and Y. L. Doz (1979). 'Strategy Formulation: A Social and Political Process', in D. E. Schendel and C. W. Hofer (eds.), *Strategic Management: A New View of Business and Planning*. Boston, Mass.: Little Brown.
3. J. L. Bower (1970). *Managing the Resource Allocation Process*. Boston, Mass.: Harvard Business School Press, 52–7.
4. Herbert A. Simon (1957). *Models of Man*. New York: John Wiley & Sons. R. A. Cyert and J. A. March (1963). *A Behavioral Theory of the Firm*. Englewood Cliffs, NJ: Prentice Hall.
5. Net Present Value (NPV) calculates the present value of an investment's future net cash flows minus the initial investment, using a given discount rate. Economic Value Added (EVA) is the monetary value of an entity at the end of a time period minus the monetary value of that same entity at the beginning of that time period. Both NPV and EVA are designed to measure and compare project and firm-level performance.
6. This finding was first reported in Bower, *Managing the RAP*, 57–60.
7. Note that this is not always wise. In later chapters, we discuss ways in which managers have learned to deal with the challenge posed by their ignorance of critical substance.

3

The Role of Strategy Making in Organizational Evolution

Robert A. Burgelman

1. Introduction

A narrow, technical view of strategy involves using resources and deploying capabilities to achieve objectives and to prevail in competition. A broader organizational view includes making a rational determination of a company's purposes and vital interests that are essential to its continued survival as an institution. In this view, strategy involves external and internal forces that have the potential materially to affect a company's destiny.[1] Adopting an evolutionary theoretical perspective to study how strategy comes about and what its role is in shaping a company's destiny focuses on strategy making as an organizational process[2] and raises several important questions not readily contemplated by other perspectives. For instance: What strategy-making processes produce survival-enhancing strategic change? How do generic and substantive corporate strategies co-evolve? How do strategy process and strategy content co-evolve? What are the consequences of periods of extraordinary success for strategy making as adaptive organizational capability? What is the link between strategy making and organizational inertia? Answers to these questions, which extend the frontier of the field of strategic management, and can be addressed with the help of conceptual frameworks that evolutionary organization theory provides.[3]

This chapter discusses three conceptual tools rooted in evolutionary organization theory and briefly summarizes findings of longitudinal research of Intel Corporation's evolution that used them.[4] Intel is one of the most important firms of the digital age, and its evolution highlights the fundamental technological and economic forces that characterize digital industries.[5] The study identified three major epochs in Intel's history: Epoch I: Intel the memory company (1968–85); Epoch II: Intel the microprocessor company (1985–98); and Epoch III: Intel the Internet building block company (beyond 1998). The three epochs correspond roughly to the tenure of Gordon Moore, Andy Grove, and Craig Barrett as Intel's CEOs. The study compared the strategy-making approach of these successive CEOs and examined their efficacy within the extended context of Intel as an evolving system.

The chapter is organized as follows. Section 2 briefly discusses key processes that constitute the analytical core of evolutionary organization theory and two of its approaches: organizational ecology and organizational learning. Both approaches are especially useful for studying strategy making. Section 3 describes three conceptual tools that, together, serve as an evolutionary research lens for studying the role of strategy making in firm evolution. Sections 4–5 summarize the research findings generated by applying these tools to the study of Intel's evolution. Section 7 discusses the implications of these findings for potentially important inescapable dilemmas in the natural dynamics of organizational adaptation discovered in previous research. Section 8 examines the theoretical and practical implications of an evolutionary perspective on the role of strategy making in organizational adaptation. Section 9 offers some conclusions and directions for further research.

2. Strategy Making and Evolutionary Organization Theory

Variation, selection, retention, and competition are the key processes of evolutionary organization theory.[6] They are generic, not necessarily biological, processes that can be fruitfully applied to organizational evolution.[7] That these key processes are necessary and sufficient for organizations to emerge and evolve is the central axiom of evolutionary organization theory. They occur simultaneously at the organization, population, and community levels of analysis. Strategy making cast in terms of intra-organizational variation, selection, retention, and competition adds an additional level of analysis that can be studied in its own right as well as in relation to the other levels. Purposeful variations at the intra-organizational level, for instance, may sometimes look like emergent variations at the organizational level, and intra-organizational selection processes can lead to organization-level adaptation.

Organizational Ecology and Strategy Making

In the mid-1970s, organizational ecology emerged as a new theoretical approach.[8] The key argument of the original formulation of the theory went roughly as follows. Organizational change must be understood at the level of entire populations of similar organizations and as the result of replacement and selection rather than of adaptation. For instance, suppose one measured the average characteristics of companies in a particular population, say the semiconductor industry, in 1960 and did so again in 2000. And suppose one found significant differences in average company characteristics. Organizational ecology posits that these differences do not come about because the incumbent companies have changed but because of an ongoing process of selection (incumbent companies exiting the industry usually because of failure) and replacement (new companies with different characteristics entering the industry). Incumbent companies fail in the face of environmental change because organizational inertia prevents them from adapting. In short, organizational inertia causes companies to be selected against. The rates of founding and disbanding drive strategic change.

During the 1980s, the organizational ecology argument was subtly modified,[9] in part, because the original formulation begged the question of why companies would be inert in the first place. The major reason for inertia proposed in the revised formulation of the theory is that companies need to develop routines and procedures that make their behavior reliable, predictable, and accountable to key constituencies, such as customers, suppliers, employees, industry analysts, and so on. These attributes allow companies to overcome the liabilities of being new, give them legitimacy, and lead them to be selected by the environment against others that are not reliable, predictable, and accountable. The very efforts to be reliable, predictable, and accountable, however, make it difficult for companies to change in major ways after they have been selected. Hence, the new argument was that environmental selection leads to organizational inertia. There is strong empirical evidence in support of organizational ecology. Organizational ecology, however, continues to raise a challenge because even in the revised theory there is little room for adaptation based on strategy.

The premise of the research summarized in this chapter is that a fruitful integration of organizational ecology and strategy is possible.[10] The argument, briefly, runs as follows. Almost all companies start small and are subject to liabilities of newness (they are unknown, untested, lacking legitimacy, and so on). The major force faced by small, new companies is environmental selection. Most small, new companies do not survive external selection pressures. Organizational ecology provides a useful theoretical framework within which the evolutionary dynamics of small, new companies can be more clearly understood. Some companies, however, do survive and become large and established. Although large, established companies remain subject to the selection force of the external environment—and many succumb to it in the long run—they have gained the opportunity to substitute internal selection for external selection. Each established company constitutes an ecology in its own right, and its survival and success depends on how well it takes advantage of its internal ecological processes. Strategy making is an important part of these processes which, similar to the processes at the level of organizational populations, are based critically on their ability to enter into new businesses and exit from failing businesses over time.[11]

Intra-organizational variation comes about as the result of individuals (or small groups) seeking expression of their special skills and career advancement by pursuing strategic initiatives. These initiatives draw on existing and/or new competencies and routines and take shape as new organizational units (e.g. functional, product-based, geographical) within the organization. Selection works through administrative and cultural mechanisms regulating the allocation of resources and paying attention to different strategic initiatives and associated competencies, routines, and organizational units. Selection operates on competencies and routines as well as on the organizational units containing them. Retention, which concerns the initiatives that survive in the external environment and grow to be important within the company, takes the form of organizational-level learning about the factors that account for their success. Internal competition arises from different strategic initiatives struggling to obtain resources necessary to grow and increase in importance in the company. Internal competition between strategic initiatives more or less can be tightly linked to the external competition these initiatives encounter.

Strategy Making and Organizational Learning

Adopting an evolutionary perspective implies that outcomes are indeterminate and can be explained only after the fact. This seems almost the exact antipode of the traditional view of strategy, which is to determine in advance the ensemble of strategic actions that will achieve desired outcomes. There is no conflict, however, when strategy making is viewed as an organizational learning process. Strategy becomes real when consequential action is taken—often by multiple strategic actors simultaneously. Consequential action commits the company to a course of action that is difficult to reverse.[12] Of course, thorough preparatory work on deciding such a course of action is important. Equally important, however, is the work that comes after a course of action has been decided. In highly dynamic industries, the unpredictable interaction and correlation of forces make most strategic plans unreliable by the time they are implemented.[13] In such environments, effective strategists must be able to understand quickly why their plan-based actions produce particular, often unanticipated outcomes. Strategic recognition provides a basis for taking further strategic actions. Sometimes this involves abandoning the course of action—for instance, exiting from a failing business.

The capacity consistently to align action with stated strategy is the hard-won gain of an organizational learning process. Top management learns what the company's distinctive competencies are, in which product-markets the company can win, what core values provide safe guidance when faced with ambiguous choices, and which objectives are meaningful and worth reaching for. That part of the strategy-making process through which strategic action is deliberately driven in a more or less foreseeable pattern toward desired outcomes is called the induced-strategy process (see below). But strategy making also manifests itself as a learning process through the autonomous-strategy process (see below). Strategic action at higher levels in the management hierarchy benefits from interpretation of the outcomes of strategic action at lower levels. Progress in this social-learning process depends on multilevel interplay between action and cognition. The effectiveness of the sequence of interplay depends on correctly interpreting the results of strategic action at each level, which makes it possible to articulate strategic content for that level. That strategic content then becomes the stepping stone for more encompassing strategic action at the next managerial level, and so on. The autonomous part of the strategy-making process integrates lower-level strategic action to achieve company-level strategic rationality.[14] Ratification of the outcomes of the autonomous-strategy process by top management provides a basis for amending the corporate strategy.

3. Evolutionary Theoretical Lens: Three Conceptual Tools

In the realm of theory, the processes of variation, selection, retention, and competition are general, abstract, and non-experiential. In the realm of practice, common language describing strategy making is particular, concrete, and experiential. Business leaders do not use the terminology of pure theory to think and talk about strategy making and find it difficult to relate to its formal mathematical and statistical models. Scholars, on the other hand, find it difficult to gain deeper insight when limited to common language and like to do more than produce a coherent and complete narrative of best practice. Conceptual frameworks, which help bridge the gap between pure theory and best practice,[15] are specific, substantive, and suggestive. Both business leaders and scholars more readily understand and relate to the boxes-and-arrows charts used to represent conceptual frameworks.

The longitudinal study of Intel's strategic evolution used three conceptual tools that bridged the general, abstract, and non-experiential concepts of evolutionary organization theory and the particular, concrete, and experiential narrative of strategy making at Intel. The three tools formed an evolutionary research lens to identify and analyze the role of strategy making in firm evolution at three levels of analysis: Tool I: company–environment interface level, Tool II: company level, and Tool III: intra-company level. The evolutionary research lens had strong 'zooming' capabilities: from industry and company interface-level forces and their interactions to company-level induced and autonomous-strategy processes and their evolving balance to the intra-company-level details of strategic leadership activities involved in these processes. Figure 3.1 shows the tools.[16]

4. Tool I: Forces Driving Firm Evolution

The framework of dynamic forces driving company evolution (Tool I in Fig. 3.1) served to analyze industry-level and company-level processes of variation, selection, retention, and competition and their interplay throughout Intel's evolution.[17]

Harmony and Disharmony among the Dynamic Forces

During Epoch I, Japanese new entrants deploying manufacturing-based strategies in the dynamic random access memory (DRAM) business represented an industry-level variation. Industry-level selection processes (customer choice) favored these variations. As a result, the basis of competitive advantage in the DRAM industry changed fundamentally and eroded Intel's strategic position. Intel's internal-selection environment favored DRAM variations based on the company's distinctive competencies (circuit design and process

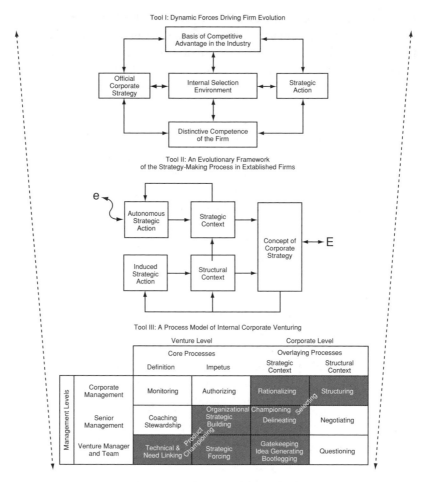

Figure 3.1 Evolutionary lens on strategy making

Source: Tool I: Adapted from R. A. Burgelman, 'Fading Memories: A Process Theory of Strategic Business Exit', *Administrative Science Quarterly* 39 (1994: 31). Tool II: Adapted from id. 'A Model of the Interaction of Strategic Behavior, Corporate Context, and the Concept of Strategy', *Academy of Management Review* 8 (1983: 65). Tool III: Adapted from id. 'A Process Model of Internal Corporative Venturing in the Diversified Major Firm', *Administrative Science Quarterly* 28 (1983: 230).

technology) that were not consistent with the variations selected at the industry level, leading the company to being selected out of the DRAM industry and replaced with new competitors. Even though Intel's internal-selection environment motivated strategic action that moved scarce manufacturing resources away from DRAM, Intel's official strategy continued to retain DRAM as a core business for several years after Intel had stopped being a major player in the industry.

External variation, selection, retention, and competition processes became inconsistent with Intel's internal variation, selection, retention, and competition processes. A growing disharmony among the dynamic forces driving Intel's evolution characterized Epoch I. The basis of competitive advantage in the industry diverged from Intel's distinctive competencies, and Intel's official strategy diverged from its strategic actions. Intel's eventual exit from DRAM was consistent with the predictions of organizational ecology, which were premised on strong forces of strategic inertia.

Generic and Substantive Corporate Strategies

The interplay between industry-level and internal variation, selection, retention, and competition processes illuminated the link between generic[18] and substantive corporate strategies. The study of Intel's transformation during Epoch I revealed the powerful inertial force associated with generic strategy and suggested that generic strategy was a more enduring feature of a company than its substantive strategy. Intel's generic strategy, based on differentiation and product leadership, endured in DRAM for several product generations in the face of the changing basis of competitive advantage in the industry, which favored the cost leadership-based generic strategy of the new entrants. After the exit from DRAM, the differentiation-based generic strategy still remained in force, having found in microprocessors a new substantive expression.

Strategy Making Shapes Destiny

There was life—Epoch II—for Intel after DRAM. The exit from DRAM did not cause Intel to disband. Microprocessors were an autonomous internal variation that was consistent with Intel's differentiation-based generic strategy and opened up a new viable niche in the external environment. Success in the external-selection environment caused Intel's internal-selection environment to favor microprocessors. During the 1970s, microprocessors were slow to develop into a major new business. In 1980, IBM's selection of Intel's 8088 microprocessor for the first PC was a fortuitous event, but one that was related to Intel's distinctive competencies in developing complete products and vigorously pursuing design wins. The fast growth of the PC market segment during the early 1980s was an exogenous factor that made the new niche very attractive. By the time Intel was ready to exit the DRAM business in 1984–5, microprocessors already had been retained as its new de facto substantive strategy. Strategic renewal through exiting from existing and entering into new businesses through the internal ecological processes of the strategy-making process redefined the company's destiny. Strategy making thus shaped destiny.

Destiny Shapes Strategy Making

As Epoch II unfolded, the basis of competitive advantage in the microprocessor market segment continued to be closely aligned with Intel's traditionally strong distinctive competencies in design and process technology and newly found strength in manufacturing. Top management also closely aligned strategic action with official corporate strategy. These alignments strengthened Intel's strategic position in the microprocessor industry and reinforced retention of microprocessors as Intel's new substantive corporate strategy. Throughout Epoch II, Intel maintained harmony among the dynamic forces. Industry-level selection within the Intel Architecture-based PC market segment favored Intel's product variations over those of AMD and Cyrix because of several complementary strategic thrusts. Intel maintained its sole source position for several product generations through product leadership combined with effective ecosystem development and vigorous protection of intellectual property. The company also successfully built the Intel brand with end users in mind and enjoyed enormous economies of scale in manufacturing. In addition, vertical integration into chipsets and motherboards helped Intel limit the bargaining power of its OEM customers. Industry-level selection between microprocessor architectures in the personal computer market segment favored the product variations emerging from the population of IA-based suppliers, which included Intel, AMD, and Cyrix, over those of the RISC-based competitors because of increasing returns to adoption. Intel's success with its sole-source microprocessor strategy, started in 1985, triggered the coevolution[19] of its strategy and the PC market segment during Epoch II. Intel became the main driver of its product-market environment. But this coevolution, in turn, strongly shaped Intel's strategy making during Epoch II and created lock-in with the PC market segment: a positive feedback process that tied Intel's fate increasingly to that of its environment. Intel needed to make larger and larger investments in manufacturing capacity to stay ahead of the surging demand for PCs, as well as in R&D to provide the OEMs with system-level innovations necessary to enable adoption of its ever more powerful microprocessors in their product development. Coevolutionary lock-in, however, produced new forms of strategic inertia (see below). Destiny thus also shaped strategy making.

5. Tool II: An Evolutionary Framework of the Strategy-Making Process

Zooming in on Intel's strategy-making process, the framework of induced- and autonomous-strategy processes (Tool II in Fig. 3.1) further illuminated the role of internal variation, selection, retention, and competition.

Internal Ecology Model of Strategy Making

During Epoch I, induced product variations (based on circuit design and process technology innovations) in the DRAM business were favored by part of Intel's structural context (R&D resource allocation decisions) but were unsuccessful in the external-selection environment. This led these variations to be disfavored by another part of the structural context: scarce manufacturing resource allocation decisions were based on the maximize margin-per-wafer start rule, which reflected the company's generic strategy of technology-based differentiation. Autonomous-product variations (microprocessors) were successful in the external environment and also favored by manufacturing resource allocation based on the maximize margin-per-wafer start rule. Over time, the outcomes of the combined internal- and external-selection processes operating on induced and autonomous variations dissolved the strategic context of DRAM and determined the strategic context of microprocessors, thereby leading Intel to abandon DRAM and retain microprocessors. These internal ecological processes transformed Intel from a semiconductor memory company into a microprocessor company. Similar to the role of founding and disbanding as sources of population-level change in organizational ecology, entry into new businesses and exit from existing ones are sources of corporate-level transformation in the internal ecology of strategy making.[20]

Rational Actor Model of Strategy Making

During Epoch II, Intel's induced-strategy process became strongly focused on the core business. Unplanned internal competition for design resources between the core $\times 86$ microprocessor product family, which was based on the complex instruction set computing (CISC) architecture, and the autonomous initiative associated with the i860 microprocessor, which was based on the reduced instruction set computing (RISC) architecture, however, created serious confusion.

To resolve this confusion, Andy Grove decided to 'vectorize' every-body at Intel in the same direction. Grove developed a strong strategic leadership discipline for the induced-strategy process. Intel's structural context became finely tuned for executing the core business strategy. Intel's strategy making evolved from the internal ecology model to the rational actor model[21] of strategy making. Intel's in-duced-strategy process drove the PC market segment. But, as noted earlier, this created coevolutionary lock-in, which had inertial consequences. The company's structural context became tightly linked to the microprocessor strategy, which made new business de-velopment difficult. Chipsets, for instance, were initially viewed as an enabler for the core microprocessor business. During Epoch II, chipsets struggled because of scarce manufacturing resources. The strategic long-range planning process (SLRP) made it difficult, during Epoch II, for the newly emerging networking business, which was viewed as nonstrategic, to get on the agenda. In retrospect, the deter-mination of the strategic context for the networking business and its acceptance as an integral part of Intel's corporate strategy was slower than desirable.

Back to Internal Ecology Model?

The success achieved with the singular focus on the induced-strategy process during Epoch II seemed to contradict earlier findings based on the study of Epoch I, which posited the importance of both the autonomous- and induced-strategy processes for a company's adaptive capability. Toward the end of Epoch II, however, concerns of new business development beyond the core microprocessor business be-came again highly salient. Numerous autonomous strategic initiatives had sprung up during Epoch II, but Intel's capacity to turn some of these initiatives into new businesses had weakened significantly. The longitudinal research thus highlighted some of the limitations of the rational actor model of strategy making.

In Strategy Making, Process Generates Content and Content Disciplines Process

Content and process are sometimes viewed as separate vantage points from which to contemplate and study strategy. An evolutionary perspec-tive on strategy making, however, views process and content as inherently intertwined: process generates content, but content disciplines process.

During Epoch II, Andy Grove was very much concerned with the content of strategy. Grove decisively influenced Intel's focus on the PC market segment and on the distinctive competencies needed to drive its development. His deep involvement in strategy content was possible because Intel had a narrowly focused business strategy, which allowed Grove to develop deep intuition for the substantive strategy issues in the core business.[22] Grove's contribution, however, was initially based on strategic recognition rather than strategic planning. The evolutionary process of strategy making already had produced the foundation for Intel's new strategic content. The microprocessor's development had been fortuitous and its emergence as Intel's most important product gradual and unplanned. The installed base of Intel's microprocessors in the PC market segment was initially established by IBM. The force of increasing returns to adoption associated with the installed base was equally unplanned but gave Intel the opportunity to become a sole-source supplier. Once clearly established, the content of Intel's strategy then disciplined its strategy-making process, shaping the induced-strategy process to exploit fully the opportunities associated with the strategy.

Punctuated Equilibrium Reconsidered

Although the research findings do not rule out punctuated change, they do indicate that characterizing Intel's transformation during Epoch I as a sudden company-level strategic change taking place in 1984–5 would be misleading. Rather, Intel's transformation was the result of cumulative variation, selection, retention, and competition processes, which had been playing out for several years inside and outside the company before they culminated in the company-level transformation. Similarly, Intel's strategy change with respect to the networking business during Epoch II was the result of evolutionary processes that had been going on for many years. The findings thus suggest that claims involving punctuated equilibrium patterns should be verified with multilevel analyses of variation, selection, retention, and competition processes. What looks as punctuated change at the level of the company may look more continuous when considering also intra-organizational evolutionary processes.[23]

6. Tool III: Process Models of Strategy Making

The process model—Tool III of Fig. 3.1—helps zoom in further on the patterns of detailed strategic leadership activities involved in the internal variation, selection, retention, and competition processes associated with exiting from existing and entering into new businesses.[24] The internal corporate venturing (ICV) and strategic business exit (SBE) process models provided further theoretical insight into different mechanisms through which strategic leadership activities are coordinated in strategy making.[25] This further illuminates the process of self-organization,[26] the interplay of strategy content and process, and the role of strategic context determination and dissolution.

Coordinating Simultaneous Strategic Action

Using Tool III, the research highlighted the simultaneous strategic actions of multiple actors distributed throughout the organization involved in Intel's business exit from semiconductor memories and entry into microprocessors. The analysis showed that coordinating the simultaneous actions of multiple strategic actors into a coherent pattern of strategy making, especially in the face of environmental change, was a major challenge. During Epoch I, coordination was achieved primarily through the internal-selection environment. During Epoch II, Intel achieved coordination through strategic direction set by top management.

Internal-Selection Environment as Coordinating Mechanism   During Epoch I, Intel was in some ways successful in coordinating the strategic actions of different managers without strong direction from top management. The analysis showed that inertial deployment of distinctive competencies in the induced-strategy process led to unlinking product characteristics from evolving customer needs in Intel's successive DRAM offerings. This in turn led to unsuccessful efforts to reposition Intel's DRAM as niche products. Some middle-level managers systematically shifted manufacturing resources away from DRAM in response to structural context forces, which further undermined Intel's position in DRAM. Other middle-level managers, whose critical choices involved uncoupling commodity DRAM from further process technology development, exacerbated this. Together, these various activities dissolved the strategic context for DRAM and provided an opening for determining the strategic context for microprocessors within Intel. On the face of it, Intel's strategy making during Epoch I looked chaotic. However, the internal-selection environment—the structural and strategic contexts—coordinated the activities of various middle-level managers in a way that was survival enhancing for the company in the face of the radically changing semiconductor memory industry. As a result,

Intel was able to exit from a business that no longer was consistent with its differentiation-based generic strategy and product leadership culture and to enter into a new business that corresponded to a new propitious niche in the external environment. Strategic recognition on the part of top management made retroactive rationalization of these strategic actions possible.

Coordination through internal selection is a powerful manifestation of self-organization, which depends on 'mutually dependent criteria of action (utility functions)'.[27] Such criteria seem closely related to the idea of 'focal points', which are used by some scholars to give operational meaning to culture.[28] The various actors involved in the DRAM exit process all had the interest of Intel in mind. Some responded directly to the maximize margin-per-wafer-start rule, which served as a focal point in the company given Intel's generic strategy of technology-based differentiation and product leadership. Others had to make more complex trade-offs in the technology choices they faced, but they did so with the long-term interest of the company in mind. From the perspective of evolutionary organization theory, the analysis based on Tool III suggests that the internal-selection environment, self-organization, and culture are closely related concepts.

Strategic Direction as Coordinating Mechanism   During Epoch II, Andy Grove realized that Intel had been, to some extent, lucky to get the new opportunities associated with microprocessors. He exerted more centralized strategic leadership to exploit them. Grove formulated the content of Intel's strategy in a decisive way. He restructured Intel's strategic long-range planning process (SLRP) to communicate the corporate strategy and to get all senior executives to respond to it. He strongly focused Intel's induced-strategy process on the core microprocessor business and concentrated strategic decision making at the top, thereby limiting the role of lower levels mostly to the execution of the official corporate strategy. During Epoch II, Intel did not have to rely to the same extent on the self-organizing capacity of its internal ecology of strategy making as during Epoch I. Although tightly coordinated and extremely successful in executing the core business strategy, Intel's strategy-making process also became severely constraining. This was demonstrated by analyses based on process models of new business development concerning videoconferencing (ProShare) and consumer electronics (Hood River). These analyses demonstrated the overwhelming influence of the core business strategy and associated structural context on the definition of new business opportunities.

During Epoch II, the process model analysis of the networking business was able to document the potential limitations of Intel's rational actor model of strategy making. This analysis showed that during this extraordinarily successful period, Intel's capacity to manage the autonomous-strategy process had withered. Technical and need linking, product championing, and strategic forcing were effectively performed at the operational level, leading the networking business to grow to several hundred million dollars in revenue by the mid-1990s. Middle-level managers operating outside Intel's intensely focused induced-strategy process, however, found it difficult to engage effectively in strategic building and organizational championing activities necessary to activate strategic context-determination processes. As a consequence, the networking business was not able to grow commensurately with the industry, leading Cisco and others to dominate Intel. The chipset business, on the other hand, although initially not supported by Andy Grove, was able to complete effectively the strategic context-determination process by quickly demonstrating its importance for the core business at the time of the launch of the Pentium processor.

7. Dilemmas of Organizational Adaptation

The research findings obtained with the help of Tools I, II, and III provide insight into several inescapable dilemmas associated with the natural dynamics of organizational adaptation discovered in previous research.

The Position Versus Competence Dilemma

Research in organizational ecology on competitive intensity suggests a potential trade-off between positional advantages and advantages based on distinctive competencies.[29] Companies that rely on positional advantages shield themselves from competitive pressures and do not necessarily have to develop strong distinctive competencies in order to succeed. However, they are potentially vulnerable to new competitors using novel strategies to attack their niche. On the other hand, companies that rely on distinctive competence development to compete better with similar others may be able to hone sharply these competencies and become best in class. However, such distinctive competencies may become a trap and make the company vulnerable to new competitors with different distinctive competencies.[30] Intel, for instance, lost its strategic position in DRAM in part because of inertial deployment of its distinctive competencies (circuit design and process technology) in the face of new entrants competing on different distinctive competencies (large-scale precision manufacturing). Intel's distinctive competencies, however, also spawned a new product variation—microprocessors—that gave it the opportunity to get on a profitable growth trajectory in a new propitious niche. This time Intel also developed the manufacturing competencies necessary to defend its strategic position against competitors and potential new entrants. Considering the role of both the induced- and autonomous-strategy processes helps address this dilemma. Companies that have a strong induced-strategy process can attempt to match the competitive intensity they experience in their existing businesses. At the same time, companies need to develop the capacity to capitalize on new opportunities emerging in the autonomous-strategy process. Opportunities, which are often based on new distinctive competencies, allow companies to occupy new strategic positions and face weaker competitive pressures.

The Multibusiness Dilemma

An intriguing implication of the evolutionary ecological perspective on competition is that established companies comprising multiple businesses face the hazard of protecting some of the businesses from the severity of competitive pressures that stand-alone businesses encounter.[31] This may be the result simply of inertial tendencies or of political pressures. In either case, multibusiness companies may end up weakened overall. This dilemma can be addressed in the context of the framework of dynamic forces (Tool I) by considering further the role of the internal-selection environment. In principle, portfolio planning was devised in strategic management to bring more discipline to resource-allocation processes traditionally based on capital-budgeting processes. Strategic business exit is a key option in portfolio planning. However, as the current and other studies show, exit is difficult for a variety of reasons. For instance, as in the case of DRAM, strategic business exit as a product-market strategic decision can have strong potential implications for the company's distinctive competencies. The politics of resource allocation also are well documented.[32] These types of forces lead companies to shield some of their businesses from competitive reality in ways that stand-alone businesses would not be able to do. An important normative implication of Tool I is that a multibusiness firm's internal-selection environment should match the competitive intensity of the external-selection environment while simultaneously sharing and transferring best practices more rapidly and more efficiently than could happen in the external-selection environment.[33] Single-business firms may find it easier to remain focused than multibusiness firms and therefore may develop greater competitive intensity for some time. As their opportunity set declines, however, single-business firms also may find it more difficult to develop new business opportunities. In the long run, multibusiness firms able to withstand the competitive intensity of the focused players they encounter in each of their businesses may have an adaptive advantage.

The Narrow Business Strategy Dilemma

This, in turn, raises the dilemma of focus in strategy. Some economists have proposed a mathematical model of the profit-maximizing firm from which strong benefits of a narrow, top-driven business strategy could be deduced.[34] These scholars propose that in order to improve profits, firms have to have access to innovative projects. This, in turn, depends on the willingness of employees to develop projects. However, if they are worried that the firm will not adopt their projects and therefore they will not be rewarded for their efforts, employees are unlikely to spend effort in the first place. Adopting a clearly defined strategy is a means to overcoming employees' worries. Employees of a firm that commits itself to a general pattern of project adoption— a well-defined strategy that strictly rejects projects outside its scope—are reassured and therefore more motivated to pursue innovative projects in the set that corresponds to the pattern. The normative implications of this model correspond well to Intel's strongly focused induced-strategy process during Epoch II, which resembled a strategy vector. Andy Grove was able to drive Intel in the intended direction with a total force that was the sum of all the forces at its disposition. Intel's strongly focused induced-strategy process, however, resulted in coevolutionary lock-in with its product-market environment and engendered strategic inertia.

   In recent work, these same scholars show that, under certain conditions, a strategy-making process allowing for successful strategic initiatives outside the existing corporate strategy to amend the corporate strategy has greater profit-maximizing potential than one based on a narrow business strategy.[35] In this mathematical model, the firm employs a visionary CEO who is consistently biased in favor of certain projects and against others, but who leaves the door open for pursuing sufficiently good opportunities outside the existing vision. These scholars show the important role objective middle managers willing to support promising projects outside the CEO's vision play. They also show that the biased CEO must not interfere with the autonomy of these middle managers in allocating resources to projects. This model supports the potential value of the autonomous-strategy process in a company's efforts to secure long-term profitable growth, as well as for countering the inertial tendencies of coevolutionary lock-in.

The Coevolutionary Lock-in Dilemma (Exploitation vs. Exploration)

Highly successful narrow business strategies may engender coevolutionary lock-in, which exacerbates the difficulties in maintaining a balance between exploitation (induced strategy) and exploration (autonomous strategy) processes in organizational learning.[36] Both processes compete for limited resources, and company leaders necessarily make trade-offs between them. Given the extraordinary opportunities Intel faced in the core business, focusing on learning that increased its mean performance rather than on learning that could increase the variance of performance seemed rational.[37] Also, Andy Grove's ability to vectorize everybody at Intel in the same direction led to quick convergence of individual beliefs (strategic initiatives) and the organizational code (the corporate strategy).[38] Intel experienced a reasonable amount of turnover because low individual performers were systematically replaced, but this also made sure that the socialization of new employees to Intel's organizational code was rapid. Overall, Intel's induced-strategy process during Grove's tenure as CEO favored organizational learning that was maximally concerned with exploitation.

Exploration involves experimentation. It is viewed here through the lens of the autonomous-strategy process, which dissects exploration into autonomous strategic initiatives and the process of strategic context determination. The distinction between exploratory initiatives and the strategic context-determination process helps explain the mixed record of new business development during Intel's Epoch II. In spite of Andy Grove's efforts to drive everybody at Intel in the same strategic direction, numerous autonomous strategic initiatives continued to emerge, indicating continued attempts at exploration. Intel's reduced capacity to activate strategic context-determination processes, however, prevented the company from exploiting the more viable autonomous initiatives.

The Insufficient Variation Dilemma

Still another dilemma that established companies face, according to organizational ecology, even those with an active autonomous-strategy process, is that they will eventually not be able to match all the variations generated in the external environment. Some of these variations pose the threat of substitution; others are potential complements that carry the opportunity for moving the industry forward in advantageous directions. For example, simply witness the enormous variation spawned by the Internet in recent years, which no single established company could possibly match. Autonomous variations, while fortuitous, do not emerge randomly; they find their origin in companies competencies and resources. Hence, the amount of new variation that the autonomous-strategy process can generate is limited.

To avoid the strategic threats and/or capitalize on the opportunities associated with external variations, some companies in high-technology industries developed an acquisition capability[39] and sometimes adopted corporate venture capital approaches. Intel, for instance, through its Corporate Business Development group, has in recent years developed a new acquisition capability to augment its strategic thrust into the communications industry. It also made venture capital investments of hundreds of millions of dollars in start-up companies that have the potential to influence the evolution of the information-processing industries in directions favorable to Intel's microprocessors. In order to effectively help the established company adapt, these external variations must be linked to its corporate strategy, which depends on its ability to activate and complete strategic-context determination processes.

The Disruptive Technology Dilemma

Recent research outside the evolutionary ecological tradition has discovered an innovator's dilemma associated with disruptive technologies[40] that can be fruitfully subsumed under it. This dilemma, not unlike the one associated with the inertia of coevolutionary lock-in, indicates that resource allocation in well-managed companies is naturally driven by positive feedback from the external-selection environment and by concerns that top management can understand in light of the existing strategy. Both phenomena underscore the importance of developing the organization's capacity to activate strategic context-determination processes as a means for addressing strategic initiatives (potential substitutes/disruptive technologies as well as complements) that fall outside the corporate strategy at that particular time and that are usually highly uncertain. Strategic context-determination processes serve to counter this natural tendency of the resource-allocation process and to address explicitly the attendant evolutionary dilemmas.[41]

8. Strategy Making and Organizational Adaptation

The insights generated with the three evolutionary tools and the light they shed on several important dilemmas occurring in the course of the dynamics of organizational adaptation raise further questions: How many resources should a company devote, over time, to the induced- and autonomous-strategy processes, respectively? How does a company manage the difficulties of balancing opposing orientations within the strategy-making process? These questions have potentially important theoretical implications for typology-based approaches to strategy making. They also have normative implications for designing the internal ecology of strategy making as adaptive organizational capability.

Managing the Evolutionary Path of the Strategy-Making Process

Resource Allocation to Induced and Autonomous Processes   Strategy making as adaptive organizational capability depends on the combination of induced- and autonomous-strategy processes throughout a company's evolution. This of course does not imply that the weights on these two processes should be constant over time. During any given period, and given a specific resource level, top management explicitly or implicitly makes trade-offs in resources allocated to induced- and autonomous-strategic initiatives. In principle, the changing weights reflect the key strategic challenges a company faces during a particular period: Whether exploitation of existing opportunities or development of new ones is the dominant concern, both processes should be in play at all times.[42] Figure 3.2 illustrates the path surmised (not measured) of Intel's strategy making over the three Epochs of its evolution.

During Epoch I, Intel faced a large unexplored technological opportunity set and accordingly allocated resources to induced and autonomous initiatives in a fairly balanced way. During Epoch II, Intel faced the enormous opportunity set associated with microprocessors for the PC market segment and shifted resource allocation almost exclusively to induced initiatives. At the start of Epoch III, Intel faced declining relative growth opportunities associated with the PC market segment

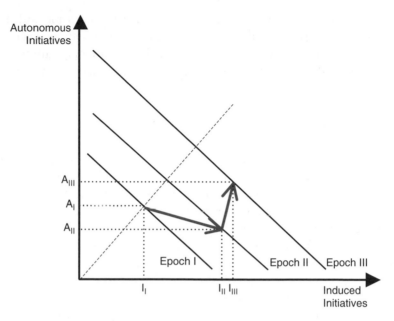

Figure 3.2 Expansion path of resource allocation in Intel's strategy making

but a new large opportunity set associated with communications technologies, and accordingly reestablished somewhat the balance between induced and autonomous initiatives.

Viewed as a rational choice problem, different analytical approaches may be helpful in establishing an appropriate quantitative balance in the resource allocation to induced- and autonomous-strategic initiatives. The basic structure of the problem can be viewed in terms of the two-arm bandit class of problems in decision theory[43] or in terms of long-term versus short-term regulation in optimal control and self-organization theory.[44] In theories of limited rationality, aspiration levels play an important role in allocating resources to search (exploration).[45] On a project-by-project basis, some rational choice approaches rely on real options theory.[46]

Managing Simultaneity in Strategy Making: The Role of Strategic Context

Even if the optimal proportion of induced- and autonomous-strategic initiatives could be calculated at any given time, the question still lingers whether the behaviors associated with induced- (variation reducing) and autonomous- (variation increasing) strategy processes are fundamentally at odds with one another or can be effectively pursued simultaneously. Strategic context-determination processes appear to be the crucial nexus between exploration and exploitation and key to balancing effectively induced- and autonomous-strategy processes. They help turn exploration efforts into new exploitation opportunities. Strategic context-determination processes complement a company's structural context in important ways. They offer the possibility of suspending the selective effects of the structural context, which almost unavoidably tends to become fine-tuned for supporting top management's current strategic intent.[47] And they serve to create linkages between autonomous strategic action and the company's strategy, thereby amending it. The capacity to activate and successfully complete such processes depends critically on the cognitive, political, and general management abilities of middle-level executives. A company's ability to activate and complete strategic context determination and dissolution processes can be usefully viewed as a measure of the intelligence of its internal-selection environment. These processes may be at the very heart of strategy making as adaptive organizational capability.[48]

Strategy Making and Organizational Typologies

An evolutionary perspective also sheds light on whether the strategy-making process may make a company take on significantly different features over time, or whether a company's type is fixed and fundamentally constrains its strategy-making process. Evolutionary theory implies the former,[49] but typologies that distinguish between firm types persist in the strategic management literature. One well-known typology distinguishes 'Prospector', 'Defender', 'Analyzer', and 'Reactor' types.[50] During Epoch I, Intel's autonomous-strategy process played a prominent role, and Intel resembled the 'Prospector' type, almost continually searching for new product-market opportunities in a rapidly changing environment. During Epoch II, Intel's induced-strategy process became extremely dominant, and Intel morphed into the 'Defender' type, narrowing its product-market domain in a dynamic but predictable environment. At the start of Epoch III, Intel seemed to be trying to restore the balance between its induced- and autonomous-strategy processes and to be moving toward the 'Analyzer' type, simultaneously operating in a relatively stable environment (the PC market segment) and more rapidly changing ones (networking and communications). Intel's evolution seems to suggest that the typical features a company exhibits during different epochs in its history may be driven more by its strategy-making process than the other way around.

Strategy Making as Long-Term Adaptive Organizational Capability
The evolution of Intel's strategy-making process suggests its importance as an emergent property of organizations. As Intel's Epoch II shows, the approach of the CEO and the top management team strongly influences the strategy-making process. The inertial consequences of CEO Andy Grove's success in driving Intel's strategy-making process during Epoch II in ways that approximated the classical rational actor model, however, also provided further support for a perspective that views strategy making as adaptive organizational capability in terms of an internal ecology model. The research showed that an organization's long-term adaptation, spanning multiple generations of CEOs, critically depends on maintaining the strategic renewal capability of its internal ecology of strategy making. This conceptual separation between the strategy-making process as emergent property and the influence of any given top management team in the course of a company's history provides a foundation for novel directions in further research about the role of strategy making in firm evolution.[51]

9. Conclusion

This chapter summarized insights obtained from studying Intel's strategy making and resource allocation throughout its history, with the lens of evolutionary organization theory. The three tools of the evolutionary lens, together, form a conceptual bridge between the key processes of evolutionary organization theory and strategic management. The insights have implications for many important theoretical issues in the strategy field. For instance, these tools offered the opportunity to address important questions concerning the forms that resource allocation takes that are not readily contemplated by other perspectives, in particular in allocating resources to induced- and autonomous-strategic initiatives and balancing these resource commitments over time. They helped draw attention to the coevolution of generic and substantive corporate strategies, provided increased understanding of the interplay between process and content in strategy making, and shed additional light on punctuated equilibrium views.

They also helped address several strategic dilemmas discovered in previous evolutionary research.

Perhaps the most important contribution of the evolutionary perspective consists in showing that the internal ecology of strategy making is an emergent property of organizations. The research findings showed that this process may be strongly influenced by the approach of the CEO and the top management team during any particular period of the company's evolution, even approximating the classical rational actor model. But they also show that its long-term adaptive capacity, that is, spanning multiple generations of CEOs, depends on maintaining a balance in resource allocation between induced- and autonomous-strategy processes. This chapter thus suggests that a conceptual separation between characteristics of the strategy-making process as emergent property and the characteristics of the particular top and senior executives that employ it during any period in the firm's history is useful. This conceptual separation offers a foundation for novel directions in further research about the role of strategy making in firm evolution.

The theoretical insights generated by the evolutionary research lens do not of course exhaust all that can be learned from the history of Intel's strategy making. Alternative research lenses may discover valuable additional insights. The insights produced by the evolutionary lens, however, link theory of strategy making more closely to evolutionary organization theory and provide at least one clear avenue for cumulative knowledge development. Further research, for instance, could focus on the characteristics of the internal-selection environment that are associated with high adaptiveness or, conversely, engender inertial tendencies in established companies. In particular, further research could focus on the role of strategic context determination and dissolution processes in helping established companies cope with internal and external variation and associated dilemmas identified by research in organizational ecology and the economic theory of the firm. Further study of leadership activities that constitute these processes, and of the external and internal forces that shape them, offers the prospect of adding meaningfully to the knowledge base for strengthening the strategic leadership capability of large, complex organizations.

Endnotes

1. R. A. Burgelman (2002). *Strategy Is Destiny: How Strategy Making Shapes a Company's Future.* New York: Free Press.
2. Peter Paret in the introduction to the 1986 sequel to *Makers of Modern Strategy* (Princeton University Press, 1943), a classic of the military strategy literature,

points out that once the broader historical context is considered, it might be better to title the book 'The Making of Modern Strategy'. In the field of strategic management, Henry Mintzberg was among the first to pay systematic attention to strategy as an organizational process. See: 'Patterns in Strategy Formation', *Management Science* 24 (1978): 934–48.

3. In 1962, Alfred D. Chandler offered 'strategy' as the unifying theoretical concept for studying a company's development. See A. D. Chandler III (1962). *Strategy and Structure*. Cambridge, Mass.: MIT. Chandler's historical analysis offered insight into the process through which companies develop internal competencies and capabilities in response to exogenous external growth opportunities. He argued that companies then deliberately seek to exploit these through diversification and that they develop new structural and administrative arrangements to support their diversification strategy. In 1959, Edith Penrose elucidated the endogenous dynamics of a company's growth. See E. T. Penrose (1968). *The Theory of the Growth of the Firm*. Oxford: Basil Blackwell. Penrose's business economics analysis offered novel insights into the managerial actions that constitute a company's internal impulse to grow. The fundamental research questions raised here extend the dynamic perspective on strategy introduced by Chandler and Penrose. They complement those raised by Rumelt, Schendel, and Teece as the defining ones of the field of strategy. See R. P. Rumelt, D. E. Schendel, and D. J. Teece (1994). *Fundamental Issues in Strategy*. Boston, Mass.: Harvard Business School Press.

4. For a complete report of the research method and findings, see Burgelman, *Strategy Is Destiny*.

5. See e.g. B. Arthur (1987). 'Competing Technologies: An Overview', in G. Dosi (ed.), *Technical Change and Economic Theory*. New York: Columbia University Press, 590–607.

6. Howard Aldrich offers a definition and discussion of these evolutionary processes. Variation 'is a departure from routine or tradition and may be intentional or blind'. Intentional variations result from the deliberate attempts of people or organizations to generate alternative opportunities and seek solutions to problems. Blind variations, on the other hand, 'result from accidents, chance, luck, conflict, malfeasance, creative exploration, and so forth'. Selection is generated by forces 'that differentially select or selectively eliminate certain types of variations'. Selection occurs within organizations as well as at the organization and population (e.g. industry) levels. Retention 'occurs when selected variations are preserved, duplicated, or otherwise reproduced so that the selected activities are repeated on future occasions or the selected structures appear again in future generations.' Finally, competition (struggle) for scarce resources occurs between strategic initiatives within organizations, between organizations, and between populations. See Howard E. Aldridge (1999). *Organizations Evolving*. London: Sage. The first systematic linking of the strategy-making process and the key processes of evolutionary organization theory

can be found in R. A. Burgelman (1983). 'A Model of the Interaction of Strategic Behavior, Corporate Context and the Concept of Strategy'. *Academy of Management Review* 8: 61–70. For a more recent sampling of evolutionary studies in strategy, see: W. P. Barnett and R. A. Burgelman (Summer 1996). *Strategic Management Journal* Vol. 17, Special Issue: 'Evolutionary Perspectives on Strategy', 5–19. For a broad overview of perspectives of evolutionary organization theory, see J. A. C. Baum and B. McKelvey (eds.) (1999), *Variations in Organization Science: In Honor of Donald T. Campbell*. Thousand Oaks, Calif.: Sage.

7. Stephen Jay Gould explains why biological evolution is a bad analog for cultural change. See S. J. Gould (1991). *Bully for Brontosaurus: Reflections in Natural History*. New York: W. W. Norton, 64–5. Gould nevertheless uses evolutionary analogy effectively to elucidate some important findings in the adoption of particular technologies. Other evolutionary scientists have pursued the implications of evolutionary theory for understanding the behavior of social systems. See e.g. R. Dawkins (1986). *The Blind Watchmaker*. New York: W. W. Norton.

8. Several contributions have helped clarify the dual inheritance mechanism in cultural evolution. Cultural entities evolve not only because of the transmission of a genetic heritage, but also because of learning processes. See R. Boyd and P. J. Richerson (1985). *Culture and the Evolutionary Process*. Chicago: University of Chicago Press.

9. See M. T. Hannan and J. Freeman (1977). 'The Population Ecology of Organizations'. *American Journal of Sociology* 83: 929–84.

10. See M. T. Hannan and J. Freeman (1984). 'Structural Inertia and Organizational Change'. *American Sociological Review* 49: 149–64.

11. For a first effort at integration, see R. A. Burgelman (1990). 'Strategy Making and Organizational Ecology: A Conceptual Integration', in J. V. Singh (ed.), *Organizational Evolution: New Directions*. Newbury Park, Calif.: Sage. More generally, linking substantive research in strategic management to discipline-based intellectual traditions in organization theory and organizational economics may offer the best opportunity for developing cumulative knowledge. This is, of course, not necessary to make the research findings useful or to legitimate the research in the first place. For instance, important aspects of the work of Clark and Wheelwright on product and process development, such as the product development funnel concept, could be discussed in terms of the variation, selection, retention, and competition processes of evolutionary organization theory, but they do not do so. See K. B. Clark and S. C. Wheelwright (1993). *Managing New Product and Process Development: Text and Cases*. New York: Free Press.

12. For an early discussion of the intraorganizational ecology model in strategic management, see R. A. Burgelman (1991). 'Intraorganizational Ecology of Strategy Making and Organizational Adaptation: Theory and Field Research'. *Organization Science* 2: 239–62. Viewing the

strategy-making process as an internal opportunity structure provides a rational basis for explaining both induced and autonomous strategic initiatives within the internal ecology of strategy making. Recent research suggests that autonomous strategic initiatives may be influenced by external opportunity structures as well as by internal ones. See A. H. Taylor (May 2000). 'A Process Study of the Influence of Competition between New Product Initiatives on Innovation and Organizational Learning'. Doctoral Dissertation, Graduate School of Business, Stanford University. For a recent overview of research adopting an intraorganizational ecological perspective, see: C. Galunic and J. Weeks, 'Intraorganizational Ecology', in J. Baum (ed.), *Blackwell's Companion to Organizations* (forthcoming).

13. For a somewhat different but consistent view of strategy as consequential action, see P. Ghemawat (1991). *Commitment: The Dynamic of Strategy*. New York: Free Press.

14. Leo Tolstoy in *War and Peace* provides perhaps the most compelling articulation of the limitations of strategic planning in war, arguably the most dynamic strategic situation imaginable. He asks, for instance, 'What science can there be where everything is vague and depends on an endless variety of circumstances, the significance of which becomes manifest all in a moment, and no one can foretell when that moment is coming?' (London: Penguin Books (1978): 762).

15. See R. A. Burgelman (1988). 'Strategy Making as a Social Learning Process: The Case of Internal Corporate Venturing'. *Interfaces* 18: 74–85.

16. See S. Winter (1987). 'Knowledge and Competence as Strategic Assets', in D. J. Teece (ed.), *The Competitive Challenge: Strategies for Industrial Innovation and Renewal*. Cambridge, Mass.: Ballinger, 180.

17. The three tools are the outcome of more than twenty years of grounded theorizing efforts (for a discussion of grounded theorizing, see B. G. Glaser and A. L. Straus (1967). *The Discovery of Grounded Theory*. Chicago: Aldine). Tool III was developed first, based on field research of the internal corporate venturing (ICV) process. Relating the insights of the ICV process model to the findings of Chandler (1962), *Strategy and Structure*. MIT Press and Penrose (1959), *Theory of Growth* (New York: John Wiley & Sons), as well as to the emerging literature on evolutionary organization theory (see Aldrich, *Organizations Evolving*) provided the basis for Tool II. Tool I resulted from the field-based research of Intel's defeat in the DRAM business and its transformation from a memory to a microprocessor company. Even though developed independently from Tools II and III, it became clear afterwards that Tool I could subsume Tool II, just as Tool II had been able to subsume Tool III—hence, the evolutionary lens. The research of Intel's defeat in DRAM also provided the basis for developing a process model of strategic business exit. See R. A. Burgelman (1996). 'A Process Model of Strategic Business Exit: Implications for an Evolutionary Perspective on Strategy'. *Strategic Management Journal*, Special Issue: 193–214. Hence, the conceptual

usefulness of Tool III extends beyond internal corporate venturing. To avoid cluttering Fig. 3.1, however, only the process model of internal corporate venturing is shown here as Tool III.

18. See R. A. Burgelman (1994). 'Fading Memories: A Process Theory of Strategic Business Exit in Dynamic Environments'. *Administrative Science Quarterly* 39: 24–56. The 'basis of competitive advantage in the industry' of Tool I relates directly to Michael Porter's framework of industry forces. See M. E. Porter (1980). *Competitive Strategy*. New York: Free Press. Tool I thus provides a way for linking internal and external strategic forces. Other external forces include technology, complementors, and nonmarket forces such as government regulation.

19. For the original discussion of generic strategy, see M. E. Porter, *Competitive Strategy*.

20. Coevolution refers to the process whereby particular units of analysis evolve in a reciprocal influence relationship, affecting each other's evolutionary success. See e.g. J. A. C. Baum and J. V. Singh (eds.) (1994). *Evolutionary Dynamics of Organizations*. New York: Oxford University Press. See R. A. Burgelman (2002). 'Strategy as Vector and the Inertia of Coevolutionary Lock-in'. *Administrative Science Quarterly* 47: 325–57.

21. See Burgelman, 'Intraorganizational Ecology'.

22. The Rational Actor model of strategy making is often viewed as the ideal one. It assumes a comprehensively rational CEO who clearly formulates the strategy and organizational participants who simultaneously and in concert act to implement the strategy. For the original discussion of the Rational Actor model, see G. Allison and P. Zelikow (1990). *Essence of Decision: Explaining the Cuban Missile Crisis*, 2nd edn. New York: Addison Wesley Longman. For commentary and further discussion, see J. Bendor and T. H. Hammond (1992). 'Rethinking Allison's Models'. *American Political Science Review* 86: 301–22. Also, Burgelman, *Strategy Is Destiny*, 4–6.

23. In multibusiness firms, the CEO is less likely to be able to determine strategy content and more likely to focus on managing the strategy process. In highly diversified corporations such as General Electric, for instance, it is virtually impossible for the CEO to direct the strategies of the multitude of businesses in the corporate portfolio. Jack Welch had to concern himself primarily with core values and corporate objectives, and with the selection of the business leaders. Content-wise, his strategic influence was limited to asking sharp questions about the businesses and to the introduction of general themes that could cut across all businesses. The corporate discipline associated with the core values (including strong emphasis on executive development), corporate objectives, and the imposition of frontier management approaches and techniques—mostly process elements—ultimately determined the value added of being part of GE for each of the businesses. As Intel enters

Epoch III and becomes a more diversified company, CEO Craig Barrett faces the issue of how much to emphasize content versus process in his strategic leadership approach.

24. For various viewpoints on applying the 'punctuated equilibrium' model, adopted from biology, in organization theory, see e.g. M. L. Tushman and E. Romanelli (1985). 'Organizational Evolution: A Metamorphosis Model of Convergence and Reorientation', in B. Staw and L. L. Cummings (1985). *Research in Organizational Behavior*. Greenwich, Conn.: JAI vii. 439–65; C. J. G. Gersick (1991). 'Revolutionary Change Theories: A Multilevel Exploration of the Punctuated Equilibrium Paradigm'. *Academy of Management Review* 16: 10–36; and S. L. Brown and K. M. Eisenhardt (1997). 'The Art of Continuous Change: Linking Complexity Theory and Time-Paced Evolution in Relentlessly Shifting Organizations'. *Administrative Science Quarterly* 42: 1–34.

25. The first generation of the process model resulted from Joseph Bower's efforts to conceptualize the strategic resource allocation process in large diversified major corporations. See J. L. Bower (1970). *Managing the Resource Allocation Process*. Boston, Mass.: Harvard Business School Press. Several of Bower's doctoral students further refined the resource allocation process model. See J. L. Bower and Y. L. Doz (1979). 'Strategy Formulation: A Social and Political Process', in D. E. Schendel and C. W. Hofer (eds.), *Strategic Management: A New View of Business and Planning*. Boston, Mass.: Little Brown.

26. The second generation of the process model resulted from efforts to conceptualize the complete set of fine-grained strategic leadership activities involved in the internal corporate venturing process in large diversified major firms in terms of the resource allocation process model. To be able to encompass the complete set of leadership activities, however, it was necessary to include strategic context determination as a new subprocess. This made it possible to generalize the process model as a tool for studying the strategy-making process. See R. A. Burgelman (1983). 'A Process Model of Internal Corporate Venturing in the Diversified Major Firm'. *Administrative Science Quarterly* 28: 223–44. This extended version of the process model is shown in Fig. 3.1. Further research showed that the extended-process model also was useful to conceptualize the strategic business exit process. See R. A. Burgelman (1996). 'A Process Model of Strategic Business Exit: Implications for an Evolutionary Perspective on Strategy'. *Strategic Management Journal*, Special Issue: 193–214. For a discussion of the place of the Bower–Burgelman process model in the strategic management literature, see H. Mintzberg, B. Ahlstrand, and J. Lampel (1998). *Strategy Safari*. New York: Free Press.

27. For research discussing self-organization, see e.g. R. A. Thietart and B. Forgues (1995). 'Chaos Theory and Organization'. *Organization Science* 6: 19–31. Ilya Prigogine, Nobel laureate in Chemistry, uses the Lotka–Volterra equations of prey–predator competition, which are part

of the conceptual foundation of organizational ecology, in a discussion of self-organization to examine 'structural stability'. Structural stability, according to Prigogine, 'seems to express in the most compact way the idea of innovation, the appearance of a new mechanism and a new species, which were initially absent in the system.' See Y. Prigogine (1980). *From Being to Becoming: Time and Complexity in the Physical Sciences*. San Francisco: W. H. Freeman, 109. Prigogine views 'structure' as resulting from the actions (choices) of multiple actors, having 'in part at least mutually dependent criteria of action (utility functions)' (ibid. 126). Referring to the baroque of the natural world, Prigogine posits 'ecosystems contain many more species than would be "necessary" if biological efficiency alone were an organizing principle. This "over creativity" of nature emerges naturally from the type of description being suggested here, in which "mutations" and "innovations" occur stochastically and are integrated into the system by the deterministic relations prevailing at the moment. Thus we have in this perspective the constant generation of "new types" and "new ideas" that may be incorporated into the structure of the system, causing its continual evolution' (ibid. 128). Keeping in mind the pitfalls of the fallacy of unwarranted analogy, there seems nevertheless to exist a potentially interesting isomorphism between Prigogine's analysis and the analysis of the role of the induced and autonomous processes in strategy making. Autonomous initiatives generate innovations (new ideas) in the organization, but they are viable only if they can be integrated into the corporate strategy and eventually become part of the induced-strategy process. Strategic context determination is the part of the process through which this integration is attempted. How strategic context determination works and what the determinants are of its success may be the central issues in a theory of corporate entrepreneurship. See R. A. Burgelman (1983). 'Corporate Entrepreneurship and Strategic Management: Insights from a Process Study'. *Management Science* 29: 1349–64. Also id. (June 1984). 'Strategy Making and Evolutionary Theory: Toward A Capabilities-Based Perspective'. *Research Paper 755*, Stanford Business School.

28. See Prigogine, *From Being to Becoming*, 126.
29. According to Schelling, focal points facilitate coordination without communication. More generally, they are ideas, values, criteria, and the like around which the organization's members naturally coalesce or toward which they naturally converge. In the case of Intel, the maximize margin-per-wafer-start resource allocation rule can be viewed as a focal point. Focal points are useful for operationalizing corporate culture as a rational concept. See T. C. Schelling (1963). *The Strategy of Conflict*. Cambridge, Mass.: Harvard University Press; also D. M. Kreps (1990). 'Corporate Culture and Economic Theory', in J. Alte and K. Shepsle (eds.), *Rational Perspectives on Positive Political Economy*. Cambridge: Cambridge University Press, 90–143.

30. See: W. P. Barnett, (1997). 'The Dynamics of Competitive Intensity'. *Administrative Science Quarterly* 42: 128–80. Barnett's research sheds further light on the debate between the so-called resource-based view of the firm, which emphasizes competence as the basis of competitive advantage, and the industrial organization economics view, which emphasizes position. Barnett's findings suggest that there may be a trade-off between seeking an advantageous strategic position and developing strong competitive skills. Building on earlier work in evolutionary biology, his research also suggests that competitive processes in the business world often have consequences similar to those described by the Red Queen in Lewis Carroll's *Through the Looking Glass*. (In a fast world, one must run just to stand still.) See W. P. Barnett and M. T. Hansen (Summer 1996). 'The Red Queen in Organizational Evolution'. *Strategic Management Journal* 17, Special Issue: 139–58.

31. This form of inertia is related to 'competency traps' (see B. Levitt and J. G. March (1988). 'Organizational Learning', in W. R. Scott (ed.), *Annual Review of Sociology* 14: 319–40) and 'core rigidities' (see D. Leonard-Barton (Summer 1992). 'Core Capabilities and Core Rigidities: A Paradox in Managing New Product Development'. *Strategic Management Journal*, Special Issue, 13: 248–66).

32. See W. P. Barnett, H. R. Greve, and D. Y. Park (1994). 'An Evolutionary Model of Organizational Performance'. *Strategic Management Journal* 15: 139–57.

33. See Bower (1970), *Managing the Resource Allocation Process*. Boston, Mass.: Harvard Business School Press.

34. Jack Welch's strongly enforced criterion that every GE business must be 'number one or number two' in its industry combined with his insistence on best practice sharing among GE's businesses is perhaps the best-known example.

35. See J. J. Rotemberg and G. Saloner (1994). 'The Benefits of Narrow Business Strategies'. *American Economic Review* 84: 1330–49.

36. See J. J. Rotemberg and G. Saloner (2000). 'Visionaries, Managers, and Strategic Direction'. *Rand Journal of Economics* 31: 693–716.

37. See James G. March (1991). 'Exploration and Exploitation in Organizational Learning'. *Organization Science* 2: 71–87.

38. Ibid. 82.

39. Ibid. 75.

40. Acquisition of winning external variations is the strategy that Cisco Systems has successfully pursued throughout the 1990s. Cisco was able quickly to observe which technology-based variations in the external-selection environment were successful and to use its highly valued shares to acquire these emergent winners. Cisco developed a distinctive competency related to integrating acquisitions into its strategy-making process. The integration task was probably facilitated by the fact that these were by and large young, relatively small companies—sometimes encompass-

ing mostly a product team of scientists and engineers—with little institutional history and still inchoate cultures. See e.g. N. Tempest and C. G. Kasper (1999). 'Cisco Systems, Inc. Acquisition Integration for Manufacturing (A)'. *Harvard Business School Case*. In either case—corporate venture capital or acquisitions—the problem of strategic context determination for outside ventures raises just the same as it does for internal ones.

41. See C. Christensen (1997). *The Innovator's Dilemma*. Boston, Mass.: Harvard Business School Press. 'Disruptive technologies' focus on a different subset of performance dimensions in a product's multidimensional performance space. These technologies typically are rejected by a company's existing customers and therefore are not further supported within the company's resource allocation process. Often the internal entrepreneurs associated with such initiatives leave the company to start a new one. After finding new customers interested in the different performance characteristics of the technology, performance on the other dimensions also improves over time. As a result, the customers that earlier were not interested are likely eventually to find the new technology 'good enough' and may switch. This leaves the incumbent companies still working with the old technology in a difficult strategic situation.

42. For examples of successful and unsuccessful strategic context determination processes in a different corporate context, see T. Noda and J. L. Bower (Summer 1996). 'Strategy Making as Iterated Processes of Resource Allocation'. *Strategic Management Journal* 17, Special Issue: 159–92.

43. See Burgelman, 'Corporate Entrepreneurship and Strategic Management'.

44. See March, 'Exploration and Exploitation', for a discussion of rational choice approaches and standard references.

45. See Y. Prigogine and D. Sahal (1979). 'A Unified Theory of Self-Organization'. *Journal of Cybernetics* 9: 127–42. These are reviewed in Burgelman, 'Corporate Entrepreneurship and Strategic Management'.

46. March, 'Exploration and Exploitation'.

47. The applicability of real options theory in strategic management is currently a topic of scholarly debate. See e.g. R. Adner and D. A. Levinthal (2004). 'What is Not a Real Option: Considering Boundaries for the Application of Real Options to Business Strategy'. *Academy of Management Review* 29: 74–85.

48. Burgelman, 'Strategy as Vector', 325–57.

49. Strategic context determination and dissolution processes provide a potentially fruitful link to network theory. Network methodology could help measure strategic context determination and dissolution in terms of growing, respectively declining, networks of supporting senior executives in the company over time. From the perspective of network theory, research of strategic context determination and dissolution processes

could provide additional substantive content. For a theoretical discussion of network theory and methodology see e.g. R. S. Burt (1992). *Structural Holes*. Cambridge, Mass.: Harvard University Press. For an early effort to apply network ideas to strategic context determination, see M. E. D. Hutt, P. H. Reingen, and J. J. Ronchetto, Jr. (1988). 'Tracing Emergent Processes in Marketing Strategy Formation'. *Journal of Marketing* 52: 4–19.

50. E. Mayr (2001). *What Evolution Is*. New York: Basic Books.

51. See R. E. Miles and C. C. Snow (1978). *Organizational Strategy, Structure, and Process*. New York: McGraw-Hill. See also Burgelman, 'Corporate Entrepreneurship and Strategic Management'.

52. It would seem that companies that have maintained strong innovative capabilities over long periods of time, such as 3M and Johnson and Johnson, have a strategy-making process that resembles the internal ecology model.

4

Anomaly-Seeking Research: Thirty Years of Development in Resource Allocation Theory

Clark G. Gilbert and Clayton M. Christensen

Introduction

Our purpose in writing this chapter is twofold. First, we wish to describe the process by which theory is built, using as an example the thirty-five years of research that commenced with Bower's 1970 model of the resource allocation process (RAP). Second, we hope to familiarize the reader with a series of important findings concerning the management of strategic process that enabled researchers to think about the model in new ways. (In the final chapter of this book, Bower and Gilbert use these findings to revisit the RAP model and formally map its evolution.) We hope that the pattern of research process presented here might provide a common language that helps readers visualize how independently derived insights on the resource allocation process accumulated. Also we hope that this description will help other scholars of management build upon each other's work more effectively. The pattern of research process that we present has strong normative pedagogical implications—for both how we train our students and how we learn from and teach each other through publication. It has normative implications also for the kinds of research questions and research designs that are more or less likely to build useful theory.[1]

A review of the research on the theory of resource allocation shows a striking incidence of field-based, small-sample research designs. In fact, Bower and Burgelman published studies based on a *single* firm. Many other scholars studied small samples within a single industry. A question that might arise is: How can you have developed a reliable theory based on repeated small-sample, even single-firm studies? One response is that studying a process that is distributed over several levels of an organization and plays out over time is costly in elapsed time and research effort. But scarce resources alone do not justify small-sample observation. Another response is that the cumulative effort of each of these studies established a much larger data-set of cases that, taken collectively, and through repeated observation across *all* the research, provide a more reliable body of findings. Moreover, many of these field-based, small-sample findings were examined in large-sample research studies conducted by the original authors themselves. For example, Christensen tested his original findings around disruptive innovation against the entire population of firms in the disk-drive industry (Christensen and Bower 1996). Eisenmann (2002) used a large sample from the cable industry to analyze risk under uncertainty, and Gilbert (2001) derived similar statistical analysis on the top 100 US newspapers in his study on cognitive framing. These large-sample, quantitative studies all improved or confirmed important aspects of our understanding of the resource allocation process.

There are, however, more profound reasons why so much of the research is process based and involves relatively small samples. The phenomenon of resource allocation had not been observed until Bower's 1970 study. In a sense, much of what this research has done is simply describe the process that is resource allocation. If the collective work had done nothing more than describe this complex phenomenon, and built a foundation for future research, the research would have made a significant contribution. By looking carefully in a few firm settings at processes that had previously gone unobserved, we now have data both to confront and contradict propositions derived from existing theory and to induce new propositions altogether. As in medicine, clinical observation often precedes theoretical explanation.

As the work progressed, it moved well beyond its original efforts to articulate and describe the phenomenon. The result of cumulative observation and revision is a model that increasingly can predict firm behavior in a wide range of circumstances and conditions. Following a path of observation, confrontation, and inductive explanation, which we describe below as 'anomaly-seeking' research designs, scholars have found behavior or outcomes not predicted by the model as originally observed.[2] The anomalous observations led to an improved understanding of the different situations or circumstances in which managers may find themselves when wrestling with the allocation of resources and strategic change. That improved understanding has yielded theories that managers can use to determine the correct set of actions that must be taken, given the circumstances in which they find themselves. Thus, it is our central hypothesis that the repeated observation of anomalies to the original models of RAP has been the key to the field's development over the last thirty-five years.

A Crisis in Management Research

Some scholars of management, organizations, and markets expend significant energy disparaging and defending various research methods. Debates about deductive vs. inductive theory-building, the objectivity of information from field observation vs. large-sample numerical data, and qualitative vs. quantitative research are polarities that surface almost daily in the lives of those of us whose research is reviewed and who review the work of others. Despite this preoccupation with research methodology, some of the most respected members of our profession (e.g. Bennis and O'Toole (2005), Pfeffer and Fong (2002), Simon (1985), Solow (1985), and others) have expressed deep concern that our collective efforts have produced a paucity of theory that is intellectually rigorous, practically useful, and able to stand the test of time and changing circumstances.

We suspect that many scholars who read this chapter will think that they see little new in it. At some point in their past, they probably read Kuhn (1962), Glaser and Strauss (1967), Yin (1984), and a number of other treatises on the design and execution of research, and feel quite comfortable in their own understanding of this process. Although we may not dispel this belief, we sense that the scientific method has, for many of us, been replaced with a kind of scientific *rigidity* (Bourdieu and Wacquant 1992: 227). We observe this rigidity at different levels. For example, doctoral students, even from the most reputable programs, who apply for faculty positions often seem to have received extraordinary training in methods of modeling and data collection and analysis, but they seem almost diffident about defining good research questions and deploying research designs that are likely to yield new insight into theory. They seem unschooled in what theory is and how it is built. We often observe in personal interviews and the literature reviews in their theses that they recite long lists of articles in 'the literature'. But they struggle when asked to diagram within that body of work which scholar's work builds upon which prior scholar's effort; whose results contradicted whose, and why. They often stumble because they have not structured their work or even their literature review in terms of the prior cycles of observation, categorization, theory-building, and anomaly discovering in their fields. The same can be said for most literature citations at the beginning of published papers. If we indeed understood how theory is built, then we would change the way we approach our own research and evaluate the work of others.

In this chapter, we first present a model of the process by which bodies of understanding are built. This model is not our own, but is a synthesis of models that scholars of the research process developed in a range of fields: A. Kaplan (1964), Roethlisberger (1977), and Weick (1989) in organizational and social sciences; Kuhn (1962) and Popper (1959) in the natural sciences; and Simon (1976), R. Kaplan (1986), Eisenhardt (1989), and Van de Ven (2000) in the study of strategy and management practice. The model presented here is not based on primary research of our own, but rather is a secondary synthesis of insights from the work of these other scholars. This synthesis of their work does not include or recite every aspect of all that these scholars have written. In instances where the scholars disagree, we have chosen one view and ignored others. We have, however, drawn on those dimensions of their work that, in our opinion, describe in a general way the process by which understanding is built. Where none of these scholars offered an insight that adequately characterized an important dimension of the problem, we have added our own thoughts.

We then explore this model and show how it has been useful in the development of theory on resource allocation. Not always have the RAP scholars intended to follow this model, nor do we argue that each study follows the pattern perfectly. But we do find a reasonably consistent pattern in the thirty-five years of research. By examining how this pattern relates to a broader view of how theory develops, we illustrate that view and provide a framework for understanding how theory has developed within the field of resource allocation.

A Theory of Theory Building

The process of theory building can be divided into several stages that repeat. In the earliest stages of theory building, the best that researchers can do is to observe phenomena and to carefully describe, measure, and record what they see. Many of the early Harvard Business School case studies written in the 1940s and 1950s had this characteristic—they simply described problems that managers faced. At the time, they could do little else—few theories about management had yet been developed. An important element of work at this stage is the careful description of the phenomena with words and numbers. This is extremely important, because if subsequent researchers cannot agree on the descriptions of phenomena, then improving theory will prove difficult. Indeed, much of Bower's original contribution was his description of the phenomenon. By making it apparent that resource allocation was a *process*, not an event, Bower was able to observe and articulate the structure of the process in a way that enabled subsequent theory to develop.

With the phenomenon observed and described, researchers then can classify the phenomena into categories with similar characteristics. Solid, liquid, gas, and plasma comprise one such categorization scheme in physical science; and juvenile vs. adult-onset diabetes is an example from medicine. Incremental vs. radical and sustaining vs. disruptive technological changes are categorization examples from the study of innovation. Categorization schemes attempt to simplify and organize the world in ways that highlight the consequential differences among phenomena. Researchers in this stage also work to measure the phenomena, primarily for categorization and, as noted below, prediction.

In the next phase, researchers build theories that explain the behavior of the phenomena. A theory is a statement of what causes what, and why. If the theory is built upon a sound categorization scheme, it can explain how this causality might vary by *circumstance*. In fact, it is often the understanding of differences in circumstance that enables researchers to understand the causal relationships that constitute the theory. And it is the attempt to articulate statements of cause and effect that helps the researcher determine which categorization systems are and are not useful.

Researchers of management often use different terms for the categorization and theory-building stages of research described above. The term *framework* maps closely to our term *categorization*. The word *model* is closely associated with *theory* as it is defined here— whether the model is in the form of a regression equation that specifies how causal variables affect the dependent variable, or in the form of a 2×2 matrix whose axes represent the causal variables in a specified relationship. The model of resource allocation introduced in Ch. 2 and developed in this book is a theory of how strategy is created in large, complex firms. Good theory defines what is most important to pay attention to in any given circumstance. Theory has value for researchers and managers in proportion to its predictive power—its ability to help researchers foresee what events or actions will result in what outcomes.

The Process of Building Better Theory

Once a theory has been articulated, how is it improved? Armed with a theory that is built upon a categorization scheme, researchers then use the theory to predict what they will observe under various conditions. If the theory accurately predicts what they actually observe, this 'test' offers one specific confirmation that the theory is useful under the circumstances in which the data or phenomena were observed.[3] As Fig. 4.1 suggests, the theory is then situationally confirmed, but the theory itself remains *unimproved*.

In their efforts to use theory to predict what they will see, researchers often observe something that the theory did *not* lead them to expect—resulting in a paradox or *anomaly*. This discovery forces patient and thorough researchers to cycle back into the categorization stage with a puzzle such as: 'There's something else going on here'; or 'These two things we thought were the same, really aren't'. The results of this effort typically include: (1) more accurately describing what the phenomena are and are not; (2) defining a revised categorization scheme, or specifying ways to measure more accurately the attributes by which the phenomena are classified; and/or (3) articulating a new statement of causality and how it varies by circumstance. The objective of this process is to revise theory so that it accounts for the phenomena that the prior theory did not explain; and, in addition, predict accurately the phenomena that, to the unimproved theory, had appeared to be anomalous.

The worth of anomalies depends on what researchers are trying to accomplish. Researchers whose goal is to 'prove' a theory's validity are likely to view discovery of an anomaly as failure. In contrast, researchers whose objective is to *improve* theory will view uncovering an anomaly as an opportunity for progress—because the discovery of phenomena that the existing theory cannot explain is the enabling event that allows researchers to end the cycle with a better theory.

This cycle repeats itself as theory-building researchers, like runners in a relay race, circle around this track. Sometimes they keep the baton as individuals, and sometimes they hand the baton to others to continue to improve their ability to predict what will cause what, and why, and how that chain of causality might differ across circumstances.

Thomas Kuhn (1962) observed that after researchers have circled around the theory-building track successfully enough so that a broad community comes to trust that the theory has reliable and accurate predictive power, it evolves towards a *paradigm*—an explanation of

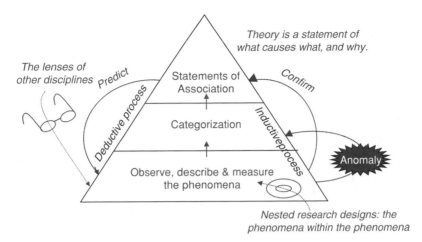

Figure 4.1 The process of building theory

causality that is so generally accepted that it affects the way people view and operate in the world. After a paradigm has emerged, researchers continue to circle around this observation-categorization-theory track, but in a mode that Kuhn labeled 'normal science'.

Our model treats normal science as a special case within the general process noted above. There are pre-paradigmatic and post-paradigmatic cycles of theory building. In both, researchers strive to improve the theory's ability to predict what causes what, and why, under each different category of circumstance. In pre-paradigmatic cycles, the most productive emphasis of researchers is on *finding* anomalies, to improve the definition of categories. They spend time learning how to measure the phenomena for categorization, but this is done to facilitate their other work.

Researchers studying the resource allocation process have been largely pre-paradigmatic, and that has shaped the way research has been designed and developed over the last thirty years.[4] Researchers in post-paradigmatic cycles, in contrast, expend much more effort figuring out how to measure the phenomena for categorization and prediction, developing instruments to do that work, and so on—because the categorization schemes have been broadly accepted. Post-paradigmatic researchers continue to discover anomalies, but typically they are not explicitly seeking them as they might in the pre-paradigm state. More often, anomalies are encountered accidentally when technological progress enables researchers unintentionally to observe phenomena that previous scholars were unable to see. Improvements in the precision with which we can measure phenomena and constructs often cause anomalies to surface.

Many researchers of management, organizations, and markets think of their work as being of this 'normal science' genre. It appears to us, however, that there are few fields within these realms of inquiry where a true paradigm exists because robust categorization schemes have yet to be defined to underpin theory. Further, in many areas, there remains a remarkable lack of understanding of the underlying phenomenon being studied. This suggests that some of the 'normal science' energy expended in management research not only might be premature, but also impede the overall theory building process. This is one reason why so many scholars of the resource allocation process continue to influence other areas of management research. They are re-exploring *phenomena* others have missed and reconsidering the underlying systems of categorization.

For example, Bower's research began with the observation that the assumptions underlying the theory of long-range planning and those underlying the theory of capital budgeting were contradictory. Using two years of field observations, he was able to build a more comprehensive and accurate model because he had studied a more complete set of situations than previous research. In another example, Gilbert reconsidered conflicting research on the role threat played in response to discontinuous change. Whereas research in strategic management suggested that threat perception enabled response, research in social psychology showed that threat constrained response. Why the contradiction? Gilbert's study showed that both streams of research had missed an underlying categorization scheme that was critical to explaining response. His research demonstrated that the predictions of strategic management scholars were related to a change in resource investment, whereas the predictions of social psychology scholars were related to a change in organizational routines. By recategorizing the basic phenomenon observed, the contradiction was resolved.

Movement up and down the pyramid of Fig. 4.1 essentially defines the 'scientific method'. A key tenet of such methods is that theory must be falsifiable. In our parlance, a theory must be capable of yielding anomaly, in order for the theory to constitute a foundation for better theory. By our definition, therefore, certain important concepts, particularly in economics, would be termed 'constructs', not theories, because they cannot be falsified. The construct of utility maximization, which asserts that all people in all situations act to maximize utility, is one example. But because utility can be defined in any way that is consistent with the outcome, the construct can be used to build tautological predictions. In this sense, specifying the categories of utility maximization is critical to improving theory.

Anomalies vs. Exceptions

There is a tendency among some researchers to cite 'exceptions' to a theory's predictions as evidence that it is invalid. Not all exceptions are anomalies. For example, the observation that airplanes fly is an exception to the general assertion that the earth's mass pulls things down towards its core. Do these exceptions disprove the law of gravity? No. The fact that aviators need airfoils that harness Bernoulli's principle in order to counteract the pull of gravity is an exception that supports the theory. In the realm of management, does the observation that Hewlett Packard, the leading maker of laser printers, also became the leading vendor of disruptive ink-jet printers, invalidate Christensen's (1997) assertion that listening to your best customers and investing where profit margins are greatest causes industry leaders to fail when faced with disruptive technology? Even though this is an exception to the general tendency Christensen observed, it is not an anomaly because HP had to create an autonomous business unit for ink-jet printers in order to cope with the forces he described.

Yin (1984) distinguished between *literal* replications of a theory—instances where the outcome is exactly what the theory predicts—and *theoretical* replications, where the predicted outcome did not occur, but for reasons that the theory can explain. Airplanes flying and Hewlett Packard's ink-jet success are both theoretical replications of the respective theories. It is when an exception is observed that a theory cannot account for as a literal *or* theoretical replication, that an anomaly has been identified.

Designing Anomaly-Seeking Research

Although some productive anomalies might be obvious from the outset, the task of theory-building scholars often is to design their research to maximize the probability that they will be able to find anomalies. Here we outline three ways to design anomaly-seeking research. The first is to look at the phenomena through the lenses of other methods or disciplines. The second is to look at the phenomena *within* the phenomena (to execute a nested research design). The third is to look at a broader variety of phenomena than previous researchers were able to examine.

The Lenses of Other Disciplines

One of Kuhn's (1962) most memorable observations was that the anomalies that led to the toppling of a reigning theory or paradigm almost invariably were observed by researchers whose backgrounds were in different disciplines than those comprising the traditional training of the leaders in the field. The beliefs of adherents to the prior theory about what was and was not possible seemed to shape so powerfully what they could and could not see that they often went to their graves denying the existence or relevance of the very anomalous phenomena that led to the creation of improved theory. Examining a situation through the lenses of a different discipline is a mechanism that leads researchers to look for different things than scholars within the existing dominant discipline instinctively look for. It enables them to attach meaning and significance to phenomena that, when not viewed through new lenses, might appear inconsequential.

In the work presented here on resource allocation, we see several examples of this. Bower demonstrated this with his original efforts to bring political and behavioral theory into a model of resource allocation. Burgelman made the connection to evolutionary theory in his study of induced and autonomous process. Authors in this book have used the lenses from still other literatures, including: innovation theory (Christensen 1997), agency theory (Eisenmann 2002), and cognitive psychology (Gilbert 2001), see Table 4.1. Note that in each of these instances, using the lens of a discipline had a dual payoff, adding new insight into the resource allocation model as well as the literature with which it connected.

Examining a situation through the lenses of other academic disciplines does not just improve the chances of observing anomalies that lead to better theory. It leads to more *valid* theory. One of the most important objectives of theory-building researchers is to establish the *internal validity* of their theories (Yin 1984). A theory with strong internal validity is one in which the statements of cause and effect are unambiguous. Internal validity is established when a researcher has examined all plausible alternative hypotheses of what could have led to the outcomes in the study and has shown that those alternative theories all lead to anomalies. In other words, the process of looking at a

Table 4.1 *Examples of anomaly-seeking designs in resource allocation research*

Research	New lens	Nested research design	Broadened range of phenomena
Bower	Process View and Politics	Original multilevel design: Corporate, Middle, and Operating levels within a single firm	Studied resource allocation decisions prior to the actual budgeting meeting at the corporate level
Burgelman	Evolutionary Theory	Multilevel research of corporate venture, nested within division and corporate levels	Studied strategic initiatives that were both induced and autonomous
Christensen	Resource Dependence Theory	Study of individuals, within ventures, within firms, across firms	Studied innovation phenomenon where incumbents had both failed and triumphed in the face of modular, architectural, and radical change
Noda	Capital Market Theory	Study of corporate venture, nested within corporate level, nested within capital markets	Studied resource allocation decisions across different firms where only the capital market context varied
Sull	Institutional Theory	Study of individuals, within divisions, within firms, across an industry	Studied cases of divestment vs. previous research on investment decisions
Eisenmann	Agency Theory	Study of individuals, within divisions, within firms, across an industry	Examined cases where the bottom-up process failed to produce impetus for valid projects
Gilbert	Threat Rigidity Theory	Study of individuals, within ventures, within firms, across an industry	Studied cases where resources were committed to disruptive technology

situation through the lenses of relevant theories in other disciplines is the process by which the internal validity (or invalidity) of a theory is enhanced.

Studying the Phenomena within the Phenomena

A second method for researchers to increase the probability that they can surface anomalies in order to build better theory is to execute *nested* research designs. Rather than study industries *or* companies *or* divisions *or* groups *or* individuals, a nested research design entails studying how individuals act and interact within groups and how the interaction among groups and the companies within which they are embedded affects the actions of individuals, and so on. Many anomalies and the consequent improved understanding of causality will emerge only from studying second-order interactions and relations across levels within a nested design. Researchers who look only at a single level of the phenomena cannot see these anomalies.

The research reported in Johnson and Kaplan's *Relevance Lost* (1987), which led to the concept of activity-based costing, is a remarkable example of the fruits born of nested research designs. Most prior researchers in managerial accounting and control had conducted their research at a single level—the numbers printed in companies' financial statements. Johnson and Kaplan essentially said: 'Yes, I see this number on the page just like you do. But where did that number come from?' What they were able to see is that nested beneath each of those numbers was a labyrinth of political, negotiated, judgmental processes that led to those numbers—processes that quite readily could have yielded very different numbers and that could systematically lead to inaccurate numbers. In many ways, Johnson and Kaplan's study did for accounting what Bower's research had done earlier for capital allocation theory. Bower asked, 'Where do these numbers that we see in the net present value (NPV) calculations come from?' As described in Chs. 1 and 2, by observing behavior representing nested levels of analysis carried out long before the capital budgeting meeting, well below the level of senior management, Bower was able to gain his insights into the process of resource allocation.

Future studies in resource allocation continued to benefit from nested research designs. Much of this came from Bower's basic observation that the resource allocation process was multilevel and many of the studies included within-firm nested designs. Burgelman's multilevel study of Intel is a good example. Others built nested research designs that explored not only within-firm observation, but also across a major industry. Noda's research on the Regional Bell Operating Companies, which were formed simultaneously at the break-up of AT&T, was an ideal natural experiment that employed a nested research design. He used the multilevel, multirole model of resource allocation described earlier to explore the process of re-source commitment to cellular telephony in the seven very similar newly formed companies. Through comparison, he was able to derive insights into the way in which iterative resource allocation shapes strategy.

An added benefit of such nested designs is that they allow for comparisons across nested levels of analysis. This can increase the chances of observed anomaly. Again, Noda's research is an excellent example. The capital market viewed the seven otherwise similar newly born firms quite differently. This external context led to very different strategic outcomes. The differences across nested phenomena led to the observed anomaly.

Observing a Broad Range of Phenomena

The third mechanism that researchers can employ to surface an anom-aly is to execute a research design that looks at a broader, more diverse range of phenomena than prior scholars examined. Christensen's (1997) work on disruptive technology, for example, used the theory of Henderson and Clark (1990) to examine an even broader range of situations than they had studied—in which incumbent disk-drive makers had both failed and triumphed when faced with modular, architectural, and radical technological change. This led to a model based on theories of resource dependency and resource allocation that augmented the previous theory. A key insight was that customers can effectively capture the process of impetus that drives resource alloca-tion: 'The inability of some successful firms to *allocate sufficient re-sources* to technologies that initially cannot find application in mainstream markets, but later invade them, lies at the root of the failure of many once-successful firms' (Christensen and Bower 1996: 1998, italics added). Gilbert's follow-on research examined yet a broader range of phenomena. In his study, firms *were* able to allocate sufficient resources to such technologies, but only when they were framed as a threat to the core business. This observed anomaly then led to the recognition of the role that cognitive frames play in the resource allocation process.

Sometimes broadening the range of phenomena involves looking for *failures* in predicted outcomes. Many of the research studies in this volume look for cases of the resource allocation process failing in some way. They used these failures to start asking questions that eventually led to revisions in existing theory. In fact, part II of this book focuses exclusively on why the bottom-up process sometimes fails to adapt to changes in the external environment. These studies led to the discovery that other forces beyond structural and strategic context shape the bottom-up processes of definition and impetus.

The Role of Anomaly in the Development of Resource Allocation Theory

One of the propositions of our Theory of Theory Development is that anomalies present opportunities to *improve* theory. Bower's original observation that the process of resource allocation was inseparably connected to strategy has been an organizing insight for a continuous stream of research that has followed. Similarly, the observation that the process was a complex, multilevel, and multirole phenomenon led many subsequent scholars to employ field intensive explorations into subsequent strategic phenomenon. But more importantly, and following our theory of theory development, these scholars designed research that was anomaly seeking in its intent. Noted earlier, many of these studies benefited from viewing their research through the lens of another discipline, employed nested research designs, and expanded the base of the phenomena originally observed (refer to Table 4.1). And whereas each author helped contribute to the different streams of research across a wide range of disciplines, they also contributed to the cumulative theory-building process within the research on the resource allocation model itself (see Table 4.2).

In the language of our theory-building model, Bower's (1970) landmark work, *Managing the Resource Allocation Process*, was the foundation of the pyramid. His was an insightful description of how the resource allocation process worked within a single large chemical company. Bower's work yielded such powerful descriptions of the phenomena because his research design was *nested*; he studied the phenomena within the phenomena. Bower's constructs such as *structural context*, for example, provided an instant, common language that allowed subsequent users readily to communicate, cite, and build upon each other's work. And by exploring the phenomena at a level that most scholars of capital allocation theory had avoided or ignored, Bower was able to see two key anomalies to then existing theory. First, capital allocation decisions were not made just in the boardroom, but were part of a complex process that developed across multiple levels of the firm, constructed by managers with sometimes conflicting roles, and that the middle managers often did the true selecting among projects long before corporate level managers saw any proposals. Second, the way this process was structured shaped the way strategy developed in the firm—in essence, structure shaped strategy. Previous thinking suggested the opposite.

A few years after Bower's work, Burgelman initiated his twenty-year stream of contributions to our understanding of resource allocation (Burgelman 1983). He began his work as Bower did, by carefully observing the processes of innovation and resource allocation in the new ventures group of a major corporation. He clarified and amplified some of Bower's phenomenological constructs—concluding, for example, that Bower's notion of *structural context* needed to be augmented by the *strategic* context within which the decision makers were working. Burgelman took the research enterprise further up the pyramid by describing categories of circumstance: the innovations that managers were attempting to commercialize either fit or did not fit these contexts. He then articulated a theory about what types of internal ventures could and could not succeed, depending on their fit within the corporate context. Clayton Christensen's (1997) work paralleled and built upon Burgelman's work in several respects. He also noted the link between the company's strategic context and the way that resources could and could not be allocated within the firm. He was able to see these phenomena because he looked at the internal allocation of resources through a different theoretical lens than others had yet used— resource dependence—and chronicled the power that customers and shareholders had over the investments that companies can and cannot undertake. Christensen proposed new names for the categories that emerged from Burgelman's early work. He termed innovations and investments that fit the strategic and structural context of the company *sustaining technologies*. Innovations that did not fit those contexts were termed *disruptive* technologies. He then noted that if a strategically important innovation did not fit the company's strategic and structural context—if it was disruptive—then the only way the company could succeed was to set up a new organization whose context fit the innovation.

What Tomo Noda (Noda and Bower 1996) taught us about the phenomena at the base of the pyramid is that the resource allocation that determines a company's ultimate strategic direction is not a single-shot decision. Resources are allocated *iteratively* across repeated rounds of resource allocation in the annual budgeting cycle. Noda was also the first of several scholars to show how the capital market context influenced the resource allocation process, thus extending Christensen's original linkages to resource dependency. Sull demonstrated this in the tire industry (Sull 1999) and Eisenmann observed the same tendency in the cable industry (2002). All these scholars observed anomalies where the bottom–up process of resource allocation broke down and required corporate level intervention. This led to Eisenmann and Bower's concept of the Entrepreneurial M-form (2000). Finally, Gilbert observed an anomaly in the basic premise of the RAP model itself. In his study of the US newspaper industry, firms seemed repeatedly able to commit resources to disruptive ventures, something not predicted by Christensen and Bower's (1996) earlier findings. By looking at the phenomena through the lens of social psychology, Gilbert showed that when disruptive ventures were framed as a threat, impetus coalesced behind proposals that would otherwise fail in resource allocation.

Unfortunately, and despite the intense resource commitment observed, threat framing confined the firm's response to the existing structural and strategic context. Gilbert's insights about threat impetus and threat rigidity resolved an anomaly that Christensen had been unable to explain: why established companies almost always try to 'cram' disruptive technologies as sustaining innovations into their mainstream business model. His observations also expanded the model to show that strategic response goes beyond the commitment of resources, but includes the cognitive architecture that underlies that commitment as well (see Table 4.2).

One of the things that impressed us as we reviewed this body of research on the resource allocation process is that the research design of those who did this cumulative theory-building work nearly always reinforced the process of anomaly discovery and theory development discussed in this chapter. Their projects were triggered by anomalous observations that the prior body of research could not explain well. Each of the scholars reinserted themselves at the bottom of the pyramid by painstakingly adding to the description of the resource allocation process that Bower and Burgelman had given them. In the process, they saw new things that prior scholars had missed, either because they examined a broader range of phenomena, or they looked at the same phenomena through the lens of another discipline. Every study employed a nested research design. And each of the scholars sought a circumstance-contingent explanation of cause-and-effect. We believe it is because this community of scholars followed this method of theory

Table 4.2 *Anomaly-seeking research and the development of the RAP model*

Author	Anomaly	Implications for the RAP Model
Bower	There is a complex process that leads to the submission and evaluation of budgetary proposals that is entirely more complicated than traditionally viewed by capital market theory	Resource allocation is a *process*, not an *event* The structure of this process shapes the strategy realized Original RAP model: definition, impetus, and structural context operating at multiple levels
Burgelman	Activity outside the existing structural context is not explained by the original model	Development of the strategic context
Christensen	Innovation anomalies exist when theories on modular, architectural, or radical change did not explain incumbent firm failure.	Customers shape the resource allocation process and the category of disruptive vs. sustaining innovation
Noda	Funding decisions are not a one-time event. They develop not only simultaneously, but also through multiple iterations across time.	Resource allocation is iterative over time
Sull	The bottom up process fails in the face of institutional barriers around sources of capital	Capital markets shape the resource allocation process
Eisenmann	The bottom-up process fails in the face of highly volatile and uncertain investment decisions	The Entrepreneurial M-form and the role of corporate intervention
Gilbert	Strategy goes beyond resource commitment and is reflected in the cognitive architecture that underlies that commitment	Cognitive framing shapes the resource allocation process

building that they have been able to build, through independent and loosely coordinated work, such a powerful and useful body of knowledge about how executives can effectively direct strategy by managing the resource allocation process. As you read through the rest of this volume, look for instances of how each of these researchers has used anomaly-seeking research to revise or improve our theory of resource allocation. In the final chapter of the book, Bower and Gilbert capture this collective learning and present a revised model of the resource allocation process.

Endnotes

1. Note that this chapter draws heavily on the ideas developed by Carlile and Christensen (2005) on theory development.
2. Defined here, an anomaly is an outcome that is different from what existing theory would predict (Popper 1959).
3. Popper asserted that a researcher in this phase, when the theory accurately predicted what he observed, can only state that his test or experiment of the theory 'failed to disconfirm' the theory.
4. To be sure, not all the resource allocation scholars have used anomaly-seeking research as their primary form of investigation. Further, many of these scholars (Christensen 1997; Eisenmann 2002; and Gilbert 2001) all explored and tested their categorizations of the underlying phenomenon using methods that were predictive in design. And within the categorization schemes observed, these studies moved to become increasingly post-paradigmatic in intent. Nonetheless, most of the research as it pertains to our development of the resource allocation model has tended to develop much more in the pre-paradigmatic role.

References

Bennis, W. G., and O'Toole, J. (2005). 'How Business Schools Lost their Way'. *Harvard Business School* 83(5): 96–104.

Bower, J. L. (1970). *Managing the Resource Allocation Process*. Boston, Mass.: Harvard Business School Press.

Bourdieu, P., and Wacquart, L. (1992). *An Invitation to Reflexive Sociology*. Chicago: University of Chicago Press.

Burgelman, R. (1983). 'A Model of the Interaction of Strategic Behavior, Corporate Context, and the Concept of Strategy'. *Academy of Management Review*, 3/1: 61–9.

Carlile, P. R., and Christensen, C. M. (2005). 'Practice and Malpractice in Management Research'. Working Paper.

Christensen, C. M. (1997). *The Innovator's Dilemma: When New Technologies Cause Great Firms to Fail*. Boston, Mass.: Harvard Business School Press.

—— and Bower, J. L. (1996). 'Customer Power, Strategic Investment, and the Failure of Leading Firms'. *Strategic Management Journal* 17: 197–218.

Eisenhardt, K. M. (1989). 'Building Theories from Case Study Research'. *Academy of Management Review* 14/4: 532–50.

Eisenmann, T. R. (June 2002). 'The Effects of CEO Equity Ownership and Diversification on Risk Taking'. *Strategic Management Journal* 23: 513–34.

—— and Bower, J. L. (May–June 2000). 'The Entrepreneurial M-Form: Strategic Integration in Global Media Firms'. *Organizational Science* 11/3: 348–55.

Glaser, B., and Straus, A. (1967). *The Discovery of Grounded Theory: Strategies of Qualitative Research*. London: Weidenfeld & Nicolson.

Gilbert, C. G. (2001). 'A Dilemma in Response: Examining the Newspaper Industry's Response to the Internet'. *The Academy of Management Best Paper Proceedings Series*.

Henderson, R. M., and Clark, K. B. (March 1990). 'Architectural Innovation: The Reconfiguration of Existing Systems and the Failure of Established Firms'. *Administrative Science Quarterly*, 9–30.

Johnson, H. T., and Kaplan, R. (1987). *Relevance Lost*. Boston, Mass.: Harvard Business School Press.

Kaplan, A. (1964). *The Conduct of Inquiry: Methodology for Behavioral Research*. Scranton, Pa.: Chandler.

Kaplan, R. (1986). 'The Role for Empirical Research in Management Accounting'. *Accounting, Organizations and Society* 4/5: 429–52.

Kuhn, T. (1962). *The Structure of Scientific Revolutions*. Chicago: University of Chicago Press.

Noda, T., and Bower, J. L. (1996). 'Strategy Making as Iterated Processes of Resource Allocation'. *Strategic Management Journal* 17: 169–92.

Pfeffer, J., and Fong, T. (2002). 'The End of Business Schools? Less Success than Meets the Eye'. *Academy of Management Learning & Education* 1(1): 78–96.

Popper, K. (1959). *The Logic of Scientific Discovery*. New York: Basic Books.

Roethlisberger, F. (1977). *The Elusive Phenomena*. Boston, Mass.: Harvard Business School Press.

Simon, Herbert (1985). 'The Business School: A Problem of Organizational Design'. *Administrative Behavior*, 3rd edn. New York: Free Press, ch. 17.

Solow, Robert M. (May 1985). 'Economic History and Economics'. *The American Economic Review* 75/2: 328–31.

Sull, Donald N. (1999). 'The Dynamics of Standing Still: Firestone Tire and Rubber and the Radial Revolution'. *Business History Review* 73: 430–64.

Van de Ven, Andrew (2000). 'Professional Science for a Professional School', in Michael Beer and Nitin Nohria (eds.), *Breaking the Code of Change*. Boston, Mass.: Harvard Business School Press.

Weick, Karl E. (1989). 'Theory Construction as Disciplined Imagination'. *Academy of Management Review* 14/4: 516–31.

Yin, R. (1984). *Case Study Research*. Beverly Hills, Calif.: Sage.

Part II

When the Bottom-up Process Fails

Part II

5

When the Bottom-up Resource Allocation Process Fails

Donald N. Sull

A core tenet of strategy process research is that strategy results from a series of actions and decisions taken over time rather than a single 'big bet' at a given point in time (Bower 1970; Mintzberg 1978; Burgelman 1983*c*; Mintzberg and McHugh 1985; Mintzberg and Waters 1985). In a large, complex organization, these decisions generally emerge from lower levels in the organization (Bower 1970; Mintzberg 1978; Burgelman 1983*c*; Pascale 1984; Mintzberg and Waters 1985; Noda and Bower 1996).

Although these studies have been characterized as largely descriptive (Lovas and Ghoshal 2000: 892), there are sound theoretical reasons to conceive a distributed, bottom-up process to be a mechanism capable of overcoming the challenges posed by bounded rationality and dispersed knowledge (Simon 1945). Simon argues that bounded rationality prevents any single individual from collecting and processing all the relevant knowledge necessary to make an optimal decision. Bottom-up resource allocation relieves top executives of the need to collect and process all information by distributing decision rights to organization members who possess the relevant specific knowledge (Cyert and March 1963). In many complex, multiunit organizations, for example, frontline employees and middle managers will have a more detailed understanding of current customers' needs, potential market opportunities, and competitive dynamics, and therefore be better positioned to make appropriate decisions. Agents lower in the organization also have incentives to define and support successful projects, to the extent their rewards, such as promotion or job security, are a function of their reputation for identifying and lending impetus to successful projects (Bower 1970). Thus, a bottom-up process can help organizations

overcome the strategic challenges posed by bounded rationality of top
executives and dispersed knowledge.

Despite their advantages, bottom-up resource allocation processes
can fail under certain circumstances. The three chapters in this
section illustrate three specific sources of failure and contribute to a
growing body of research on the circumstances under which a bottom-up resource allocation process is liable to result in suboptimal
outcomes. Christensen's influential research focused on 'disruptive
technologies' that did not pose significant technological challenges for
incumbents but failed to address the needs of their current customers. In a careful study of the disk-drive industry, Christensen
found that incumbent producers consistently failed to commercialize
disruptive technologies. As described in Ch. 4, Christensen integrates
resource dependence and the resource allocation process perspectives
to explain an anomaly in the innovation literature regarding incumbent firm failure. Investments in disruptive technology did not serve
the needs of existing powerful customers whose business provided
critical resources to the disk-drive producers. Because they lacked
support from resource providers, these proposals failed to attract the
management support required to obtain funding. As a consequence,
they did not survive the rigors of the firms' internal resource allocation processes (RAP). The bottom-up process in resource allocation
failed because line managers could not find support for the disruptive
technology with their existing customers. As predicted by the RAP
model, this meant that most proposals with disruptive characteristics
were not defined by operating levels of management. The few proposals that did progress to middle management received no impetus.
Lack of demand from existing customers was the kiss of death. Even
when corporate-level management might have been supportive of a
disruptive investment, the bottom-up process failed to produce plans
to which resources might have been allocated.

Whereas most RAP research explores failures in *investment*, Sull, in
Ch. 7, explores why a bottom-up resource allocation process fails when
faced with the need for *disinvestment*. In a clinical study of Firestone's
response to radial tire technology, Sull found that frontline employees
and middle managers closest to the traditional business rendered obsolete by radial tires had little incentive to propose plant closure,
because it would jeopardize their own job security and that of their
colleagues and subordinates. This failure results from an asymmetry in
payoffs between investment and disinvestment proposals. Sound investment proposals create value for the organization and also enhance
the employee's intraorganizational reputation and job security (Bower

1970). Proposals for disinvestment, in contrast, may be optimal for the organization but run counter to the employees' interests (Jensen 1993). Frontline employees and middle managers also may fail to make disinvestment proposals to avoid the perception that their early actions were mistaken, leading them to escalate their commitment (Brockner 1992; Ross and Staw 1993). Although this study focuses on disinvestment in the context of capital budgeting decisions in a manufacturing company, the model predicts a similar process failure in other contexts where employee incentives and reputation are endangered by pulling resources from ongoing projects—e.g. research and development initiatives, internal corporate venturing. In most cases, disinvestment cannot, of course, be delayed forever, and the model predicts a delay in exit beyond the optimal point rather than a complete absence of disinvestment.

Whereas Christensen and Sull present specific circumstances where bottom-up resource allocation breaks down (due to powerful customers in the first and misaligned incentives for disinvestment in the second), Kuemmerle, in Ch. 8, presents a more general cause of bottom-up process failure. In comparing the international R&D investment decisions of established companies in the electronics and pharmaceutical industries with a matched pair sample of start-up firms, Kuemmerle finds important differences in the structure of their resource allocation decisions. Even though both types of firm can have effective bottom-up processes blocked by autocratic imposition of top management, the layer of middle management of more established companies—not present in start-ups—were an added source of failure. Middle managers blocked bottom-up proposals from gaining impetus, not from a lack of fit with structural or strategic context, but because of political and personal conflicts with operating managers below. Kuemmerle suggests that established companies are likely to be disadvantaged in international expansion relative to entrepreneurial firms when political conflict is high between middle and operating management, and that this probability is higher in more established, multilayered organizations. Thus, whereas middle management can play a translating role in assimilating complex, distributed knowledge, it also can prevent that knowledge from rising to the senior levels of an organization—in other words, both outcomes are possible. This challenge appears to be a general phenomenon, not a specific case. Thus, whether one considers disruptive proposals to new customers, disinvestment decisions, or other significant resource allocation decisions, the possibility of middle management playing a blocking role is a risk in resource allocation.

Later chapters in this book will identify other situations in which the internal resource allocation process fails. In a study of media firms, Eisenmann (2002) found that the bottom-up resource allocation process failed to produce required investment proposals because the magnitude of the investments required exceeded the budget authority of divisional managers. They were also reluctant to bear the risk associated with the high variance in potential payoffs of these bets. These findings are consistent with earlier research that found managers avoided risky R&D investments to improve the probability that they would achieve budget targets (Hoskisson and Hitt 1988; Hoskisson, Hitt, and Hill 1991). Eisenmann's research also suggests that investment proposals that require integration across units in a multidivisional corporation are likely to fall through the cracks because division heads lack the breadth of perspective to identify and incentives to pursue these opportunities (Eisenmann and Bower 2000). Gilbert's research on newspaper companies' response to the Internet demonstrates that an organization's framing of a contextual change as either an opportunity or a threat influences the effectiveness of the firm's bottom-up resource allocation process in responding to the change.

Several trends in these chapters signal patterns in subsequent research. First, the work since Bower's original 1970 research has become increasingly explanatory, even predictive, as opposed to descriptive. Christensen and Bower are not simply trying to describe how resource providers capture the resource allocation process, they are trying to explain the failure of incumbent firms in the face of technological change. Sull is not merely trying to describe the disinvestment process, he is trying to explain why key expenditures do not occur. This explanatory approach surfaces in much of the work that follows and can be seen in the chapters by Noda and Bower, Gilbert, and Eisenmann and Bower later in the book.

The second trend the reader will notice is that the chapters presented in this section represent a common research approach used by many of the RAP scholars that followed Bower. In Ch. 4, Gilbert and Christensen describe this as a pattern of anomaly-seeking research. The authors of the chapters in this section all use breakdowns in the resource allocation process as a way of shedding light on the workings of the process itself. In this sense, the focus on 'failure' is really the search for anomaly, where the researcher recognizes, 'I would have expected x, but I'm observing y.' Gilbert and Christensen described this process of anomaly seeking as creating opportunities to improve theory. In this section, we now see the continuation of this process of observed anomaly leading to revisions in the original model. Christensen and Bower use this to capture how customers shape the resource allocation process, and Sull reports similar findings with capital markets. Note also that Sull tries to use these new observations to reconsider the model itself. Although he leaves the core components of RAP unchanged, he tries to capture the various forces that shape the process of definition and impetus. And whereas the model will continue to evolve through repeated efforts of anomaly-driven research, in Sull we see the first effort to move toward a revised model.

References

Bower, J. L. (1970). *Managing the Resource Allocation Process*. Boston, Mass.: Harvard Business School Press.

Brockner, I. (1992). 'The Escalation of Commitment to a Failing Course of Action: Toward Theoretical Progress'. *Academy of Management Review* 17/1: 39–61.

Burgelman, R. A. (1983c). 'A Process Model of Internal Corporate Venturing in the Diversified Major Firm'. *Administrative Science Quarterly* 28: 223–44.

Cyert, R. M., and March, J. G. (1963). *A Behavioral Theory of the Firm*. Englewood Cliffs, NJ: Prentice-Hall.

Eisenmann, T. R. (2002). 'The Effects of CEO Equity Ownership and Diversification of Risk Taking'. *Strategic Management Journal* 23: 513–34.

—— and Bower, J. L. (2000). 'The Entrepreneurial M-Form: Strategic Integration in Global Media Firms'. *Organizational Science* 11: 348–55.

Hoskisson, R., and Hitt, M. (1988). 'Strategic Control Systems and Relative R&D Investments in Large Multiproduct Firms'. *Strategic Management Journal* 9: 605–21.

—— —— and Hill, C. (1991). 'Managerial Risk Taking in Diversified Firms: An Evolutionary Perspective'. *Organization Science* 2: 296–314.

Jensen, M. C. (July 1993). 'The Modern Industrial Revolution, Exit, and the Failure of Internal Control Systems'. *The Journal of Finance*, 831–80.

Lovas, B., and Ghoshal, S. (2000). 'Strategy as Guided Evolution'. *Strategic Management Journal* 21: 875–96.

Mintzberg, H. (1978). 'Patterns in Strategy Formation'. *Management Science* 24: 934–48.

—— and McHugh, A. (1985). 'Strategy Formulation in an Adhocracy'. *Administrative Science Quarterly* 30: 160–97.

—— and Waters, J. A. (1985). 'Of Strategies, Deliberate and Emergent'. *Strategic Management Journal* 6/3: 257–72.

Noda, T., and Bower, J. L. (1996). 'Strategy Making as Iterated Processes of Resource Allocation'. *Strategic Management Journal*, Summer Special Issue 17: 159–92.

Pascale, R. T. (Spring 1984). 'Perspectives on Strategy: The Real Story Behind Honda's Success'. *California Management Review*, 47–72.

Ross, J., and Staw, B. M. (1993). 'Organizational Escalation and Exit: Lessons from the Shoreham Nuclear Power Plant'. *Academy of Management Journal* 36: 701–32.

Simon, H. A. (1945). *Administrative Behavior*. New York: Macmillan.

6

Customer Power, Strategic Investment, and the Failure of Leading Firms

Clayton M. Christensen and Joseph L. Bower

Students of management have marveled at how hard it is for firms to repeat their success when technology or markets change, for good reason: there are lots of examples. For instance, no leading computer manufacturer has been able to replicate its initial success when subsequent architectural technologies and their corresponding markets emerged. IBM created and continues to dominate the mainframe segment, but it missed by many years the emergence of the minicomputer architecture and market. The minicomputer was developed, and its market applications exploited, by firms such as Digital Equipment and Data General. While very successful in their initial markets, the minicomputer makers largely missed the advent of the desktop computer: a market which was created by entrants such as Apple, Commodore, and Tandy, and only later by IBM. The engineering workstation leaders were Apollo and Sun Microsystems, both entrants to the industry. The pioneers of the portable computing market— Compaq, Zenith, Toshiba, and Sharp—were not the leaders in the desktop segment.

And yet even as these firms were missing this sequence of opportunities, they were *very* aggressively and successfully leading their industries in developing and adopting many strategically important and technologically sophisticated technologies. IBM's leadership across generations of multichip IC packaging, and Sun Microsystems' embrace of RISC microprocessor technology, are two instances. There are many other examples, discussed below, of firms that aggressively stayed at the forefront of technology development for extended periods, but whose industry leadership was later shaken by shifting technologies and markets.

The failure of leading firms can sometimes be ascribed to managerial myopia or organizational lethargy, or to insufficient resources or expertise. For example, cotton-spinners simply lacked the human, financial, and technological resources to compete when DuPont brought synthetic fibers into the apparel industry. But in many instances, the firms that missed important innovations suffered none of these problems. They had their competitive antennae up; aggressively invested in new products and technologies; and listened astutely to their customers. Yet they still lost their positions of leadership. This chapter examines why and under what circumstances financially strong, customer-sensitive, technologically deep, and rationally managed organizations may fail to adopt critical new technologies or enter important markets—failures to innovate which have led to the decline of once-great firms.

Our conclusion is that a primary reason why such firms lose their positions of industry leadership when faced with certain types of technological change has little to do with technology itself—with its degree of newness or difficulty, relative to the skills and experience of the firm. Rather, they fail because they listen too carefully to their customers—and customers place stringent limits on the strategies firms can and cannot pursue.

The term 'technology', as used in this chapter, means the processes by which an organization transforms labor, capital, materials, and information into products or services. All firms have technologies. A retailer such as Sears employs a particular 'technology' to procure, present, sell, and deliver products to its customers, while a discount warehouse retailer such as the Price Club employs a different 'technology'. Hence, our concept of technology extends beyond the engineering and manufacturing functions of the firm, encompassing a range of business processes. The term 'innovation' herein refers to a change in technology.

A fundamental premise of this chapter is that patterns of resource allocation heavily influence the types of innovations at which leading firms will succeed or fail. In every organization, ideas emerge daily about new ways of doing things—new products, new applications for products, new technical approaches, and new customers—in a manner chronicled by Bower (1970) and Burgelman (1983a, 1983b). Most proposals to innovate require human and financial resources. The patterns of innovation evidenced in a company will therefore mirror to a considerable degree the patterns in how its resources are allocated to, and withheld from, competing proposals to innovate.

We observe that because effective resource allocation is market-driven, the resource allocation procedures in successful organizations provide impetus for innovations known to be demanded by current customers in existing markets. We find that established firms in a wide range of industries have tended to lead in developing and adopting such innovations. Conversely, we find that firms possessing the capacity and capability to innovate may fail when the innovation does *not* address the foreseeable needs of their current customers. When the initial price/performance characteristics of emerging technologies render them competitive only in emerging market segments, and not with current customers, resource allocation mechanisms typically deny resources to such technologies. Our research suggests that the inability of some successful firms to allocate sufficient resources to technologies that initially cannot find application in mainstream markets, but later invade them, lies at the root of the failure of many once-successful firms.

Earlier Views of Factors Influencing Patterns of Resource Allocation in the Innovation Process

Our research links two historically independent streams of research, both of which have contributed significantly to our understanding of innovation. The first stream is what Pfeffer and Salancik (1978) call *resource dependence*: an approach which essentially looks *outside* the firm for explanations of the patterns through which firms allocate resources to innovative activities. Scholars in this tradition contend that firms' strategic options are constrained because managerial discretion is largely a myth. In order to ensure the survival of their organizations, managers lack the power to do anything other than to allocate resources to innovative programs that are required of the firm by external customers and investors: the entities that provide the resources the firm needs to survive. Support for this view comes from the work of historians of technological innovation such as Cooper and Schendel (1976) and Foster (1986). The firms they studied generally responded to the emergence of competitively threatening technologies by intensifying their investments to improve the conventional technologies used by their current customers—which provided the resources the firms needed to survive over the short term.

The second stream of ideas, originally taught by Bower (1970) and amplified by Burgelman (1983a, 1983b), describes the resource allocation process internal to the firm. These scholars suggest that most strategic proposals—to add capacity or develop new products or processes—take their fundamental shape at lower levels of hierarchical organizations. Bower observed that the allocation of funding amongst projects is substantially shaped by the extent to which managers at middle levels of the organization decide to support, or lend *impetus*, to some proposals and to withhold it from others. Bower also observed that risk management and career management were closely linked in the resource allocation process. Because the career costs to aspiring managers of having backed an ultimately unsuccessful project can be severe, their tendency was to back those projects where the demand for the product was assured.

Our study links these two streams by showing how the impetus that drives patterns of resource allocation (and hence innovation) within firms does not stem from autonomous decisions of risk-conscious managers. Rather, whether sufficient impetus coalesces behind a proposed innovation is largely determined by the presence or absence of current customers who can capably articulate a need for the innovation in question. There seems to be a powerful linkage from: (1) the expectations and needs of a firm's most powerful customers for product improvements; to (2) the types of innovative proposals which are given or denied impetus within the firm and which therefore are allocated the resources necessary to develop the requisite technological capabilities; to (3) the markets toward which firms will and will not target these innovations; which in turn leads to (4) the firms' ultimate commercial success or failure with the new technology.

A primary conclusion of this chapter is that when significant customers demand it, sufficient impetus may develop so that large, bureaucratic firms can embark upon and successfully execute technologically difficult innovations—even those that require very different competencies than they initially possessed.[1] Conversely, we find that when a proposed innovation addresses the needs of small customers in remote or emerging markets that do not supply a significant share of the resources a firm currently needs for growth and survival, firms will find it difficult to succeed even at innovations that are technologically straightforward. This is because the requisite impetus does not develop, and the proposed innovations are starved of resources.

Our findings build upon the work of earlier scholars who have addressed the question of why leading firms may fail when faced with technological change. Cooper and Schendel (1976) found that new technologies often are initially deployed in new markets, and that these were generally brought into industries by entering firms. They observed that established firms confronted with new technology often intensified investment in traditional technical approaches, and that those that did make initial resource commitments to a new technology rarely maintained adequate resource commitments. Foster (1986) noted that at points when new technologies enter an industry, entrants seem to enjoy an 'attacker's advantage' over incumbent firms. Henderson and Clark (1990) posited that entrant firms enjoyed a particular advantage over incumbents in architectural technology change.

We hope to add additional precision and insight to the work of these pioneering scholars, by stating more precisely the specific sorts of technological innovations that are likely initially to be deployed in new applications, and the sorts that are likely to be used in mainstream markets from the beginning; and to define the types of innovation in which we expect attackers to enjoy an advantage, and the instances in which we expect incumbents to hold the upper hand. By presenting a model of the processes by which resource commitments are made, we hope partially to explain a puzzle posed but not resolved by each of these authors: *why* have incumbent firms generally intensified their commitments to conventional technology, while starving efforts to commercialize new technologies—even while the new technology was gaining ground in the market? Finally, by examining why established firms do these things, we hope to provide insights for how managers can more successfully address different types of technological change.

Research Methods

Three very different classes of data were used in this study, to establish solid construct validity (Yin 1989). The first was a database of the detailed product and performance specifications for every disk-drive model announced by every firm participating in the world industry between 1975 and 1990—over 1400 product models in all. These data came from *Disk/Trend Report*, the leading market research publication in the disk-drive industry, and from product specification sheets obtained from the manufacturers themselves. The tables and other summary statistics reported in this chapter were calculated from this database, unless otherwise noted. This data-set is not a statistical sample, but constitutes a complete census of companies and products for the world industry during the period studied.

The second type of information employed in the study relates to the strategies pursued, and the commercial success and failure, of each of the companies that announced the development of a rigid disk drive between 1976 and 1990. *Disk/Trend* reported each firm's rigid disk-drive sales in each of these years, by product category and by market segment. Each monthly issue between 1976 and 1990 of *Electronic Business* magazine, the most prominent trade publication covering the magnetic recording industry, was examined for information about disk-drive manufacturers, their strategies and products. We used this information to verify the completeness of the *Disk/ Trend* data,[2] and to write a history of the disk-drive industry describing the strategies and fortunes of firms in the industry (Christensen 1993).

The third type of information employed in this study came from over seventy personal, unstructured interviews conducted with executives who are or have been associated with twenty-one disk-drive manufacturing companies. Those interviewed included founders; chief executives; vice presidents of sales and marketing, engineering, and finance; and engineering, marketing, and managerial members of pivotal product development project teams. The firms whose executives were interviewed together account for over 80 per cent of the disk drives produced in the world since the industry's inception. Data from these interviews were used to reconstruct, as accurately as possible, the decision-making processes associated with key innovations in each company's history. Wherever possible, accounts of the same decision were obtained from multiple sources, including former employees, to minimize problems with *post hoc* rationalization. Multiple employees were interviewed in sixteen of the twenty-one companies.

The *Disk/ Trend* data enabled us to measure the impact that each new component and architectural technology had on disk-drive performance. Furthermore, it was possible to identify which firms were the first to develop and adopt each new technology, and to trace the patterns of diffusion of each new technology through the world industry over time, amongst different types of firm. When analysis of the *Disk/ Trend* data indicated a particular entrant or established firm had prominently led or lagged behind the industry in a particular innovation, we could determine the impact of that leadership or followership on the subsequent sales and market shares, by product-market segment, for each company.

Analysis of these data essentially enabled us to develop a theory of *what* will happen when different types of technological change occur— whether we would expect entrant and established firms to take leadership in their development. We then used our interview data to write case histories of key decisions in six companies to understand *why* those patterns of leadership and followership in technology development occur. These case studies covered entrant and established firms, over an extended period of time in which each of them made decisions to invest, or delay investing, in a variety of new technologies. These cases were selected in what Yin (1989) calls a multi-case, nested experimental design, so that through pattern-matching across cases, the external validity of the study's conclusions could be established. Table 6.3 describes this pattern-matching.

We studied the disk-drive industry because its history is one of rapid change in technology and market structure. The world rigid disk-drive market grew at a 27 per cent annual rate to over $13 billion between 1975 and 1990. Of the seventeen firms in the OEM industry in 1976, only one was still in operation in 1990. Over 130 firms entered the industry during this period, and more than 100 of them failed. The cost per megabyte (MB) of the average drive in constant 1990 dollars fell from $560 in 1976 to $5 in 1990. The physical size of a 100 MB drive shrank from 5,400 to 8 cubic inches over the same period. During this time, six architecturally distinct product generations emerged, and a new company rose to become market leader in four of these six generations. A description of disk-drive technology that may be helpful for some readers is provided in Appendix 1.

Typologies of Technological Change

Earlier scholars of technology change have argued that incumbent firms may stumble when technological change destroys the value of established technological competencies (Tushman and Anderson 1986), or when new architectural technologies emerge (Henderson and Clark 1990). For present purposes, however, we have found it useful to distinguish between those innovations that *sustained* the industry's rate of improvement in product performance (total capacity and recording density were the two most common measures), and those innovations that *disrupted* or redefined that performance trajectory (Dosi 1982). The following two sections illustrate these concepts by describing prominent examples of trajectory-sustaining and trajectory-disrupting technological changes in the industry's history. The subsequent sections then describe the role these innovations played in the industry's development; the processes through which incumbent and entrant firms responded to these different types of technological change; and the consequent successes and failures these firms experienced.

Sustaining Technological Changes

In the disk-drive industry's history, most of the changes in competent technology, and two of the six changes in architectural technology, sustained or reinforced established trajectories of product performance improvement. Two examples of such technology change are shown in Fig. 6.1. The left-most graph compares the average recording density of drives that employed conventional particulate oxide disk technology and ferrite head technology, vs. the average density of drives that employed new-technology thin film heads and disks, that were introduced in each of the years between 1976 and 1990. The improvements in the conventional approach are the result of consistent incremental advances such as grinding the ferrite heads to finer, more precise dimensions; and using smaller and more finely dispersed oxide particles on the disk's surface. Note that the improvement in areal density obtainable with ferrite/oxide technology began to level off in the period's later years—suggesting a maturing technology S-curve (Foster 1986). Note how thin film head and disk technologies emerged to sustain the rate of performance improvement at its historical pace of 35 per cent between 1984 and 1990.

The right-most graph in Fig. 6.1 describes a sustaining technological change of a very different character: an innovation in product architecture. In this case, the 14-inch Winchester drive substituted for removable disk packs, which had been the dominant design between 1962 and 1978. Just as in the thin film-for-ferrite/oxide substitution, the impact of Winchester technology was to sustain the historically established rate of performance improvement. Other important innovations, such as embedded servo systems, RLL & PRML recording codes, higher RPM motors and embedded SCSI, SMD, ESDI, and AT interfaces, also helped manufacturers sustain the rate of historical performance improvement that their customers had come to expect.

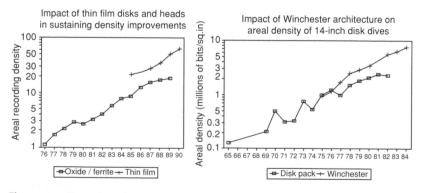

Figure 6.1 Examples of sustaining technological change in componentry (left) and product architecture (right). Reprinted with permission from *Business History Review* 67 (1993: 557).

(The examples of technology change presented in Fig. 6.1 and 6.2 introduce some ambiguity to the unqualified term 'discontinuity', as it has been used by Dosi (1982), Tushman and Anderson (1986), and others. The innovations in head and disk technology described in the left graph of Fig. 6.1 represent *positive discontinuities* in an established technological trajectory, while the development of trajectory-disrupting technologies charted in Fig. 6.2 represent *negative* discontinuities. As will be shown below, established firms seemed quite capable of leading the industry over positive discontinuities. The negative ones were the points at which established firms generally lost their positions of industry leadership.) Hereafter in this chapter, technological changes that have such a sustaining impact on an established trajectory of performance improvement are called *sustaining technologies*.

Disruptive Technological Changes

Most technological change in the industry's history consisted of sustaining innovations of the sort described above. In contrast, there were just a few trajectory-disrupting changes. The most important of these from a historical viewpoint were the architectural innovations that carried the industry from 14-inch diameter disks to diameters of 8, 5.25, and then 3.5 inches. The ways in which these innovations were disruptive are illustrated in Table 6.1. Set in 1981, this table compares the attributes of a typical 5.25-inch drive—a new architecture that had been in the market for less than a year at that time—with those of a typical 8-inch drive, which by that time had become the standard drive used by minicomputer manufacturers. Note that along the dimensions of performance which were important to established minicomputer manufacturers—capacity, cost per megabyte, and access time—the 8-inch product was vastly superior. The 5.25-inch architecture did not address the needs of minicomputer manufacturers, as they perceived their needs at that time. On the other hand, the 5.25-inch architecture *did* possess attributes that appealed to the desktop personal computer market segment that was just emerging in 1980–2. It was small and lightweight—important features for this application. And it was priced at around $2,000, which means it could economically be incorporated in desktop machines. Hereafter in this chapter, technologies such as this, which disrupt an established trajectory of performance improvement, or redefine what performance means, are called *disruptive technologies*.

Table 6.1 *The disruptive impact on performance improvement of the 5.25-inch vs. the 8-inch architecture*

Attribute	8-inch drives	5.25-inch drives
Capacity (megabytes)	**60**	10
Volume (cubic inches)	566	*150*
Weight (pounds)	21	*6*
Access time (ms)	**30**	160
Cost per megabyte	**$50**	$200
Total unit cost	*$3,000*	*$2,000*

Notes: Attributes valued highly in the minicomputer market in 1981 are presented in boldface. Attributes valued in the emerging desktop computing market in 1981 are shown in *italics*.

Source: *Analysis of Disk/Trend Report* data; from Christensen (1992a: 90).

In general, sustaining technological changes appealed to established cutomers in existing, mainstream markets. They provided these customers with more of what they had come to expect. In contrast, disruptive technologies rarely could initially be employed in established markets. They tended instead to be valued in remote or emerging markets. This tendency consistently appears not just in disk drives, but across a range of industries (Rosenbloom and Christensen 1995).

The Impact of Sustaining and Disruptive Technologies on Industry Structure

The history of sustaining and disruptive technological change in the disk-drive industry is summarized in Fig. 6.2. It begins in 1974, the year after IBM's first Winchester architecture model was introduced to challenge the dominant disk-pack architectural design. Almost all drives then were sold to makers of mainframe computers. Note that in 1974 the median-priced mainframe computer was equipped with about 130 MB of hard disk capacity. The typical hard disk storage capacity supplied with the median-priced mainframe increased about 17 per cent per year, so that by 1990 the typical mainframe was equipped with 1300 MB of hard disk capacity. This growth in the use of hard disk memory per computer is mapped by the solid line emanating from point A in Fig. 6.2. This trajectory was driven by user learning and software developments in the applications in which mainframes were used (Christensen and Rosenbloom 1995).

The dashed line originating at point A measures the increase in the average capacity of 14-inch drives over the same period. Note that

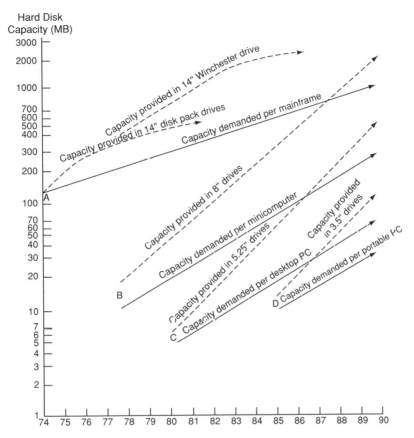

Figure 6.2 Patterns of entry and improvement in disruptive disk-drive technologies. Reprinted with permission from *Business History Review* 67 (1993: 559).

although the capacity of the average 14-inch drive was equal to the capacity shipped with the typical mainframe in 1974, the rate of increase in capacity provided within the 14-inch architecture exceeded the rate of increase in capacity demanded in the mainframe market—carrying this architecture toward high-end mainframes, scientific computers, and supercomputers. Furthermore, note how the new 14-inch Winchester architecture sustained the capacity trajectory that had been established in the earlier removable disk-pack architecture. Appendix 2 describes how these trajectories were calculated.

The solid trajectories emanating from points B, C, and D represent the average hard disk capacity *demanded* by computer buyers in each market segment, over time.[3] The dashed lines emanating from points B, C, and D in Fig. 6.2 measure trends in the average capacity that disk-drive manufacturers were able to *provide* with each successive disk-drive architecture. Note that with the exception of the 14-inch Winchester architecture, the maximum capacity initially available in each of these architectures was substantially *less* than the capacity required for the typical computer in the established market—these were *disruptive* innovations. As a consequence, the 8, 5.25, and 3.5-inch designs initially were rejected by the leading, established computer manufacturers, and were deployed instead in emerging market applications for disk drives: minicomputers, desktop PCs, and portable PCs, respectively. Note, however, that once these disruptive architectures became established in their new markets, the accumulation of hundreds of sustaining innovations pushed each architecture's performance ahead along very steep, and roughly parallel, trajectories.[4]

Note that the trajectory of improvement that the technology was able to *provide* within each architecture was nearly *double* the slope of the increase in capacity *demanded* in each market. As we will see, this disparity between what the technology could provide and what the market demanded seems to have been the primary source of leadership instability in the disk-drive industry.

Leaders in Sustaining and Disruptive Technological Innovations

To understand better why leading firms might successfully pioneer in the development and adoption of many new and difficult technologies, and yet lose their positions of industry leadership by failing to implement others, we compared the innovative behavior of *established* firms with that of *entrant* firms, with respect to each of the sustaining and disruptive technological innovations in the history of the disk-drive industry. Building upon the approach employed by Henderson and Clark (1990), established firms were defined as firms that had previously manufactured drives which employed an older, established technology, whereas entrant firms were those whose initial product upon entry into the industry employed the new component or architectural technology being analyzed. This approach was used because of this study's longitudinal character, looking at the performance of incumbents and entrants across a sequence of innovations.

In spite of the wide variety in the magnitudes and types of sustaining technological changes in the industry's history, the firms that led in their development and adoption were the industry's leading, established firms. Table 6.2(a) depicts this leadership pattern for three representative sustaining technologies. In thin-film head technology, it was Burroughs (1976), IBM (1979), and other established firms that first successfully incorporated thin-film heads in disk drives. In the 1981–86 period, when over sixty firms entered the rigid disk-drive industry, only five of them (all commercial failures) attempted to do so using thin-film heads as a source of performance advantage in their initial products. All other entrant firms—even aggressively performance-oriented firms such as Maxtor and Conner Peripherals—found it preferable to cut their teeth on ferrite heads in the entry products, before tackling thin-film technology in subsequent generations.

Note the similar pattern in the development and adoption of RLL codes—a much simpler development than thin-film head technology— which consumed at most a few million dollars per firm. RLL enabled a 30 per cent density improvement, and therefore represented the type of inexpensive path to performance improvement that ought to be attractive to entrant firms. But in 1985, eleven of the thirteen firms which introduced new models employing RLL technology were established firms, meaning that they had previously offered models based on MFM technology. Only two were entrants, meaning that their initial products employed RLL codes. Table 6.2(a) also notes that six of the first seven firms to introduce Winchester architecture drives were established makers of drives employing the prior disk pack architecture.[5]

The history of literally every other sustaining innovation—such as embedded servo systems, zone-specific recording densities, higher RPM motors and the 2.5-inch Winchester architecture—reveals a similar pattern: the established firms led in the adoption of sustaining technology be it in componentry or architecture. Entrant firms followed. In other words, the failure of leading firms to stay atop the disk-drive industry generally was not because they could not keep pace with the industry's movement along the dashed-line technological trajectories mapped in Fig. 6.2. The leading incumbent firms effectively *led* the industry along those trajectories even though many of these were competency-destroying progressions in terms of technologies, skills, and manufacturing assets required (Tushman and Anderson 1986).

In contrast, the firms that led the industry in introducing *disruptive* architectural technologies—in the moves to points B, C, and D in Fig. 6.2—tended overwhelmingly to be *entrant*, rather than established firms. This is illustrated in Table 6.2(b). It shows, for example, that in 1978 an entrant offered the industry's first 8-inch drive. By the end of the second year of that architecture's life (1979), six firms were offering 8-inch drives; two-thirds of them were entrants. Likewise, by the end of the second year of the 5.25-inch generation's life, eight of the ten firms offering 5.25-inch drives were entrants. Entrants similarly dominated the early population of firms offering 3.5-inch drives. In each of

Table 6.2 *Trends in technology leadership and followership in sustaining vs. disruptive technologies*

	1974	1975	1976	1977	1978	1979	1980	1981	1982	1983	1984	1985	1986	1987	1988
(a) Numbers of established and entrant firms introducing models employing selected trajectory-sustaining technologies															
Thin-film heads Entrants										1	2	1		1	4
Established		1			1	1	3	5	6	8	12	15	17	22	
RLL codes Entrants										1	2	3	6	8	
Established										4	11	20	25	26	
Winchester Entrants			1	4	9										
architecture Established	1		3	3	7	11									
(b) Numbers of established and entrant firms introducing models based upon disruptive architectural technologies															
8-inch Entrants					1	4	6	8							
Established					0	2	5	5							
5.25-inch Entrants							1	8	8	13					
Established							1	2	8	11					
3.5-inch Entrants										1	2	3	4		
Established											0	1	1	4	

Note: Data are presented in these tables only for those years in which the new technologies were gaining widespread acceptance, to illustrate tendencies in technology leadership and followership. Once the technologies had become broadly accepted, the numbers of firms introducing models using them are no longer reported. Twelve years are covered in the thin-film head category because it took that long for thin film heads to become broadly used in the marketplace. Only five years of history are reported for RLL codes because by 1988 the vast majority of established *and* entrant firms had adopted RLL codes. Four years of data are shown for new architectures, because any established firms that had not launched the new architecture within four years of its initial appearance in the market had been driven from the industry.

these generations, between half and two-thirds of the established manufacturers of the prior architectural generation *never* introduced a model in the new architecture. And those established drivemakers that did design and manufacture new architecture models did so with an average two-year lag behind the pioneering entrant firms. In this fast-paced industry, such slow response often proved fatal.

These patterns of leadership and followership in sustaining and disruptive technologies are reflected in the commercial success and failure of disk-drive manufacturers. The ability of established firms to lead the industry in the sustaining innovations that powered the steep technological trajectories in Fig. 6.2 often were technologically difficult, risky, and expensive. Yet in the history of this industry, there is no evidence that the firms that led in sustaining innovations gained market share by virtue of such technology leadership (Christensen 1992*b*). This leadership enabled them to maintain their competitiveness only within specific technological trajectories. On the other hand, entrant firms' leadership advantages in disruptive innovations enabled them not only to capture new markets as they emerged, but (because the trajectories of technological progress were steeper than the trajectories of performance demanded) to invade and capture established markets as well.

Hence, all but one of the makers of 14-inch drives were driven from the mainframe computer market by entrant firms that got their start making 8-inch drives for minicomputers. The 8-inch drive makers, in turn, were driven from the minicomputer market, and eventually the mainframe market, by firms which led in producing 5.25-inch drives for desktop computers. And the leading makers of 5.25-inch drives were driven from desktop and minicomputer applications by makers of 3.5-inch drives, as mapped in Fig. 6.2.

We began this chapter by posing a puzzle: why it was that firms which at one point could be esteemed as aggressive, innovative, customer-sensitive organizations could ignore or attend belatedly to technological innovations with enormous strategic importance. In the context of the preceding analysis of the disk-drive industry, this question can be sharpened considerably. The established firms were, in fact, aggressive, innovative, and customer-sensitive in their approaches to sustaining innovations of every sort. But why was it that established firms could not lead their industry in disruptive architectural innovations? For it is only in these innovations that attackers demonstrated an advantage. And unfortunately for the leading established firms, this advantage enabled attacking entrant firms to topple the incumbent industry leaders each time a disruptive technology emerged.[6]

To understand why disruptive technological change was so consistently vexing to incumbent firms, we personally interviewed managers
who played key roles in the industry's leading firms, as incumbents or
entrants, when each of these disruptive technologies emerged. Our
objective in these interviews was to reconstruct, as accurately and
from as many points of view as possible, the forces that influenced
these firms' decision-making processes relating to the development and
commercialization of disruptive architectural technologies. We found
the experiences of the firms, and the forces influencing their decisions,
to be remarkably similar. In each instance, when confronted with
disruptive technology change, developing the requisite *technology* was
never a problem: prototypes of the new drives often had been developed before management was asked to make a decision. It was in the
process of allocating scarce resources amongst competing product and
technology development proposals, however, that disruptive projects
got stalled. Programs addressing the needs of the firms' most powerful
customers almost *always* pre-empted resources from the disruptive
technologies, whose markets tended to be small and where customers'
needs were poorly defined.

In the following section we have synthesized the data from case studies
of the six firms we studied in particular depth, into a *six*-step model that
describes the factors that influenced how resources were allocated across
competing proposals to develop new sustaining vs. disruptive technology in these firms. The struggle of Seagate Technology, the industry's
dominant maker of 5.25-inch drives, successfully to commercialize the
disruptive 3.5-inch drive, is recounted here to illustrate each of the steps
in the model. Short excerpts from a fuller report of other case histories
(Christensen 1992*a*) are also presented to illustrate what happened in
specific companies at each point in the process. Table 6.3 describes how
the findings from each of the case studies support, or do not support, the
principal propositions in the model. In Yin's (1989) terms, the high
degree of literal and theoretical replication shown in Table 6.3, and the
extent of 'pattern matching' across case studies where more than one
firm encountered the same technological change, lend high degrees of
reliability and external validity to the model.[7]

A Model of the Resource-Allocation Process in Established Firms Faced with Disruptive Change

1. Although entrants were the leaders in *commercializing* disruptive
technology, it did not start out that way: the first engineers to develop

Table 6.3 *Support of key elements of model found in each of six in-depth case studies*

Companies Studied:	Prototypes of disruptive architecture drive developed internally, well before widespread industry adoption (model step 1)	Marketers show early prototypes to lead customers of prior architecture; they reject product; marketing issues pessimistic forecast (model step 2)	Project to commercialize disruptive product is shelved; company aggressively pursues sustaining innovations (model step 3)	New firms are established to commercialize disruptive architecture; they find new markets, where product's attributes are valued (model step 4)	Entrant firms which initially sold product only in new market improve performance faster than initial market requires, enabling them to attack established markets (model step 5)	In response to entrants' attack, established firms belatedly introduce disruptive product. Sales are largely to existing customers, cannibalizing sales of prior architecture products (model step 6)
Quantum Corp.	L	L	L, T	L, T	L	L, T
Conner Peripherals	L	L	L	L	L	
Miniscribe		L		L	L	L
Seagate Technology	L	L	L	L	L	L
Micropolis	T	L	L, T	L, T	L	T
Control Data	L	L	L, T	L, T	L	L, T

Note: An 'L' in the matrix indicates that this step was a clear, explicit element in that firm's case history—ir Yin's (1989) terms, a 'literal replication'. Where 'T' is shown, the firm avoided the fate described in the model by explicitly recognizing the factors in the model, and dealing with them in the manner described in the final section of this chapter. These constitute what Yin calls 'theoretical replications' of the model. Where no 'L' or 'T' is shown, that step was not a clear o˙ prominent part of the firm's encounter with the disruptive technology being studied. Some firms studied confronted only one disruptive architecture. Miniscribe, for example, started making 5.25-inch drives generally in the pattern indicated by our model; and was subsequently driven from the industry. Other firms, such as Quantum and Control Data, confronted a series of disruptive innovations, and dealt with some of them differently than they did with others, as described in the last section of the chapter. In such instances, an 'L' and a 'T' are entered in the matrix. As Yin points out, when multiple case studies are used to support a multi-element model, as in this study, each cell in a matrix such as this constitutes an independent 'observation'. Hence, the model is supported in 32 of the 36 observations.

Source: Yin (1989: 35–7).

the disruptive architectures generally did so while employed by a leading established firm, using bootlegged resources. Their work was rarely initiated by senior management. While architecturally innovative, these designs almost always employed off-the-shelf components. For example, engineers at Seagate Technology, the leading 5.25-inch drive maker, were the second in the industry to develop working prototype 3.5-inch models, in 1985. They made over eighty prototype models before the issue of formal project approval was raised with senior management. The same thing happened earlier at Control Data, the dominant 14-inch drive maker. Its engineers had designed working 8-inch drives internally, nearly two years before they appeared in the market.

2. The marketing organization then used its habitual procedure for testing the market appeal of new drives, by showing prototypes to lead customers of the existing product line, asking them to evaluate the new models.[8] Again drawing on the Seagate case, marketers tested the new 3.5-inch drives with IBM and other makers of XT- and AT-class desktop personal computers—even though the drives, as shown in Fig. 6.2 above, had significantly less capacity than the mainstream desktop market demanded.

These customers showed little interest in the disruptive drives, because they did not address their need for higher performance within the established architectural framework. As Fig. 6.2 shows, the established customers needed new drives that would take them *along* their existing performance trajectory. As a consequence, the marketing managers were unwilling to support the disruptive technology and offered pessimistic sales forecasts.

Generally, because the disruptive drives were targeted at emerging markets, initial forecasts of sales were small. In addition, because such products were simpler and offered lower performance, forecast profit margins were also lower than established firms had come to require. Financial analysts in established firms, therefore, joined their marketing colleagues in opposing the disruptive programs. As a result, in the ensuing allocation process resources were explicitly withdrawn, and the disruptive projects were slowly starved.

For example, when Seagate's main customer, IBM's PC division, rejected Seagate's 3.5-inch prototypes for insufficient capacity, sales forecasts were cut and senior managers shelved the program—just as 3.5-inch drives were becoming firmly established in laptops. 'We needed a new model,' recalled a former Seagate manager, 'which could become the next ST412 (a very successful product generating $300 million sales annually in the desktop market that was near the end of its life cycle). Our forecasts for the 3.5-inch drive were under $50 million because the laptop market was just emerging—and the 3.5-inch product just didn't fit the bill.' And earlier, when engineers at Control Data, the leading 14-inch drive maker, developed its initial 8-inch drives, its customers were looking for an average of 300 MB per computer, whereas CDC's earliest 8-inch drives offered less than 60 MB. The 8-inch project was given low priority, and engineers assigned to its development kept getting pulled off to work on problems with 14-inch drives being designed for more important customers. Similar problems plagued the belated launches of Quantum's and Micropolis's 5.25-inch products.

3. In response to the needs of current customers, the marketing managers threw impetus behind alternative *sustaining* projects, such as incorporating better heads or developing new recording codes. These would give their customers what they wanted, could be targeted at large markets, and generate the sales and profits required to maintain growth. Although they generally involved greater development expense, such sustaining investments appeared *far* less risky than investments in the disruptive technology, because the customers were there. The rationality of Seagate's decision to shelve the 3.5-inch drive in 1985–6, for example, is stark. Its view downmarket (in terms of Fig. 6.2) was at a $50 million total market forecast for 3.5-inch drives in 1987. What gross margins it could achieve in that market were uncertain, but its manufacturing executives predicted that costs per megabyte in 3.5-inch drives would be much higher than in 5.25-inch products. Seagate's view upmarket was quite different. Volumes in 5.25-inch drives with capacities of 60–100 MB were forecast to be $500 million in size by 1987. And companies serving the 60–100 MB market were earning gross margins of 35–40 per cent, whereas Seagate's margins in its high-volume 20 MB drives were between 25 and 30 per cent. It simply did not make sense for Seagate to put resources behind the 3.5-inch drive, when competing proposals to move upmarket to develop its ST251 line of drives were also actively being evaluated.

After Seagate executives shelved the 3.5-inch project, it began introducing new 5.25-inch models at a dramatically accelerating rate. In the years 1985, 1986, and 1987, the numbers of new models it introduced each year as a percentage of the total number of its models on the market in the prior year were 57, 78, and 115 per cent, respectively. And during the same period, Seagate incorporated complex and sophisticated new component technologies such as thin-film disks, voice coil actuators, RLL codes, and embedded, SCSI interfaces. In each of our other case studies as well, the established firms introduced new models in their established architectures employing an array of new component technologies at an accelerating rate, after the new architectures began to be sold. The clear motivation of the established firms in doing this was to win the competitive wars against each other, rather than to prepare for an attack by entrants from below.

4. New companies, usually including members of the frustrated engineering teams from established firms, were formed to exploit the disruptive product architecture. For example, the founders of the leading 3.5-inch drive maker, Conner Peripherals, were disaffected employees from Seagate and Miniscribe, the two largest 5.25-inch manufacturers. The founders of 8-inch drive maker Micropolis came from Pertec, a 14-inch manufacturer; and the founders of Shugart and Quantum defected from Memorex.[9] The start-ups were as unsuccessful as their former employers in interesting established computer makers in the disruptive architecture. Consequently, they had to find *new* customers. The applications that emerged in this very uncertain, probing process were the minicomputer, the desktop personal computer, and the laptop (see Fig. 6.2). These are obvious markets for hard drives in retrospect. But at the time, whether these would become significant markets for disk drives was highly uncertain. Micropolis was founded before the market for desk-side minicomputers and word processors, in which its products came to be used, emerged. Seagate was founded two years before IBM introduced its PC, when personal computers were simple toys for hobbyists. And Conner Peripherals got its start before Compaq knew the portable computer market had potential. The founders of these firms sold their products without a clear marketing strategy, essentially to whomever would buy them. Out of what was largely a trial-and-error approach to the market, the ultimately dominant applications for their products emerged.

5. Once the start-ups had found an operating base in new markets, they found that by adopting sustaining improvements in new component technologies,[10] they could increase the capacity of their drives at a faster rate than was required by their new market. As shown in Fig. 6.2, they blazed trajectories of 50 per cent annual improvement, fixing their sights on the large, established computer markets immediately above them on the performance scale. As noted above, the established firms' views downmarket, and the entrant firms' views upmarket, were asymmetrical. In contrast to the unattractive margins and market size the established firms saw when eyeing the new markets for simpler drives as they were emerging, the entrants tended to view the potential volumes and margins in the upscale, high-performance markets

above them as highly attractive. Customers in these established markets eventually embraced the new architectures they had rejected earlier, because once their needs for capacity and speed were met, the new drives' smaller size and architectural simplicity made them cheaper, faster, and more reliable than the older architectures. For example, Seagate, which started in the desktop personal computer market, subsequently invaded and came to dominate the minicomputer, engineering workstation, and mainframe computer markets for disk drives. Seagate, in turn, was driven from the desktop personal computer market for disk drives by Conner and Quantum, the pioneering manufacturers of 3.5-inch drives.

6. When the smaller models began to invade established market segments, the drive makers that had initially controlled those markets took their prototypes off the shelf (where they had been put in step 3), and defensively introduced them to defend their customer base in their own market.[11] By this time, of course, the new architecture had shed its disruptive character, and had become fully performance-competitive with the larger drives in the established markets. Although some established manufacturers were able to defend their market positions through belated introduction of the new architecture, many found that the entrant firms had developed insurmountable advantages in manufacturing cost and design experience, and they eventually withdrew from the market. For those established manufacturers that did succeed in introducing the new architectures, survival was the only reward. None of the firms we studied was ever able to win a significant share of the new market whose emergence had been enabled by the new architecture; the new drives simply cannibalized sales of older, larger-architecture products with existing customers. For example, as of 1991 almost none of Seagate's 3.5-inch drives had been sold to portable/laptop manufacturers: its 3.5-inch customers still were desktop computer manufacturers, and many of its 3.5-inch drives continued to be shipped with frames permitting them to be mounted in XT- and AT-class computers that had been designed to accommodate 5.25-inch drives. Control Data, the 14-inch leader, never captured even a 1 per cent share of the minicomputer market. It introduced its 8-inch drives nearly three years after the pioneering start-ups did, and nearly all its drives were sold to its existing mainframe customers. Miniscribe, Quantum, and Micropolis all had the same cannibalistic experience when they belatedly introduced disruptive-technology drives. They failed to capture a significant share of the new market, and at best succeeded in defending a portion of their prior business.

There are curious asymmetries in the *ex post* risks and rewards associated with sustaining and disruptive innovations. Many of the sustaining innovations (such as thin-film heads, thin-film disks, and the 14-inch Winchester architecture) were *extremely* expensive and risky from a *technological* point of view. Yet because they addressed well-understood needs of known customers, perceived market risk was low; impetus coalesced; and resources were allocated with only prudent hesitation. Yet, although these innovations clearly helped the innovators retain their customers, there is no evidence from the industry's history that any firm was able to gain observable market share by virtue of such technology leadership.[12]

On the other hand, disruptive innovations were technologically straightforward: several established firms had already developed them by the time formal resource allocation decisions were made. But these were viewed as extremely risky, because the markets were not 'there'. The most successful of the entrants that accepted the risks of creating new markets for disruptive innovations generated billions in revenues upon foundations of architectural technology that cost at most a few million dollars to put into place.

We argue that although differences in luck, resource endowments, managerial competence, and bureaucratic agility matter, the patterns of technology leadership displayed by established and entrant firms in the disk-drive industry accurately reflect differences in the fully informed, rational *ex ante* perceptions of risks and rewards held by managers in the two types of firm. In each of the companies studied, a key task of senior managers was to decide which of the many product and technology development programs continually being proposed to them should receive a formal allocation of resources. The criteria used in these decisions were essentially the total return perceived in each project, adjusted by the perceived riskiness of the project, as these data were presented to them by mid-level managers. Projects targeted at the known needs of big customers in established markets consistently won the rational debates over resource allocation. Sophisticated systems for planning and compensation ensured that this would be the case.[13]

The contrast between the innovative behavior of some *individuals* in the firm, vs. the manner in which the firm's *processes* allocated resources across competing projects, is an important feature of this model.[14] In the cases studied, the pioneering engineers in established firms that developed disruptive-architecture drives were innovative not just in technology, but in their view of the market. They intuitively perceived opportunities for a very different disk drive. But organizational processes allocated resources based on rational assessments of data about returns and risks. Information provided by innovating engineers was at best hypothetical: without existing customers, they could only guess at the size of the market, the profitability of products, and required product performance. In contrast, current customers could articulate features, performance, and quantities they would purchase with *much* less ambiguity. Because of these differences in information clarity, firms were led toward particular sorts of innovations—many of which were extremely challenging and risky— and away from others. In the firms studied here, the issue does not seem so much to be innovativeness *per se*, as it is what *type* of innovation the firms' processes could facilitate.

In light of this research, the popular slogan, 'Stay close to your customers' (which is supported by the research of von Hippel 1988 and others), appears not always to be robust advice. One instead might expect customers to lead their suppliers toward sustaining innovations, and to provide no leadership—or even to explicitly *mis*lead—in instances of disruptive technology change. Henderson (1993) saw similar potential danger for being held captive by customers in her study of photolithographic aligner equipment manufacturers.

We close our discussion of the model with a final note. Neglect of disruptive technologies proved damaging to established drive makers because the trajectory of performance improvement that the technology *provided* was steeper than the improvement trajectory *demanded* in individual markets (see Fig. 6.2.) The mismatch in these trajectories provided pathways for the firms that entered new markets eventually to become performance-competitive in established markets as well. If the trajectories were parallel, we would expect disruptive technologies to be deployed in new markets and to stay there; each successive market would constitute a relatively stable niche market out of which technologies and firms would not migrate.

The Linkage between Models of Resource Dependence and Resource Allocation

We mentioned at the outset that a contribution of this chapter is in establishing a linkage between the school of thought known as *resource dependence* (Pfeffer and Salancik 1978) and the models of the resource allocation process proposed by Bower (1970) and Burgelman (1983*a*, 1983*b*). Our findings support many of the conclusions of the resource dependence theorists, who contend that a firm's scope for strategic change is strongly bounded by the interests of external entities (customers, in this study) who provide the resources the firm needs to survive. We show that the mechanism through which customers wield this power is the process in which impetus coalesces behind investments in sustaining technologies, directing resources to innovations that address current customers' needs.

But although our findings lend support to the theory of resource dependence, they decidedly do not support a contention that managers are powerless to change the strategies of their companies in directions that are inconsistent with the needs of their customers as resource providers (Pfeffer and Salancik 1978: 263–5).[15] The evidence from this study is that managers can, in fact, change strategy—but that they can successfully do so only if their actions are consistent with, rather than in counteraction to, the principle of resource dependence. In the disk-drive industry's history, three established firms achieved a measure of commercial success in disruptive technologies. Two did so by spinning out organizations that were completely independent, in terms of customer relationships, from the mainstream groups. The third launched the disruptive technology with extreme managerial effort, from within the mainstream organization. This chapter closes by summarizing these case histories and their implications for theory.

Distinct Organizational Units for Small Drives at Control Data

Control Data (CDC) was the dominant manufacturer of 14-inch disk pack and Winchester drives sold into the OEM market between 1975 and 1982: its market share fluctuated between 55 and 62 per cent. When the 8-inch architecture emerged in the late 1970s, CDC missed it by three years. It never captured more than 3–4 per cent of the 8-inch market, and those 8-inch drives that it did sell were sold almost exclusively to its established customer base of mainframe computer manufacturers. The reason given by those interviewed in this study was that engineers and marketers kept getting pulled off the 8-inch program to resolve problems in the launch of next-generation 14-inch products for CDC's mainstream customers.

CDC also launched its first 5.25-inch model two years after Seagate's pioneering product appeared in 1980. This time, however, CDC located its 5.25-inch effort in Oklahoma City—according to one manager, 'not to escape CDC's Minneapolis engineering culture, but to isolate the (5.25-inch product) group from the company's mainstream customers. We needed an organization that could get excited about a

$50,000 order. In Minneapolis (which derived nearly $1 billion from the sale of 14-inch drives in the mainframe market) you needed a million-dollar order just to turn anyone's head.' Although it was late and never reascended to its position of dominance, CDC's foray into 5.25-inch drives was profitable, and at times it commanded a 20 per cent share of higher-capacity 5.25-inch drives.

Having learned from its experience in Oklahoma City, when CDC decided to attack the 3.5-inch market it set up yet another organization in Simi Valley, California. This group shipped its first products in mid-1988, about eighteen months behind Conner Peripherals, and enjoyed modest commercial success. The creation of these stand-alone organizations was CDC's way of handling the 'strategic forcing' and 'strategic context determination' challenges described by Burgelman (1983*b*, 1984).

Quantum Corporation and the 3.5-inch Hardcard

Quantum Corporation, a leading maker of 8-inch drives sold in the minicomputer market, introduced its first 5.25-inch product three years after those drives had first appeared in the market. As the 5.25-inch pioneers began to invade the minicomputer market from below, for all the reasons described above, Quantum launched a 5.25-inch product and was temporarily successful in defending some of its existing customers by selling its 5.25-inch drive to them. But it never sold a single drive into the desktop PC market, and its overall sales began to sag. In 1984 a group of Quantum engineers saw a market for a thin 3.5-inch drive plugged into an expansion slot in IBM XT- and AT-class desktop computers—drives that would be sold to end-users, rather than OEM computer manufacturers. Quantum financed and retained 80 per cent ownership of this spin-off venture, called Plus Development Corporation, and set the company up in different facilities. Plus was extremely successful. As sales of Quantum's line of 8-inch drives began to evaporate in the mid-1980s, they were offset by Plus's growing 'Hardcard' revenues. By 1987, sales of 8- and 5.25-inch products had largely evaporated. Quantum purchased the 20 per cent of Plus it did not own; essentially closed down the old corporation, and installed Plus's executives in Quantum's most senior positions. They then reconfigured Plus's 3.5-inch products to appeal to desktop computer makers such as Apple, just as the capacity vector for 3.5-inch drives was invading the desktop, as shown in Fig. 6.2. By 1994 the new Quantum had become the largest unit-volume producer of disk drives in the world. Quantum's spin-out of the Hardcard effort and its subsequent strategic reorientation appears to be an example of the processes of strategy change described in Burgelman (1991).

Micropolis: Transition through Managerial Force

Managers at Micropolis Corporation, also an 8-inch drive maker, employed a very different approach in which senior management initiated a disruptive program within the mainstream organization that made 8-inch drives. As early as 1982, Micropolis's founder and CEO, Stuart Mabon, intuitively saw the trends mapped in Fig. 6.2 and decided the firm needed to become primarily a maker of 5.25-inch drives. While initially hoping to keep adequate resources focused on the 8-inch line that Micropolis could straddle both markets,[16] he assigned the company's premier engineers to the 5.25-inch program. Mabon recalls that it took '100% of his time and energy for 18 months' to keep adequate resources focused on the 5.25-inch program, because the organization's own mechanisms allocated resources to where the customers were: 8-inch drives. By 1984 Micropolis had failed to keep pace with competition in the minicomputer market for disk drives, and withdrew its remaining 8-inch models. With Herculean effort, however, it did succeed in its 5.25-inch programs. Fig. 6.3 shows why this was necessary: in the transition, Micropolis assumed a position on a very different technological trajectory (Dosi 1982). In the process it had to walk away from every one of its major customers, and replace the lost

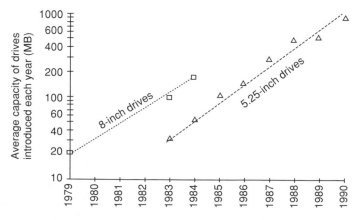

Figure 6.3 The disruptive impact of 5.25-inch drives on the market position of Micropolis Corp.

revenues with sales of the new product line to an entirely different group of desktop computer makers. Mabon remembers the experience as the most exhausting of his life. Micropolis aborted a 1989 attempt to launch its first 3.5-inch drive, and as of 1992 the company still had not introduced a 3.5-inch product.

Table 6.4 arrays the experiences of the six companies we studied in depth, as they addressed disruptive technologies from within their mainstream organization, and through independent organizations. Companies are classed as having been successful in this table if their market share in the new market enabled by the disruptive disk-drive technology was at least 25 per cent of its percentage share in the prior, established market in which it was dominant. Hence, Control Data, whose share of the 14-inch mainframe computer disk-drive market often exceeded 60 per cent, was classed as a failure in its attempt to sell 8-inch drives, because its share of minicomputer disk drives never exceeded 3 per cent. Its share of 5.25-inch drives sold to the desktop workstation market, however, reached 20 per cent, and it was therefore classed as a success in that effort. An organization was defined as being independent from the mainstream if it was geographically separated; was held accountable for full profit and loss; and included within it all of the functional units of a typical company: sales and marketing, manufacturing, finance, human resources, engineering, and so on.

In addition to the six firms studied in depth, Table 6.4 lists other firms (shown in *italic type*), whose histories were researched through public sources and a more limited number of personal interviews. The 'L' and 'T' shown next to each company in the table, as in Table 6.3, denotes whether that firm's experience lends literal or theoretical support (Yin 1989) to the proposition that managers can effect a strategy change despite resource dependence, by creating independent organizations that depend exclusively upon resources in the targeted market. Micropolis's transition from 8- to 5.25-inch drives is classed as a theoretical replication, because of the enormous managerial effort that was required to counteract the force of resource dependence in that transition.[17] Note that in every instance except Micropolis's 5.25-inch entry, firms that *fought* the forces of resource dependence by attempting to commercialize disruptive technology from within their mainstream organizations failed, as measured by *Disk/Trend* data. And the firms that *accounted for* the forces of resource dependence by spinning out independent organizations succeeded.

Note in Table 6.4 that there do not seem to be strong firm or managerial effects, compared to the organizational effect. Control Data, Quantum, and Micropolis encountered multiple disruptive tech-

Table 6.4 *The success and failure of companies addressing disruptive technologies through mainstream vs. independent organizations*

Succeeded	Control Data 5.25-inch (L) Control Data 3.5-inch (L) Quantum 3.5-inch (L) *Maxtor 3.5-inch (L)*	Micropolis 5.25-inch (T)
Failed		Control Data 8-inch (L) Quantum 5.25-inch (L) Miniscribe 3.5-inch (L) Seagate 3.5-inch (L) Micropolis 3.5-inch (L) *Memorex 8-inch (L)* *Memorex 5.25-inch (L)* *Priam 5.25-inch (L)* *Century Data 8-inch (L)* *Ampex 8-inch (L)* *Ampex 5.25-inch (L)*
	Commercialized from within an independent organization	Commercialized from within the mainstream organization

nologies; and *the same general managers sat atop these organizations across each of these transitions.* What seems to have distinguished these firms' successful from failed attempts to commercialize these disruptive technologies was not the talent of the managers *per se*, but whether the managers created organizationally distinct units to accomplish the task—where the forces of resource dependence could work in their favor, rather than against them. The successful cases cited here are the only ones in the industry's history in which a leading incumbent stayed atop its market when faced with disruptive technological change—and as a result, the number of data points in the top half of the matrix is limited. But these findings do suggest that, while the forces of resource dependence act as strong constraints on managerial discretion, managers can in fact manipulate those constraints effectively in order to achieve strategic change.

Conclusions

This study highlights an important issue for managers and scholars who strive to understand the reasons why strong, capably managed firms stumble when faced with particular types of technological change. While many scholars see the issue primarily as an issue of *technological competence*, we assert that at a deeper level it may be an issue of *investment*. We have observed that when competence was lacking, but impetus from customers to develop that competence was sufficiently strong, established firms successfully led their industries in developing the competencies required for sustaining technological change. Importantly, because sustaining technologies address the interests of established firms' existing customers, we saw that technological change could be achieved without strategy change.

Conversely, when technological competence existed, but impetus from customers was lacking, we saw consistently that firms were unable to commercialize what they already could do. This is because disruptive technologies initially tend to be saleable only in different markets whose economic and financial characteristics render them unattractive to established firms. Addressing these technologies therefore requires a change in strategy in order to attack a very different market. In the end, it appears that although the stumbles of these established firms are *associated* with technological change, the key issue appears to be firms' disabilities in changing strategy, not technology.

Our model is not presented as the path every firm follows when faced with disruptive technology. We believe, however, that it may contribute several insights for scholars interested in the factors that affect strategic change in firms. First, it notes that the allocation of resources to some product development and commercialization programs, and the denial of resources to others, is a key event or decision in the implementation of strategy. The model highlights the process by which impetus and consequent resources may be denied to technological opportunities that do not contribute to the needs of prominent customers. These findings suggest a causal relationship might exist between resource allocation processes, as modeled by Bower (1970) and Burgelman (1983a, 1983b), and the phenomenon of resource dependence (Pfeffer and Salancik 1978). Our findings suggest that despite the powerful forces of resource dependence, however, managers can, in fact, wield considerable power, and wield it effectively, in changing the strategic course of their firms in directions other than those in which its resource providers are pulling it. By understanding the processes that link customer needs, impetus, and resource allocation, managers can align efforts to commercialize disruptive technology (which entails a change in strategy) with the forces of resource dependence. This involves managing disruptive technology in a manner that is out of the organizational and strategic context of mainstream organizations—where of necessity, incentives and resource allocation processes are designed to nourish sustaining innovations that address current customers' needs. In this way, the model and these case studies illustrate the mechanisms through which autonomous and induced strategic behavior (Burgelman 1983*a*) can affect, or fail to affect, a company's course.

Much additional research must be done. Efforts to explore the external validity and usefulness of the model through studies of sustaining and disruptive technological change in other industries has begun (Rosenbloom and Christensen 1995), but much more is required. In addition, we hope that future researchers can develop clearer models for managerial action and strategic change in the face of disruptive technology change that are consistent with the principles of resource dependence and the processes of resource allocation.

Acknowledgements

We gratefully acknowledge the financial support of the Harvard Business School Division of Research in conducting the research for this chapter, and thank the editors of *Disk/Trend Report* for sharing their industry data with us. We are indebted to Professors Robert Burgelman of Stanford University, Rebecca Henderson of the Massachusetts Institute of Technology, David Garvin and several of our other colleagues at the Harvard Business School, as well as the anonymous referees, for invaluable suggestions for improving earlier versions of this chapter. Any remaining deficiencies are our sole responsibility.

Endnotes

1. Evidence supporting this conclusion is provided below. In making this statement, we contest the conclusions of scholars such as Tushman and Anderson (1986), who have argued that incumbent firms are most threatened by attacking entrants when the innovation in question destroys, or does not build upon, the competence of the firm. We observe that established firms, though often at great cost, have led their industries in developing critical competence-destroying technologies, when the new technology was needed to meet existing customers' demands.

2. *Disk/Trend Report* identified 133 firms that participated in the disk-drive industry in the period studied. The search of *Electronic Business* magazine yielded information on one additional firm, Peach Tree Technology, that never generated revenues and somehow had escaped detection by the *Disk/ Trend* editors.

3. These trajectories represent the disk capacity *demanded* in each market because in each instance, greater disk capacity could have been

supplied to users by the computer manufacturers, had the market demanded additional capacity at the cost for which it could be purchased at the time.

4. The parallel impact of sustaining innovations across these architectural generations results from the fact that the same sustaining technologies, in the form of componentry, were available simultaneously to manufacturers of each generation of disk drives (Christensen 1992*b*).

5. Note that the statistics shown in Table 6.2 are not a sample—they represent the entire population of firms in each of the years shown offering models incorporating the technologies in question. For that reason, tests of statistical significance are not relevant in this case.

6. We believe this insight—that attacking firms have an advantage in disruptive innovations but not in sustaining ones—clarifies but is not in conflict with Foster's (1986) assertions about the attacker's advantage. The historical examples Foster uses to substantiate his theory generally seem to have been disruptive innovations.

7. For readers who are unfamiliar with the work of scholars such as Yin (1989) and Campbell and Stanley (1966) on research methodology, a *literal* replication of a model occurs when an outcome happens as the model would predict. A *theoretical* replication of the model occurs when a different outcome happens than what would have been predicted by the model, but where this outcome can be explained by elements in the model. In the instance here, the success of entrants and the failure of established forms at points of disruptive technology change are directly predicted by the model, and would be classed as literal replications. Instances where an established firm succeeded in the face of disruptive technological change because it acted in a way that dealt with the factors in the model that typically precipitated failure, would be classed as *theoretical* replications of the model. Several of these instances occurred in the industry's history, as explained later in this chapter.

8. This is consistent with Burgelman's observation that one of the greatest difficulties encountered by corporate entrepreneurs was finding the right 'beta test sites', where products could be interactively developed and refined with customers. Generally, the entrée to the customer was provided by the salesman who sold the firm's established product lines. This helped the firm develop new products for established markets, but did not help it identify new applications for its new technology (Burgelman and Sayles 1986: 76–80). Professor Rebecca Henderson pointed out to us that this tendency always to take new technologies to mainstream customers reflects a rather narrow *marketing* competence—that although these issues tend to be framed by many scholars as issues of technological competence, a firm's disabilities in finding new markets for new technologies may be its most serious innovative handicap.

9. Ultimately, nearly all North American manufacturers of disk drives can trace their founders' genealogy to IBM's San Jose division, which developed and manufactured its magnetic recording products (Christensen 1993).

10. In general, these component technologies were developed within the largest of the established firms that dominated the markets above these entrants, in terms of the technology and market trajectories mapped in Fig. 6.2.

11. Note that at this point, because the disruptive innovation invading below had become fully performance-competitive with the established technology, the innovation had essentially acquired the character of a sustaining innovation—it gave customers what they needed.

12. Christensen (1992*b*) shows that there was no discernible first-mover advantage associated with trajectory-sustaining innovations, to firms in the disk-drive industry. In contrast, there were *very* powerful first-mover advantages to leaders in trajectory-disruptive innovations that fostered the creation of new markets.

13. It is interesting that twenty years after Bower's (1970) study of resource allocation, we see in leading-edge systems for planning and compensation the same bias against risk taking. Morris and Ferguson's description of how IBM allowed Microsoft to gain control of PC operating system standards is centered on the role of mainframe producers in IBM's resource allocation process. In a 1990 interview with one of the authors, one of the most successful innovators in IBM history recounted how time and again he was forced to battle the controlling influence of middle-management's commitment to serve commercial mainframe customers.

14. We are indebted to Professor Robert Burgelman for his comments on this issue. He has also noted, given the sequence of events we observed—where engineers inside the established firms began pursuing the disruptive product opportunity before the start-up entrants did—that timing matters a lot. It may be that when individuals in the established firms were pressing their ideas internally, they were too far ahead of the market. In the year or two that it took them to leave their employers, create new firms, and create new products, the nascent markets may have become more ready to accept the new drives.

15. In ch. 10 of Pfeffer and Salancik's (1978) book, for example, they assert that the manager's most valuable role is symbolic, and they cite a hypothetical example. When external forces induce hard times in a company, managers can usefully be fired—not because bringing in a new manager will make any difference to the performance of the organization, but because of the symbolic content of that action. It creates the *feeling* in the organization that something is being done to address this problem, even though it will have no effect. The evidence from these case studies does not support this assertion about the ability of managers to change the course of their organizations. *As long as managers act in a manner consistent with the forces of resource dependence*, it appears that they can, indeed, wield significant power.

16. The failure of Micropolis to maintain simultaneous competitive commitments to its established technology while adequately nurturing the 5.25-

inch technology is consistent with the technological histories recounted in Utterback (1994). Utterback found historically that firms that attempted to develop radically new technology almost always tried simultaneously to maintain their commitments to the old; and that they almost always failed.

17. The success or failure of these other firms at each point of disruptive technology change was unambiguously determinable from *Disk/Trend Report* data. Similarly, whether these firms managed the launch of disruptive technology products from within their mainstream organization, or through an organizationally separate unit, was a matter of public record and general industry knowledge. Hence, there were no subjective judgments involved in constructing Table 6.4.

References

Bower, J. (1970). *Managing the Resource Allocation Process*. Homewood, Ill.: Irwin.

Burgelman, R. (1983*a*). 'A Model of the Interaction of Strategic Behavior, Corporate Context, and the Concept of Strategy', *Academy of Management Review* 3/1: 61–9.

——(1983*b*). 'A Process Model of Internal Corporate Venturing in the Diversified Major Firm', *Administrative Science Quarterly* 28: 223–44.

——(1984). 'Designs for Corporate Entrepreneurship in Established Firms', *California Management Review* 26 (Spring), 154–66.

——(1991). 'Intraorganizational Ecology of Strategy-Making and Organizational Adaptation: Theory and Field Research', *Organization Science* 2: 239–62.

——and Sayles, L. (1986). *Inside Corporate Innovation*. New York: Free Press.

Campbell, D. T., and Stanley, J. C. (1966). *Experimental and Quasi-Experimental Designs for Research*. Boston, Mass.: Houghton Mifflin.

Christensen, C. M. (1992*a*). 'The Innovator's Challenge: Understanding the Influence of Market Demand on Processes of Technology Development in the Rigid Disk Drive Industry'. Unpublished DBA dissertation. Graduate School of Business Administration, Harvard University.

——(1992*b*). 'Exploring the Limits of the Technology S-Curve', *Production and Operations Management* 1: 334–66.

——(1993). 'The Rigid Disk Drive Industry: A History of Commercial and Technological Turbulence', *Business History Review* 67: 531–88.

——and Rosenbloom, R. S. (1995). 'Explaining the Attacker's Advantage: Technological Paradigms, Organizational Dynamics, and the Value Network', *Research Policy* 24: 233–57.

Cooper, A., and Schendel, D. (Feb. 1976). 'Strategic Responses to Technological Threats', *Business Horizons* 19: 61–9.

Data Sources: The Comprehensive Guide to the Information Processing Industry (annual). New York: Ziff-Davis.

Disk/Trend Report (annual). Disk/Trend, Inc., Mountain View, Calif.

Dosi, G. (1982). 'Technological Paradigms and Technological Trajectories', *Research Policy* 11: 147–62.

Foster, R. J. (1986). *Innovation: The Attacker's Advantage*. New York: Summit Books.

Henderson, R. M. (1993). 'Keeping Too Close to Your Customers', working paper, Sloan School of Management, Massachusetts Institute of Technology.

—— and Clark, K. B. (1990). 'Architectural Innovation: The Reconfiguration of Existing Systems and the Failure of Established Firms', *Administrative Science Quarterly* 35: 9–30.

Pfeffer, J., and Salancik, G. R. (1978). *The External Control of Organizations: A Resource Dependence Perspective*. New York: Harper & Row.

Rosenbloom, R. S. and Christensen, C. M. (1995). 'Technological Discontinuities, Organizational Capabilities, and Strategic Commitments', *Industrial and Corporate Change* 4: 655–85.

Tushman, M. L., and Anderson, P. (1986). 'Technological Discontinuities and Organizational Environments', *Administrative Science Quarterly* 31: 439–65.

Utterback, J. (1994). *Mastering the Dynamics of Innovation*. Harvard Business School Press, Boston, Mass.

von Hippel, E. (1988). *The Sources of Innovation*. New York: Oxford University Press.

Yin, R. K. (1989). *Case Study Research: Design and Methods*. Newbury Park, Calif.: Sage.

Appendix 1: A Brief Primer on How Disk Drives Work

Rigid disk drives are comprised of one or more rotating disks—polished aluminum platters coated with magnetic material—mounted on a central spindle. Data are recorded and read on concentric tracks on the surfaces of these disks. Read/write heads—one each for the top and bottom surfaces of each disk on the spindle—are aerodynamically designed to fly a few millionths of an inch over the surface of the disk. They generally rest on the disk's surface when the drive is at rest; 'take off' as the drive begins to spin; and 'land' again when the disks stop. The heads are positioned over the proper track on the disk by an actuator motor, which moves the heads across the tracks in a fashion similar to the arm on a phonograph. The head is essentially a tiny electromagnet which, when current flows in one direction, orients the polarity of the magnetic domain on the disk's surface immediately beneath it. When the direction of current through the electromagnet reverses, its polarity changes. This induces an opposite switch of the polarity of the adjacent domain on the disk's surface as the disk spins beneath the head. In this manner, data are written in binary code on the disk. To read data, changes in the magnetic field on the disk as it spins beneath the head are used to induce changes in the direction of current—essentially the reverse process of writing. Disk drives also include electronic circuitry enabling computers to control and communicate with the drive.

As in other magnetic recording products, *areal recording density* (measured in megabits per square inch of disk surface area, or mbpsi) was the pervasive measure of product performance in the disk drive industry. Historically, areal density in the industry has increased at a steady 35 per cent annual rate. A drive's total capacity is the product of the available square inches on the top and bottom surfaces of the disks mounted on the spindle of the drive, multiplied by its areal recording density. Historically, the capacity of drives in a given product architecture has increased at about 50 per cent annually. The difference between the 35 per cent increase in areal density and the 50 per cent increase in total capacity has come from mechanical engineering innovations, which enable manufacturers to squeeze additional disks and heads into a given size of drive.

Appendix 2: Calculation of the Trajectories Mapped in Fig. 6.2

The trajectories mapped in Fig. 6.2 were calculated as follows. Data on the capacity provided with computers in the mainframe, minicomputer, desktop personal computer, and portable computer classes were obtained from *Data Sources*, an annual publication that lists the technical specifications of all computer models available from each computer manufacturer. Where particular models were available with different features and configurations, the manufacturer provided *Data Sources* with a 'typical' system configuration, with defined RAM capacity, performance specifications of peripheral equipment (including disk drives), list price, and year of introduction. In instances where a given computer model was offered for sale over a sequence of years, the hard disk capacity provided in the typical configuration generally increased. *Data Sources* divides computers into mainframe, mini/midrange, desktop personal, portable and laptop, and notebook computers. For each class of computers, all models available for sale in each year were ranked by price, and the hard–disk capacity provided with the median–priced model was identified, for each year. The best-fit line through the resultant time series for each class of computer is plotted as the solid lines in Fig. 6.2. These single solid lines are drawn in Fig. 6.2 for expository simplification, to indicate the trend in typical machines. In reality, of course, there is a wide band around these lines. The leading and trailing edges of performance—the highest and lowest capacities offered with the most and least expensive computers—were substantially higher and lower, respectively, than the typical values mapped in Fig. 2.

The dotted lines in Fig. 2 represent the best-fit line through the unweighted average capacity of all disk drives introduced for sale in each given architecture, for each year. These data were taken from *Disk/Trend Report*. Again, for expository simplification, only this average line is shown. There was a wide band of capacities introduced for sale in each year, so that the highest-capacity drive introduced in each year was substantially above the average shown. Stated in another way, a distinction must be made between the full range of products available for purchase, and those in typical systems of use. The upper and lower bands around the median and average trajectories in Fig. 6.2 are generally parallel to the lines shown.

Because higher-capacity drives were available than the capacities offered with the median-priced systems, we state in the text that the solid-line trajectories in Fig. 6.2 represent the capacities 'demanded' in each market. In other words, the capacity per machine was not constrained by technological availability. Rather, it represents a *choice* for hard disk capacity, made by computer users, given the prevailing cost.

7

No Exit: The Failure of Bottom-up Strategic Processes and the Role of Top-down Disinvestment

Donald N. Sull

Introduction

Scholars in the field of strategic management have extensively studied how organizations initiate new activities such as acquisitions, international expansion, or investment in new technology. Researchers have devoted far less attention, however, to studies of organizational exit from existing operations (Ross and Staw 1993; Burgelman 1996). Much of the research on exit focuses on how organizations that get out of a business altogether through strategic business exit (Burgelman 1994, 1996), divestiture of businesses within a diversified portfolio (Gilmour 1973; Hoskisson, Johnson, and Moesel 1994), or de-escalation of commitment from a new strategic initiative (Ross and Staw 1993). This research, in contrast, addresses the process of disinvestment whereby organizations remove resources from an ongoing business. Disinvestment entails the reduction of productive capacity such as closure of factories, retail bank branches, local offices, or hospitals without exiting the business altogether.

Strategy content researchers have explored the question of the optimal product-market position when an industry faces predictable declines in primary demand (Porter 1980; Harrigan 1981; Lieberman 1990; Ghemawat and Nalebuff 1985, 1990). This research, which takes a complementary approach, explores disinvestment from a strategy process perspective. Specifically, we view the process of removing resources from an ongoing business as part of the evolutionary process that takes place within an organization (Burgelman 1991; Miner 1994;

Lovas and Ghoshal 2000). Organization theorists have productively applied evolutionary theory to social sciences by using a general framework of variation, selection, and retention to explain how individual organizations or populations evolve over time (Campbell 1969; Aldrich 1979; Weick 1979). Viewed from this perspective, disinvestment poses an interesting dilemma because it requires an organization to reverse its retention mechanisms. A study of disinvestment, therefore, may shed light on the broader theoretical question of how organizations let go of previously selected and retained units.

An evolutionary perspective can serve as an overarching framework for integrating diverse theoretical traditions (Barnett and Burgelman 1996). This chapter introduces a grounded theory of the disinvestment process that draws on two theoretical streams: the intra-firm resource allocation process (RAP) model developed by Bower and Burgelman (Bower 1970; Burgelman 1983*a*; 1983*b*; 1983*c*) and resource dependence (Pfeffer and Salancik 1978). The proposed model of the disinvestment process has five components—the core resource allocation process and four factors that influence it (see Fig. 7.1).

The center component of the framework is the process within the organization for allocating resources. This process is considered strategic because the allocation of resources is a powerful mechanism for selecting among alternative initiatives that subsequently set the organization's strategic trajectory (Burgelman 1991). Bower and Burgelman modeled the intra-firm RAP as taking place in predictable stages across levels in the organizational hierarchy, and researchers have found the Bower–Burgelman framework to be a robust model for studying diverse strategic processes, including firms' response to disruptive

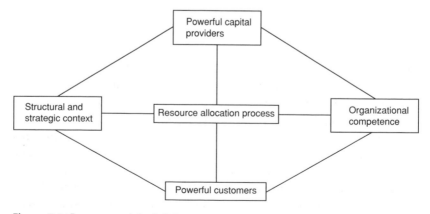

Figure 7.1 Process model of disinvestment

technology (Christensen and Bower 1996; Gilbert 2002), internal corporate venturing (Burgelman 1983*c*), business development (Noda and Bower 1996), and others (see Bower and Doz 1979 for a comprehensive review of earlier research using this framework).

The second component is the established internal context. An organization's resource allocation process is shaped by the structural and strategic context within the firm. In evolutionary terms, the context is the enduring set of cognitive frames, rules, and processes that shape which strategic initiatives are identified and defined—i.e. variation—and which receive support from middle managers and ratification from top executives—i.e. selection and retention (Burgelman 1991). *Structural context* refers to organizational levers, such as information systems, performance goals, organizational design, and compensation plans that top executives can manipulate to influence indirectly what type of strategic initiatives are defined and selected (Bower 1970). *Strategic context* refers to an organization's official strategy, which induces initiatives consistent with the strategy while discouraging autonomous strategic initiatives that fall outside an organization's official strategy (Burgelman 1983*c*).

The third component in the model is an organization's distinctive competence (Teece, Pisano, and Shuen 1997). Initiatives that build on an organization's competence are more likely to be defined, selected, and retained, those that do not or actually destroy existing competencies are less likely to be defined or selected (Tushman and Anderson 1986; Burgelman 1994).

The final two components consist of customers and investors who provide the financial resources necessary for an organization's survival. *Resource-dependence* theory posits that managers' decisions will be influenced by the demands of external stakeholders who provide resources necessary for continued survival (Pfeffer and Salancik 1978). Christensen and Bower (1996) explicitly linked resource-dependence theory with the Bower–Burgelman model of resource allocation. They found that incumbent firms were unlikely to commercialize new technologies that failed to serve the demands of their largest customers, even when these innovations posed only modest technical challenges to commercialize. According to resource-dependence theory, providers of financing, including investors and lenders, represent another critical source of resources required for an organization's survival. Although earlier studies noted the influence of capital markets (see for example Noda and Bower 1996: 173), that research did not explicitly incorporate the role of investors and lenders in the resource allocation process. Our research integrates providers of capital—along with customers, competence, and context—as an important factor shaping the resource allocation process.

The process model of disinvestment is grounded in an in-depth clinical study of a single company over twenty-eight years. Three primary findings emerged from this study. First, a bottom-up resource allocation process that effectively generated, selected, and retained investment proposals failed to produce necessary disinvestment. Second, a top-down resource allocation process led by an active CEO who defined and implemented exit decisions was necessary to remove resources from the core business. Third, powerful investors and lenders played a critical role in selecting and supporting the CEO who led the top-down disinvestment process.

Methods

Studying an organization's internal resource allocation process poses significant methodological challenges. The process is a complex unit of analysis incorporating activities across multiple levels in the organizational hierarchy and external resource providers. The process takes place within the firm and precludes exclusive reliance on public archival data. Moreover, strategically important outcomes, such as investment in a new technology or exit from an existing business, can unfold over many years and require an extended observation period that introduces systematic biases in retrospective accounts arising from past rationalization or faulty memory (Golden 1992). This study was designed to address these challenges.

Research Setting

The research was conducted at Firestone Tire & Rubber Company. Firestone, founded in 1900 in Akron, Ohio, had emerged by 1917 as one of the four largest tire producers in the United States (Chandler 1990: 640). The study analyzed how Firestone responded to the introduction of radial tire technology into the US market. Radial tire adoption required domestic competitors to remove resources from their ongoing tire businesses by closing factories devoted to manufacturing the traditional product design (known as 'bias tires'). The observation period began in 1960—a few years prior to the introduction of radials into the US market—and extended through 1988 when Firestone was acquired by the Japanese tire manufacturer Bridgestone.

This clinical study is part of a broader research project studying the response of incumbent US tire companies to radial technology that includes a comparative case study (Sull, Tedlow, and Rosenbloom 1997) and a statistical analysis of the predictors of plant closure (Sull 1997).

Research Design

The need for in-depth data on the intra-firm process suggested a single case design. The selection of Firestone among incumbent tire makers was based on the quality of archival data and my level of access. Of the three companies that offered unlimited access to their corporate archives (i.e. Firestone, B. F. Goodrich, and General Tire), Firestone had the most comprehensive archives. The study was based on a longitudinal, nested design with the resource allocation process as the focal unit of analysis (Yin 1989; Leonard-Barton 1990). The research consisted of two stages that combined inductive and deductive approaches to develop the conceptual model (Burgelman 1996; Lovas and Ghoshal 2000). In the first stage, I collected archival data on Firestone's response to radial tire technology. This largely inductive stage resulted in a purely descriptive case study (Sull 1999). In the second stage, I drew on existing theories of strategic processes (Bower 1970; Burgelman 1983c), resource dependence (Pfeffer and Salancik 1978; Christensen and Bower 1996), and intra-organizational ecology (Burgelman 1991; Lovas and Ghoshal 2000). These theoretical readings provided the conceptual building blocks I used to construct the process model of disinvestment. Using these building blocks, I then reinterpreted the data and further refined my emerging model. The iterative cycling between inductive case data and existing theory enables researchers to develop conceptual models characterized by high levels of internal validity and links to existing literature (Eisenhardt 1989b; Strauss and Corbin 1994).

Data Collection

Firestone's internal corporate archives provided the primary source of data for this study. (See Table 7.1 for a summary of archival data sources.) These records included detailed transcripts of discussions as well as all exhibits and analyses presented in the monthly board of directors, the biannual finance committee, and weekly executive

Table 7.1 *Summary of Firestone archival data sources*

Data source	Period covered	Frequency	Description
Board of Directors Minutes	Jan. 1960– Mar. 1988	monthly	Near verbatim minutes of discussion of Firestone's board of directors. These archives also include copies of all exhibits and analyses presented in the meetings.
Executive Committee Minutes	Jan. 1960– Oct. 1980	bi-weekly	Near verbatim minutes of discussions by Firestone's Executive Committee, which consisted of Firestone's top six executives and was charged with considering all investment and disinvestment decisions. The Committee was dissolved in 1980. Minutes include all exhibits and analyses presented in meetings.
Internal financial reports	Oct. 1960– Oct. 1980	annual	A comprehensive report of financial data (e.g. revenues, profits, inventories) for each division. The report also includes budget for comparison to actual performance. Discontinued in 1980.
Finance Committee Minutes	Mar. 1981– Dec. 1987	bi-annual	Minutes of meetings by committee established in 1981 to oversee capital budgeting, financial performance, and capital structure. Includes detailed financial information.
Remarks of CEO to annual shareholders' meeting	Jan. 1960– Feb. 1987	annual	Verbatim transcript of Chairman's address to Stockholders.
Annual Reports	Oct. 1945– Dec. 1987	annual	Including 10k and proxy statements.

committee meetings. The executive committee consisted of the six most senior Firestone executives and existed to 'review and take action upon all appropriations and all [proposals for] new plants, major expansions, acquisitions...including major capital spending or other matters of corporate policy' (Firestone by-laws, 1970). The deliberations of this committee provided a productive focal point for my analysis. I read the transcripts in strict chronological order to attempt to recreate the flow of events as they unfolded over time (Van de Ven 1992; Pettigrew 1990).

I supplemented the archival data with over twenty taped interviews with Firestone directors, executives, front-line employees, and customers. Interviews, which lasted between one and eight hours, included both open-ended questions and targeted enquiries about specific events such as the discussion in a particular meeting or the respondent's rationale for a decision. I relied on follow-up interviews to explore discrepancies between the respondents' retrospective accounts and my chronology based on archival data. I conducted a literature search for articles written about Firestone in the major business press—i.e. *The Wall Street Journal, Fortune, Business Week*—industry trade journals—i.e. *Modern Tire Dealer, Elastomerics, Rubber and Plastics News*, and Akron's daily newspaper, the *Akron Beacon Journal*. The United Rubber Workers Union and the Rubber Manufacturers' Association provided additional data on Firestone and the tire industry as a whole. I collected documents and articles for the period 1960–88 and summarized and coded approximately 1,000 articles and entered them into an Excel database. These articles allowed me to triangulate using internal reports of corporate activity and study external parties' responses to these actions (Jick 1979). I also collected internal and external financial reports for the period 1960–88, including financial presentations to the board, 10Ks, and proxy statements, to create a schedule of the company's balance sheet, income statement, and cash-flow position over time. Daily stock price data on Firestone, its major competitors, and the S&P Index allowed analysis of Firestone's stock performance and investors' response to specific announcements.

Data Analysis

The data were analyzed using a grounded-theory approach that included iteration between rich clinical data and existing theoretical frameworks to categorize and structure the emerging findings (Glaser and Strauss 1967; Eisenhardt 1989*b*). In the first stage, archival, interview, and public source data were assembled into a chronology in a spreadsheet that became the basis for a descriptive narrative organized by years (Strauss and Corbin 1990: 116). In the second stage, I drew on existing theory for conceptual categories that formed the components of the process model of disinvestment. It was at this stage that I recognized that the existing strategy process literature did not incorporate the role of capital providers and that the explicit inclusion of capital markets as an influence on the intra-organizational resource allocation process would be necessary to model my clinical data.

Process Model of Disinvestment

This section uses the process model described in the introduction to structure the findings from the clinical research. The focus of the model, to recap, is the intra-firm resource allocation process as well as the four variables that influence the process—i.e. strategic and structural context, distinctive competence, powerful customers, and powerful capital providers. The findings are organized into these five categories and the events divided into three separate eras: Firestone's initial response to radial technology (1960–72), the company's subsequent delay in closing unnecessary capacity (1973–9), and the ultimate capacity reduction by an outside CEO (1979–88). This section develops the model by elaborating how each of the five elements shaped Firestone's response to the new technology and attendant need for disinvestment. (See Table 7.2 for a summary.)

Initial Response to Radial Technology (1960–1972)

Entering the 1960s, Firestone's 25 per cent share of the domestic tire market made it the second-largest competitor. In the 1960s, the US tire industry could be described as a stable oligopoly facing steadily rising demand. Demand—as measured by domestic tire unit shipments—grew at a rate of 5.2 per cent compound annual growth between 1960 and 1972. The top five domestic tire firms—Goodyear, Firestone, B. F. Goodrich, Uniroyal, and General Tire—together accounted for over 80 per cent of industry capacity and shipments and captured nearly all the growth in volume over this period. Between 1960 and 1972 these five companies responded to increased demand by building eighteen new domestic tire plants.

Table 7.2 Process model of disinvestment by era

	More of the same (1960–72)	Stalling in reverse (1973–9)	Cuts from above (1979–88)
Intraorganizational resource allocation process	Bottom-up process results in proposals to extend existing technology to forestall radial adoption	Bottom-up process continues to produce investments in radial tire production and other proposals intended to increase revenues	Outside CEO imposes top-down resource allocation process that produces disinvestment
	Bottom-up process results in rapid investments in radial production when automobile manufacturers demand the new technology	Front-line employees and middle managers fail to define and lend impetus to proposals for reducing bias tire capacity	Top down process fails to achieve revenue growth targets, in part because it fails to capture specific knowledge at lower levels in the organization
Strategic and structural context	Strategic focus on tires and closely related businesses	Executives maintain strategic focus on tires despite high investment necessary to convert to radials and low projected returns	New CEO maintains focus on tire industry and invests in company-owned stores to increase sales
	Psychological contract of job for life buffers managers from capital market implications of investment decisions.	Perceived obligation to protect employees' job security hinders executives from disinvestment	New CEO breaks psychological contract of job for life and replaces it with market-based incentives
	Focus on revenue growth	Continued emphasis on revenue growth	New CEO emphasizes debt reduction and cash generation over revenue growth

(Continues)

Table 7.2 (*Continued*)

	More of the same (1960–72)	Stalling in reverse (1973–9)	Cuts from above (1979–88)
Powerful customers	Automobile manufacturers initially accept belted-bias tires, but ultimately demand radial tires from Firestone and its competitors	Automobile manufacturers continue to demand radial tires, but do not apply pressure for disinvestment from bias tire production	Automobile manufacturers do not apply pressure to disinvest from bias production
Organizational competence	Leverages its existing manufacturing competence by producing belted-bias tires Attempts to use existing equipment to manufacture radials	Delays in closing bias tire factories do not stem from desire to preserve necessary competencies, since radial tire production requires unlearning of bias tire manufacturing processes	New CEO does not rely on middle managers and front-line employees in assessing which competencies should be preserved
Powerful capital providers	Firestone's dependence on external sources of capital was limited because the company generated sufficient cash flows to cover investments Managers occupy more board seats than Firestone family representatives, and no outside directors until 1972	Firestone becomes more dependent on outside sources of financing to fund investment in radial capacity and mounting losses from bias tire factories Number and influence of outside directors steadily increases	Firestone's major investors and lead bank work through the board to appoint an outside CEO and then support in his efforts to disinvest Outside directors constitute a majority of the board

During the 1960s, Firestone and the other domestic tire producers faced a threat—radial tires lasted twice as long as the bias tire technology they replaced in addition to increasing fuel-efficiency, handling, and tire safety (*Consumer Reports*, 1968). Longer-lasting tires depressed demand for replacement tires and required incumbent tire manufacturers to close bias tire plants as they replaced bias tire sales with radials. French tire maker Michelin pioneered the radial tire and used its superior safety, wear, and ride to increase market share throughout Western Europe. In the mid-1960s, Michelin turned its sights on the US market. Michelin, which contracted with Sears to manufacture radial tires under the Allstate label, announced its intention to build a $100 million radial tire factory in North America. Domestic rival B. F. Goodrich introduced domestically produced radials as an opportunity to gain market share from larger rivals Firestone and Goodyear (Blackford and Kerr 1996: 276).

Resource Allocation Process   Between 1960 and 1972, Firestone's process for allocating resources conformed closely to the bottom-up model predicted by the Bower–Burgelman model. Frontline employees— primarily marketing or sales representatives—identified opportunities to sell additional tires to Firestone's existing customers. Middle managers selected among these proposals and presented them for approval to Firestone's executive committee, which met on a weekly basis to review investment proposals. Throughout this period, the executive committee served as a *de facto* surrogate for the board of directors, because all members of the executive committee served as directors, where they constituted a majority throughout the 1960s and 1970s. The executive committee approved nearly all the proposals it reviewed, according to executives' retrospective accounts of the committee's deliberations between 1960 and 1972.[1]

Consistent with earlier research (Cooper and Schendel 1976), Firestone and Goodyear initially responded to radial tires by introducing a slightly modified version of the traditional tire technology. Goodyear introduced the product—known as the belted-bias tire—in 1967 and promoted it heavily as an alternative to radial tires. Firestone introduced its own belted-bias tire a few months later. Firestone's bottom-up resource allocation process quickly approved the requests for investments required to modify existing production equipment to manufacture belted-bias tires. Lee Brodeur, a Firestone executive during this period, later recalled that manufacturing belted-bias tires required 'a certain amount of development and improvement, but nothing major. It was pretty much business as usual' (Brodeur, interview, 1994).

The tire manufacturers' promotion of belted-bias tires delayed the adoption of radial tires but did not halt their acceptance altogether. In 1972, General Motors announced its intention to place radial tires on all models over the coming years, following a similar decision that Ford had announced a few months earlier. The tire companies knew that the automobile original equipment manufacturers (OEMs) were considering radials. During the 1960s, General Motors and Ford had both created internal task forces to evaluate radial tires for US automobiles, and Ford had made radials standard on the high-end Lincoln Continental model in 1970. General Motors and Ford even explored the possibility of manufacturing their own radial tires and sent surveys to their dealers to gauge their support for the proposal (*Modern Tire Dealer* 1971). Although tire industry executives were aware of the OEMs' interest in radial tires, they hoped for a gradual transition, and the abruptness of General Motors' announcement and the speed of the transition caught them off guard.

Firestone's bottom-up resource allocation process rapidly responded to the OEMs' demand for radials. Firestone's executive committee met in November 1972 to discuss their reaction to the auto manufacturers' demand (executive committee minutes, 3 November 1972). Mario DiFederico, the vice-president of manufacturing, informed the committee that the marketing managers already had committed to providing 433,000 radial tires to Ford and General Motors within seven months and noted that the marketing department saw an opportunity to sell even more tires if Firestone could manufacture them. The committee instructed DiFederico to purchase required equipment immediately and bring a formal request to the committee as soon as possible, in effect approving the proposal prior to formal review by the committee or the board.

One month later, the committee met formally to consider the proposal to invest $90 million for a new radial plant and $56 million to convert existing plants to radial production. The proposal was promptly approved (executive committee minutes, 6 December 1972). The committee's discussion focused on the details of ramping up radial production rather than an analysis of the strategic implications of the large investment in the new technology. The strategic issue, 'whether management wants to invest the substantial capital to provide the additional capacity that will be required', was placed in a footnote to the ninth page of DiFederico's proposal. The minutes did not record, nor did participants in the meeting report, any discussion of the strategic implications of the large investment or the need to close existing bias capacity.

Strategic and Structural Context   *Strategic context* refers to an organization's official strategy that induces initiatives consistent with their strategic intent (Burgelman 1983*c*). Firestone managers' decision to invest in belted-bias and then radial technology were consistent with their official corporate strategy of remaining a 'tire company', and were therefore induced by the strategic context. Between 1945 and 1972, Firestone had remained focused on the tire business, which accounted for 80 per cent of its revenues (annual reports, various years). Whereas many large corporations diversified their portfolios during the takeover wave of the 1960s (Ravenscroft and Scherer 1987), Firestone executives limited their diversification to closely related businesses (e.g. steel wheels, external sales of synthetic rubber).

Structural context refers to 'the various organizational and administrative mechanisms put in place by corporate management to implement the current corporate strategy' (Burgelman 1983*c*: 229), including formal organizational structure, information systems, and metrics (Bower 1970: 262–9). Performance measures and rewards, a critical component of the structural context, can exert a strong influence on proposals defined by frontline employees and lent impetus by middle managers (ibid. 265–9; Eisenhardt 1989*a*). In many cases, these agreements are not formalized in explicit contracts, but rather take the form of widely understood tacit agreements or 'psychological contracts' (Rousseau 1995). At Firestone, the psychological contract with managers and employees was characterized by one former executive as: 'Simple and widely understood—if you did nothing wrong, you had a job for life.' A modest percentage of managers' total compensation— typically 5–8 per cent—was linked to performance through a bonus, and stock ownership was limited to the officers of the company who sat on the executive committee.[2]

Performance goals are another important component of an organization's structural context. The behavioral theory of the firm (Cyert and March 1963) posits that managers establish performance goals that specify the relevant metrics and set aspiration levels for future performance against chosen metrics.[3] Goals represent an important component of context because a gap between an organization's aspiration and current performance will stimulate a search for initiatives to close this gap, and the choice of performance metric will guide the search. Firestone's executives, who focused on revenue growth as the principal performance metric throughout the 1960s, invested heavily to keep pace with increasing demand for tires. Between 1960 and 1970, the company built five new tire factories, erected four new dedicated component plants, and acquired or built over 500 company retail stores (internal financial reports, 1960–70). Revenue growth, rather than shareholder returns or profits, was the primary performance metric discussed by the chairman in his speech to stockholders each year that decade. He concluded the 1960s with a forecast of future growth: 'We are confident that the progress made in all areas of our operations during the past year and decade has given us a solid foundation for growth. As we enter the new decade, we believe our company is on the threshold of one of the greatest growth periods in our history' (annual report, 1969: 3).

Powerful Customers   Radial tires were not a disruptive technology because they served the same set of customers and represented a material improvement over existing technology (Christensen and Bower 1996). Consistent with resource-dependence theory, however, Firestone's resource allocation process was clearly shaped by its relationship with powerful customers, in this case automobile manufacturers. Automobile manufacturers accounted for approximately 25 per cent of Firestone's unit sales throughout the 1960s and early 1970s.

Although Firestone initially introduced the belted-bias tire to prevent radial adoption, the company rapidly invested in radials when the automobile manufacturers demanded them in 1972. Firestone made this investment despite the low projected returns on the proposals. Firestone had lost money selling tires to OEMs on an operating profit basis (i.e. prior to deducting corporate overhead) for four of the five years preceding their initial investment in radial production (internal financial reports, 1968–72).

Organizational Competence   Radial tires represented a competency-destroying technology (Tushman and Anderson 1986) because they required a significantly higher level of precision in the tire assembly process (Dick 1980). Firestone's existing competencies shaped its response in two ways. First, Firestone responded to the radial tire with the belted-bias tire, which leveraged its existing manufacturing capabilities. Belted-bias tires could be manufactured with minor modifications of existing production equipment, and Firestone made only minor increases in its capital spending in tires in 1968 and 1969 to retool its factories to accommodate belted-bias production. Second, Firestone managers also initially decided to manufacture radials using modified bias tire equipment. This decision allowed Firestone rapidly to ramp up its radial production capacity to narrow the gap with Michelin and meet automakers' requirements, but also may have contributed to subsequent quality problems (Love and Giffels 1998).

Providers of Capital Between 1960 and 1972, capital providers played a limited role in Firestone's resource allocation process, because Firestone funded most of its investment with internally generated funds. Even in the years 1970–2, as Firestone executives began investing in radial tire production, the net operating profit after taxes and internal cash reserves funded over 90 per cent of investment in the business (i.e. capital expenditure in excess of depreciation, increase in working capital) and financing expenses such as dividends, stock repurchases, interest, and principal repayment (internal financial reports, 1960–72). Firestone increased its long-term debt by only $89 million over this period. At the end of 1972, debt constituted 30 per cent of Firestone's combined long-term debt and market capitalization (see Fig. 7.2).

Stalling in Reverse: Failure of Resource Allocation Process to Disinvest (1973–1979)

Radial tire adoption decreased demand for the bias and belted-bias tires they replaced. Between 1973 and 1979, unit shipments of bias tires decreased a compound average of 11.6 per cent per year. By 1979, industry average capacity utilization fell from an estimated 77 per cent in 1973 to 60 per cent. US manufacturers cut prices to gain market share of the declining market and thereby improve capacity utilization Between 1973 and 1979, the resulting price competition depressed the median price (in real dollars) of bias and belted-bias tires approximately 50 per cent (National Tire Dealer and Retreader Association, various years). The combination of declining demand, low capacity utilization, and falling prices drove the per-unit profit to zero or even less (board minutes, 13 March 1980). Like its competitors, Firestone had capacity in excess of its demand for nonradial tires. Firestone's resource allocation process failed, however, to close unneeded bias tire factories. Firestone had thirteen nonradial factories in the United States in 1973 and had closed only one of them by the end of 1979. Goodyear, in contrast, closed four of its thirteen US nonradial plants over the same period.

Resource Allocation Process Firestone's resource allocation process failed to produce necessary disinvestment in part because proposals to close plants did not emerge from the existing bottom-up resource allocation process. Frontline employees and middle managers knew their factories were underutilized but had little incentive to propose closing their operations because it would jeopardize their job security.

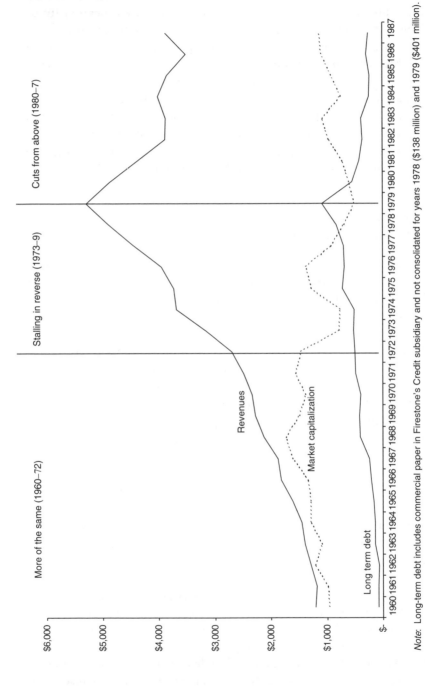

Note: Long-term debt includes commercial paper in Firestone's Credit subsidiary and not consolidated for years 1978 ($138 million) and 1979 ($401 million).

Figure 7.2 Firestone revenues, market capitalization, and long-term debt by era, 1960–1987 ($m)

One senior Firestone executive recalled that employees would not propose disinvestment because they thought: 'It's my wife and kids that need my income . . . so we didn't have situations where someone in the Decatur plant volunteered to be shut down because it was good for the company.' Instead, employees in money-losing factories consistently requested additional investments to restore their factories to profitability (executive committee minutes, various dates, 1973–9). In the absence of bottom-up definition or support for plant closure proposals, the burden for proposing and implementing disinvestment fell on Firestone's top executives whose job security was not threatened by the closure of individual plants. Firestone's top executives, however, failed to take the initiative in closing unneeded capacity.

Strategic and Structural Context   Top executives' reluctance stemmed in part from a desire to honor the psychological contract to protect employees' job security. Most research on psychological contracts to date has analyzed their effect on employees' expectations (Robinson, Kraatz, and Rousseau 1994; Rousseau 1995; Robinson 1996). Psychological contracts, however, also can create a sense of obligation to honor those expectations on the part of the organizational agents who make them (Rousseau 1995: 24–6). One executive observed that Firestone's CEO, Richard Riley, 'would linger and linger, trying to hold on to his people. A CEO who rose through the ranks and played golf with the employees for years is naturally going to try hard to protect them and their jobs.'[4] Riley explicitly referred to employees as part of the 'Firestone family' and stated in the 1974 shareholders' meeting that: 'For close to 75 years, the Firestone Tire and Rubber Company has been able to successfully manage its business in good times and bad for the benefit of its stakeholders, its employees, and its customers, and we expect to continue to do so' (remarks, 18 January 1975: 15).

From 1973 to 1979, there was no change in Firestone's strategic context. No discussion of exiting the tire business was recorded in the transcripts of the board or executive committee meetings, nor did respondents recall any such discussions.[5] Firestone executives also continued to focus on revenue growth. Riley cited sales growth as the company's primary objective in six of his seven addresses as CEO (1978–9). The continued emphasis on revenue growth induced a series of investment proposals to increase sales, including entering new segments such as heavy truck tires, increasing new product development, and diversifying into related businesses (board minutes, 21 February 1978). Few of these investments provided the anticipated growth, and almost none earned an adequate return. The president of

Firestone's North American Tire Operations (NATO) expressed his frustration in a 1979 executive committee meeting when he noted: '[We are] not spending enough money to keep the domestic tire business healthy, and yet [I have] difficulty in promising a satisfactory rate of return on the money actually being spent because of the adverse nature of the market.'

Providers of Capital   Failure to disinvest produced a severe deterioration in Firestone's financial position. Between 1973 and 1979, Firestone's stock declined an average of 13.9 per cent per year vs. an annual average decline of 9.2 per cent for the tire industry as a whole and 1.3 per cent decline for the S&P Index. Firestone issued debt to finance the operating losses and investments in radial capacity, and bond rating agencies downgraded Firestone's bonds and commercial paper four times between 1977 and 1979 (see Fig. 7.2). As banks refused to make loans to Firestone, management resorted to off-balance-sheet funding, including $400 million of short-term commercial paper used to finance capital spending and cover losses.

Investors and lenders had strong incentives to improve Firestone's financial performance and worked through the company's board of directors to pressure top executives for change. Throughout the 1960s, Firestone's board consisted exclusively of corporate executives and family representatives, some of whom were also corporate executives. The Firestone family as a whole controlled approximately one-third of the company's stock. The first outside director, Willard Butcher, joined the board in 1972 and was joined by a second outside director one year later (see Fig. 7.3).[6] Family representatives on the board dropped from five members in 1970 to three by 1973. Between 1973 and 1976, inside managers (5–6 seats) equaled or exceeded the number of seats held by outsiders and family representatives combined.

Willard Butcher, the president of Firestone's lead bank Chase Manhattan, was the most vocal board member in pressuring executives for change. In 1976, he proposed that the company hire an outside CFO. The new CFO outlined the severity of Firestone's financial position in a series of board meetings, but failed to secure agreement with the rest of the top management team on a long-term financial plan (board minutes, 25 May 1976; 16 November 1976; 21 August 1979). Butcher repeatedly urged Firestone executives to reduce bias capacity to improve the company's profitability. He requested plant-level profit and loss statements to identify which plants were losing money and repeatedly recommended that Firestone executives close plants to improve utilization and boost profits (board minutes, various dates 1977–9). He

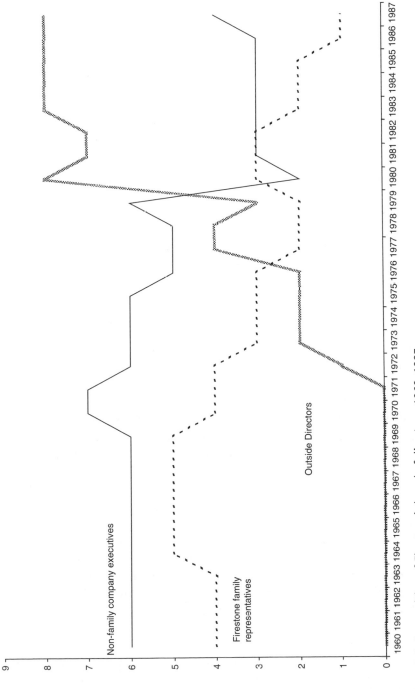

Figure 7.3 Composition of Firestone's board of directors, 1960–1987

argued in a March 1978 board meeting, for example, that: 'The investment made in North America in the last few years meant that the radial tire had been given to the motoring public for nothing, because the old bias tire capacity was still in place and the radial tire capacity had been added at enormous expense to it.'

Firestone's top executives resisted board pressure to reduce capacity. Executive board members stalled in providing the directors with plant-level financial data, prompting one director to observe that sixteen months had elapsed since the initial request for data (board minutes, 16 October 1979). In 1977, the outside board members and family representatives invited the chairman of Borg-Warner and one of his colleagues to join the board, bringing the total number of outside board members to four. The following year, the outside board members proposed a merger between Firestone and Borg-Warner, in which the merged entity would be run by Borg-Warner executives. The merger failed after Firestone's CEO increased the consideration for Firestone stock and then halted negotiations when Borg-Warner refused to accept the higher implied valuation (board minutes, 20 April 1979).

Organizational Competence   One possible explanation for delays in plant closure may have been executives' desire to preserve critical competencies (Tushman and Anderson 1986; Burgelman 1994). This was not the case, however, in the transition from bias to radial tires. The patent on the radial product designs expired in 1967, so Firestone and other domestic competitors were able to replicate the product design. Michelin, however, had invested heavily in process improvements to maintain their lead. 'Anybody can make a radial tire,' one Michelin executive noted, 'but to make 100 of them of uniform quality is our secret' (Harkelroad 1978: 2). Successfully manufacturing radial tires required greater accuracy and consistency in the production process. Thus, radial tire production required unlearning existing manufacturing processes and replacing them with new, more demanding routines. To achieve changes in manufacturing competencies, Firestone managers negotiated reductions in job classifications and changes in work rules in the factories that were converted to radial production (Jeszeck 1986; United Rubber Workers 1988).

Powerful Customers   Automobile manufacturers exerted pressure to invest in radials but did not exert a similar pressure to disinvest from bias capacity. Other important customers, such as mass retailers (including Sears and J. C. Penney) that continued to sell some bias tires, had incentives to encourage manufacturers to continue production because industry-level manufacturing overcapacity allowed retailers to negotiate more favorable prices (National Tire Dealer and Retreaders Association, various years).

Top-down Disinvestment (1979–1988)

Firestone's financial performance continued to deteriorate. In December 1979, the board appointed John Nevin as the first outside president in Firestone's seventy-nine-year history. In his first two years with the company, Nevin closed six North American tire factories and eight tire component factories, dramatically reduced the breadth of Firestone's product portfolio, and cut total headcount by nearly 25 per cent (see Table 7.3). These disinvestments initially improved financial performance. Long- and short-term debt fell from 72 per cent of enterprise value at the end of 1979 to 43 per cent two years later, and average annual returns to shareholders (including dividends and stock buybacks) of 41 per cent outpaced the 32 per cent increase for the tire industry and 14 per cent for the S&P Index. After the initial restructuring period, however, Firestone executives were unable to achieve revenue growth targets or maintain margins. Between 1982 and 1987, Firestone's average annual returns to shareholders were 9.3 per cent, lower than both the tire industry as a whole of 15.9 per cent and the S&P Index of 15.1 per cent. Firestone was the target of two unsolicited takeover bids in 1982, and in 1988 was acquired by Japanese tire manufacturer Bridgestone.

Providers of Capital   In contrast to investment decisions, which originated with customers and emerged through Firestone's bottom-up resource allocation process, pressure for disinvestment came from investors and banks and was channeled through a top-down process. In 1979, representatives of the Firestone family and the company's banks orchestrated the early retirement of president and heir-apparent to the CEO and initiated a search for an outsider. The three outside board members subsequently formed a search committee chaired by Chase Manhattan Chairman Butcher. The committee nominated John Nevin—the former CEO of Zenith—and the board voted to elevate Nevin to the CEO position six months after he joined as president. Nevin had spent seventeen years in the finance department at Ford before assuming the presidency at Zenith, where he closed factories and laid off 5,500 employees in response to industry overcapacity.

Table 7.3 Measures of Firestone's investment and disinvestment, 1960–1987

	1960–72	1973–9	1980–1	1981–7
Increase/(decrease) in North American tire manufacturing plants	7	1	(6)	(4)
Total tire plants at end of period	19	20	14	10
Increase/(decrease) in world-wide tire component facilities	5	1	(8)	(3)
Total component facilities at end of period	23	24	16	13
Increase/(decrease) in North American controlled tire dealers	513	0	(287)	447
Total Firestone controlled dealers at end of period	1,400	1,400	1,113	1,560
Increase/(decrease) in number of tire SKUs	2,700	1,128	(5,228)	(1,150)
Total tire SKUs at end of period	6,700	7,828	2,600	1,450
Increase/(decrease) in number of employees	46	2	(34)	(19)
Total Firestone employees at end of period	105	107	73	54

Note: Tire components include tire textiles, wire, synthetic rubber, and natural rubber.

Source: Firestone Annual reports, internal financial documents.

Between May and December 1979, the board also nominated or appointed four outside directors, which meant that outsiders would constitute a majority on the board beginning in 1980 for the first time in the company's history (see Fig. 7.3).

Investors and bankers also supported the new president in his efforts to improve profitability. Three months after joining the company, Nevin proposed closing six of the company's twenty North American tire factories as well as a synthetic rubber facility. Firestone executives at the board meeting opposed the proposal, but vigorous support from Butcher and Leonard Firestone (who represented the Firestone family's investment) persuaded the board to adopt Nevin's proposal (board minutes, 18 March 1980). Nevin later recalled that meeting:

When I started to read the letter to the board on shutting down the six tire plants... I was very conscious of the fact that I was a 45-day wonder asking these guys to take responsibility and approve a massive cutback... The second paragraph said 'the actions will generate $600 million in cash through the liquidation of the business and lead to a commensurate reduction in debt.'... Bill Butcher interrupted me after I read that and said 'John, if that's the only damn thing it does, I am 100% for it—you've got to deal with that debt problem, and I'm glad you're facing it.'

Resource Allocation Process　In defining his plan to restructure Firestone, Nevin did not rely on information that emerged through the existing bottom-up resource allocation process, because middle managers and frontline employees were 'often less than forthcoming with data', in the words of a manager hired by Nevin. Instead, Nevin assembled a team of six staff executives who reported directly to him and helped him gather and analyze information. Nevin prohibited these managers from discussing their work with any other staff or operating executives and relied instead on an outside management consulting firm to assist in collecting industry data. The director of the consulting engagement recalled: 'You could almost determine the need to restructure on the back of an envelope—at a general level it was pretty simple to figure out that the company had overcapacity and which plants were worst.' In his first few months as president, Nevin himself met with the company's top 100 middle managers; over 100 field sales executives; more than 200 dealers and store managers; and representatives from Ford, General Motors, and Chrysler. Nevin wrote a twelve-page memorandum (with twenty-two supporting exhibits) entitled 'North America Tire Restructuring' that laid out his disinvestment proposal. He presented it directly to the board without consulting the executive committee or operating managers beforehand. Lee Brodeur, then the president of NATO, recalled: 'We were shocked—he made one big move and bango, we closed those plants.'

After circumventing Firestone's bottom-up resource allocation process to implement his initial disinvestment plan, Nevin subsequently replaced it with a top-down process. Eight months after joining Firestone, Nevin proposed a plan to restructure the executive committee. The proposed amendments to the by-laws mandated that three of the six members of the executive committee be outside directors, and that the committee meet less frequently to accommodate directors' schedules (board minutes, 19 August 1980). The board approved the proposals. Nevin subsequently consolidated the control of resource allocation into his own hands. In February 1981, he assumed the chair of the executive committee and decreased its membership to himself, one other Firestone executive, and three outside board members (board minutes, 28 February 1981). Nevin later recalled that he gathered data himself to evaluate proposals for capital investments independently rather than relying on data generated through the bottom-up process. All Firestone executives agreed that Nevin personally made decisions on capital investment and unilaterally sent back requests for capital if he was dissatisfied with the underlying assumptions or analyses. For example, Nevin decided which of Firestone's nontire divisions would be sold without consulting other managers in the business. 'Decisions were made and Nevin handed them down,' recalled Brodeur. 'I remember time and time again in staff meetings that he would have with key managers, he would completely dominate and control us.'

Organizational Competence   The top-down resource allocation process imposed by Nevin sheds some light on Firestone's inability to grow revenues between 1982 and 1987. The top-down process failed to capture the specific knowledge possessed by long-time managers lower in the organization about the competencies that could provide future growth. Nevin decided to sell Firestone's steel wheels, foam rubber, and plastics businesses over the strong objections of long-time executives familiar with their operations. These businesses earned an average annual return on equity of 15–50 per cent, were first or second in their respective domestic markets based on superior technology, and offered significant revenue growth potential (internal financial reports, various years). Although these nontire divisions accounted for only 20 per cent of Firestone's revenue through the late 1970s, they contributed between 55 and 70 per cent of operating profits and an even higher percentage of cash flow.

Strategic and Structural Context   Nevin shifted Firestone's structural context to institutionalize capital market pressure throughout the organization. He replaced the company's psychological contract—stressing employment guarantees—with compensation packages that rewarded financial performance and stock appreciation. Senior executives and middle managers received stock options and performance-based bonuses, which could reach 25–50 per cent of their base salary if managers met or exceeded their budget. Nevin later explained his rationale: 'Philosophically, I believed very deeply that executives should be rewarded in some direct relationship to shareholder value . . . So I used stock options very extensively and very low in the organization.' Nevin emphasized strengthening the balance sheet and restoring NATO to profitability rather than growth in revenues as the key metrics of success. Nevin restructured the finance department to obtain better data and instill discipline in the investment process. He replaced nearly the entire department with executives hired from outside the company and replaced the CFO three times in as many years until he found one whom he considered sufficiently aggressive in instilling financial discipline throughout the organization.

The consolidation of the resource allocation process in one person left Firestone's resource allocation process vulnerable to the cognitive frames of the individual setting the strategic context. Nevin maintained the company's strategic focus on the tire industry, but believed strongly that Firestone-owned retail outlets provided an opportunity for profitable growth. Nevin apparently developed this frame based on his experience at Zenith before joining Firestone. Two months after joining Firestone, he told stockholders: 'I concluded long ago that a first-rate retailing organization is an absolute requisite for the success of any consumer product manufacturer' (remarks to stockholders, 9 February 1980: 2). After pruning 287 unprofitable retailers between 1980 and 1981, Firestone subsequently proceeded to acquire an additional 322 stores and build 125 new outlets in the following years. One senior executive reported: 'John loved the stores . . . he was completely irrational on the subject'—an observation that was echoed by other observers. Several managers at the time argued against the investment in retail operations, citing the division's historically low returns despite favorable transfer prices. Firestone's large investment in retail operations failed to earn an acceptable return. In 1981, Nevin forecast earnings of $147 million from the retail stores for the year 1985. Actual earnings were $18 million.

Conclusion and Discussion

Limitations

In-depth clinical research on a single company can generate grounded theory with a high level of internal validity (Campbell and Stanley 1963; Eisenhardt 1989*b*). Such research suffers, however, from limited external validity—i.e. the researcher's ability to generalize findings beyond the immediate case study. Yin (1989: 43–4) distinguishes between *analytical generalization* (in which a researcher generalizes from a specific set of results to a broader theory) and *statistical generalization* (in which the researcher generalizes from a sample to a larger population). In this chapter, my primary focus is analytical generalization, and implications for selected theoretical streams are discussed below. The findings from the study, however, also provide opportunities for statistical generalization by testing hypotheses derived from the process model on a large sample. Researchers could, for example, test the hypothesis that higher levels of dependence on capital markets for financing (as measured by interest coverage, for example, or a higher percentage of outside directors) would increase the speed of disinvestment.

Implications for Strategy Process Research: Role of Top Management

The Firestone case demonstrates that the bottom-up resource allocation process can stall in reverse—i.e. when faced with the need for disinvestment. Frontline employees and middle managers closest to the existing bias factories lacked incentives to propose disinvestment. Plant closures would jeopardize their own job security and that of colleagues and subordinates, and, in many cases, have a material adverse effect on host communities. Proposals for disinvestment in this case were optimal for the organization but ran counter to the employees' interests (Jensen 1993). Disinvestment proposals also may be delayed because managers wish to avoid the perception that their early actions were mistaken, leading them to escalate their commitment (Brockner 1992; Ross and Staw 1993).

An important assumption of most models of bottom-up strategic processes is that top executives play a relatively limited role (Bower 1970; Quinn 1980; Burgelman 1983*c*, 1991, 1994; Noda and Bower

1996), although recent research has posited a more active role for top management (Eisenmann and Bower 2000; Eisenmann 2002; Lovas and Ghoshal 2000). Top executives, according to these models, rarely intervene directly in the resource allocation process, but rather shape the process indirectly by manipulating the organizational context, often retrospectively, after major shifts have already occurred. Top executives can frame the strategic context for the organization as a whole (Lovas and Ghoshal 2000) or for specific new initiatives (Noda and Bower 1996). They also manage the tension between autonomous initiatives and the established strategic context, sometimes 'retroactively rationalizing' projects that emerged outside the official strategy or dissolving the organization's existing strategic frame altogether (Burgelman 1994, 1996). Top executives also can shape an organization's structural context through actions such as the organization of tasks (Chakravarthy and Doz 1992; Lovas and Ghoshal 2000) and performance metrics and compensation (Bower 1970: 266; Noda and Bower 1996). Top executives' ability to exert even indirect influence on strategic processes by manipulating context is limited, however, by structural inertia (Hannan and Freeman 1984) and path-dependence resulting from previous decisions (Noda and Bower 1996).

The findings from this study, however, document a CEO who exerted direct influence on the resource allocation process. After initially circumventing the bottom-up process, Nevin subsequently dismantled it and replaced it with a top-down process in which he personally gathered information and made investment and disinvestment decisions. Nevin also influenced the structural context by resetting aspirations, changing compensation, and hiring outside employees to complement his direct intervention in the process. These findings, which are at odds with the existing literature, raise two related questions: why might a top-down process be required for disinvestment and what are the limitations of such a process?

Disinvestment decisions differ from investments in three ways, and these differences shed light on why a top-down process might be appropriate for disinvestment. First, front-line employees and middle managers often lack incentives to promote disinvestment to the extent such actions would limit their job security, promotion opportunities, and reputation. Thus, a bottom-up process is prone to failure in promoting disinvestment. Second, a top-down process is well suited to disinvestment because these decisions require more general than specific knowledge. Jensen and Meckling (1992) distinguish between specific knowledge (difficult to codify and costly to transfer) and general knowledge (easily codified and transferred) and argue that decision rights should be colocated with the knowledge required to make the best decision. Many investment decisions require specific knowledge of a complex set of technical, customer, and competitive factors and should, as a result, be optimally decentralized. Disinvestment decisions, in contrast, may be made with general knowledge that can be assembled and analyzed more easily by top executives. In the Firestone case, Nevin was able to decide that disinvestment was necessary and identify the best operations to close based on a 'back-of-the-envelope' analysis. The need for disinvestment was more obvious in the Firestone case than typically might be the case, because it was not complicated by uncertainty around future demand or the need to preserve existing competencies (Burgelman 1996). Although the Firestone case is extreme, it is by no means an isolated example of delayed disinvestment in the face of a relatively clear imperative for exit (Baden-Fuller and Longley 1988; Deily 1991; Grant 1990; Jensen 1993; Dial and Murphy 1995).

The third way disinvestment differs from investment is in the level of 'buy-in' required by frontline employees and middle managers to implement these decisions. The ultimate success of a new strategic initiative (e.g. internal corporate venture, new product or service) depends to a large extent on the level of effort exerted by the frontline employees and middle managers charged with implementing the decision. Thus, the allocation of financial capital is a necessary but not sufficient condition for the initiative's success. Employees also must allocate their focus and effort to these new initiatives, and these commitment decisions are by their nature highly decentralized. Thus, a bottom-up strategic process would not only serve to colocate decision rights on capital investments with specific knowledge, but also increase the chances that employees and middle managers will focus their effort on the initiatives. Disinvestment, in contrast, requires limited commitment from employees. Differences in incentives, specificity of knowledge, and level of buy-in required, in summary, suggest that a bottom-up process may be optimal for investment decisions, whereas a top-down process may be more appropriate for disinvestment.

The difference between investment and disinvestment decisions poses a serious challenge for organizations that must make both. Lovas and Ghoshal (2000) document a project-based organization in which employees at various levels in the organization could select which initiatives they would work on and also decide whether to withdraw their support, thereby ending a project. Although this structural context is well suited to project-based activities with limited duration (such as new product development efforts), it is less feasible for routinized activities such as logistics, manufacturing, or service provision. In some circumstances, it may be optimal to impose a top-down resource allocation process for a period to drive disinvestment and return to a bottom-up process to pursue new growth opportunities after necessary disinvestment is complete.[7] According to this logic, Firestone's failure to achieve growth and profitability targets after the initial restructuring may have resulted from Nevin's maintaining the top-down process beyond the optimal point to revert to a bottom-up one. The costs of switching from a bottom-up process to a top-down one and back again suggest that it may be optimal to concentrate disinvestment decisions in time, which would lead to a pattern of long periods of growth punctuated by brief episodes of disinvestment (Tushman and Romanelli 1985).

Role of Capital Providers in the Resource Allocation Process   Early models of strategy process focused primarily on the intra-organizational dynamics, but recent research has expanded the scope of enquiry to examine how external forces influence the intra-organizational strategy processes. The research to date has focused primarily on product market influences (Mintzberg 1978; Pascale 1984; Mintzberg and McHugh 1985; Mintzberg and Waters 1985; Christensen and Bower 1996; Burgelman 2002). The Firestone case demonstrates, however, that powerful investors and lenders also can influence the resource allocation process. Owners and lenders have clear incentives to influence a company's strategic decisions if they believe delays in disinvestment will destroy shareholder value or increase the default risk of outstanding debt. They also will possess the necessary information to the extent that the need for disinvestment can be inferred from general knowledge that is publicly available or presented to board members (e.g. corporate financial reports, industry capacity utilization). Investors and lenders cannot, of course, directly intervene in intra-firm processes. They can, however, influence the timing of top executive turnover as well as the choice of new CEO selected (Furtado and Karan 1990). In the Firestone case, representatives of the Firestone family and lead bank exerted their influence through the executive selection process in the board of directors, but providers of capital also can precipitate a change of management by supporting a takeover bid.

Executives also can incorporate capital market pressure into a firm's context. After joining Firestone, Nevin took a series of steps to institutionalize capital market pressure in the company's decision making. He articulated a new set of financial goals, increased the use of incentives linked to corporate financial performance, and changed the role and increased the power of Firestone's finance function. These actions, along with his consolidation of resource allocation into his own hands, had the effect of dramatically increasing the importance of capital providers' influence on investment and disinvestment decisions. Nevin's actions to incorporate the capital providers' interests in Firestone's resource allocation process, however, highlights that top executives can exercise some discretion in intensifying or buffering intra-organizational processes from capital market pressure.

At the extreme, executives can voluntarily enter into relationships with investors or lenders that will sharply constrain future managerial discretion on allocating resources. Top executives can, for example, assume a high burden of debt or enter into highly restrictive debt covenants that cap future levels of capital spending or require bank approval for major acquisitions (Baker and Wruck 1989; Wruck 1994). A manager's ability voluntarily to enter into binding relationships with capital providers has an interesting implication for resource-dependence theory. Pfeffer and Salancik (1978) argue that managers make decisions that satisfy the needs of external stakeholders who provide the resources necessary for organizational survival. This theory assumes the preexistence of resource-dependency relationships. These relationships do not, however, arise *ex nihilo*. Rather, they are the result of earlier actions that brought the organization into the position of resource dependence in the first place. Of course, few organizations can avoid resource dependency altogether, nor can executives foresee all the consequences of their decision to bind their organization to a powerful resource provider. Executives can, however, exercise some discretion when entering into these relationships. The process by which managers evaluate alternative resource providers and decide whether and when to enter into resource-dependence relationships is an interesting topic for further research.

Investors' and lenders' influence on intra-organizational resource allocation processes is not limited to disinvestment decisions within established firms. If anything, providers of capital may exert more influence on the investment decisions of start-up ventures. Entrepreneurs often lack the financial resources necessary to pursue an opportunity and therefore tap outside parties such as angel investors, venture capitalists, or corporate partners for funding (Stevenson and Jarillo 1990). These capital providers may require terms such as board seats or veto rights on investments that allow them actively to intervene in the new venture's resource allocation process. Their influence may be functional or dysfunctional. Seasoned investors might, for example, provide a valuable perspective on the value-creation potential of opportunities. On the other hand, investors may impose inappropriate biases on the process. Many Silicon Valley venture capitalists, for example, shared an assumption that Internet start-ups would need to get big fast to succeed, an assumption that may have contributed to investments in advertising that were higher than optimal (Eisenmann 2003). The role of investors and lenders in the intra-organizational resource allocation process represents an exciting opportunity for future research.

Implications for Evolutionary Theory

Toward a More Active View of Inertia   In recent years, the population ecology perspective has emerged as an influential stream of research for understanding how groups of organizations change over time (Hannan and Freeman 1989; Carroll 1988). A central tenet of this literature stream is that organizations are characterized by structural inertia that prevents them from changing rapidly enough to adapt when their environment shifts (Hannan and Freeman 1984). The findings from the Firestone study, however, suggest a more nuanced conceptualization of inertia may be more appropriate in describing established organizations' response to disruptions in their environment. Firestone's response to radials cannot be characterized simply as a delayed response to the introduction of radial technology. The company responded rapidly to radials by introducing and promoting a modified version of their core technology and immediately approving investments in radials once their largest customers demanded them. The delay was limited to the disinvestment. I have elsewhere introduced the term *active inertia* to describe an organization's tendency to respond to major shifts in their environment by accelerating activities that proved successful in the past (Sull 2003).

Active inertia is related to constructs such as strategic momentum (Kelly and Amburgey 1991; Amburgey and Miner 1992) and escalating commitment (Ross and Staw 1993; Brockner 1992) that posit organizational persistence in an established trajectory. Active inertia, however, goes further to posit rapid investment in the face of a major shift in the environment. This investment, however, is channeled through the existing resource allocation process and shaped by the organization's existing context, competence, and customer preferences.[8] Although rapid, there is no guarantee that these investments will be adaptive. In the case of Firestone, the most adaptive response may well have been to exit the tire business and redeploy the resources in the more profitable and faster growing (albeit smaller) related businesses, and, in fact, this is precisely what Firestone's Akron-based rival B. F. Goodrich did (for reasons that are discussed below). This alternative was essentially unthinkable for Firestone, however, given the strategic assumption that Firestone meant tires, revenue growth was the most important metric of success, employees were entitled to a job for life, and automakers were the most important customers. To generalize beyond the specifics of the Firestone case, research analyzing the micro-processes within organizations can provide important insights that enrich our understanding of how organizations respond to changes in their environment (Burgelman 1994; Christensen and Bower 1996; Gilbert 2002).

Reversing Retention   Evolutionary theorists have applied the variation-selection-retention framework to analyze competition for resources within an organization (Burgelman 1991, 1994; Barnett and Burgelman 1996; Lovas and Ghoshal 2000). Much of the research to date, however, has focused on how an organization's context, competence, and customers shape which initiatives will be proposed (i.e. variation) or selected (Burgelman 1991). The process of retention, and particularly of reversing retention, has received relatively less attention. To some extent, the conceptual lens of evolutionary theory draws researchers' attention away from the issue of reversing retention. The underlying assumption is that once a trait is selected and retained, it is permanent and difficult or impossible to change (Campbell 1969; Hannan and Freeman 1989). The question of how organizations might reverse previously retained traits is important both to scholars and practitioners.

This study provides two insights on reversing retention. First, powerful forces prevent disinvestment proposals from emerging out of a bottom-up resource allocation process for a simple reason. By proposing exit, the individuals with the richest specific knowledge of a project, division, or factory may endanger their job security or reputation for competence (and subsequent ability to secure resources). As a result, employees and managers may instead propose investments to improve their project or division's fortunes, even if exit were the more adaptive response at the organizational level. It is, of course, possible that an organization's structural context will mitigate this tendency. Burgelman (1994, 1996), for example, documents that Intel shifted resources from fabricating memory chips to microprocessors because the firm's structural context included a rule for allocating fabrication plant capacity based on margins generated. This contextual factor resulted in a gradual shift from commodity memory chips to the more profitable microprocessors. This rule took effect, however, only when combined demand for the two types of chip exceeded Intel's fabrication capacity (Burgelman 1994: 43). In cases such as Firestone's, when the need for disinvestment stems from excess capacity and implies closure and layoffs, the probability of process failure is much higher.

The second insight on reversing retention concerns the role of managerial decision in evolutionary theory. Early applications of eco-logical models in organization theory had a strongly deterministic flavor (Hannan and Freeman 1989), although subsequent research has elaborated the role of managerial discretion within the confines of evolutionary theory (Burgelman 1991, 1994, 2002; March 1991; Lovas and Ghoshal 2000). Earlier research has argued that managers influence internal variation, selection, and retention processes indirectly by ma-nipulating contextual variables (Burgelman 1991, 1994; Noda and Bower 1996; Lovas and Ghoshal 2000). The Firestone case illustrates that managers also can directly intervene in intra-organizational re-source allocation processes. This finding is consistent with Gilmour's (1973) study of sales of business units by diversified companies. Gil-mour found that in each case he studied, the decision to sell divisions was made and implemented by top managers rather than emerging from a bottom-up process. This is not, of course, to argue that direct intervention is without risks. Recall in the Firestone case how a top-down resource allocation process failed to capture specific knowledge embedded at lower levels in the organization and also left the process susceptible to the cognitive biases of the outside CEO.

The Firestone case does, however, clearly demonstrate that direct intervention is possible and may even be optimal under certain cir-cumstances. A comparison of the disinvestment process in the present study (and Gilmour's) with Burgelman's findings from Intel's exit from memory chips provides interesting insights on the condition under which direct managerial intervention may be appropriate. In the Firestone case, general knowledge (i.e. 'back-of-the-envelope') was sufficient to identify the need for disinvestment, and lower-level man-agers and employees lacked the incentives to propose disinvestment. At Intel, in contrast, the need for exit was complicated by technological uncertainty and the need to preserve distinctive competence that cut across the memory and microprocessor businesses. To the extent fabrication capacity was shifted from one use to another without loss of job security or damage to reputation, employees had no incentive to oppose this reallocation of resources. This contrast suggests that managerial intervention may be necessary when the need for disinvestment is fairly obvious and uncomplicated by the preservation of cross-unit competencies and when employees lack incentives to propose exit. These conditions are more likely to prevail in slower-moving traditional industries such as chemicals, automotive, building materials, hospitals, or commercial banking.

Capital Market Influence   The Firestone case illustrates how pressure from capital providers can influence the intraorganizational process of reversing retention. To the extent organizations are dependent on investors and lenders rather than customers for funding, these capital providers potentially can exert an influence on a firm's resource allocation process either directly (e.g. review rights on major investments, caps on expenditures) or indirectly by increasing financial executives' power within the organization and shaping which proposals would be considered acceptable.

Contrasting the Firestone case with that of B. F. Goodrich illustrates how differences in the timing of capital market pressure can influence the speed of reversing retention. Like Firestone, B. F. Goodrich was an established tire producer (founded in 1870) and headquartered in Akron. Throughout the 1960s, Goodrich executives invested heavily to keep pace with larger rivals Goodyear and Firestone, although the company's smaller size depressed its earnings relative to its larger rivals. As a result, Goodrich was unable to fund its investments out of retained earnings and borrowed heavily (Blackford and Kerr 1996: 267). In the late 1960s, interest payments represented 43 per cent of net income. Goodrich's poor financial performance attracted a hostile takeover bid in January 1969.

Although Goodrich executives successfully defeated the takeover bid, the company's outside directors recognized that dramatic changes were necessary to improve the company's financial performance (Blackford and Kerr 1996: 289–96). In contrast to Firestone, outside directors constituted a majority of the Goodrich board in 1969 and included prominent financiers John L. Weinberg of Goldman Sachs and Paul C. Cabot of the State Street Investment Corp. Goodrich's directors rapidly took actions to improve the company's financial position. In 1970, Goodrich initiated private negotiations with Michelin to merge the two companies' tire operations, although the discussions ended when Michelin insisted on full control of any combined entity (Blackford and Kerr 1996: 278–9). In 1971, the board replaced the incumbent CEO with a financial executive from the oil industry who in turn replaced Goodrich's top management team with outsiders.

After divesting several businesses, the new CEO applied increased scrutiny to the financial returns earned on investments in the tire business (B. F. Goodrich 1977). Based on this analysis of financial returns, Goodrich executives decided against building a new factory dedicated to radial production, closed a larger percentage of bias factories than the other leading tire companies (and did so two years before its competitors), and ultimately decided to stop providing tires to automobile manufacturers (although these customers accounted for 10 per cent of revenues). These actions allowed B. F. Goodrich to move from the least profitable major US tire company in 1971 to the most profitable in 1981. Five years later, the company merged its tire operations with those of Uniroyal, and subsequently sold its stake in the merged entity.

Reversal of retention in the form of disinvestment took place in Firestone and Goodrich, but the latter began the process nearly a decade before the former. Goodrich's earlier response appears to have resulted from early capital market pressure in the form of a corporate raid, earlier dependence on capital markets for funding, and an outside-led board that included powerful financiers. These cases illustrate the important role powerful providers of capital can play in evolutionary processes within an organization.

Endnotes

1. Several Firestone executives described the process as one of 'rubber stamp' or 'automatic'. (Lee Brodeur, interview with author, tape recording, Akron, Ohio, 11–13 August 1994, and Mario DiFederico, interview with author, tape recording, Akron, Ohio, 10 May 1995.) An analysis of investment proposals supports the executive retrospective accounts. In the late 1960s, the executive committee approved 93 per cent of all proposals considered. There was no evidence that the committee applied greater scrutiny to larger investments, because the mean and median value of the projects approved during this period was more than twice the value of rejected proposals.
2. The top six Firestone officers who constituted the executive committee typically owned between 2,000 and 30,000 shares of common stock during the 1960s and 1970s. The stock price ranged between $17.50 and $33.30 (proxy statements, various years).
3. Although strategic context and performance goals are often conflated, they are conceptually distinct. Strategic context specifies the domain in which an organization will compete without elaborating how performance will be measured (e.g. profits, revenue growth). Performance goals, in contrast, can specify aspirations without providing any guidance on how to achieve these goals.

4. The concern for employees' welfare was manifest in the way Firestone closed the one factory they did shut between 1973 and 1979. An internal study revealed the factory had operating and plant-level overhead costs that were approximately twice that of the average domestic plant, which resulted in consistent losses. To avoid any layoffs, Firestone executives decided to invest capital to reduce costs and then phase out production over several years through a hiring freeze, planned retirements, and transfer of employees to an adjacent factory. The plant continued to lose money throughout this period (board minutes, 21 March 1978: exhibits).

5. From a purely financial perspective, this is somewhat surprising because Firestone's nontire business on average contributed 40 per cent of total corporate operating income over this period while accounting for less than 15 percent of book assets (internal reports, various years).

6. In 1964, the president of the Cleveland Trust Bank joined the Firestone board, and he or his successor in that position occupied a board seat until 1985. Cleveland Trust owned approximately 12 per cent of Firestone's outstanding stock in trust for Firestone family members. The Cleveland Trust representative is thus coded as a family representative rather than outside board member.

7. The reversion to the bottom-up process assumes that at some point the organization will face growth opportunities. If this is not the case (e.g. the proverbial buggy-whip manufacturer), it might be optimal to retain a top-down process to manage the liquidation of the company.

8. Capital providers may or may not influence these investments based on the organization's dependence on external sources of financing for the investments.

References

Aldrich, H. E. (1979). *Organizations and Environments*. Englewood Cliffs, NJ: Prentice-Hall.

Amburgey, T. L., and Miner, A. S. (1992). 'Strategic Momentum: The Effects of Repetitive Positional and Contextual Momentum on Merger Activity'. *Strategic Management Journal* 13/5: 335–51.

B. F. Goodrich (1977). 'Post-completion Study of Capital Budgeting Projects'. B. F. Goodrich Corporate Archives, Akron, Ohio.

Baden-Fuller, C., and Longley, R. (1988). 'Predicting Plant Closure in European Industry'. *Long Range Planning* 1: 90–6.

Baker, G. P., and Wruck, K. M. (1989). 'Organizational Changes and Value Creation in Leveraged Buyouts: The Case of O.M. Scott and Sons Company'. *Journal of Financial Economics* 25: 163–90.

Barnett, W. P., and Burgelman, R. A. (1996). 'Evolutionary Perspectives on Strategy'. *Strategic Management Journal* 17: 5–19.

Blackford, M. G., and Kerr, K. A. (1996). *BF Goodrich: Tradition and Transformation, 1870–1995*. Columbus, Ohio: Ohio State University Press.

Bower, J. L. (1970). *Managing the Resource Allocation Process*. Boston, Mass.: Harvard Business School Press.

——and Doz, Y. (1979). 'Strategy Formulation: A Social and Political Process', in D. E. Schendel and C. W. Hofer (eds.), *Strategic Management: A New View of Business Policy and Planning*. Boston, Mass.: Little Brown, 152–66.

Brockner, I. (1992). 'The Escalation of Commitment to a Failing Course of Action: Toward Theoretical Progress'. *Academy of Management Review* 17/1: 39–61.

Burgelman, R. A. (1983*a*). 'Corporate Entrepreneurship and Strategic Management: Insights from a Process Study'. *Management Science* 19: 1349–64.

——(1983*b*). 'A Model of the Interaction of Strategic Behavior, Corporate Context and the Concept of Strategy'. *Academy of Management Review* 8: 61–7.

——(1983c). 'A Process Model of Internal Corporate Venturing in the Diversified Major Firm'. *Administrative Science Quarterly* 28: 223–44.

——(1991). 'Intraorganizational Ecology of Strategy Making and Organizational Adaptation: Theory and Field Research'. *Organization Science* 2: 239–62.

——(1994). 'Fading Memories: A Process Theory of Strategic Business Exit in Dynamic Environments'. *Administrative Science Quarterly* 39: 24–56.

——(1996). 'A Process Model of Strategic Business Exit: Implications for an Evolutionary Perspective on Strategy'. *Strategic Management Journal* 17: 193–214.

——(2002). 'Strategy as Vector and the Inertia of Co-evolutionary Lock-in'. *Administrative Science Quarterly* 47/2: 325–57.

Campbell, D. T. (1969). 'Variation and Selective Retention in Socio-cultural Evolution'. *General Systems* 16: 69–85.

——and Stanley, J. C. (1963). *Experimental and Quasi-Experimental Design*. Boston, Mass.: Houghton-Mifflin.

Carroll, Glenn R. (1988). *Ecological Models of Organizations*. Cambridge, Mass.: Ballinger.

Chakravarthy, B. S., and Doz, Y. (1992). 'Strategy Process Research: Focusing on Corporate Self-renewal'. *Strategic Management Journal*, Summer Special Issue 13: 5–14.

Chandler, A. D. (1990). *Scale and Scope: The Dynamics of Industrial Capitalism*. Cambridge, Mass.: Harvard University Press.

Christensen, C. M., and Bower, J. L. (1996). 'Customer Power, Strategic Investment, and the Failure of Leading Firms'. *Strategic Management Journal* 17: 197–218.

Consumer Reports (1968). 'Tires'. *Consumer Reports*, August 1968: 404–9.

Cooper, A. C., and Schendel, D. E. (Feb. 1976). 'Strategic Responses to Technological Threats'. *Business Horizons*, 61–3.

Cyert, R. M., and March, J. G. (1963). *A Behavioral Theory of the Firm*. Englewood Cliffs, NJ: Prentice-Hall.

Deily, M. E. (1991). 'Exit Strategies and Plant-closing Decisions: The Case of Steel'. *RAND Journal of Economics* 22: 250–63.

Dial, J., and Murphy, K. J. (1995). 'Incentives, Downsizing, and Value Creation at General Dynamics'. *Journal of Financial Economics* 37: 261–314.

Eisenhardt, K. M. (1989*a*). 'Agency Theory: An Assessment and Review'. *Academy of Management Review* 14/1: 57–74.

——(1989*b*). 'Building Theories from Case Study Research'. *Academy of Management Review* 14/4: 532–50.

Eisenmann, T. R. (2002). 'The Effects of CEO Equity Ownership and Diversification on Risk Taking'. *Strategic Management Journal* 23: 513–34.

——(2003). 'Internet Companies' Growth Strategies: Determinants of Investment Intensity and Long-term Performance'. *Harvard Business School Working Paper No. 03–110.*

——and Bower, J. L. (2000). 'The Entrepreneurial M-Form: Strategic Integration in Global Media Firms'. *Organizational Science* 11: 348–55.

Firestone Tire & Rubber Company (various dates, 1960–80). *Minutes of the Executive Committee*. Firestone Corporate Archives, Akron, Ohio. Cited in text as 'executive committee minutes'.

——(various dates, 1960–88). Minutes of the board of directors meetings. Firestone Corporate Archives, Akron, Ohio. Cited in text as 'board minutes'.

——(1945–87). *Annual Reports*. Cited in text as 'annual report'.

——(various dates, 1960–80). Internal financial reports. *Firestone Corporate Archives, Akron, Ohio.*

——(various dates, 1960–80). Remarks of CEO to annual stockholders meetings. *Firestone Corporate Archives, Akron, Ohio. Cited in text as 'remarks'.*

Furtado, E. P. H., and Karan, V. (1990). 'Causes, Consequences and Shareholder Wealth Effects of Management Turnover: A Review of the Empirical Evidence'. *Financial Management* 19/2: 60–75.

Ghemawat, P., and Nalebuff, B. (1985). 'Exit'. *Rand Journal of Economics* 16: 184–94.

—— ——(1990). 'The Devolution of Declining Industries'. *Quarterly Journal of Economics* 105: 167–86.

Gilbert, C. (2002). 'Beyond Resource Allocation: Towards a Process Model of Response to Disruptive Change'. *Harvard Business School Working Paper.*

Gilmour, C. S. (1973). 'The Disinvestment Decision Process'. Unpublished Doctoral Dissertation, Harvard Business School, Boston, Mass.

Glaser, B. G., and Strauss, A. L. (1967). *The Discovery of Grounded Theory.* Hawthorne, NY: Aldine de Gruyter.

Golden, B. R. (1992). 'The Past Is the Past—Or Is It? The Use of Retrospective Accounts as Indicators of Past Strategy'. *Academy of Management Journal* 35: 848–60.

Grant, R. M. (1990). 'Exit and Rationalization in the British Cutlery Industry, 1974–1985', in C. Baden-Fuller (ed.), *Managing Excess Capacity*. Cambridge: Basil Blackwell.

Hannan, M. T., and Freeman, J. H. (1984). 'Structural Inertia and Organizational Change.' *American Sociological Review* 82: 149–64.

—— —— (1989). *Organizational Ecology*. Cambridge, Mass.: Harvard University Press.

Harkelroad, D. (1978). *Pneumatiques Michelin II*. INSEAD Case Services, Imprint 438.

Harrigan, K. R. (1981). 'Deterrents to Divestiture'. *Academy of Management Journal* 24: 306–23.

——Johnson, R. A., and Moesel, D. D. (1994). 'Corporate Divestiture Intensity in Restructuring Firms: Effects of Governance, Strategy and Performance'. *Academy of Management Journal* 37: 1207–51.

Jensen, M. C. (July 1993). 'The Modern Industrial Revolution, Exit, and the Failure of Internal Control Systems'. *The Journal of Finance*.

—— and Meckling, W. H. (1992). 'Specific and General Knowledge, and Organizational Structure'. In Lars Werin and Hans Wijkander (eds.), *Contract Economics*. Oxford: Basil Blackwell, 251–74.

Jeszeck, C. (1986). 'Structural Changes in Collective Bargaining: The U.S. Tire Industry'. *Industrial Relations* 25/3: 229–47.

Jick, T. (1979). 'Mixing Qualitative and Quantitative Methods: Triangulation in Action'. *Administrative Science Quarterly* 24: 602 61.

Kelly, D., and Amburgey, T. L. (1991). 'Organizational Inertia and Momentum: A Dynamic Model of Strategic Change'. *Academy of Management Journal* 34/3: 591–612.

Leonard-Barton, D. (1990). 'A Dual Methodology for Case Studies: Synergistic Use of a Longitudinal Single Site with Replicated Multiple Sites'. *Organization Science* 1/3: 248–66.

Lieberman, M. B. (1990). 'Exit from Declining Industries: "Shakeout" or "Stakeout"?' *RAND Journal of Economics* 21: 538–54.

Lovas, B., and Ghoshal, S. (2000). 'Strategy as Guided Evolution'. *Strategic Management Journal* 21: 875–96.

Love, S., and Giffels, D. (1998). *Wheels of Fortune: The Story of Rubber in Akron*. Akron, Ohio: University of Akron Press.

March, J. G. (1991). 'The Evolution of Evolution', in J. A. C. Baum and J. V. Singh (eds.), *Evolutionary Dynamics of Organizations*. New York: Oxford University Press, 39–49.

Miner, A. S. (1994). 'Seeking Adaptive Advantage: Evolutionary Theory and Managerial Action', in J. A. C. Baum and J. V. Singh, (eds.), *Evolutionary Dynamics of Organizations*, New York: Oxford University Press, 76–89.

Mintzberg, H. (1978). 'Patterns in Strategy Formation'. *Management Science* 24: 934–48.

—— and McHugh, A. (1985). 'Strategy Formulation in an Adhocracy'. *Administrative Science Quarterly* 30: 160–97.

—— and Waters, J. A. (1985). 'Of Strategies, Deliberate and Emergent'. *Strategic Management Journal* 6/3: 257–72.

Modern Tire Dealer (November 1971). 'Is the Ford Tire Coming?'

National Tire Dealer and Retreader Association (various years). National Survey of Wholesale Prices, National Tire Dealers Association, Washington, DC.

Noda, T., and Bower, J. L. (1996). 'Strategy Making as Iterated Processes of Resource Allocation'. *Strategic Management Journal*, Summer Special Issue 17: 159–92.

Pascale, R. T. (Spring 1984). 'Perspectives on Strategy: The Real Story Behind Honda's Success'. *California Management Review*, 47–72.

Pettigrew, A. M. (1990). 'Longitudinal Field Research on Change: Theory and Practice'. *Organization Science* 1: 267–92.

Pfeffer, J., and Salancik, G. R. (1978). *The External Control of Organizations: A Resource Dependence Perspective*. New York: Harper & Row.

Porter, M. E. (1980). *Competitive Strategy*. New York: Free Press.

Quinn, J. B. (1980). *Strategies for Change: Logical Incrementalism*. Homewood, Ill.: Irwin.

Ravenscroft, D. J., and Scherer, F. M. (1987). *Mergers, Selloffs and Economic Efficiency*. Washington, DC: Brookings Institution.

Robinson, S. L. (1996). 'Trust and Breach of the Psychological Contract'. *Administrative Science Quarterly* 41: 574–99.

—— Kratz, M. S., and Rousseau, D. M. (1994). 'Changing Obligations and the Psychological Contract: A Longitudinal Study'. *Academy of Management Journal* 37: 137–52.

Ross, J., and Staw, B. M. (1993). 'Organizational Escalation and Exit: Lessons from the Shoreham Nuclear Power Plant'. *Academy of Management Journal* 36: 701–32.

Rousseau, D. M. (1995). *Psychological Contracts in Organizations*. London: Sage.

Stevenson, H. H., and Jarillo, J. C. (1990). 'A Paradigm of Entrepreneurship: Entrepreneurial Management'. *Strategic Management Journal* 11: 17–27.

Strauss, A., and Corbin, J. (1994). 'Grounded Theory Methodology: An Overview', in N. K. Denzin and Y. S. Lincoln (eds.), *Handbook of Qualitative Research*. Thousand Oaks, Calif.: Sage, 273–85.

—— —— (1990). *Basics of Qualitative Research: Grounded Theory Procedures and Techniques*. Newbury Park, Calif.: Sage.

Sull, D. (1997). 'No Exit: Overcapacity and Plant Closure in the U.S. Tire Industry'. *The Academy of Management Best Paper Proceedings*, 45–9.

—— (1999). 'The Dynamics of Standing Still: Firestone Tire and Rubber and the Radial Revolution'. *Business History Review* 73: 430–64.

—— (2003). *Revival of the Fittest: Why Good Companies Go Bad and How Great Managers Remake Them*. Boston, Mass.: Harvard Business School Press.

—— Tedlow, R., and Rosenbloom, R. (1997). 'Managerial Commitments and Technological Change in the U.S. Tire Industry'. *Industrial and Corporate Change* 6: 461–501.

Teece, D. J., Pisano, G., and Shuen, A. (1997). 'Dynamic Capabilities and Strategic Management'. *Strategic Management Journal* 18: 509–34.

Tushman, M. L., and Anderson, P. (1986). 'Technological Discontinuities and Organizational Environments'. *Administrative Science Quarterly* 31: 439–65.

—— and Romanelli, E. (1985). 'Organizational Evolution: A Metamorphosis Model of Convergence and Reorientation', in L. L. Cummings and B. M. Staw (eds.), *Research in Organizational Behavior* Greenwich, CT: JAI, vii. 171–222.

United Rubber Workers (1988). 'The Changing U.S. Tire Industry'. Unpublished manuscript, United Rubber Workers, Akron, Ohio.

Van de Ven, A. H. (1992). 'Suggestions for Studying Strategy Process: A Research Note'. *Strategic Management Journal,* Summer Special Issue, 13: 169–88.

Weick, K. E. (1979). *The Social Psychology of Organizing.* Boston, Mass.: Addison-Wesley.

Wruck, K. M. (1994). 'Financial Policy, Internal Control and Performance: Sealed Air Corporation's Leveraged Special Dividend'. *Journal of Financial Economics* 36: 157–92.

Yin, R. K. (1989). *Case Study Research: Design and Methods.* Newbury Park, Calif.: Sage.

8

The Process of International Expansion: Comparing Established Firms and Entrepreneurial Start-ups

Walter Kuemmerle

Introduction

The study of processes of international expansion of firms has a long tradition within the process literature. Yet, this stream of research is somewhat thin when compared to the overall body of work on resource allocation processes (RAP) as well as when compared to research on motives for international expansion of firms. There are several possible explanations for this. First, process research typically includes a substantial component of fieldwork. This type of research is hard enough when it is performed within one country, and considerably more challenging when it involves extended visits to multiple countries. Also, process research typically examines rather complex phenomena, and researchers might deliberately limit themselves to one country in order to control for variance.

So, research on international expansion processes might be challenging, but it is also quite insightful—and increasingly important as more and more firms establish significant operations outside their home country (OECD 1996). The purpose of this research is to investigate how firms, large and small, make resource allocation decisions for international expansion. The research seeks to address a gap in the process literature, not just on the international dimension, regarding differences and similarities between large established firms and fast-growing entrepreneurial firms.

This chapter consists of four sections. I will first review the relevant literature on international expansion and argue that large established firms have traditionally followed a product-life-cycle model even though the opportunities and needs have changed over the last decade. Entrepreneurial start-up firms, on the other hand, have only recently started to expand abroad. I will also review the literature on resource allocation and argue that established firms have generally followed a resource allocation process dominated by firm-specific structures. But entrepreneurs, or a few key individuals around them, often drove resource allocation decisions in entrepreneurial firms. The second section examines larger samples of resource allocation decisions in established firms and in entrepreneurial start-up firms. The third section compares some qualitative evidence from the two samples in detail. The fourth section concludes.

International Expansion and Resource Allocation Processes

The Rationale for International Expansion

Why do firms expand abroad? Essentially, there are two reasons. Either firms seek to sell products and services in foreign markets or they seek to source certain inputs abroad that are simply unavailable or much more expensive at home. Firms might also carry out both activities, and in fact, many firms do so over time. The next question then becomes: why are not all firms present everywhere around the world? The basic answer is that national borders continue to represent distinct barriers to factor mobility. These barriers include language, customs, norms, different time zones, geographic distance, and many other factors not existing within countries, at least not to the same degree as across borders. Many of these barriers are firm-specific. For example, an older firm might have a broader stock of managerial knowledge about its products and processes that enables it to expand into an additional country at lower cost than a start-up firm. In addition, many of these barriers are unilateral at the country level. For example, it is still more difficult to sell an American manufactured car in Japan than it is to sell a Japanese manufactured car in the United States. Thus, barriers to factor mobility across country borders and heterogeneity in firm-specific capabilities continue to exist and lead to observed heterogeneity in cross-border expansion of firms.

Despite powerful trade blocks such as the EU and NAFTA in the late twentieth century, international trade is still very costly (Ghemawat 2001). Even in such well-integrated goods market pairs as the United States and Canada, there is considerable price volatility.

According to one estimate, to create the price volatility caused by the US–Canada border requires more than 2,500 miles within the United States (Engel and Rogers 1996). International trade is still the simplest form of international expansion. Not as simple is establishing and maintaining a cross-border network of manufacturing and R&D sites. A cross-border network is much more complex and costly than international trade because a firm needs to create a dense mesh of intrafirm connections among different units to make such a network fruitful (Bartlett and Ghoshal 1989; Doz and Prahalad 1991).

Yet, many costs of doing business on an international scale have decreased substantially over the years. For example, a three-minute telephone call from New York City to London cost $717.70 in 1927 and $0.84 in 1999 (all in 1999 US dollars).[1] Shipping a 150-pound parcel by air from New York City to Hong Kong cost $2,188.00 in 1960 and decreased to $389.00 by 1999 (in 1999 US dollars). Even more dramatic, transporting a container via ship from Los Angeles to Hong Kong cost $10,268.00 in 1970 and a mere $1,900.00 in 1999 (in 1999 US dollars) (US Department of Commerce 1971, p. 57; 2000, p. 164; U.S. Bureau of Census 2001, p. 716; 1929, p. 153; Air Traffic Conference of America 2000, p. 32; 1961, p. 58). These developments have enabled all types of firm to expand activities across borders at an unprecedented rate.

In earlier work, I developed and tested a distinction of motives for foreign direct investment based on knowledge flows. I found that firms carried out foreign direct investment either to create new capabilities or to exploit existing firm-specific capabilities. I labeled the former motive home-base-augmenting and the latter motive home-base-exploiting (Kuemmerle 1999a). Home-base-augmenting investment occurs when firms seek to capture spillovers in a foreign environment with the intention of enhancing the firm's capabilities. An example would be a firm establishing a research site in proximity to the home base of a major foreign competitor or in proximity to a major university. A firm typically will choose a home-base-augmenting investment over acquiring a technology license if the firm expects to create new and valuable knowledge at that site that could not be licensed from anywhere or only at a higher cost. Home-base-exploiting investment occurs when a firm seeks to exploit its capabilities through a local presence rather than through exporting or granting technology licenses. An example would be a manufacturing plant in a foreign country established to benefit from lower labor cost or to shorten response times to local market demand.

I showed that between 1955 and 1996, the frequency of home-base-augmenting investments relative to home-base-exploiting investments had increased dramatically for a group of thirty-two multinational enterprises. Between 1955 and 1965, only 7 per cent of new investments in R&D sites abroad by these firms were home-base-augmenting; but between 1986 and 1995, that number had increased to 40 per cent (Kuemmerle 1999*b*). Note that whereas that investigation pertained only to new R&D sites, the general finding is applicable to manufacturing sites and sales subsidiaries as well. Many manufacturing sites abroad might be established primarily to exploit firm-specific capabilities in a country where labor and other costs are lower. We can categorize these investments as home-base-exploiting. For example, this is the case with many pharmaceutical manufacturing facilities in Puerto Rico and with BMW's manufacturing plant in Thailand. Other manufacturing facilities might have a strong home-base-augmenting intention where the firm actively seeks to learn from the local environment. Northpole, the world's largest maker of camping tents, operates a large facility in China. This is not just to benefit from low labor costs, but also to monitor potential spillovers from a large number of suppliers of raw materials such as fiber, fabrics, and dyestuffs in the region.

The literature on international expansion reflects the shift towards home-base-augmenting investments. In the 1960s and 1970s, scholars described and analyzed a cycle where firms would first manufacture at home for domestic consumption, then export, then move to establish factories abroad for local consumption and finally, once these factories had reached a sufficient quality level, service even the home market with goods manufactured abroad (Hymer 1976; Vernon 1979). More recent studies have focused on alternative motives for international expansion, namely on investments that are home-base-augmenting in nature (Cantwell 1991; Chung and Alcacer 2001; Kuemmerle 1999*b*; Wesson 1993).

Home-base-augmenting investments became more prevalent for three reasons. First, and as documented above, the cost of doing business across borders declined dramatically because of technological progress and because of the elimination of a wide range of tariffs, at least between major industrialized and emerging market countries. Second, a supply-side shift of knowledge occurred. The quantity and quality of spillovers that firms could capture from universities and from other firms increased. Universities around the world started to actively develop, offer, and price intellectual property for use by firms, and firms sought such spillovers (Hakanson and Nobel 1993; Henderson

and Cockburn 1996; Jaffe 1989). Third, a perceived demand-side shift
for knowledge occurred. In many instances, firms realized that their
technological knowledge stock at the home base, although superior in
quality, would not enable them to survive in the long run. Knowledge
in entirely separate fields of technology was becoming increasingly
relevant for new products in the long run. Fumio Kodama has labeled
this phenomenon 'technology fusion' (Coombs, Narandren, and
Richards 1996; Kodama 1992).

It should come as no surprise that for an established firm home-base-
augmenting international expansion typically entails higher levels of
uncertainty than home-base-exploiting investments. In the latter case,
the firm typically has a good understanding of the technology and of
the requirements for making such an investment successful. By contrast, in the case of home-base-augmenting investments, firms seek to
capture spillovers that are generally only vaguely defined *ex ante* and
often do not even exist yet by the time the firm makes an expansion
decision. In addition, there is uncertainty about how well the firm's
home base will be able to absorb and process the newly created
knowledge. The not-invented-here syndrome has been described as a
powerful inhibitor of knowledge absorption and exploitation within the
firm (Katz and Allen 1982). As I will discuss below, this has important
implications for the resource allocation process.

For start-up firms, the opposite applies: home-base-augmenting
investments typically involve less uncertainty than home-base exploiting ones. First, start-up firms typically do not have a large number of
entrenched organizational routines that would make intrafirm knowledge absorption difficult. Rather, start-up firms do not have a lot firm-
specific capabilities yet and are in a learning mode (Bhide 1999).
Second, home-base-exploiting investments at start-up firms typically
involve considerable fixed costs, not just for capital equipment but also
for creating a minimum set of administrative routines between the
foreign site and the firm's home-base. These costs can put the entire
firm's survival at risk if free cash flows are still volatile or, even worse, if
free cash flows are negative and remaining funds might not be sufficient
to reach break-even.

The Resource Allocation Process and International Expansion

The expansion of firms across country borders is associated with
considerable uncertainty about benefits and costs of such a decision.
In practice, the basic economic aspects of an international expansion
decision are generally more clouded by a lack of hard data than

comparable domestic expansion decisions. This lack of reliable data affects both established firms and start-ups, but there are important differences between the two types of firms. This section will first discuss the international expansion of established firms and then focus on the international expansion of start-up firms.

In established multinational enterprises, at least several, if not many, individuals are involved in the decision-making process for a new subsidiary. Additional uncertainty arises from conflicting views among the managers involved (Cyert and March 1963). Essentially, all the classic challenges described by studies of resource allocation processes apply here. These include: (1) a lack of transparency regarding the long-term outcome of managerial decisions, and (2) a lack of alignment between managerial incentives (at different levels within the firm) and the overall strategy of the firm (Bower 1970; Burgelman 1983). Because organizations are 'fundamentally political entities' (Pfeffer 1992), senior managers should strive to design resource allocation processes that make constructive use of multiple managerial perspectives at different levels in the organization and that encourage an open dialogue about (sometimes radically) different choices, all while rewarding managers involved for their relative contribution to the decision. This is, of course, much easier said than done. For example, several researchers have documented that investments that enhance an established firm's current competences are undertaken more rapidly than investments that jeopardize existing firm competences for the benefit of establishing new ones (Christensen and Bower 1996; Tushman and Anderson 1986).

In the international context, these typical challenges are compounded by all the issues that make international business more complex than domestic business: national culture, business practices, consumer preferences, different local factor conditions, and differences in the rule of law.

What do we know specifically about resource allocation processes in an international context? It turns out, quite little. An early study had documented the haphazard nature of foreign expansion (Aharoni 1966), whereas other authors had argued that international expansion was a gradual process where discrete expansion decisions were not necessarily well planned or rational. Furthermore, only in very few instances did managers involved in an expansion decision really consider overall firm strategy and synergies with the rest of the firm's existing international network. This lack of rationality in expansion decisions seemed to be more pronounced in larger firms and if a larger number of individuals were involved in the decision making (Johanson and Vahlne 1990; Malnight 1995).

At the same time, managers seem to learn from international expansion, even though their initial investment decisions might be unsuccessful. In my own research, I have found that managers often systematically underestimated the cost of geographic expansion (Kuemmerle and Ellis 1999). In line with this finding, a study of established multinational firms documented that these firms had a reduced risk of failure as they sought *further* to expand their presence, whereas firms taking their first expansion steps often failed (Mitchell, Shaver, and Yeung 1992). These findings suggest a punctuated equilibrium of either a sizeable international presence or no presence abroad at all. Also, cross-border joint ventures seem to be a somewhat inferior alternative to fully owned subsidiaries, at least as far as the management of intrafirm knowledge is concerned. A recent study has argued quite convincingly that fully owned subsidiaries are better facilitators of knowledge flows across country borders than cross-border joint ventures (Almeida 2002).

In general, process rather than structure seems to be the important driver of success in multinational firms. Bartlett and Ghoshal have argued that the transnational corporation is successful because it prepares managers for natural conflicts that arise in an ever-changing matrix structure (Bartlett and Ghoshal 1990). A study of cross-border joint ventures also has argued that process variables, such as resource allocation and knowledge internalization, have a stronger effect on the success of a cross-border joint venture than structural variables such as duration or ownership (Hamel 1991).

With this in mind, how do resource allocation processes for international expansion in large multinational firms and in fast-growing entrepreneurial firms compare? The literature on this topic is very small, presumably because the phenomenon of young firms expanding abroad is relatively new. However, the number of so-called global start-ups has risen sharply over the last five years. Global start-ups can be defined as firms that establish dedicated sites abroad during the first year of their existence (Kuemmerle 2002). Dramatically lower costs of doing business across borders have created the opportunity for entrepreneurs to expand abroad early and to preempt competitors from copying the basics of a business idea.

Global start-ups are different from established multinational firms in at least three important ways. First, it is typical that they are strongly influenced by the personalities of the founders; and during the early days of the firm, the founders' capabilities dominate relative to the capabilities of the firm as a whole. Thus, resource allocation decisions to expand abroad are driven primarily by the founders and their vision or by early employees of the firm who often have risk profiles similar to the founders. Several studies have found that prior international exposure of founders has a strong positive influence on a young firm's propensity to expand abroad (McDougall and Oviatt 1996). Organizational routines and the internal structural context, as defined by Bower, play a less important role in start-ups than in established firms (Bower 1970).[2] This might give the start-up firm some advantages, because decision-making processes are faster and less encumbered by structural context factors than in established firms. However, it can also put start-up firms at a disadvantage because, presumably, not all structural context is bad. The inability of many start-up firms eventually to become a successful multinational firm often has a lot to do with the lack of attention that the founders paid to the nurturing of a conducive structural context inside the firm.

Second, start-up firms are quite resource-constrained and carry little overhead because of their small size. This makes resource allocation decisions more transparent than in large firms. Budgeting systems in large firms typically use an internal benchmark that is set by the CFO's office, such as a rate of return or a payback period, to evaluate projects. Not surprisingly, most expansion projects that reach the relevant decision-making body show that they pass these previously set hurdles. Often, this is not a reflection of the true nature of the project, but a result of 'gaming' the system—forecasts get tweaked so that the project passes the hurdle. This happens particularly when the firm does not have a reliable system of *ex-post* evaluation for past expansion decisions. In start-up firms, things are different. There are hardly any set return hurdles; typically, the most important constraint is available cash. And because the firm is in survival mode, it monitors its cash carefully. Because of the small size of the firm, the entrepreneurs are almost always directly involved in important expansion decisions, especially regarding geographic expansion (Kuemmerle 2002). And their continued involvement in the firm ensures a post-investment review of the critical assumptions. In summary, in start-up firms there are few, if any, set hurdles in the first place. Also, start-up firms are sufficiently small that those who make a geographic expansion decision will be directly confronted with its outcome.

Third, most entrepreneurs and senior managers in start-up firms readily acknowledge that they are in a learning mode. This has a rather fundamental effect on their approach toward resource allocation processes. Most decisions will be seen as trials and therefore monitored more carefully than in many large firms (Bhide 1992; Sahlman, Stevenson, and Roberts 1999). In learning mode, start-up firms generally have an easier time reversing an international expansion decision. Online auction firm eBay recently shut down its operations in Japan, a country where Yahoo had developed a leading market share because of eBay's late entry and because Yahoo's auctions were free of charge. It is doubtful that the average established multinational firm would have taken such a drastic exit decision so quickly.

Venture capital funding, which many start-ups receive, is further conducive to a learning mode. Venture capital financiers prefer to release financing to entrepreneurial firms in stages. This encourages spending discipline and a periodic thorough review of the business. It is likely that start-up firms benefit from this initial spending discipline even beyond the time during which venture capitalists are involved in the firm.

All this is not to say that established firms always fall short in their resource allocation processes when it comes to competing against entrepreneurial start-ups. Some established firms succeed in maintaining the entrepreneurial culture of their resource allocation process throughout their international expansion. One detailed case study documented that at 3M a combination of several factors led to a uniquely entrepreneurial resource allocation process. It included a transparent information system and simple but ambitious performance goals, as well as an understanding among senior managers that their most important role was to coach junior managers as they learned how to allocate resources and a culture that cherished well-intended failure (Bartlett and Mohammed 1994).

Another study examined the corporate venturing process in an established firm and found that an internal structural context that allowed for entrepreneurial activity at the operational level and enabled middle managers to understand conceptually the link between such activity and outcomes was conducive to successful corporate venturing (Burgelman 1983). Finally, a study of foreign subsidiaries of diversified multinational firms found that the performance of these subsidiaries was positively correlated with the presence of local entrepreneurial culture within the subsidiary (Birkinshaw, Hood, and Jonsson 1998).

Overall, it seems challenging for established firms to keep their resource allocation processes flexible and transparent over time, particularly when it comes to investment projects in untried areas that require improvisation (Scott 1987). A key problem in such projects is that ideas get intercepted and do not 'bubble up' from the front line of management to the top of the firm.

Comparing International Expansion Decisions

I have argued that in established firms home-base-augmenting investments are typically associated with a higher level of uncertainty than home-base exploiting investments. First, because the outcome of a learning effort (and that is what home-base-augmenting investments are about) is generally less predictable than the application of an existing capability to a market opportunity. Second, because the not-invented-here syndrome might limit the absorption of new knowledge into the firm. Also, the internal structural context probably drives managers to suggest predictable projects (i.e. home-base-exploiting ones) rather than uncertain projects.

I have also argued that in start-up firms the opposite is true, and home-base-exploiting investments are associated with higher degrees of uncertainty than home-base-augmenting ones. Start-ups are generally very resource constrained, and most home-base-exploiting investments involve considerably higher fixed costs than home-base-augmenting ones do. Furthermore, start-up firms typically have fewer specific capabilities that they can exploit internationally, and there is more uncertainty associated with the long-term value of these existing capabilities than in large established firms. In eBay's early days, for example, it was not at all clear that running online auctions was a capability that would be difficult to replicate for others and hence valuable. It was even less clear whether this capability had a similar value outside the United States. Would consumers in the United Kingdom and Japan accept eBay's business model as enthusiastically as they did in the United States? Thus, eBay's decision to expand abroad was more risky than the decision of an established auction house such as Sotheby's to set up shop in an additional country would have been.

Finally, most start-up firms that decide to expand beyond their borders will probably first invest abroad with a home-base-augmenting objective, because their business at home is still very much in an experimental mode and there is much to be learned by further refining the business model. Using the framework of Cohen and Levinthal, one can argue that start-up firm's 'absorptive capacity' is high (Cohen and Levinthal 1994) and that this reduces the uncertainty of home-base-augmenting investments.

If one maps the two types of investments on a matrix where one axis measures the degree of stability of the internal structural context for resource allocation processes and where the other axis measures the degree of uncertainty associated with the investment, Fig. 8.1 emerges.

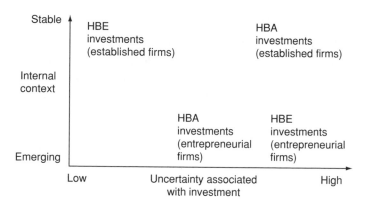

HBA = Home-Base-Augmenting investments intended to increase the firms' set of capabilities
HBE = Home-Base-Exploiting investments intended to make better use of firms' capabilities

Figure 8.1 Resource allocation for international expansion: start-up firms vs. established firms

This is a behavioral model derived from the careful examination of a number of case studies and from the existing literature. It suggests that for established firms, the relative uncertainty of home-base-augmenting investments versus home-base-exploiting investments is larger than for start-up firms. It also suggests that for start-up firms, home-base-augmenting investments are less uncertain than home-base-exploiting investments.

One way to verify the information in Fig. 8.1 would be to study a number of expansion cases in detail and to measure the degree of uncertainty associated with each. Because there are considerable measurement problems associated with this approach, I suggest a simple alternative measure: relative timing of home-base-augmenting versus home-base-exploiting investments. One would imagine that established firms and start-ups alike would carry out the *less uncertain* type of investment *first*, even though the motives for this behavior might differ.

In established firms, the tendency towards carrying out less uncertain expansion investments first might be driven by operating managers' seeking to maximize their private benefits. If intrafirm information systems are imperfect and if the internal structural context is more focused on punishing failure (well intended or not) than rewarding success, operating managers will prefer to propose and champion low uncertainty expansion investments. In start-up firms, on the other hand, the tendency toward carrying out less uncertain geographic expansion investments most likely will be driven more by the firm's desire to survive during its critical early stages than by a manager's desire to maximize private rather than firm benefits. The reason is that maximizing private benefits by managers is detected more easily in start-up firms, and very often the principals themselves rather than the agents make key resource allocation decisions. And the principals (i.e. the founders) are strongly focused on firm survival.

The assumption that more uncertain investments will be undertaken later than less uncertain investments hinges on the premises that the state of the world at more distant points in time is more difficult to predict than at closer points in time and that managers and entrepreneurs have a strong interest in the survival of their firms. There is little doubt about the two premises in the mainstream literature on economics and sociology.

The question arises, however, why either type of firm would carry out the more uncertain type of investment at all. In established firms, the answer lies in the fact that in the long run top managers will advocate the more uncertain type of investment and that under their influence the internal structural context for this type of investment becomes more favorable. Often, such a change in internal structural context will be temporary because it is associated with the newness of a significant change, such as a new CEO taking charge (Khurana and Nohria 2002). In start-up firms, the answer lies in the fact that if the young firm survives, its core business presumably stabilizes and generates free cash flows that can be used for geographic expansion decisions involving high fixed costs.

This reasoning leads to three hypotheses:

H1. In established firms, geographic expansion decisions of home-base-exploiting nature will occur before geographic expansion decisions of home-base-augmenting nature.

H2. In start-up firms, geographic expansion decisions of home-base-augmenting nature will occur before geographic expansion decisions of home-base-exploiting nature.

H3. In start-up firms, the time-lag between geographic expansion of low and high levels of uncertainty is shorter than in established firms.

Data and Analysis

Data for the established firms is drawn from an analysis of all R&D sites that a sample of thirty-two multinational firms in the electronics and pharmaceutical industries established up to 1995 anywhere outside of their home countries. The firms were domiciled in the United States, Japan, and Europe and are among the largest in their respective industry and country (or region, for Europe.) I sampled for firm size; and whenever a firm declined to cooperate on the detailed survey, I approached the next-largest firm. The two industries were selected because they were technologically intensive and because previous case studies had reported a high level of cross-border investment activity in these industries. The United States, Japan, and Europe were selected because the world's leading firms in these industries are domiciled in those countries.

Altogether, 156 expansion decisions across borders were examined. I also examined eighty-two domestic R&D sites. The sites abroad were established in nineteen different host countries with a preference towards industrialized host nations. Each firm made on average about five investments in R&D sites abroad. In a survey, senior R&D managers at all thirty-two firms were asked to provide detailed data on all R&D sites and to quantify to what degree these sites carried out either home-base-exploiting or home-base-augmenting activities. The majority of sites fell clearly into either category. The survey was complemented through multiple (typically three) structured interviews with managers at each firm. During these structured interviews, we sought further information on the international expansion process and clarified any open questions from the survey.

Ninety-six sites were primarily of a home-base-augmenting nature, whereas sixty sites were primarily of a home-base-exploiting nature (Kuemmerle 1999*b*). Each site represented a sizeable investment. Home-base-augmenting sites were significantly more likely (t-test, $p > 0.001$) to be located close to a university, whereas home-base-exploiting sites were significantly more likely to be located close to an important market and/or a previously existing manufacturing plant. As mentioned earlier in this chapter, the relative importance of home-base-augmenting sites increased particularly between the years 1986 and 1995. This is in line with the argument that, over time, home-base-augmenting expansion became easier to accomplish or more necessary, or both.

The mean establishment date for home-base-exploiting sites was 1981 (standard deviation: 10.7 years) and for home-base-exploiting sites 1985 (standard deviation: 7.0 years). The comparative statistics confirm our first hypothesis. On average, home-base-augmenting sites were established about four years after home-base-exploiting sites (t-test, $p = 0.06$). These are average values for all sites established.[3]

Data for the start-up firms comes from a sample of firms I studied between 1996 and 2002. In constructing this sample, I intentionally selected entrepreneurial start-ups with a wide geographic variety of home bases. I also sought out firms that had some cross-border orientation of their founders (but not necessarily any cross-border activity.) Overall, I sought a sample that represented firms from most major industrialized countries as well as firms from a wide range of emerging markets countries. The firms in the sample were active in twenty-six countries, and the sample represents eighteen home-base countries. Sixteen out of the twenty-seven companies have their home base in industrialized countries.

Together with a research associate I visited and studied each firm in great detail. Just as in the sample of established firms, all cross-border activities were documented and classified after multiple interviews at each firm. Two researchers coded international expansion activities (home-base-augmenting, home-base-exploiting, timing of expansion, etc.). Initial inter-rater reliability was very high. Wherever differences occurred, we went back to the original interview data and archival data and sought to clarify differences. Also, we checked that the results described below are not materially affected if the few instances where coding differences occurred are included in either category of expansion decision.

In contrast to the sample of established firms that were all domiciled in industrialized countries, nine out of twenty-seven firms in the start-up sample were domiciled in emerging markets countries. Also, even though I sampled for firm size in the sample of established firms, I sampled for firms' cross-border activity potential in the start-up sample. The approach of sampling for variance in cross-border activity potential makes sense because it would have been virtually impossible to study the entire population of start-up firms in just one country, let alone several countries, at the level of detail needed to answer the research questions of this chapter.

Results indicate that twenty-four out of twenty-seven firms carried out home-base-augmenting activities. These activities, contrary to the sample of established firms, involve *less* uncertainty than home-base-exploiting activities, which were carried out by twenty-three firms. Twenty out of twenty-seven firms (74%) carried out both types of activity, and in these cases home-base-augmenting activities preceded home-base-exploiting activities by 1.5 years on average (t-test; p = 0.0004). In seventeen out of twenty cases, home-base-augmenting activities preceded home-base-exploiting ones. This offers support for the second hypothesis that start-up firms will perform less uncertain activities first, just as established firms do.

In contrast to established firms, the mean time difference between performing the less and more uncertain activities is only 1.5 years as opposed to four years (t-test, p = 0.0001.) This offers support for the third hypothesis. In combination with data from field interviews, this suggests that start-ups (relative to established firms) pursue more risky international expansion more aggressively.

Finally, it is interesting that all home-base-augmenting expansions by start-up firms occurred into industrialized countries. Field interviews revealed that in these countries, consumer demand was sufficiently sophisticated and technology was sufficiently developed that the entrepreneurs felt they could capture spillovers. Recent research on the legal rules covering the protection of corporate shareholders and creditors has argued that common law countries generally have the strongest level of such protection and French civil law countries the weakest, with German and Scandinavian civil law countries falling somewhere in the middle (La Porta *et al.* 1998). It is possible that these legal traditions also will affect the ability of foreign entrants to capture local spillovers. I found that most home-base-augmenting investments in both the established firm sample and start-up sample were carried out into common law and German civil law countries, thus supporting the hypothesis that legal regimes affect not just shareholder protection but also the ability to capture spillovers. This question warrants further detailed investigation.

Qualitative Evidence on the Resource Allocation Process for International Expansion

Decisions on highly uncertain cross-border investments pose considerable threats to the managers and entrepreneurs involved in them. Managers fear for their personal future within the firm, and entrepreneurs for their personal fortune and legacy. Even though these investments might make economic sense in the long term for the firm as a whole, managers and entrepreneurs might shy away from them. This raises the question of what aspects of the internal structural context are conducive to such decisions being taken in the interest of the firm's long-term survival and growth. As discussed above, previous research outlined two elements of successful resource allocation processes: (1) transparency of the link between decisions and outcomes, and (2) an alignment of individual managerial incentives with overall long-term performance of the firm at all levels. But what specifically does this mean?

In this section, I will present four case studies on international expansion decisions that were derived from studying the firms in the sample. Certain elements of the cases have been disguised, but this does not materially affect the aspects of the cases relevant to this discussion. The purpose of these cases is twofold. First, the cases identify and illustrate some salient features of internal structural context. Second, the cases further support the argument that home-base-augmenting investments were more uncertain in established firms, whereas home-base-exploiting investments were more uncertain in start-up firms. Two cases concern established firms and two cases concern start-up firms. For each category of firm, I present one case where the resource allocation process for international expansion can be considered successful and where it can be considered unsuccessful.

An Investment by Company A

Company A is a large research-intensive pharmaceutical firm based in Europe. The firm employed 3,200 people in R&D and already operated two home-base-exploiting facilities abroad by the time a number of bench scientists suggested that the firm open its first home-base-augmenting facility in the United States. Their initiative was triggered by the fact that a large US-based rival had recently developed genetically engineered human insulin in collaboration with a biotechnology firm. Scientists at Company A felt strongly that their firm should seek to capture similar spillovers by establishing an R&D site in either Boston, San Francisco, or San Diego. Two capable researchers in their early thirties approached their group leader with the idea and prepared an informal memorandum.

Company A's internal structural context was quite hierarchical in terms of both resource allocation and communication processes. Most senior managers originally had trained as scientists and completed a science career track within the firm before shifting to a management career track. Relative to Company B (see below) career paths at Company A were clearly delineated. Also, corporate staff played a key role in the interactions between operating managers and top management.

Hierarchical and structured information flow also affected the proposed project. The scientists' group leader approached his boss. This person in turn approached a member of corporate staff who managed the investment review committee for the pharmaceuticals division. Informal feedback from this member of corporate staff was negative. He argued that the investment was too risky and that top management already had considered and rejected similar plans in the past. The plan died.

Eighteen months later, the scientists were surprised when they learned that a member of the executive board had just struck a deal with a leading scientist at a US university to establish a sixty-person R&D center on that university's hospital campus. The deal was structured as a ten-year joint venture. The decision primarily had been driven by the executive's decision 'to finally get something done in the U.S.'. Negotiations with the university were managed almost single-handedly by the executive and two senior members of his staff who were trained and had worked as scientists but had moved on to managerial functions more than eight years earlier. After corporate staff prepared a formal proposal, the investment committee approved the decision. In fact, in this case the investment proposal was less of a proposal and more of a document that was rubberstamped *ex post*. Figure 8.2 visualizes the rough sequence of events.

From its very start, the new lab had lacked deep connections to the firm's bench scientists, and it was always viewed as the pet project of the executive board member who had initiated it. Staff at the lab realized during its early phase of operation that there was an unexpected level of independence from the firm's home base. One staff member felt that she was working at a university lab, but without the teaching requirement. This set the tone for the lab's working climate and thrust of productivity towards scholarly achievement and scientific publications. The new lab did not do very well for Company A. Even though its scientific output was quite respectable, almost none of the results made it into the firm's product pipeline.

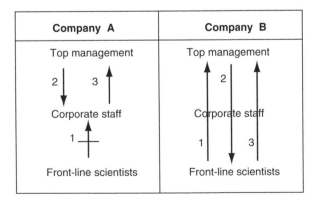

Figure 8.2 Resource allocation for home-base augmenting facilities in established firms

It is not clear whether the original bottom-up initiative by the two scientists would have fared better. In Company A, the perceived uncertainty of a home-base-augmenting investment was caused not so much by underlying technical uncertainty of the science covered in the new lab but by the firm's difficulties to absorb knowledge created at a new site in a foreign country. Two factors contributed to these difficulties. First, there was a desire by managers and scientists at the firm's home base to assert the home base's capabilities, the innate not-invented-here syndrome. Second, and possibly more importantly, the process of the lab's establishment was handled in a top-down fashion, yet top management did not play an active and nurturing role in integrating the lab into the firm's network. Specifically, top management did not succeed in framing the decision to establish a home-base-augmenting site in a way that encouraged operating managers to take ownership of the decision. Better framing would have reduced barriers to communication and knowledge transfer within the firm.

An Investment by Company B

Company B, also a European pharmaceutical firm, expanded into the United States with its first home-base-augmenting site. A combination of ambitious goals and open communication pathways characterized Company B's culture. Several operating managers I interviewed characterized the firm's culture as 'tough but fair'. Also, top management took a strong interest in day-to-day activities. During the interviews, one scientist who had worked at both Company A and Company B suggested that the likelihood of a meaningful ad-hoc hallway conversation with a top manager was more likely in Company B than in Company A.

The firm employed approximately 3,000 people in pharmaceutical research at its home base. In 1975, it already had several bench scientists arguing that a home-base-augmenting facility in the United States would make sense for the firm. Top management at the time felt that, whereas in principle this seemed like a good idea, there was not enough knowledge available within the firm on where and how to best invest. However, the project was kept on the radar screen by top management and periodically discussed with bench scientists. My interviews revealed that during these discussions, the success of the firm's potential first home-base-augmenting site was perceived as considerably more uncertain than had been the case for the firm's first home-base-exploiting site fifteen years earlier.

Then the firm's chemicals division acquired a chemicals company in the United States. The acquired firm operated a manufacturing site close to New Haven, Connecticut. Over a period of about one year after the acquisition, and at the initiative of bench scientists with support from corporate staff, a task force evaluated to what degree the acquired firm might offer a base to set up a home-base-augmenting site.

When the formal investment proposal was finally submitted for a site near New Haven, the plan called for an initial size of eighty employees with an expansion to 300 employees over the following eight years. The proposal was accepted, and a taskforce kept working throughout the site's launch to create tight informal connections with the home base.

There were some glitches and mishaps in communication and hiring. For example, some of the initial discoveries at the lab were not transferred to the home base in a timely manner because the managers in charge of the lab wanted to make sure the lab's first output was perfect rather than just good enough. Also, managers who had considerable knowledge about the firm's local manufacturing operations, but knew little about the required profile of scientists, influenced some of the early hiring. Overall, however, the site is considered a success and has contributed considerably to the firm's portfolio of chemical entities. Figure 8.2 shows the sequence of events.

An Investment by Company C

Company C is an entrepreneurial firm started by a telecommunications engineer in Japan to design chips for pagers and cellphones. Due to a variety of factors, including the rigid organization of its employment system and the social perception of failure, Japan has generated few entrepreneurs in the last four decades. Those who started their own firms generally struggled against the odds, especially in their quest to hire qualified employees from established firms. In addition, a lack of sources of external financing led most entrepreneurs to rely on internal financing. This strategy entailed slower growth of entrepreneurial firms.

The entrepreneur at Company C was fairly typical. He had started his firm in 1990 and by 1996 employed about thirty people. Growth had deliberately been slow, but the company was profitable from its early days. Fully aware of the need to import innovative chip design ideas from the booming US telecommunications market, the entrepreneur had started a home-base-augmenting effort by hiring a small group of engineers in the United States. This relationship worked out well, partly because the entrepreneur himself had spent a considerable period of time working in the United States before starting his own firm. The internal structural context for decision making, especially expansion decisions, was fairly patriarchal. The entrepreneur would discuss issues with his coworkers, but he had a 'determined' decision-making style, as one employee called it, and all the entrepreneur's coworkers knew about it. Even though some financing had been provided externally in 1994, financiers were not actively involved in the oversight of the firm.

In 1996, the entrepreneur was asked to design a whole array of chips for a wireless communications system in India. This offer came through a US firm that was selected to supply most of the hardware, such as antennas and transmitters. Prior to that time, Company C had applied its capabilities only in the Japanese market. Bidding for and accepting this order from India would involve frequent trips, as well as a deeper understanding of the country context. Employees within Company C considered this deal to involve a high level of uncertainty, especially when compared to the firm's first home-base augmenting initiative (a design joint venture with a US-based independent chip designer), which had been started a few years earlier. Even though Company C had reached considerable size (manufacturing and a part of the design work were subcontracted), there was no formal feedback loop for investment decisions. The firm had done reasonably well with its ad-hoc style, or so the entrepreneur thought. He decided to go for this opportunity.

The home-base-exploiting effort to India was not successful. Development costs of the product were much higher than expected. But more importantly, the firm's project staff felt overwhelmed by the task of coordinating a project in India. None of them had ever traveled there prior to the project, and few employees were familiar with international business in general. Although this experience did not break the firm, it endangered its survival. The firm had gained its first international expansion experience through a reasonably successful home-base-augmenting site, but it turned out that home-base-exploiting activities were much more challenging than anticipated. The entrepreneur realized that he had overestimated the firm's capabilities, not so much on a technical but on an organizational level.

The case of Company C suggests that staff might have been able to counterbalance the entrepreneur's optimistic estimates; but despite the firm's small size, the internal structural context was not conducive to a formal review of the founder-entrepreneur's assessment. Thus, small firm size, even though it might facilitate direct information flows between operating managers and top management, does not guarantee an internal structural context that is conducive to successful resource allocation under high uncertainty.

An Investment by Company D

Company D is a catalogue-based business-to-business distributor of office supplies in Argentina. Two young entrepreneurs started the company in mid-1996 with funding from experienced local business angels. *Prior* to actually starting operations in early 1997, the entrepreneurs undertook their first home-base-augmenting effort through an extensive visit to various distributors of office supplies in the United States. Their goal was to learn as much as possible about the business because it did not exist in similar form in Argentina at that time and to reduce uncertainty for the initial stages of the business. By contrast, any home-base-exploiting effort at that stage or at a slightly later stage probably would have increased uncertainty for the young firm.

This visit and the contacts that resulted from it turned out to be a very important learning experience for the entrepreneurs, especially because the US firms they visited were quite willing to share knowledge and insights with the two entrepreneurs. From the very start, the company was characterized by ambitious goals (becoming the largest office supply distributor in Argentina, avoiding corruption, providing an opportunity for employees to grow), but also by a strong sense of realism and open communication channels. The company hired a sales staff (divided into 'hunters' and 'gatherers'), created a simple but effective warehouse management system, and outsourced physical distribution to independent truck drivers. By the end of 1999, the firm employed about 200 people and had just reached break-even. The company is one of the few firms I have come across in my studies of entrepreneurial firms that actually met sales and profitability targets from the original business plan.

In late 1999, the company was considering its first home-base-exploiting expansion, and Brazil seemed like the most logical country to expand into. Its market was large, its economy was growing fast, and it was adjacent to Argentina. After a series of negotiations, the company decided to merge with a newly created (and apparently successful) Internet retailer in Brazil. The company decided to do so partly because it was concerned about the challenges of establishing itself in Brazil independently. The two entrepreneurs and several senior employees felt that a local partner might be helpful. About a year later the merger was dissolved because the business of the Internet retailer was not doing well and another objective of the merger, a joint IPO, had to be postponed indefinitely. However, by that time Company D already had established a foothold in Brazil and, with the help of the Internet retailer's brand name, had been able to attract strong local management.

Throughout the home-base-exploiting expansion process, communication within the firm had been open, and all senior staff I interviewed felt that their concerns and views were taken into serious consideration before the entrepreneurs made a decision. The entrepreneurs and senior employees also considered the governance provided by the original investors in Company D helpful. This governance occurred during regular board meetings as well as through informal communications. Despite its relative success in entering Brazil, the company intended to approach future home-base-exploiting investments into other Latin American countries very carefully. This approach would possibly be through franchising, because the entrepreneurs and managers had realized that costs associated with such investments were difficult to estimate.

Figure 8.3 gives an idea of the way in which the investment process worked for uncertain investments in Companies C and D. In the case of Company C, the entrepreneur initiated the decision and pushed it through. There was little input or resistance from his team, quite likely because the team was not expecting that its view would matter much. In Company D, the two entrepreneurs from the very start created an internal structural context geared at considering staff's views in their decisions. They did so even when the company was still very small.

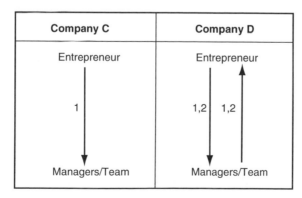

Figure 8.3 Resource allocation for home-base exploiting facilities in start-up firms

The climate at Company D was as ambitious as at Company C, but at Company D communication about highly uncertain investments could be initiated at all levels. This early grooming is most likely going to give Company D an advantage as the firm grows larger and even as additional layers of management are created within the firm.

Resource Allocation and the Role of Internal Structural Context

The four cases suggest that the nature of the internal structural context is a critical determinant for the outcomes of the international expansion decision process, especially when a decision entails significant resource commitments and high levels of uncertainty for the firm. Three aspects of this context are particularly relevant.

First, ideas and investment proposals need to 'bubble up' from operating managers to top management without distortion. The entire resource allocation process needs to be framed as an opportunity to operating managers and corporate staff. This entails a deep understanding among corporate staff not only about the resource allocation process itself but also about substantive matters in an investment proposal and about sources of uncertainty in it. In an ideal case, corporate staff will amplify the pieces of information in the proposal that need particular attention by top management.

Second, top management needs to follow a decision-making process that addresses the uncertainty of an investment proposal by involving all parties within the firm who can contribute to the decision in a sensible way and who will most likely be involved in its implementation. In other words, the resource allocation process needs to be framed as a process that copes with uncertainty partly by creating early ownership of the project among a variety of constituencies within the firm.

Third, top management and operating managers should be keenly aware that highly uncertain investments, such as R&D sites abroad, need intensive monitoring and nurturing immediately after the investment decision. If the investment decision is negative, a consensus should evolve that the quality of the decision-making process was high. This happens primarily through clear and open intra-firm communication and prepares the way for future successful decisions. If the investment decision is positive, the decision needs to be framed so that voluntary ownership for the project evolves almost immediately after the decision at various levels in the firm. Company A represents an example where such a sense of ownership did not evolve.

Established firms face challenges regarding all three aspects. Due to their larger size, established firms have more layers of hierarchy and more formal communication channels than small firms. Thus, it is more likely that investment ideas get distorted or never reach decision makers. Also at large firms, it is more complex to include all parties that might be involved in the implementation in the decision-making process, quite simply because they are numerous. Finally, the implementation and nurturing of the international site during its early phases is challenging because of limited management attention in a large firm.

Entrepreneurial firms face different challenges, especially along the second aspect, i.e. the involvement of all constituencies that can contribute to a sensible investment outcome. Even though investment proposals generally bubble up fairly quickly to entrepreneurs and often even originate from them, a young firm typically lacks the capabilities necessary to assess the international expansion decision. This is particularly true for home-base-exploiting decisions that require a deep understanding of cost structures and actual pace of ramp-up of a local site. Even though all relevant constituents within the firm (operating managers and entrepreneurs) might be involved in the resource allocation process, the entrepreneur often dominates this process so much that a balanced assessment is difficult. Thus, the very strengths of the entrepreneurial firm, namely its smaller size and less formal routines, can represent a disadvantage because they do not give enough voice to those managers who might be able to counterbalance a lopsided view by the entrepreneur. Company C exemplifies this.

Entrepreneurial firms often make up for this lack of deep knowledge about the true risk profile of an expansion decision through a rapid trial and error process. The entrepreneur can thus quickly reverse a decision that proves not tenable. Company D's decision to unmerge from its Brazilian partner after one year represents an example for this behavior. Despite its flexibility, however, the entrepreneurial firm is quite exposed to judgment errors by the entrepreneur with little or no intra-firm counterbalancing process in place. As mentioned earlier, venture capitalists can serve an important role in providing such a counterbalancing force from the outside.

Even though established and entrepreneurial firms' investment processes differ regarding the relative importance of middle management and corporate staff, one common aspect of successful investment processes I studied was the permeability of organizational structures for ideas and feedback. In more established firms, top managers need to pay attention to making and keeping structures permeable for ideas and feedback. In entrepreneurial firms, the challenge is to design permeability into geographic expansion processes and to maintain this permeability as the firm grows larger and as additional layers of management are added in the middle. It could also mean for entrepreneurs deliberately to limit the size of managerial units, even during periods of rapid growth, in order to maintain the circumspect quality of decision-making processes during geographic expansion.[4]

Conclusion

I have argued that the international expansion of firms has materially changed over the last decade. Established firms in technologically intensive industries need to expand abroad in order to augment their home base. Often, they will face new managerial challenges and considerable uncertainty. Start-up firms need to expand abroad earlier than ever, either in order to augment or to exploit the knowledge base, with the latter activity typically being more uncertain. I have shown that both established and entrepreneurial firms expanded first with the less uncertain type of activity, but that eventually, in most cases, the more uncertain type of activity followed.

I have further argued that established firms and start-ups need to pay close attention to the internal structural context and framing for decision making. In the ideal case, this context will allow ideas to bubble up, to get assessed by a broad and relevant intra-firm constituency, and to get executed swiftly with a focus on nurturing early success. If the right internal structural context is lacking, however, the firm will likely make the wrong expansion decisions, which are often those suggested by optimistic senior managers in ignorance of the real capabilities of the firm.

So, is it easier for a top manager in an established firm or for an entrepreneur in a start-up to manage international expansion? Recent research on disruptive technologies has shown that intra-firm inertia to disruptive technologies can be so formidable that only a geographically and organizationally separate initiative will enable the firm to create sufficient capabilities in the disruptive technology domain early enough to lead in that domain once it reaches full commercial bloom (Christensen 1997). This suggests that internal structural context in established firms is very difficult to change. Does this mean that entrepreneurial start-ups have an advantage over established firms? As discussed above, this is not necessarily the case, because in entrepreneurial start-ups most of the decision-making process is centered on one person, the entrepreneur. Also, as the entrepreneurial firm matures, it needs to build its own middle-level structures and routines. Hopefully, the entrepreneurs are aware of the continued need to design processes for permeability. Also, not all routines that exist in established firms are bad for international expansion. For example, established firms are generally quite good at estimating the costs of international expansion, whereas most start-ups struggle mightily with this issue. The challenge for top managers in established firms is to mobilize the rich intra-firm knowledge at the right time.

There are ample opportunities for future research on this topic. First, there is the question to what degree the process of geographic expansion by start-up firms and established firms is mediated by the cultural distance between the countries involved. Although there is a body of literature on the effect of cultural distance on expansion decisions, the comparative analysis of entrepreneurial and established firms most likely will shed additional light on this question. Second, there is an interesting question about a general array of factors that are conducive to designing processes for permeability of ideas and feedback, especially in entrepreneurial firms. We know that many entrepreneurial firms hit a growth ceiling at some point, not so much because they run out of markets or ideas, but because the decision-making processes within these firms do not keep up with the intricacies of larger size. As more entrepreneurial firms expand abroad, and as established firms increasingly acquire entrepreneurial firms around the world to support their own growth and profitability, these questions are salient and timely.

Endnotes

1. The cost for a 3-minute telephone call from New York City to San Francisco also declined, from $136.80 (in 1999$) in 1920 to $0.90 in 1999. Thus, the cost of a call from New York City to London declined by a factor of 854, whereas the cost for a call from New York City to San Francisco declined by a factor of 152 over a roughly comparable period of time.

2. Bower in his process model of resource allocation defines three factors/phases: definition, impetus, and structural context. *Definition* is the process of determining the basic technical and economic characteristics of a project. *Impetus* refers to the rate at which general managers within the firm publicly commit to the project, and *structural context* is defined as a set of organizational forces that influence the process of definition and impetus. In Bower's model it is particularly the structural context and its elements that top management can shape.

3. Interestingly, a similar relationship holds for domestic sites away from the firm's home base. The less uncertain type of site for established firms was

established on average seven years before the more uncertain type of site (t-test, p = 0.008). This suggests that the argument made in this chapter applies not just across country borders but, probably in a moderated form, also across geographic distance.

4. There are several examples for such behavior. The industrial textile manufacturer Gore, Inc. for example, deliberately limits the size of each new manufacturing facility to a workforce of about 200 employees, even if technical economies of scale might suggest a site designed for a larger workforce (*Industry Week* 1983).

References

Aharoni, Yair (1966). *The Foreign Investment Decision Process*. Boston, Mass.: Harvard Business School Press.

Air Traffic Conference of America (1961). *Air Cargo*. Washington, DC: Air Traffic Conference of America.

—— (2000). *Air Cargo*. Washington, DC: Air Traffic Conference of America.

Almeida, Paul (2002). 'Are Firms Superior to Alliances and Markets? An Empirical Test of Cross-Border Knowledge Building'. *Organization Science* 13/2: 147–61.

Bartlett, Christopher, and Afroze, Mohammed (1994). *3M Optical Systems: Managing Corporate Entrepreneurship*. Boston, Mass.: Harvard Business School Publishing.

—— and Ghoshal, S. (1989). *Managing Across Borders: The Transnational Solution*. Boston, Mass.: Harvard Business School Press.

—— —— (1990). 'Managing Innovation in the Transnational Corporation', in C. A. Bartlett, Y. Doz, and G. Hedlund (eds.), *Managing the Global Firm*. London: Routledge.

Bhide, Amar (1992). 'Bootstrap Finance: The Art of Start-ups'. *Harvard Business Review* (Nov.–Dec.), 110–17.

—— (1999). *The Origin and Evolution of New Business*. Oxford: Oxford University Press.

Birkinshaw, J., Hood, N., and Jonsson, S. (1998). 'Building Firm-Specific Advantages in Multinational Corporations: The Role of Subsidiary Initiative'. *Strategic Management Journal* 19/3: 221–41.

Bower, J. L. (1970). *Managing the Resource Allocation Process: A Study of Corporate Planning and Investment*. Boston, Mass.: Harvard Business School Press.

Burgelman, R. A. (1983). 'A Process Model of Internal Corporate Venturing in the Diversified Major Firm'. *Administrative Science Quarterly* 28: 223–44.

Cantwell, John (1991). 'The International Agglomeration of R&D', in M. Casson (ed.), *Global Research Strategy and International Competitiveness*. Oxford: Basil Blackwell.

Christensen, C. M. (1997). *The Innovator's Dilemma: When New Technologies Cause Great Firms to Fail*. Boston, Mass.: Harvard Business School Press.
—— and Bower, J. L. (1996). 'Customer Power, Strategic Investment and the Failure of Leading Firms'. *Strategic Management Journal* 17: 197–218.

Chung, Wilbur, and Alcacer, Juan (2001). *Knowledge Seeking and Location Choice of Foreign Direct Investment in the United States (Working Paper)*. New York: New York University.

Cohen, W. M., and Levinthal, D. A. (1994). 'Fortune Favors the Prepared Firm'. *Management Science* 40/2: 227–52.

Coombs, R., Narandren, P., and Richards, A. (1996). 'A Literature-Based Innovation Output Indicator'. *Research Policy* 25: 403–13.

Cyert, R. M., and March, J. G. (1963). *A Behavioral Theory of the Firm*. Englewood Cliffs, NJ: Prentice-Hall.

Doz, Y. L., and Prahalad, C. K. (1991). 'Managing DMNCs: A Search for a New Paradigm'. *Strategic Management Journal* 12: 145–64.

Engel, C., and Rogers, J. (1996). 'How Wide is the Border?' *American Economic Review* 86.

Ghemawat, Pankaj (September 2001). 'Distance Still Matters: The Hard Reality of Global Expansion'. *Harvard Business Review*, 137–47.

Hakanson, L., and Nobel, R. (1993). 'Determinants of Foreign R&D in Swedish Multinationals'. *Research Policy* 22: 396–411.

Hamel, Gary (Summer 1991). 'Competition for Competence and Inter-Partner Learning Within International Strategic Alliances'. *Strategic Management Journal* 12: 83–103.

Henderson, Rebecca, and Cockburn, Iain (Spring 1996). 'Scale, Scope, and Spillovers: The Determinants of Research Productivity in Drug Discovery'. *The Rand Journal of Economics* 27: 32–59.

Hymer, S. H. (1976). *The International Operations of Multinational Firms: A Study of Foreign Direct Investment*. Boston, Mass.: MIT.

Industry Week (1983), Oct. 17: 48–9.

Jaffe, A. B. (1989). 'Real Effects of Academic Research'. *American Economic Review* 79/5: 957–70.

Johanson, J., and Vahlne, Jan-Erik (1990). 'The Mechanism of Internationalisation'. *International Marketing Review* 7/4: 11–24.

Katz, R., and Allen, T. J. (1982). 'Investigating the Not Invented Here (NIH) Syndrome: A Look at the Performance, Tenure, and Communication Patterns of 50 R&D Project Groups'. *R&D Management*, 7–19.

Khurana, Rakesh, and Nohria, Nitin (2002). *The Performance Consequences of CEO Turnover (Working Paper)*. Boston, Mass.: Harvard Business School Press.

Kodama, Fumio (July/Aug. 1992). 'Technology Fusion and the New R&D'. *Harvard Business Review*.

Kuemmerle, Walter (1999a). 'The Drivers of Foreign Direct Investment into Research and Development'. *Journal of International Business Studies* 30/1: 1–24.

Kuemmerle, Walter (1999*b*). 'Foreign Direct Investment in Industrial Research in the Pharmaceutical and Electronics Industries—Results from a Survey of Multinational Firms'. *Research Policy* 28/2–3: 179–93.

—— (2002). 'Home Base and Knowledge Management in International Ventures'. *Journal of Business Venturing* 17: 99–122.

—— and Ellis, C. (1999). *Internet Securities, Inc.: Financing Growth (9-899-149)*. Boston, Mass.: Harvard Business School Press.

La Porta, Rafael, Lopez-de-Silanes, Florencio, Shleifer, Andrei, and Vishny, Robert W. (1998). 'Law and Finance'. *Journal of Political Economy* 106/6: 1113–55.

McDougall, Patricia P., and Oviatt, Benjamin M. (1996). 'New Venture Internationalization, Strategic Change and Performance: A Follow-Up Study'. *Journal of Business Venturing* 11: 23–40.

Malnight, T. W. (1995). 'Globalization of an Ethnocentric Firm: An Evolutionary Perspective'. *Strategic Management Journal* 16: 119–41.

Mitchell, W., Shaver, J. M., and Yeung, B. (1992). 'Getting There in a Global Industry: Impacts on Performance of Changing International Presence'. *Strategic Management Journal* 13: 419–32.

OECD (1996). *Globalization of Industry—Overview and Sector Reports*. Paris: OECD.

Pfeffer, J. (Winter 1992). 'Understanding Power in Organizations'. *California Management Review* 34: 29–50.

Sahlman, W. A., Stevenson, Howard H., and Roberts, Michael (eds.) (1999). *The Entrepreneurial Venture*. 2nd edn. Boston Mass.: Harvard Business School Press.

Scott, Richard W. (1987). *Organizations: Rational, Natural and Open Systems*. Englewood Cliffs, NJ: Prentice-Hall.

Tushman, Michael L., and Anderson, Philip (1986). 'Technological Discontinuities and Organizational Environments'. *Administrative Science Quarterly* 31/3: 439–66.

US Bureau of Census (1929). *Statistical Abstract of the United States*. Washington, DC: US Government Printing Office.

—— (2001). *Statistical Abstract of the United States*. Washington, DC: US Government Printing Office.

US Department of Commerce, Maritime Administration, Office of Trade Studies and Statistics (1971). *Containerized Cargo Statistics*. Washington, DC: US Department of Commerce.

—— (2000). *Containerized Cargo Statistics*. Washington, DC: US Department of Commerce.

Vernon, R. (Nov. 1979). 'The Product Cycle Hypothesis in a New International Environment'. *Oxford Bulletin of Economics and Statistics* 41: 255–67.

Wesson, Thomas (1993). 'An Alternative Motivation for Foreign Direct Investment'. Unpublished Dissertation. Cambridge, Mass.: Harvard University Press.

Part III

Restoring the Bottom-up Process

Part III

9

Restoring the Bottom-up Process of Resource Allocation

Clark G. Gilbert

As we look at the research presented in Part II, several important conclusions can be drawn. First, there are powerful forces shaping the bottom-up processes of definition and impetus. These forces include the structural and strategic context internal to the firm. But we also observed external forces, such as powerful customers and capital markets, which play a similar role in shaping the bottom-up process. These external forces were not incorporated in the original models of Bower (1970) and Burgelman (1983).

In Part III, we extend the discussion in several areas. First, we introduce the concept of cognitive framing, defined here as the 'underlying structures of belief, perception, and appreciation', through which information is collected, interpreted, and retained (Schön and Rein 1994: 23). In this sense, the structural and strategic context, as well as customers and capital markets, operate like cognitive frames in that they shape the collection, interpretation, and retention of information used in the resource allocation process (RAP). Second, we also recognize the existence of managerial cognition that is separate from and independent of the forces already identified. Third, managing the set of forces that shape bottom-up processes can alter the collection, interpretation, and retention of information in a way that restores the bottom-up process and redirects strategic outcomes. Finally, we consider the implications of these observations for the way we model the resource allocation process.

Cognitive Framing and the Resource Allocation Process

There is a well-established set of literatures on cognition and cognitive framing. We will explore two of these literatures: schematic and interpretive theory. Then we illustrate the parallels between cognitive frames and the forces that shape definition and impetus.

Schematic Theory

The psychology literature often describes cognitive frames as *schema*, a pattern imposed on a complex reality to help interpret and guide response (Rosch 1975; Rosch and Mervis 1975). Schemas employ three basic coding processes to respond to stimuli: abstraction, interpretation, and selection. What is encoded is 'heavily determined by a guiding schema or knowledge framework that selects and actively modifies experience in order to arrive at a coherent, unified, expectation-confirming and knowledge-consistent representation of an experience.... Only the information that is relevant and important to the currently active schema will be encoded' (Alba and Hasher 1983: 203–4).

Schema can lead to rapid interpretation of complex or ambiguous realities. Although this enables quick, even efficient response, it also risks significant self-reinforcing bias. For example, individuals can be biased toward interpreting a certain color when it is labeled or categorized, even if the hue actually changes (from red to orange for instance) (Rosch and Mervis 1975). Once labeled, schema become very robust because they bias the collection, interpretation, and retention of information to conform with the original categorization through the encoding process described above (Alba and Hasher 1983).

The Interpretive Perspective

Weick has described a process of organizational 'sense making' that is similar to the encoding process of schema theory (1979). This interpretive perspective assumes that organizations (and not just individuals) have cognitive systems and that managers use their existing cognitive frames to filter, interpret, and retain information from the environment (Daft and Weick 1984). Retained interpretation then shapes how subsequent attention is allocated, which, in turn, shapes what can be interpreted and retained in an organization. Thus, there is a reciprocal relationship between the information collected and the interpretation of that information.

What do cognitive frames, schema theory, and an interpretive perspective have to do with resource allocation and the forces that shape the bottom-up process? First, like cognitive frames, the structural and strategic context as well as customers and capital markets shape what projects get considered, how they get defined, and whether they get selected through the commitment of resources. For example, Bower (1970) showed h͟o͟w͟ ͟t͟ structure of the incentives and reporting ͟r͟ ͟ ͟ ͟ ͟ ͟ ͟ erating managers will consider, mid- ͟ ͟ ͟ ͟ ͟porate-level executives will fund. ͟re shapes strategy'. Burgelman ͟so can guide the bottom-up n's research showed that ͟ned and whether they gement.

corporate context is pe how a firm inter- ͟ld be described as a firms facing similar ͟bilities interpreted ͟nitial capital struc- ͟ret early results as pret similar results observed results, ͟ifferent strategies ͟ning. Chapter 10 ͟ttom-up process ͟s of the resource

(
s
b
al

... and Bower chapter also highlights a second parallel to research on cognition. Like cognitive frames, the forces shaping definition and impetus serve to reinforce the way projects or plans are first assessed. How a project is initially categorized perpetuates managers' perceptions until expectations are shattered. This 'stickiness' in categorization constitutes a strong conservative bias even in the face of significant environment change. Recall the tendency for self-perpetuation stated in schema theory: 'Only the information that is relevant and important to the currently activated schema will be encoded' (Alba and Hasher 1983: 204). Similarly, in the Noda and Bower study, the differences in capital market context that led to different strategies caused managers at Bell South to seek out data that confirmed their investment strategy, whereas managers at US West sought out data that confirmed their skimming strategy. Shaped by these initial categorizations, both organizations were able to collect, interpret, and retain data that validated their initial directions. This strong conservative bias can be seen in Christensen's study of disk-drive manufacturers. Existing customers had a tremendous influence on information collected for new products, how it was interpreted, and what was done about it. This self-perpetuating force repeatedly caused the established firms to conclude that disruptive technologies did not present a compelling investment opportunity. Meanwhile, a large set of entrepreneurs found equally compelling evidence that these technologies did offer a tremendous investment opportunity. A set of venture capital firms concurred and provided repeated rounds of investment. The entrepreneurs and their backers reached their conclusion because they listened to an emerging customer base that had a different set of needs than the established market. Whether it is capital markets or customers, external forces can have the same persistence as the internal forces described by Bower and Burgelman. Unless managed, the direction of their influence does not change.

In Ch. 11, we see that there are specific cognitive frames that also should be considered as forces acting on the bottom–up process. These are independent from structural and strategic context but equally powerful influences on strategic outcomes. In his study of eight newspapers responding to the emergence of digital media, Gilbert showed that whether an environmental change was perceived as an opportunity or a threat could have a tremendous impact on how projects were defined and the level or resources provided. Different cognitive frames shaped different strategic outcomes even when the structural and strategic context remained relatively stable. The behavior observed presents a paradox: when discontinuous change is framed as an opportunity, the definition process allows a flexible strategy, but yields very little resource commitment. When it is framed as a threat, resource commitment increases, but the definition process becomes rigid and inflexible. Gilbert's study helps bridge research on the resource allocation process to other work on cognition (Tripsas and Gavetti 2000; Porac and Thomas 1990) as well as the research on schema theory and interpretive theory already mentioned. His study is also an important reminder that if RAP really is the link to strategy, then it is more than just the allocation of resources (impetus), but includes the substantive content of plans to which those resources are deployed (definition).

Another implication of the chapters in Part III is that management can reframe the way projects are defined and funded. Managers can drive strategic outcomes by managing the forces that shape how their operating managers and middle managers define and commit to projects. Although this can include cognitive frames, it also involves each of the forces shaping the bottom-up process. Bower, Christensen, and Gilbert all suggest that changes in the structural context can lead to changes in strategy. If 'structure shapes strategy' then changes in structure lead to changes in strategy. Conversely, managers intending to change strategy without changing structure or any of the other forces that shape the bottom-up process are likely to be frustrated in their efforts.

These findings have important implications for how we model the resource allocation process. First, the forces that shape the bottom-up process of definition and impetus are greater in number and complexity than originally considered. Second, modeling these forces as separate from the processes they shape is more accurate and is likely to improve our understanding of the overall process. These are not parallel activities with definition and impetus. Rather they are metaforces that provide context and shape these bottom-up processes. Managing the resource allocation process has a great deal to do with managing these forces. Third, extending Bower's original observation that resource allocation is a process, not an event, Noda and Bower's study shows us that our modeling efforts must consider the iterative cycles of resource allocation and how initial framing shapes subsequent data collection, interpretation, and retention in ways that ultimately lead to strategic outcomes over time. In Ch. 20, we apply to these observations in an effort to formally present a revised model of RAP.

References

Alba, J. W., and Hasher, L. (1983). 'Is Memory Schematic'? *Psychological Bulletin* 93: 203–31.

Bower, J. L. (1970). *Managing the Resource Allocation Process*. Boston, Mass.: Harvard Business School Press.

Burgelman, R. (1983). 'A Model of the Interaction of Strategic Behavior, Corporate Context, and the Concept of Strategy'. *Academy of Management Review* 3/1: 61–70.

Daft, R. L., and Weick, K. E. (1984). 'Toward a Model of Organizations as Interpretation Systems'. *Academy of Management Review* 12/1: 76–90.

Porac, J. F., and Thomas, H. (1990). 'Taxonomic Mental Models in Competitor Definition'. *Academy of Management Review* 16: 224–40.

Rosch, E. (1975). 'Cognitive Reference Points'. *Cognitive Psychology* 1: 532–47.

Rosch, E. and Mervis, C. (1975). 'Family Resemblances: Studies in the Internal Structure of Categories'. *Cognitive Psychology* 7: 573–605.

Schön, D. A., and Rein, M. (1994). *Frame Reflection: Toward the Resolution of Intractable Policy Controversies*. New York: Basic Books.

Tripsas, M., and Gavetti, G. (2000). 'Capabilities, Cognition, and Inertia: Evidence from Digital Imaging'. *Strategic Management Journal* 21: 1147–61.

Weick, K. (1979). *The Social Psychology of Organizing*, 2nd edn. New York: McGraw-Hill.

10

Strategy Making as an Iterated Process of Resource Allocation

Tomo Noda and Joseph L. Bower

Introduction

Despite the fact that many well-known discussions of strategy invoke the image that strategy is a course of action consciously deliberated by top management (e.g. Chandler 1962; Andrews 1971) or an analytical exercise undertaken by staff strategists (e.g. Ansoff 1965; Porter 1980), descriptive analysis of the complexity of real organizational phenomena challenges such simplified conceptualization (e.g. Allison 1971). An explicit recognition of inherent organizational complexities, often described as 'possible goal incongruence', 'information asymmetry', and 'organizational politics' (e.g. Barnard 1938; Simon 1945; Cyert and March 1963; Crozier 1964), as well as 'unpredictable' and 'uncontrollable' environments (e.g. Schumpeter 1934; Nelson and Winter 1982; Thompson 1967; Pfeffer and Salancik 1978; Miles 1982), has led some strategic management scholars to describe how strategy is actually formed instead of prescribing what it should be. Findings from their empirical studies suggest that strategy is, more or less, emergent from lower levels of organizations (e.g. Mintzberg 1978; Pascale 1984; Mintzberg and Waters 1985), whether through trial-and-error learning (Mintzberg and McHugh 1985), incrementally with logical guidance from the top (Quinn 1980), or such that small changes are often punctuated by a sudden big change in a relatively short period (Miller and Friesen 1984; Tushman and Romanelli 1985; Gersick 1991). From this *strategy process* perspective, strategy is 'a pattern in a stream of decisions and actions' (Mintzberg and McHugh 1985: 161) that are distributed across multiple levels of an organization.

Whereas some of the scholars associated with this line of research see the process as unguided or 'muddling through' (e.g. Lindbloom 1959; Wrapp 1967), others see part of top management's task as intervening in the emergent strategy process and attempting to maneuver the enterprise to a preferable course of direction. These scholars explore multilevel managerial activities that shape the strategy process, interacting with external and internal forces. Bower (1970) initiated this line of enquiry by conducting an intensive field-based study on strategic planning and capital investment in a large, diversified firm and presenting a parsimonious framework, grounded in the field data, for understanding the interplay of those managerial activities. His process model was validated by subsequent field studies in different organizational settings and on various strategic processes (see Bower and Doz 1979, for the details of these studies). It was then further extended by Burgelman (1983*a*) in his clinical study on internal corporate venturing (ICV) in a large corporation.

The Bower–Burgelman (B–B) process model of strategy making in a large, complex firm depicts multiple, simultaneous, interlocking, and sequential managerial activities over three levels of organizational hierarchy (i.e. front-line or bottom, middle, and top managers) and conceptualizes intra-organizational strategy-making processes as consisting of four subprocesses: two interlocking bottom-up core processes of 'definition' and 'impetus' and two overlaying corporate processes of 'structural context determination' and 'strategic context determination'. *Definition* is a cognitive process in which technological and market forces, initially ill defined, are communicated to the organization, and strategic initiatives are developed primarily by front-line managers who usually have specific knowledge on technology and are closer to the market (Chakravarthy and Lorange 1991; Jensen and Meckling 1992). *Impetus* is a largely sociopolitical process by which these strategic initiatives are continually championed by front-line managers, and are adopted and brokered by middle managers who, in doing so, put their reputations for good judgment and organizational careers at stake. The role of top managers is limited in that they do not necessarily have the appropriate knowledge or information to evaluate technical and economic aspects of the strategic initiatives, and tend to rely on the track records or credibility of proposing middle managers in making resource allocation decisions (Bower 1970).

Strategic initiatives therefore 'emerge' primarily from managerial activities of front-line and middle managers, as implied by the Carnegie School bottom-up problem-solving perspective (Simon 1945; Cyert and March 1963; March and Simon 1965) and suggested in many other descriptive strategy process studies. Nevertheless, top managers can exercise critical influences on these activities by setting up the *structural context* (i.e. various organizational and administrative mechanisms such as organizational architecture, information and measurement systems, and reward and punishing systems) to reflect the corporate objectives, and thereby manipulating the context in which the decisions and actions of lower-level managers are made (Bower 1970), as suggested by the Harvard top-down administrative perspective (Chandler 1962; Learned *et al.* 1965; Andrews 1971). The development of those strategic initiatives would lead to the refinement or change of the concept of corporate strategy, thereby determining 'strategic context' over time. Strategic context determination is conceived primarily as a political process through which middle managers delineate in concrete terms the content of new fields of business development for the corporation and attempt to convince top managers that the current concept of corporate strategy needs to be changed so as to accommodate successful new business development (Burgelman 1983*a*, 1983*b*).

The central feature of the B–B model is a resource allocation process in which bottom-up strategic initiatives compete for scarce corporate resources and top managers' attention to survive within the corporate contexts—structural and strategic contexts. Burgelman (1991), in his in-depth field study on Intel's corporate renewal, further developed the idea of intra-organizational competition among bottom-up initiatives and proposed an intra-organizational ecological perspective, following the variation–selection–retention framework of cultural evolutionary theory (Campbell 1969; Aldrich 1979; Weick 1979). Strategic initiatives are identified and examined in the definition process, within the corporate context (variation), are selected out in the impetus process by corporate context as 'internal selection environment' (selection), and lead to the reinforcement or modification of corporate context (retention). Burgelman (1994) argues that Intel's internal selection environment, particularly its 'maximizing margin-per-wafer-start' resource allocation rule, reflected selective pressures from the product market in ways that helped the firm exit from the increasingly competitive memory business and refocus on microprocessors.

Although the B–B model, together with insights from the intra-organizational ecology perspective, elucidates organizational dynamics, conflicts, and dilemmas and provides a useful way of understanding managerial activities in the emergent strategy process, it leaves simple, but fundamental questions in theory and practice unanswered: Why is it that firms, facing similar opportunities, respond differently and come up with different strategic commitments to the business? How and why do managerial activities at multiple levels of organization, which add up to such different emergent concepts of corporate strategy, differ among these firms? Most past studies which contributed to the establishment of the model compared different capital investment projects (e.g. Bower 1970; Ackerman 1970), different intracorporate ventures (e.g. Burgelman 1983a), and different business units (e.g. Haspeslagh 1983; Hamermesh 1986) within a single firm to develop an in-depth understanding of the inner workings of a complex organization, particularly at the levels of project, venture, and business units. What is missing are studies tracing the efforts of multiple firms to respond with new ventures or business units to the same market opportunity—precisely the data needed to provide insight into the inter-firm comparative questions.

The study presented in this chapter fills the critical gap and extends the B–B model to a comparative analysis of a single business across multiple firms, as opposed to multiple types of businesses within a single firm. It explores the inter-firm comparative questions in the context of new business development by comparing divergent business development experiences of two very similar firms. The next section of this chapter describes the research design and field study research methodology employed in the study. The third section presents the field data using the extended framework of the B–B process model. The Discussion section presents several propositions derived from the research. The chapter closes with implications and conclusions.

Methodology

The application of the B–B model at the firm level of analysis poses significant challenges to researchers. The inherent diversity among firms is often so dominant that the researchers find it difficult to isolate managerial activities and other critical variables that might have caused the firms to respond differently to new business opportunities. In order to overcome the difficulties in research design that impede inter-firm comparison, this study uses the contrasting experiences of BellSouth and US West—two of the seven Bell regional holding companies (RHCs) created by the break-up of the Bell system and the consequent spin-off of AT&T's telephone operating companies on 1 January 1984—in newly developing and expanding wireless communications businesses between 1983 and mid-1994.

Research Setting

The seven RHCs constitute a unique research sample: they were of the same age because they were created at the same time. At the time of break-up, they were engaged in the same core business, wired telephony or local exchange business, employing the same operational and technological capabilities. Their executives had common backgrounds, usually spending their entire business careers within the Bell system and sharing an administrative heritage developed throughout its more than 100-year history. Although they certainly differed in some respects, most notably in geographical locations (i.e. franchised regions for local exchange businesses), the significant similarities make the RHCs a relatively controlled research sample.

What is particularly unique to the RHCs are their experiences in developing cellular telephone service and other wireless communications businesses (e.g. paging service). Almost at the same time as when they started independent operations, the RHCs entered cellular telephone service business, first in major local markets within their franchised regions, using the cellular business plan inherited from the pre-break-up AT&T. Although the RHCs faced the same freedoms and constraints in developing and expanding cellular and other wireless communications businesses both nationwide (i.e. beyond their franchised region) and overseas, they responded quite differently to these growth opportunities and, consequently, came up with different strategic commitments to, or corporate-level strategies for, wireless communications businesses.

Focus on BellSouth and US West   While the fuller study (Noda 1996), from which this chapter borrows data, analyzes all seven RHCs, this chapter focuses on two of them because of its primary purpose to present an in-depth analysis of business development and strategy-making process based on the B–B model. Table 10.1 provides company profiles, at the time of break-up of Atlanta-based BellSouth, which serves nine sun-belt states as a franchised region, and Denver-based US WEST, which operates in a T-shaped franchised territory consisting of fourteen states in the Pacific Northwest, the Rocky Mountain region, and the midwest.

BellSouth and US WEST were selected for this chapter because their initial local cellular markets within the franchised regions were similar, yet they represented polar opposites regarding strategic commitments to wireless communications businesses ten years after their initial entry. Divergent business development results out of similar

Table 10.1 *Company profiles of BellSouth and US West at the time of break-up*

	BellSouth	US West
Assets as of 1 Jan. 1984	$21.4 billion	$15.6 billion
Revenues FY 1983	$10.7 billion	$7.8 billion
Net income FY 1983	$1.4 billion	$0.9 billion
ROE FY 1983	13%	12%
Debt ratio as of 1 Jan. 1984	43%	43%
Employees as of 1 Jan. 1984	99,100	75,000
Access lines as of 31 Dec. 1983	13.6 million	10.6 million
No. of BOCs as of 1 Jan. 1984	2 (Southern Bell, South Central Bell)	3 (Northwestern Bell, Mountain Bell, Pacific Northwest Bell)
No. of states served as of 1 Jan. 1984	9 (Alabama, Florida, Georgia, Kentucky, Louisiana, Mississippi, North Carolina, South Carolina, Tennessee)	14 (Arizona, Colorado, Idaho, Iowa, Minnesota, Montana, Nebraska, New Mexico, North Dakota, Oregon, South Dakota, Utah, Washington, Wyoming)

Source: Company annual reports.

starting conditions suggest that much of the variance can be expected to come from the business development and strategy-making processes.

Similar starting conditions. Recent studies on the origin of competitive advantage (e.g. Porter 1990, 1994) suggest that proximate or local markets may exercise a critical impact on a firm's subsequent business development. In entering the cellular business, the RHCs were endowed with wireline cellular licenses—one of two (wireline and nonwireline) licenses granted for each local cellular service area—for a share of the nation's thirty largest areas located within each of their franchised regions.[1] BellSouth received wireline licenses for Atlanta, Miami, and New Orleans; US WEST got Minneapolis, Denver, Seattle, and Phoenix. Table 10.2 assesses the attractiveness of these local markets for cellular operations based on population size, the number of automobile commuters, and the percentage of high-income households. Industry experts viewed these three variables (size, driving intensity, and income propensity) as major determinants of the area's attractiveness because cellular telephone service was a network business with strong economies of scale, and cellular telephones were permanently installed in cars and were very expensive 'executive toys' in the earliest days. As shown in Table 10.2, BellSouth and US WEST were quite similar, even among the seven siblings, in these variables.

Polar cases. Second and more important, these two companies had quite contrasting experiences in developing wireless communications businesses since their entry into the field in 1984, and consequently, differed significantly in regard to corporate-level strategy or strategic commitments for the businesses. Brief histories of their business development are presented in the Appendix. Table 10.3 lists chronologies of their major strategic actions (B1–33 for BellSouth and U1–19 for US WEST).

At the end of 1993, BellSouth was the largest of the seven RHCs in domestic wireless revenues, as well as in international wireless operations measured by the number of POPs (*point* of *p*resence, or *popula*tion) in areas where it held licenses. The company was also the nation's second largest paging operator. With its well-articulated 'global/mobile' strategy, it was active in a wide range of wireless communications businesses, from paging to mobile data service. In contrast, US WEST was the smallest in domestic wireless revenues of the seven companies. Although it had fairly active international cellular operations, US WEST was more committed to broadband and multimedia businesses, and did not put strategic emphasis on its wireless communications businesses. Table 10.4 compares the two companies' operation statistics of wireless communications.

Retrospective, Longitudinal, Nested Field Study Research Methodology

How did BellSouth and US WEST deal with new business opportunities presented by cellular and other wireless technologies? Why and how did BellSouth come up with a strong strategic commitment to wireless communications businesses? Why and how did US WEST take a different course of action? What was the sequence of managerial activities at multiple levels of the organizations which led them to come up with such different strategic commitments to or corporate strategies

Table 10.2 *Characteristics of initial local cellular markets of BellSouth and US West*

Initial local market (portions of US top 30 cellular service areas [ranking by population size])	Market size (1980 population in millions)	Drive intensity (drive-alone commuters as percentage of population)	Income level (earnings over $50,000 p.a. as percentage of population)
BellSouth			
Miami–Fort Lauderdale [12]	2.6	30.5	1.01
Atlanta [17]	2.0	31.3	0.95
New Orleans [29]	1.2	25.1	0.86
Total (weighted average)	5.8	29.7	0.96
US West			
Minneapolis [15]	2.1	31.3	1.04
Denver–Boulder [19]	1.6	32.6	1.14
Seattle–Everett [20]	1.6	30.7	1.05
Phoenix [26]	1.5	30.6	0.77
Total (weighted average)	6.9	31.3	1.01
Average of 7 RHCs	11.2	27.0	0.97

Source: Calculated by the authors, using the data from *1980 State and Metropolitan Area Data Book* and *1980 Census: Characteristics of Workers in Metropolitan Areas.*

Table 10.3 *Key strategic actions in wireless communications business development at BellSouth and US West*

	Date	BellSouth's strategic actions
B1	10/83	BellSouth Mobility Incorporated (BMI) was established
B2	5/84	BMI introduced cellular service in Miami, its first local service area
B3	7/85	The formation of BellSouth International was announced
B4	5/85	BellSouth lost the Communications Industries deal to Pacific Telesis. This was the first acquisition of an out-of-region nonwireline cellular license by Bell regional holding companies
B5	7/85	BellSouth agreed with Mobile Communications Corporation of America (MCCA) to form a 50–50 cellular joint venture
B6	1/86	BellSouth Enterprises was formed as a holding company to supervise BellSouth's unregulated businesses
B7	1/86	BMI added a paging business in Atlanta
B8	8/86	BellSouth International announced its plan to enter joint venture with AirCall Communications, the UK's largest independent mobile communications company (BellSouth Enterprises acquired an interest in AirCall in 11/86)
B9	9/87	BellSouth Enterprises announced acquisition of Link Telecommunications, an independent paging and telephone-answering company in Australia
B10	10/87	BellSouth International reached an agreement with TDF Radio Service, a new national paging operator in France, to provide a range of customer services for TDF
B11	2/88	BellSouth reached a definitive agreement to purchase Mobile Communications Corporation of America
B12	8/88	The consortium led by BellSouth was awarded the franchise for cellular service in Buenos Aires, Argentina, South America's first private cellular mobile communications network
B13	8/88	BellSouth purchased two paging operations in Australia to become part of Link Telecommunications
B14	2/89	BellSouth formed a consortium to compete for the private Pan-European digital cellular telephone license (D2) in the Federal Republic of Germany

(Continues)

Table 10.3 (*Continued*)

	Date	BellSouth's strategic actions
B15	7/89	BellSouth formed a consortium to bid for one of the Personal Communications Network (PCN) licenses in the UK
B16	9/89	BellSouth announced a merger with Lin Broadcasting (It terminated the merger agreement in 12/89)
B17	11/89	Buenos Aires Cellular inaugurated service
B18	3/90	The consortium, which BellSouth was part of, was awarded a cellular license in the western region of Mexico
B19	6/90	BellSouth International was awarded one of the New Zealand's cellular licenses
B20	12/90	A BellSouth-led consortium finalized a contract for the development and operation of a cellular system in Uruguay
B21	12/90	BellSouth signed a definitive agreement to purchase Graphic Scanning, a cellular and paging company
B22	1/91	BellSouth International was the highest bidder for a Venezuelan cellular license
B23	3/91	BellSouth Cellular announced a definitive agreement to acquire cellular properties from GTE Mobilnet
B24	4/91	BellSouth's paging subsidiary, MobileComm, purchased one of the three nationwide paging licenses from CellTelCo
B25	4/91	BellSouth announced the purchase from McCaw Cellular Communications of cellular properties in Indiana and Wisconsin
B26	6/91	BellSouth's consortium was awarded the nationwide digital cellular license in Denmark
B27	9/91	BellSouth Enterprises purchased Pacific Telecom's nonwireline cellular telecommunications operations in Chile
B28	10/91	BellSouth Enterprises announced an agreement with RAM Broadcasting to jointly own and operate mobile data communications networks worldwide as well as specific paging and cellular assets in the USA
B29	11/91	The consortium of BellSouth Enterprises was named the second telecommunications provider in Australia that would also provide cellular service

B30	2/93	The BellSouth consortium was awarded the second private digital cellular license in Germany
B31	3/93	BellSouth acquired a minority interest in France Telecom Mobile Data, a France Telecom subsidiary that will build and operate a mobile data network throughout France. It also announced development of a nationwide mobile data network in the Netherlands
B32	5/93	BellSouth agreed to acquire cellular operations in Wisconsin
B33	7/93	BellSouth agreed to acquire cellular operations in Indiana

US West's strategic actions

U1	9/83	US West New Vector Group was established
U2	1/84	NewVector proposed a venture outside its region, providing cellular service to the Gulf of Mexico
U3	6/84	NewVector introduced cellular telephone service first in Minneapolis
U4	9/84	NewVector announced a plan to build and operate cellular networks in Costa Rica
U5	early 85	US West International was established
U6	12/85	NewVector announced its intent to acquire from Communications Industries a cellular license and paging operations in San Diego
U7	3/86	US West Diversified Group was formed to supervise unregulated businesses
U8	5/86	US West Paging was established by acquiring paging assets in Oregon and Washington
U9	6/86	NewVector agreed to acquire a minority interest in a cellular license in Omaha
U10	12/89	US West and the Hungarian PTT signed a joint venture agreement to own and operate a national cellular telephone system in Hungary
U11	12/89	US West, with its international partners, was awarded a license to develop a Personal Communications Network (PCN) in the UK
U12	6/90	US West announced that it, along with Bell Atlantic, had been selected by the Czech and Slovak Federal Republic to build and operate a cellular telephone network

(Continues)

Table 10.3 *(Continued)*

	Date	US West's strategic actions
U13	7/90	US West announced the creation of Spectrum Enterprises to handle its domestic and international cellular, paging, and personal communications interests
U14	10/90	US West Spectrum Enterprises signed an agreement to provide a cellular telephone system in Leningrad (now St Petersburg)
U15	1/91	US West announced that its consortium was chosen as one of two cellular carriers to serve Moscow
U16	7/91	US West participated in TU-KA cellular company in Japan
U17	9/93	US West International was awarded a 900 GSM cellular license in Hungary
U18	10/93	US West announced the sale of its paging operations
U19	5/94	US West announced the formation of cellular joint venture with AirTouch Communications

Sources: Company annual reports, company documents, *Inside BellSouth* (1993) and *Inside US West* (1993), Telecom Publishing Group, Alexandria, Va.

for the wireless communications businesses? Why were such decisions and actions taken? These questions were examined by retrospective field studies—the appropriate research methodology when the subject matter is an otherwise undocumented process and the boundary between phenomena and context is not well established (Yin 1989).

The field study research method is particularly useful for theory development. It allows for a continual interplay between theory and data, whereby theory evolving during this research is *grounded* in data actually gathered and analyzed (Glaser and Strauss 1967; Eisenhardt 1989). In this instance, the study was guided by the B–B process model of strategy making in a multilevel, multibusiness organization (a large, complex firm), which was grounded in substantive areas such as strategic capital investment, internal corporate venturing, and portfolio planning within a single firm. By extending the model based on the data gathered in the new field (i.e. new business development across multiple firms), it is possible to develop a higher-order grounded theory or a more formal theory (Glaser and Strauss 1967; Vaughan 1992; Strauss and Corbin 1994).

The field study research relies on *theoretical* rather than *statistical sampling* (Glaser and Strauss 1967; Eisenhardt 1989). The use of polar cases, BellSouth and US WEST, which illustrate strong and weak

Table 10.4 *Wireless communications businesses at BellSouth and US West (1993)*

	BellSouth	US West
Wireless revenues as a percentage of total revenues	9.8%	5.5%
Domestic cellular		
Revenues ($ millions)	1150	507
Operating income ($ millions)	282	n.a.
Operating cash flow ($ millions)	483	125
Cash operating margin	42.0%	28.2%
POPs (millions)	38.8	18.2
Subscribers	1,559,132	601,000
Penetration rate	4.01%	3.30%
Domestic paging		
Revenues ($ millions)	190	0[a]
Subscribers	1,232,172	0[a]
International cellular		
POPs (millions)	55.4	13.3
Subscribers	192,181	18,200
Countries in Operation	France, Chile, Argentina, New Zealand, Uruguay, Venezuela, Denmark, Australia, Germany	Czech Republic, Slovakia, Hungary, Japan, Russia
International paging		
Subscribers	112,211	0
Other international operations	Mobile Data (UK, Australia, France, Netherlands, Belgium)	Personal Communications Network (UK)

[a] US WEST announced the sales of domestic paging operations in 1993.

Source: 1993 BellSouth Annual Report, 1994 BellSouth Source Book, 1993 US West Annual Report, 1993 US West Fact Book, *Inside BellSouth* (1993) and *Inside US West* (1993), Telecom Publishing Group, Alexandria, Va.

resultant strategic commitments to wireless communications businesses, allows researchers to explore the phenomenon of interest. The progress of the phenomenon is 'transparently observable' in such extreme situations (Pettigrew 1990). The field study research also allows for the use of a *nested* research design with multiple units of analysis (Yin 1989), which is indispensable for the analysis using the

B–B process model. Accordingly, the decisions and actions of managers were studied at multiple levels of organization. Because these decisions and actions took place over long periods, particular attention was also paid to their sequence and interconnections (Pettigrew 1990).

Data Collection

The field studies make use of multiple sources of data, both qualitative and quantitative (Yin 1989), derived from interviews and archival documents. The use of multiple sources permitted a degree of verification through triangulation. Data gathering took place between November 1992 and June 1995.

Fifty managers (thirty managers at BellSouth and twenty managers at US WEST) were interviewed. They included top corporate executives, corporate staff managers, and senior officers in the subsidiaries responsible for the domestic and international wireless communications businesses. Some senior business-unit officers supervising local exchange and other unregulated businesses were interviewed to understand better the evolution of the companies' overall strategic direction and gain insights about changes in perceptions concerning wireless communications businesses. Table 10.5 lists the job titles of the informants at the time of interview at the two companies.

The interviews, conducted by this chapter's first author, typically lasted one to two hours, some as long as four hours. A majority were conducted on site, but many of the follow-up interviews were made by telephone. All but three interviews at the two companies were taped and transcribed. Though an interview protocol ensured that the same material was covered, the interviews themselves were open ended. As key events, issues, and people were identified later in the study, interviews became more structured.

Sources of archival data included company annual reports, 10Ks, annual statistical fact books, trade journals, the general business press, and reports of market research institutions. Despite generous cooperation of executives from the two companies, the authors were not given access to the details of company documents, particularly business plans and actual capital appropriation that were not also available to regulators. The collected data provided a comparable database that served as the foundation for 'time-line' style histories of major changes in the business portfolio, organization, personnel, and other key events in the lives of the two companies. The analysis of this data in tabular and graphic form permitted the interviewer to review responses of the

Table 10.5 *List of interviewees at BellSouth and US West*

BellSouth (30 managers)

Corporate executives
  Chairman and chief executive officer
  Vice chairman and president of a holding company for unregulated businesses
  President of telephone operating companies (former vice president—strategic planning)
  Chief financial officer (former group president for mobile communications)
  Vice president and comptroller
  Vice president for strategic planning and corporate development
  Vice president—planning—of telephone companies (former vice president—strategic planning)

Corporate staff managers/functional middle managers
  Former vice president for corporate development
  Assistant vice president for strategic planning
  Assistant vice president for worldwide wireless strategy
  Five corporate planning managers
  Corporate economist (financial management)
  Director—strategic planning

Business-unit managers (wireless/international)
  Former president of wireless subsidiary
  President of international subsidiary
  Former president of international subsidiary
  Vice president for mobile date operations
  Manager of wireless subsidiary
  Anonymous wireless manager

Others
  Former group president for diversified operations
  Vice president—marketing—of telephone companies
  Executive assistant and secretary of telephone companies
  Chief strategist of advertising and publishing subsidiary
  Manager—business information systems

US West (20 managers)

Corporate executive
  Former chairman and chief executive officer
  Former executive vice president and chief financial officer
  Former corporate vice president and president of commercial development
  Vice president—strategic marketing

Corporate staff managers/functional middle managers
  Assistant vice president—public policy
  Executive director—corporate strategy

(Continues)

Table 10.5 (*Continued*)

Director—corporate strategy
Former director—financial management
Former director—corporate strategy
Manager—strategic marketing
Business-unit managers (wireless/international)
Two vice presidents of wireless subsidiary
Former executive director of wireless subsidiary
Former strategist of wireless subsidiary
Managing director for international and business development
Former president—international subsidiary
Anonymous wireless manager
Others
Former president of marketing services
Executive director for multimedia planning and development
Director for multimedia technology

informants for lapse in memory, thereby protecting against possible retrospective bias of informants.

Data Analysis and Conceptualization

The data collection and analysis components of a field study overlap, particularly in the case of theory building (Glaser and Strauss 1967; Eisenhardt 1989; Leonard-Barton 1990). In this study, the early phase of data analysis confirmed that the B–B process model basically provides a useful lens to analyze wireless communications business development at BellSouth and US WEST, and guided further data collection. At the same time, however, the inter-firm, corporate-level comparison revealed some key variables that were unobserved in past studies, and the identification of such variables challenged some elements of the B–B process model, particularly determination of strategic context. Most important, the longitudinal nature of the phenomenon of interest, in which a sequence of proposals to develop and expand wireless communications businesses over the ten year period added up to the emergence or lack of strategic commitment to the business, necessitated that the B–B process model should be applied in an iterated way so that it could capture the managerial activities involved in these multiple, sequential projects. Findings from the field studies at BellSouth and US WEST are presented below, using this iterated framework.

Strategy Making as Iterated Processes of Resource Allocation

Although the iterated framework can be conceptualized project by project, doing so would add overwhelming complexity to the analysis. For the convenience of data analysis, the experiences of BellSouth and US WEST in developing wireless communications businesses between 1983 and mid-1994 are described in three time periods: 'getting started' (the pre-break-up era to late 1985), 'unexpected growth' (early 1986 to mid-1989), and 'full bloom' (mid-1989 to mid-1994). Figure 10.1 maps the two companies' strategic actions (from Table 10.3) by each time period, and highlights their activities in domestic cellular, domestic paging, and international wireless operations. Dotted lines indicate bottom-up efforts to promote the new businesses whereas their changes into solid lines represent the emergence of corporate-level strategy for the businesses.

The First Period: Getting Started (the Pre-break-up Era to Late 1985)

At the time of the break-up, cellular telephone service was novel to American consumers. Because of rudimentary incipient network and equipment technologies and untested customer demand, development of the cellular business involved a great deal of uncertainty. Managers at BellSouth and US WEST therefore experimented with this uncertain business, first starting with the assessment or evaluation of new business opportunities presented by wireless technologies. A majority of managerial activities in this early period therefore centered around the definition process. As the companies proceeded with the preparation and introduction of cellular operations in major local markets, early 'product-championing' activities for wireless communications businesses emerged, thus providing a connection between the definition and impetus processes (Burgelman 1983*a*). Figure 10.2 compares major activities at the two companies during this time period, using the 12-cell (3-level by 4-subprocess) framework of the B–B process model.

Definition Since the commercialization of cellular technology was pursued by AT&T's cellular subsidiary, called Advanced Mobile Phone Systems (AMPS), prior to the break-up, and was transferred to the Bell regional holding companies as part of the break-up arrangement, BellSouth and US WEST did not experience 'technical/need linking activities' in the strict sense observed in Bower's (1970) study on strategic capital investment or Burgelman's (1983*a*) ICV study. Nevertheless, both faced the task of evaluating and defining the business

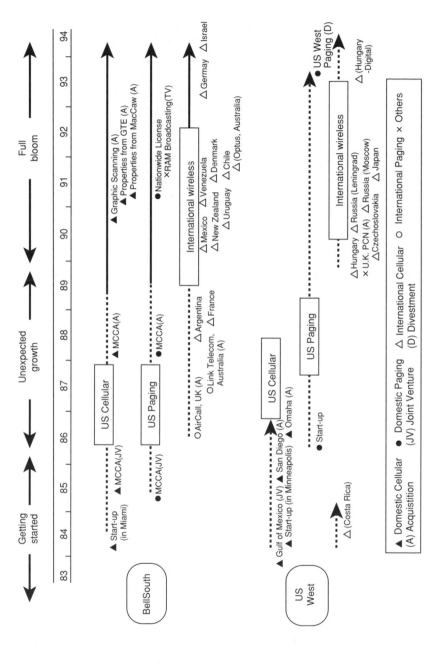

Figure 10.1 Wireless communications business development at BellSouth and US West

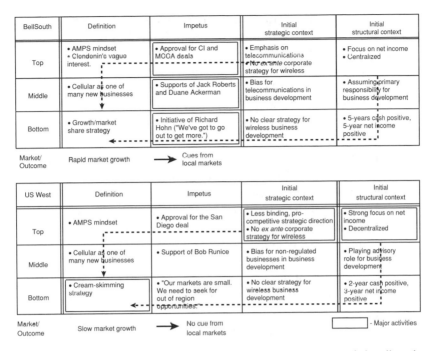

Figure 10.2 Process interpretation of field data: getting started (predivestiture—1986)

opportunities at hand and needed to answer such questions as: What are the cellular and wireless communications technologies? What is the scope of the businesses? What kind of customer needs do they serve? How much potential do the cellular and other wireless communications businesses have for profit and growth?

AMPS mind-set of top corporate executives. At this early stage of business development, top corporate executives of both BellSouth and US WEST did not pay much attention to the new wireless opportunities. The AMPS business plan inherited from AT&T assumed only 1 per cent ultimate service penetration, and envisioned the cellular and other wireless communications businesses as never achieving a big-business status. A cellular telephone was nothing but an executive toy in the eyes of these executives. Although John Clendenin, BellSouth's chief executive officer since the official January 1984 break-up, supervised Bell experiments on precellular technology at Illinois Bell early in his career, and retained an interest in cellular technology, his interest was still vague, as he recalled: 'Even with the low level of penetration anticipated in the early days, which have proved to be very conservative, cellular was still going to be a good business, and it was going to complement the rest of the telecommunications business. It was not thought, in those days, to be anything more than a complement.'

One of many new businesses for middle managers. Similarly, strategic planners and corporate development managers at BellSouth and US WEST did not pay much attention to wireless communications businesses. They were exploring and evaluating new growth opportunities in a variety of business areas from publishing and advertising, to selling telecommunications and information equipment and systems, and even to leasing and financial services and real estate services. Wireless communications businesses were therefore regarded by middle managers as just one of the new unregulated business opportunities.

Different business strategies taken by business-unit officers. The lack of relative interests of top and middle managers left the task of defining new business opportunities primarily to the officers of newly formed business units for cellular telephone service: BellSouth Mobility Incorporated (BMI) and US WEST New Vector Group (New Vector). Although these officers at the two companies were much too pessimistic in hindsight, there was an important difference in their evaluation of the new business opportunities, a difference manifested in opposite business-level strategies—a growth/market share strategy of BMI and a cream-skimming strategy of NewVector—despite the relative similarity in size and demographics of their primary local cellular markets.

BMI, located in suburban Atlanta, was headed by Bob Tonsfeldt, former chief operating officer of AMPS (B1 from Table 10.3). John Clendenin, with his personal interest in the cellular technology, had recruited Tonsfeldt, who brought Richard Hohn, AMPS's chief strategist, as his second in command. It was Hohn who strongly believed in the potential of cellular. According to Tonsfeldt:

Richard Hohn was the keeper of the [AMPS] model. Richard always felt that the AMPS numbers were too low, and he had argued with the AMPS president on that. The AMPS president wanted to make sure that whatever he promised to Charlie Brown [then AT&T's chief executive officer], he could deliver. And so we went at it [the AMPS business plan] . . . However, the model, of course, could accept any kind of parameters you wanted to put into it, so Richard and I played a lot of 'what if' games in terms of double penetration [of the AMPS business plan] and all those things. Richard was really an optimist.

The optimistic strategist and the supportive president developed a growth/market share strategy that aimed to gain customers and maximize revenues for its initial major cellular markets. Tonsfeldt explained:

We didn't have a greater vision than anybody else, except we thought that the key was to get customers... The idea was to price cheaper, to sell harder, and that's going to get customers... We paid a lot of money for customers [as commissions]. We probably paid too much... We concluded [by playing 'what if' games] that we were much better off getting more customers at a middle price than by trying to cream-skim. We also went out to get customers fast, and we tried to build bigger networks [with larger service coverage].

NewVector, located in Bellevue, Washington, was initially headed by an entrepreneurial, visionary, and aggressive president, Dick Callahan, originally from one of three Bell operating companies reorganized into US WEST (U1). Without an optimistic strategist such as Richard Hohn, the New Vector officers shared a common belief in the assumption of the AMPS business plan. They developed a kind of cream-skimming strategy for its initial major local markets. Bill Dixon, New-Vector's vice president for network and planning, explained the subsidiary's early business strategy:

We were determined not to get leveraged by the distribution channel. We tried to ensure that the business was done half through our indirect organization and half through our direct sales organization. In that way, we wouldn't have either group leveraging, saying, 'We're doing all of your business so we want bigger commissions, or we want this or that.'... We weren't sure that people were very interested in the service... we didn't think that the price would drive them to buy into cellular. There were others who believed that if you said 'air time is cheap, come buy it now, we have a special deal', you would get more people. We didn't believe that... and we purposefully kept the prices high. I think we were one of the higher-priced carriers in the industry.

Influence of Corporate Contexts on the Definition Process   Though the personal beliefs of key business-unit officers were a major reason why BMI and NewVector took such contrasting business strategies, the field data suggest strong influences of the companies' corporate contexts—structural and strategic contexts—which were designed primarily by top corporate executives. Arrows with dotted lines in Fig. 10.2 show how different corporate contexts induced different business strategies at the two companies.

Initial structural context. At the time of the break-up, BellSouth's and US WEST's organizational structure and administrative systems and processes were quite similar, both reflecting the administrative heritage of the Bell systems and conforming themselves to common institutional forces.[2] Despite many similarities, however, there were two major differences in structural context between BellSouth and US WEST.

1. *Centralized vs. decentralized structure*. One difference was the degree of delegation in decision making by the corporate office to business units. BellSouth inherited the traditional centralized management style of the Bell system, whereas US WEST adopted a strong decentralized management style, with a lean corporate office of about 160 people, reflecting the personality of Jack MacAllister, the founding CEO, who had been known as a maverick in the Bell system for his approach to leadership even before the break-up. This difference in management style between BellSouth (centralized) and US WEST (decentralized) resulted in differences in business development practices, specifically in the way business development ideas were initiated and pursued. For example, BellSouth's corporate development team, which reported to a chief planning officer, shared responsibility in identifying, initiating, and pursuing growth opportunities with the business units. In contrast, the primary responsibilities for growth opportunities were left to relevant business units at US WEST, and the role of US WEST's commercial development division was limited to provide advisory assistance to existing business units and to investigate additional opportunities that fell beyond the boundaries of these business units.

2. *Financial grip of the corporate office on business units*. The second major difference in the structural context between the two companies concerned the strength of the corporate office's financial grip on business units. Because the capital markets viewed the RHCs' stock as dividend stocks, not growth stocks, all of the RHCs were financially oriented, focusing particularly on net income. They needed constantly to increase earnings in order to satisfy investors' expectations. Moreover, many financial analysts were pessimistic about the financial prospects of the RHCs, which were left by AT&T with aging local exchange businesses, and this pessimism further fueled the RHCs' financial emphasis. Top corporate executives of BellSouth were very concerned about their enterprise's financial viability and set 'to be financial driven' as one of key strategic objectives (BellSouth 1984 *Annual Report*, 3). US WEST's financial emphasis was even stronger—much stronger. Financial analysts frequently compared the prospects of these seven siblings and ranked US WEST as the lowest in investment potential because of the company's less attractive franchised territory for local exchange business. Jack MacAllister explained:

When divestiture was announced, security analysts on the East and West coasts talked about US WEST as a company of wide-open spaces, relatively small advantage, and the least value...That really got my attention. I decided we had to meet the investment community and tell them what our philosophy was. So, even before divestiture, we had security analyst meetings...We stressed our philosophies on competition, regulation, the MFJ, and what all that meant in terms of share value. My chief financial officer and I made tour after tour not only in the US but in Europe and Japan, telling people about our focus on creating value for the share owners. We included that in our fundamental mission statement. We put more emphasis on that than anyone else because of the American security analysts' indifference to us.

Concern of US WEST's top corporate executives for financial viability imprinted the company with a particularly strong emphasis on share owner value, and hence on bottom line.

Initial strategic context. Strategic contexts of BellSouth and US WEST were initially similar in that top corporate executives of the two companies, who shared, more or less, the AMPS mind-set, had no articulated corporate-level strategy for wireless communications businesses. Yet, the field data reveal that these top executives established very rough 'overall strategic directions' for their enterprises, which slightly differed between the two companies. This corporate-level variable for strategic context, which reflected top management's personal beliefs and strategic intents, was not observed in either Bower's or Burgelman's study, presumably because it had been controlled in these studies that compared multiple projects or ventures within the same single multibusiness firm.

Binding, conservative vs. less binding, procompetitive strategic direction. BellSouth's initial overall strategic direction emphasized a familiar business territory for telephone companies, i.e. 'telecommunications'. The company's fundamental strategies announced in late 1983, for example, included 'to emphasize telecommunications, the business we know best' and 'to pursue orderly diversification' (BellSouth 1984 *Annual Report*, 3). The company viewed telecommunications as its principal business (BellSouth 1985 *Annual Report*, 1). This emphasis on telecommunications resulted from management's assessment of the company's strategic prospect. John Clendenin commented:

One of the principal differences [between BellSouth and other RHCs] was that the [BellSouth's] nine southeastern states had a much faster growth rate than other parts of the country. There was a lot of continuing growth in our core business...We began to realize that we would continue to have an active core business, which had us emphasize [what we know best], and not jump into things that were far removed until we had fully undertaken all that was in the core telecommunications business...From the start, we focused our energy on staying close to telecommunications.

US WEST, on the other hand, defined itself as 'a *diversified* tele-communications holding company' (emphasis added by the authors) that 'owns a growing base of information industry companies' (US WEST 1984 *Annual Report*, back of cover page). Although this statement seems somewhat similar to BellSouth's, it was much broader and less binding in setting a direction for the enterprise. The less attractive image of the company's territory led it to explore growth opportunities with a broader scope in a spirit best characterized by MacAllister's own words 'aim high, hit hard, and don't be afraid to raise a little dust' (the CEO's letter to share owners, US WEST 1985 *Annual Report*, 2). US WEST's overall strategic direction also differed from BellSouth's in its procompetitive, aggressive posture of moving away from regulation, reflecting MacAllister's belief in the coming of competition in telecommunications. One former corporate executive commented:

The feeling was that competitive market forces were present, and we thought at that time that they were going to move more quickly and profoundly than they actually did. The greater good for US WEST was getting more of the business out from under regulation as quickly as possible. Our CEO [MacAll-ister] had considerable experience dealing with state public service commis-sions. He believed that the solution was getting as much of the business out from under regulation as possible. He based the company on those beliefs.

Different business plans for business units. These different corporate contexts—structural and strategic—of BellSouth and US WEST resulted in different business plans for their cellular subsidiaries, and caused the subsidiaries to develop different business strategies in their initial local cellular markets.

The US WEST corporate office's particularly strong focus on net income led to a very ambitious business plan for NewVector: 'being cash positive in two years and net income positive in three years'. Under US WEST's strategy of moving away from regulated busi-nesses, the cellular business, which was mostly unregulated but was closer to regulated local exchange businesses, was assigned to generate net income rather than provide a growth vehicle for the company. This ambitious business plan led NewVector to follow a cream-skimming strategy with high cellular rates, small commissions for distributors, and small upfront capital expenditures in order to generate net income as quickly as possible.

At BellSouth, BMI, in contrast, initially agreed with its corporate office on a much less stringent business plan, which was 'being cash positive and net income positive both in five years'. The corporate office was not as insistent for early profits as US WEST's. In Bell-South's strategic context, which emphasized 'telecommunications', cellular telephone service was viewed as a small, yet complementary business to the core local exchange business, and long-term growth was considered as much as short-term profitability. Though Richard Hohn's vision, under Bob Tonsfeldt's patronage, was certainly a key driver behind BMI's growth/market share strategy, the less stringent business plan given by the corporate office allowed the subsidiary to choose this strategy as one of many possible options.

Product Championing   As cellular telephone service was introduced in their major local service areas within franchised regions (B2, U3), and as early operations results became available, BellSouth and US WEST continually reevaluated the technical and economic aspects of the cellular business and assessed the potential of other wireless communications businesses. While still busy constructing and operating cellular networks in initial local markets as well as applying for wireline cellular licenses for lower-ranked areas, some of BMI and NewVector officers were eyeing wireless opportunities beyond their existing operations and taking on the role of 'product champions'.

Different operating results in relatively similar local markets. Soon after introducing cellular operations, BMI found an unexpectedly strong customer response, particularly in Miami and Atlanta, boosted by its growth/market share strategy. The number of Mobility's total cellular subscribers consistently exceeded its projections, increasing from 6,500 (0.11% penetration) in three local areas at the end of 1984, to 26,300 (0.24% penetration) in twelve markets by the end of 1985. In contrast, New Vector did not find as strong a market response in its local markets as BMI did, due, at least partially, to its cream-skimming strategy. The number of subscribers was 5,300 total (0.09% penetration) in the initial four markets at the end of 1984, and increased to 15,500 (0.20% penetration) in eight markets at the end of 1985.[3] Although the difference in subscribers and penetration rate numbers between Mobility and NewVector was not significant, it was still important considering that the prevailing belief was that ultimate service penetration would remain a few percentage points by the turn of the century.

Product championing and early impetus. At BellSouth, encouraged by the unexpectedly strong market response particularly in Miami and Atlanta, visionary strategist Richard Hohn initiated the idea of expanding cellular telephone business by acquiring out-of-region nonwireline cellular licenses. Bob Tonsfeldt, to whom Hohn reported directly at that time, recalled: 'Richard had the idea of expansion. He was the first person to say, "We've really got to go out and buy other stuff". And I kind of said, "Good gosh, we've got enough to do here" but he kept pushing to grow.'

Shortly, Tonsfeldt and Hohn found a supporter in the corporate office, Jack Roberts, a former investment banker who had joined BellSouth as director of corporate development in September 1984. Roberts and Hohn worked together and developed business plans for acquiring wireline cellular licenses. 'Richard Hohn and Jack Roberts both had a lot of confidence in each other, and convinced each other that this [wireless business] was clearly something to take a chance on,' as one former corporate strategic planner recalled. Tonsfeldt, in the capacity of BMI's president, supported them by letting Hohn work for the corporate development group while he was still on BMI's payroll. The first proposal, pursuing the acquisition of Communications Industries (CI), a Dallas-based paging and cellular company, was rolled out and presented to senior corporate executives in early 1985. Duane Ackerman, to whom Roberts reported directly, gave it his support, and the proposal was then approved by top corporate executives, including Bill McCoy, then vice chairman for Finance, Strategy, and Administration, and John Clendenin. Although these senior executives did not then share the vision and enthusiasm of early product champions, the unexpectedly strong market growth in Atlanta and Miami helped to win their approval. According to Roberts: 'I think we were lucky. The development of our markets [Atlanta and Miami] proceeded faster early on, and they [senior corporate executives] could sense that this was a more attractive business. We had a good beginning experience, even in 1984.'

Although BellSouth's corporate development team lost Communication Industries to Pacific Telesis by a very small amount (B4), it successfully moved on to its second target (B5).

Senior officers of NewVector, primarily responsible for growth opportunities related to wireless communications, moved early to explore cellular opportunities outside US WEST's franchised region, even before the introduction of cellular service in major within-region local service areas (U2, U4). Compared with BellSouth's early moves, however, NewVector's aggressive moves were rather opportunistic.[4]

When Pacific Telesis won CI over BellSouth, it was unable to hold the CI's nonwireline license for San Diego because it had already owned wireline side in this service area. Although they had not originally pursued the CI deal, Dick Callahan, then NewVector's president, and his staff became aware of it and interested in acquiring the San Diego nonwireline license. Unlike BellSouth, negotiation with the corporate office was very tough without early favorable experiences in the major local markets. 'When we proposed the San Diego deal, everyone at US WEST, Inc. [i.e. the corporate office] thought we were crazy,' according to one senior officer of NewVector. The New-Vector managers were 'locked into a lot of boxing with the corporate office', but eventually persuaded the corporate executives to pursue the San Diego deal (U6).

The Second Period: Unexpected Growth (Early 1986 to Mid-1989)

As cellular service took off in the nation's major local areas, and the industry began to experience unexpected growth,[5] officers of BMI and New Vector continually redefined the scope of their businesses, and corporate managers reevaluated the potential of wireless communications businesses. These activities together constituted continuation of the definition process. Major managerial activities of business development during this period, however, shifted to the impetus process and early product champions of BellSouth and US WEST actively pursued further expansion of cellular and other wireless communications businesses. Figure 10.3 compares major managerial activities of the two companies during this period of unexpected growth.

Wireless proponents of the two companies had contrasting experiences in attracting the attention of their top corporate executives and obtaining necessary resources from their corporate offices. Two factors are important in explaining the difference between the two companies in the impetus process. One is the operating results of BMI and New-Vector, which were, in fact, determined largely by their initial business strategies and business plans. Another appears to have been selective forces exercised by the corporate context of the two companies. The influences of the two factors are graphically displayed in Fig. 10.3 by solid lines (results) and dotted lines and arrows (corporate context).

Continual Impetus   During this period, different business plans and strategies together brought about quite different operations results for BMI and NewVector. BMI experienced continual strong market

BellSouth	Redefinition	Continual Impetus	Determination of strategic context	Determination of structural context
Top	• "Cellular is a good business."	• Increasing confidence in wireless proponents	• Stronger bias towards "telecommunications" • Inceasing confidence in wireless business	• Cautiously checking financials in proposals
Middle	• "We do not know how further this business can grow."	• Stronger commitment • Additional supporters	• Experimenting an idea of 'global/mobile' strategy	• Reevaluating administrative systems and processes
Bottom	• "This is a great business."	• "Let's replicate success."	• Examining the scope of wireless business	• Trying to accommodate the corporate's focus on net income

| Market/ Outcome | • Consistent growth • Meeting budgets | ⟶ More resource allocation to wireless businesses |

US West	Redefinition	Continual impetus	Determination of strategic context	Determination of structural context
Top	• "Cellular is not a good business."	• Losing confidence in wireless proponents	• "Keep trying everything."	• Favoring quick net income generators (i.e. real estate and financial businesses)
Middle	• Mixture of confusion and excitement	• 'Indecisive' commitment • No additional supporter	• "Diversification is good, telecommunications is too narrow."	• Reevaluating administrative systems and processes
Bottom	• "Our performance is poor because we do not have good markets."	• "We must follow others, other markets must be more attractive."	• Examining the scope of wireless business	• Renegotiating budgets with corporate office

| Market/ Outcome | • Slow business growth • Failing to meet budgets | ⟶ Little resource allocation to wireless businesses | ☐ - Major activities |

Figure 10.3 Process interpretation of field data: unexpected growth (1986–9)

growth in its major local markets, being continually boosted by its growth/market share strategy. 'Every time a projection was done, it was exceeded . . . Every year, it went faster and faster. We kept thinking we don't really know where this is going, but it's faster than we can believe and understand,' according to Jack Roberts. In contrast, New-Vector's early cream-skimming strategy suppressed the growth of cellular business in major local markets.[6] Because comprehensive data on cellular operation by carrier or by local market were not available at that time managers relied mostly on their actual experiences in assessing the potential of cellular businesses. Consequently, the New Vector officers were slower than their BMI counterparts in recognizing the potential of cellular opportunities.

More importantly, the two cellular subsidiaries differed significantly in their accomplishment of budget and business plan, which served as preset 'aspiration levels' (e.g. Cyert and March 1963; Levitt and March 1988). BMI always met its budget. According to Bob Tonsfeldt, 'In terms of cash, we probably were on target or better. In terms of net income, we were way ahead.' In contrast, after two years of operation, NewVector failed to meet its business plan, which initially was simply too ambitious. Even after it renegotiated with its corporate office and lowered the level of the budget, NewVector still did not meet the modified budget.[7]

Strategic forcing by business-unit officers. Business-unit officers at BMI and NewVector were delighted about the booming cellular acquisitions, although their reasons differed. BMI officers, who had better-than-expected operations results, thought they should replicate success, whereas NewVector officers reasoned that their cellular operations results were unsatisfactory because they were not in major markets, and therefore the company should act to find bigger ones. At the same time, the business-unit officers of the two companies reevaluated the scope of their operations and added paging service to its portfolio (B7, U8). These officers therefore played a role of 'strategic forcing' by urging a need and rationale for acquiring cellular properties and expanding into other wireless communications businesses.

Strategic building by middle managers. As observed in past studies (Burgelman 1983a), middle managers played the most critical role of strategic building in the impetus process, capitalizing on strategic forcing activities of business-unit officers and trying to articulate a master strategy for wireless communications businesses.

At BellSouth, BMI as well as the corporate development team moved to BellSouth Enterprises, newly established as a holding company for all its unregulated businesses with Bill McCoy, formerly vice chairman, as the president (B6). In the new organization, Jack Roberts and Richard Hohn, who had left BMI to join the Roberts team, continued to pursue domestic cellular opportunities in close collaboration with Bob Tonsfeldt of BMI (B11). They soon recognized, however, that winning domestic cellular deals was becoming increasingly difficult as more companies started participating in the deals, and turned their attentions to international wireless opportunities, i.e. acquisitions of foreign paging operations (B8, B9, B10, B13). Although it was still too early for foreign countries to introduce cellular and other advanced wireless communications services, they believed that the presence as a paging operator in a country would allow BellSouth to claim expertise necessary to be qualified as cellular operators and increase the likelihood that the company would get a cellular license when the cellular service was introduced in the country. To support the strategic initiatives, Hohn developed the 'global/mobile' concept in late 1986 and discussed it with Roberts and Tonsfeldt. The concept represented a belief that mobile (wireless) communications service, including cellular and paging, would shortly be introduced everywhere in the world, and articulated the intention that BellSouth should be a leader in exploiting these opportunities world-wide. Although Hohn died suddenly of cancer in March of 1987, Jack Roberts further advocated this concept.

Faster-than-expected market growth and consistent budget accomplishment by BMI's cellular operations not only made these product champions more enthusiastic about wireless opportunities, but also helped them to gain additional support of middle managers. Charlie Coe, who became the president of BellSouth International in early 1986, and Roger Hale, the then BellSouth Enterprises' group vice president who supervised domestic wireless communications businesses, international operations, and market development, bought into the idea, and became strong advocates for the global/mobile concept. Sid Boren, who took over Duane Ackerman's position of vice president for strategic planning, provided support from the corporate side. Under the leadership of these former and new wireless proponents, BellSouth entered cellular operations in Buenos Aires, Argentina (B12).

Experiences of US WEST's wireless proponents were quite different. In 1986, Dick Callahan was called back to Denver and became group vice president for Diversified Operations, including NewVector and US WEST International (U7), and John DeFeo, the former vice president of Marketing, was promoted to president of NewVector. After the San Diego deal, Callahan and DeFeo were more excited about cellular opportunities and aggressively pursued the expansion of business. Bob Runice, the then president of the Commercial Development Division, continued to support Callahan and DeFeo from the corporate side. 'We looked at all the deals [which appeared in the market] and we were a player,' according to Runice. These products champions, however, did not find strong support from other middle or senior managers, and they were unsuccessful in pursuing the cellular deals, except a very small deal in Omaha (U9). Slower market growth of NewVector's markets and its failure to meet its budgets made many senior managers at US WEST skeptical of wireless opportunities. Even Runice, one of the few corporate supporters, became uneasy and often indecisive in his commitment to wireless opportunities. He recollected his vacillation:

I remember sitting in a Corporate Development Counsel meeting when they took votes [for cellular acquisition], and the votes were split. Feelings were so strong that I told Dick McCormick [who became COO in 1986 and succeeded Jack MacAllister later in 1990] that we shouldn't do it because there were three dissenting votes. I didn't want future discussions to be affected by these three people saying they never believed in the deal. [My belief was] if we didn't convince more than half of the voters, we hadn't convinced them that it was a good deal, and so we shouldn't do it.

Over time, wireless proponents faced increasingly strong opposition from the corporate office, particularly from the financial management group, and became inactive in the domestic cellular deals. One senior officer of NewVector, who promoted these initiatives, described this situation by saying, 'We were very aggressive and bold [in pursuing cellular opportunities], and then, all of a sudden, it changed. After the San Diego deal, they [the corporate office] clammed up.'

Confidence building by top corporate executives. Although the B–B model assumes that top management plays a passive role by saying 'yes' or 'no' (Bower 1970) or by 'authorizing' (Burgelman 1983*a*) in the impetus process, the field data of this study suggest a more active role of 'confidence building' by top corporate executives.

Even for BellSouth's wireless proponents, top corporate approval was not automatic during this period. These executives were still skeptical about the potential of wireless communications and hesitated very much to pay an 'extraordinarily expensive' price for cellular properties. BMI's favorable operating results, however, turned again to be a key in business development. Rapid growth of the business in major local markets and BMI's consistent success in meeting its budgets caused the corporate executives to gain confidence not only in wireless communications businesses but also in wireless proponents. Tonsfeldt explained:

We [BMI] were fairly successful early on—that, I think, makes a big difference. I mean, if your first city goes well, and then your second city goes well, you've got a track record that they [corporate managers] will go along with . . . Our chief financial officer was a very number-oriented person. If you meet your budgets, he loves you. If you do not meet your budgets, he hates you. It's real simple. There's no gray area; it's black and white. We kept meeting budgets like crazy.

Additionally, early actions of the expanding wireless business turned out to be successful, which further boosted the top executives' confidence. This comment of Bill McCoy on the Bakersfield deal illustrates this point:[8]

We had a chance to build out in Bakersfield California [in 1987]. We already had Los Angeles [nonwireline license] which we got with the MCCA [joint venture] deal. Bakersfield did not prove itself in our model, and we couldn't bid high enough to get it. However, we said, 'Well, isn't Bakersfield important, being where it is? We ought to put a strategic component in evaluation.' So we lowered it to a strategic level, maybe another hundred basic points, and, on the basis of that, bought it. Once again, it did better than we thought it would do. We had positive reinforcement from our properties really quickly after we got them. The more we did, the more confident we became that we knew what we were doing, so we began to get aggressive.

Although an investment in Argentine cellular operations was generally considered risky because of the Latin American country's slow recovery from its debt crisis in the early 1980s, BellSouth's top corporate executives, who had gradually gained confidence in wireless businesses and their proponents, felt comfortable enough to take risks.

The experiences of US WEST's wireless proponents in dealing with the corporate executives were contrary. Slow market growth of the cellular business in primary markets handicapped Callahan and DeFeo in proving to top corporate executives the cconomics of acquisition proposals. Most important, New Vector's failure to meet its budgets shook the confidence of its top executives; the wireless proponents lost credibility in their eyes. The New Vector's senior officer, introduced above, commented from the perspective of a wireless proponent:

When we [New Vector] didn't meet those goals [of the original business plan] in the first two years, they [the corporate office] said cellular was a terrible business. It was sort of a self-fulfilling prophecy: we didn't meet those goals, and then we brought them growth opportunities [acquisition proposals]. They said 'Why should we go and do those [cellular deals] when they [New Vector] can't even meet their goals for the business that they have? Besides that, we have some other ways that we want to invest the money.' It just got to be this big circle. [Our corporate office] was concerned only about the bottom line. It was as though, if you made the bottom line, then you earned the right to do something else.

Although New Vector's early acquisition of the San Diego cellular license turned out to be successful, the success was discounted and treated as some lucky accident by top corporate executives, who did not receive positive cues from local cellular markets and were increasingly disappointed with the company's poor performance. Howard Doerr, then executive vice president and chief financial officer, explained the situation from the perspective of a top corporate executive.

The first major acquisition we [US WEST] made was the nonwireline license in San Diego. We bought it for $24–25 per POP. Because the other cellular licenses had been given to us free of charge [by the FCC], people said we were out of our minds. Some of us also wondered if we were out of our minds . . . As more nonwireline franchises became available, NewVector executives became more aggressive in asking the board for approval to bid for licenses. We were part of five or six major bids. For some reason, we were unsuccessful within these biddings . . . Cellular performance within our [US WEST's] territory was a little slow. It took a few more years than we had predicted to become profitable . . . There were some deals we [the corporate office] should have said yes to, but they [New Vector executives] were not convincing enough with their own performance.

Although Jack MacAllister personally became more interested in cellular opportunities, he did not support these proposals strongly. MacAllister recalled with regret: 'I had the ability to over-rule [the decision of rejecting cellular proposals.] I was the CEO. Even though they [Callahan and Runice] were very interested, I was sufficiently influenced by those who weren't. I look at it as my personal decision.'

Influence of Corporate Contexts on the Impetus Process   In addition to cellular operating results, the company's structural and strategic contexts presented another critical factor in determining the fate of wireless proposals in the impetus process. These contexts together functioned as an 'internal selection environment' in choosing between competing business proposals as suggested by the intra-organizational ecological perspective (Burgelman 1991, 1994).

Selecting. At BellSouth, proposals to expand cellular and other wireless communications businesses were consistent with an overall strategic orientation to emphasize telecommunications as opposed to nontelecommunications. BellSouth's structural context, particularly its conservative, financially driven management practices, provided a cautious stoppage to the escalating expansion of wireless communications businesses, because wireless ventures—domestic acquisitions or international start-ups—usually required up-front investments of capital and caused a short-term earning dilution. Yet, it was not a fundamental deterrence for wireless proponents in pursuing domestic and international wireless opportunities.

The strategic and structural contexts of US WEST posed contrasting influences on wireless proposals. During this period, US WEST was still feeling that 'diversification is good, and telecommunications is too narrow', according to one corporate manager. Its strategic context therefore did not bind business units when exploring new growth opportunities as much as BellSouth's strategic context, which emphasized telecommunications, did. At the same time, the company's structural context of a heavy-net income focus strongly favored proposals that would allow US WEST to earn net income quickly. These corporate contexts drove US WEST into unrelated diversification, particularly real estate and later financial services, businesses that produced handsome net income almost immediately without short-term earning dilution.

Changing corporate contexts. It is important to note the iterative nature of the influence of strategic context on the impetus process. While the initial strategic context favored proposals of one business over another, the context kept changing as the operating success of a winning proposal provided further impetus, while failure of another business to obtain incremental resources fueled further operating disappointments. In contrast, structural context including many diverse organizational and administrative elements is much more stable over time.

BellSouth's emphasis on telecommunications was not readily apparent at the beginning, but took clearer shape as its business development efforts progressed. For example, like US WEST, BellSouth established subsidiaries for real estate and financial service businesses. Although the company was at one time tempted to grow these businesses, the good progress of other telecommunications-related businesses allowed top corporate executives to recognize that these diversifications were not consistent with their strategic orientation. The company continued to define itself as a 'telecommunications holding company' in the late 1980s (e.g. BellSouth 1989 Source Book, 1) although, according to Sid Boren, what telecommunications meant had become clearer and also changed to include wireless 'telecommunications'.

US WEST's expansion in real estate and financial services also progressed incrementally. These businesses turned out initially to be financially successful, enabling the company's corporate executives to gain confidence in them quickly and to approve further expansion of their operations. The development of strategic initiatives in these unrelated businesses kept the US WEST's strategic context less binding than BellSouth's. Although the company's corporate vision was to become 'a leader in the information industry' (US WEST 1987 *Annual Report*, 5), what the 'information industry' meant was not necessarily clear, even to top corporate executives. The corporate definition then evolved to 'a diversified corporation' that concentrated on 'four lines of businesses' such as communications, data solutions (e.g. software and system integration), marketing services (e.g. directory publishing), and financial services (US WEST 1988 *Annual Report*, 2).

The Third Period: Full Bloom (Mid-1989 to Mid-1994)

By mid-1989, the potential of cellular and other wireless communications businesses became obvious almost to everyone, and the industry experts started to discuss seriously the concept of a 'wireless local loop', suggesting that wireless communications service would substitute or replace wired local exchange in the near future.[9] In the meantime, many foreign governments started to introduce wireless communications services, opening their markets to foreign companies as part of their deregulation programs.

At BellSouth, major managerial activities in this period shifted to determine the strategic context. The global/mobile strategy was articulated and became an integral part of corporate strategy, which then further drove BellSouth into new wireless ventures. At US WEST, wireless proponents, who previously failed to gain the impetus to pursue domestic cellular deals, turned to new international opportunities. Their efforts to shape strategic context failed, however, due to poor performance of NewVector's domestic cellular operations, coupled with emerging strategic initiatives in the area of cable TV/telephony. Managerial activities of the two companies during this third period of full bloom of wireless communications are mapped in Fig. 10.4.

Continual Impetus and Organizational Championing   At BellSouth, the corporate development team led by Jack Roberts became more committed to wireless communications businesses and more aggressive in pursuing opportunities in the USA. The team persuaded top corporate executives to pursue a megamerger with Lin Broadcasting, though the extraordinarily high bid of McCaw Communications, then one of the largest independent cellular companies, eventually led BellSouth to withdraw from the deal (B16). The corporate development team then pursued acquiring neighborhood cellular properties in order to develop a larger 'cluster' of local cellular operations and enhance the company's competitive position (B21, B23, B25).

In the meantime, BellSouth's drive into global wireless opportunities (B14, B15) was accelerated by the successful start-up of cellular operations in Argentina, in which the undeveloped wired telephone infrastructure inspired consumers to choose available cellular service immediately rather than enter a long wait list for wired service (B17). BellSouth's wireless proponents aggressively explored wireless opportunities overseas, particularly in other Latin American countries, and further advocated the global/mobile concept (B19, B20, B22). Earl Mauldin, who succeeded Roger Hale to become a group president of mobile communications (including international), became one of the strongest voices promoting these initiatives, working actively to keep top corporate executives such as John Clendenin and Bill McCoy informed and enthusiastic about the new area of business development.

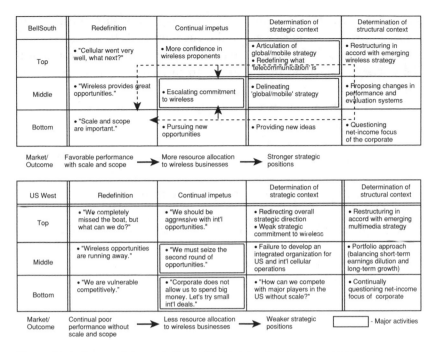

Figure 10.4 Process interpretation of field data: full blossom (1989–94)

Such 'organizational championing' activities by Mauldin and others provided a connection between impetus and determination of strategic context, thereby paving the way for the articulation of a corporate-level strategy for wireless communications businesses (Burgelman 1983a). Like the Bakersfield deal, the success in Argentina was particularly significant to top corporate executives' confidence in wireless businesses and wireless proponents.[10]

At US WEST, wireless proponents such as Callahan and DeFeo came to realize that 'the corporate office would not allow us to spend a penny [to acquire cellular licenses in the USA]', and instead turned their attention to burgeoning international opportunities. They worked hard to get a new personal communications network (PCN) license in the UK (U11) and drove the company to enter cellular operations in several Eastern European countries and Russia (U10, U12, U14, U15).[11]

International expansion was supported by some of the top corporate executives, particularly Jack MacAllister. They had come to realize that wireless communications businesses would be much bigger and more important than they had originally thought, and that they had missed initial opportunities in the USA. Seeing the second round of opportunities arising overseas, they became aggressive and supported international wireless proposals. MacAllister commented:

We had cellular opportunities first in the US. Outside of San Diego, we passed on them. It became obvious that we had been too cautious. The next opportunity was wireless and cable TV in Europe. We learned from our experience, so we became very aggressive in Europe... What I learned and did in Europe was to become very aggressive. For example, when the PCN license came up in London, there were a lot of people who said that's going to cost billions of dollars to exploit that market. We had a chance to enter that market by merely applying. Dick Callahan, Bob Runice and I worked together and decided we were going to do it. I explained to the board all the risks and opportunities. The board supported me and we pursued the license. We got it.

Determination of Strategic Context   By the late 1980s performance of the two companies' domestic cellular operations differed greatly. Bell-South's growth/market share strategy, past acquisitions of cellular properties as well as cluster strategy brought about higher penetration, a larger customer base, and a broader geographical coverage, all of which gave scale economies to cellular operations. BellSouth's full year domestic cellular operations, including acquired properties, became profitable for the first time in 1990. Additionally, by this time, Bell-South's paging properties grew to a considerable scale through acquisitions (B21), which allowed the company to enjoy scope economies associated with joint marketing of cellular and paging services. In contrast, US WEST suffered from a lack of scale and scope economies as a consequence of its early cream-skimming strategy and a lack of past major domestic acquisitions.[12] One NewVector officer commented cynically that 'They [corporate office] are paying for the past. They shouldn't complain that we don't have scope and scale advantages when they failed to give us money to buy properties.' In 1990, the last year for which NewVector disclosed the details of its financial results, the operating margin of NewVector's cellular operations was 0.59 per cent, whereas that of BellSouth's domestic operations recorded 16.36 per cent. Even in 1993, NewVector continued to suffer a net income loss.

Delineating by middle managers. While pursuing wireless opportunities worldwide, BellSouth's wireless proponents worked to develop a master strategy to support such a pursuit. Although Jack Roberts left the company shortly after the Lin Broadcasting deal and Bob Tonsfeldt retired in 1991, Eric Ensor, who joined BellSouth in 1987 and replaced the late Richard Hohn as a strategist in BellSouth Enterprises, became, with Earl Mauldin at the senior level, a primary advocate for wireless communications. Ensor and his staff built on the Hohn's global/mobile concept, and gave substance to it by scrutinizing the scope of business opportunities BellSouth should pursue and analyzing why such a scope would be strategically important. They envisioned BellSouth as a more comprehensive provider of wireless communications services ranging from tone-only paging to two-way cellular. They also upgraded the global/mobile concept by strategically repositioning BellSouth's presence in one country as a wireless provider as a 'beachhead' which would allow the company to successfully explore other telecommunications-related opportunities (e.g. second general carrier license) in that country. The steady performance of BellSouth's domestic cellular operations supported these middle managers' 'delineation' of a master strategy. In early 1990, within BellSouth Enterprises and under the direction of Eric Ensor, the BellSouth Worldwide Wireless group was formed to coordinate all wireless-related activities that were then handled by several subsidiaries and to pursue new wireless opportunities such as personal communications services in the USA (B29).

As US WEST became active in international cellular operations, Callahan and his staff in the Diversified Business Group similarly attempted to develop an integrated strategy for domestic and international operations. They worked to create Spectrum Enterprises as a holding company for both domestic and international cellular operations with John DeFeo appointed president (U13). The continuing poor performance of NewVector's domestic cellular operations, however, disrupted the idea of coordinating the two operations. Within several months, Spectrum Enterprises was dismantled, and DeFeo returned to NewVector to work on improving domestic cellular operations. Soon after, the Diversified Business Group headed by Dick Callahan was reorganized into the International and Business Development Group to focus on international opportunities, and the supervision of domestic cellular operations was transferred from Callahan to Chuck Lillis, then chief planning officer.

Strategy articulation by top corporate executives. At BellSouth, the delineating efforts of middle managers, combined with the executives' increasing confidence in wireless operations, finally resulted in a formal articulation of a corporate-level strategy for wireless communications businesses. In his letter to shareholders in BellSouth's 1988 *Annual Report*, CEO John Clendenin implied for the first time the emergence of a corporate-level wireless strategy: 'We are emerging as one of the world's largest providers of mobile communications' (p. 2).[13] The 'global/mobile' strategy of 'making BellSouth a leader in wireless worldwide' (1992 BellSouth *Annual Report*, 10), an earlier rough draft of which was first envisioned in 1986 by Richard Hohn and then promoted by Jack Roberts and Bob Tonsfeldt, materialized over time, gained additional supporters, and finally became an integral part of BellSouth's corporate strategy in the early 1990s.

For US WEST, this time period was a critical turning point for determining its overall strategic direction. The company's early diversification efforts in such areas as real estate and data solutions were unsuccessful. Like other RHCs, it also found a great deal of difficulty in expanding directory publishing and in selling telecommunications and information equipment. In the meantime, with investments in a variety of operations such as wireless and cable TV in the UK, Eastern Europe, and Russia since 1988, international activities quickly became a strategic focus. A new management team, led by Dick McCormick who became the CEO in early 1991, wanted to lead the company back to the 'network' business by shedding some unrelated businesses such as real estate. This refocus and international thrust led US WEST to pay attention to emerging cable TV/telephony opportunities. US WEST's early experience with the cable TV/telephony businesses in Europe made Callahan and his staff in the International Business Group increasingly confident that the broadband/multimedia opportunities would be 'the second wireless' in the 1990s. Learning from the UK operations was transferred back to Denver, and a 'multimedia/broadband' corporate strategy quickly gained consensus among a new management team.[14]

Accelerated/decelerated business development. At BellSouth, the articulated global/mobile strategy accelerated the company's development of wireless communications businesses (B24, B26, B29, B30, B32, B33). One notable example was a mobile-data venture with RAM Broadcasting announced in late 1991 (B28, B31). John Clendenin explained his rationale in promoting this venture:

I spend a lot of time thinking about the company's strategy and direction. I try to look over the horizon and ask what the next technology is. Cellular has done well, but what is the next version of cellular? We made a huge investment in mobile data, for example—building nationwide systems in this country and in several European countries. That's an attempt to say there's another technology coming over the horizon and that will have a significant impact on our revenue streams after I am gone.

By contrast, at US WEST, the emergent focus on the multimedia/broadband area further diverted the company's attention from wireless businesses, although the company continued to explore some international wireless opportunities (U16, U17). Consequently, the company announced the sale of its paging operations, in 1993 (U18), and its commitment to wireless communications, particularly cellular telephone service, remained very weak. Then, in July 1994, US WEST agreed with AirTouch Communications to combine their domestic cellular assets to form a joint venture, in which US WEST would take a minority (30%) ownership (U19). One anonymous US WEST cellular executive commented:

US WEST really had no idea how to deal with the wireless business. They still cannot make a decision as to what the wireless business means to US WEST. I think it [the reason why they did the AirTouch deal] was almost out of frustration. It was like, 'OK, we can't figure it out. We have an opportunity to take 30% in a bigger venture. Let's just go do this.'

Toward a Formal Process Theory of Strategy Making in Large, Complex Firms

At considerable length, we have demonstrated that the strategy making for wireless communications businesses at BellSouth and US WEST can be modeled as an iterated process of resource allocation. The iterated process model capitalizes on the B–B process model of strategy making and extends it with new insights. These insights, which help us to understand the interfirm comparative questions raised earlier in the chapters, are discussed and developed below as a series of propositions.

The Role of Corporate Context in Strategy Making

Firm-level analysis of the field data from the present study reveals the important difference in corporate—structural and strategic—context in the two Bell siblings. Structural contexts varied: financial hurdles were higher and control more decentralized at US WEST than at BellSouth. Strategic context also differed, specifically in the overall or corporate strategic direction, a variable that was not observed in earlier studies with the project/venture level of analysis: BellSouth's initial strategic context focused thinking on the telecommunications businesses, while US WEST's did not have a clear focus with its aggressive, procompetitive approach to diversification. The corporate contexts of the two companies were partially determined by the distinctive strategic and financial status of their core local exchange businesses in different local franchised territories. The growth potential of local exchange businesses in the sun-belt states allowed BellSouth's top corporate executives to pay more attention to telecommunications businesses, while the 'wide open space' of US WEST's franchised territory and the consequent disinterest of financial analysts in the company led US WEST executives to prioritize in short-term net income and consider a wider range of new growth opportunities. Nevertheless, each firm's top managers still had a certain level of discretion in designing corporate context to reflect their personal visions and beliefs (Child 1972). BellSouth's Clendenin saw the continual viability of a traditional area of telecommunications whereas MacAllister predicted forthcoming competition in that area and felt the need to explore broader opportunities. This observation therefore further validates and extends the proposition of earlier studies (Bower 1970):

> *Proposition 1a.* Top managers exercise a critical influence on the strategic initiatives of lower-level managers by setting up the context in which these managers make decisions and take actions.

What was particularly noticeable in this study is the strong impact of the corporate context on the business development processes. The difference in corporate context of the two companies resulted in their varied responses to cellular opportunities in the definition process despite the fact that they both had very similar local markets: they came up with different business plans—cash positive and net income positive in five years (BMI) and cash positive in two years and net income positive in three years (NewVector). As a response to these plans, they developed contrary business strategies—growth/market share (BMI) and cream-skimming (NewVector). The same corporate context also influenced the impetus process by functioning as an internal selection environment, that led the two companies to different courses of action. The strong net income focus of the US WEST's structural context, coupled with procompetitive strategic direction of its strategic context, favored real estate and financial service projects rather than cellular, whereas BellSouth's less stringent structural context, combined with emphasis on telecommunications, weighted more favourably toward cellular projects. Accordingly:

> *Proposition 1b.* Both strategic and structural contexts influence bottom-up initiatives in the definition process, and shape resource allocation in the impetus process in a way that virtually defines a course of business development and subsequent emergence of a corporate strategy for the new business.

Ironically, the impact of corporate context, particularly that of structural context, is so strong that it often presents a dilemma to top managers even though they were initial architects of the context. The regret of US WEST's Jack MacAllister, reported earlier in this chapter, demonstrates an interesting example for this point. Although MacAllister, unlike most of the other corporate executives who lost confidence in cellular, altered his initial pessimistic perception toward cellular and became interested in cellular acquisitions in the mid- to late 1980s, he could not support the acquisition proposals of New-Vector managers. These proposals did not meet the firm's stringent financial hurdle. Additionally, the decentralized management style, which MacAllister set up himself, prevented him from overruling the majority-based decisions rejecting the proposals. Structural context, once designed and institutionalized as part of a firm's administrative systems and processes, seems to present a strong source of a firm's inertia (Hannan and Freeman 1984, 1989) and continuously exercises strong selecting forces regardless of possible subsequent changes in top managers' intentions and brings about undesirable unanticipated consequences to the top managers.[15] Therefore:

> *Proposition 1c.* A firm's structural context is relatively stable over time and its persistent impact on the subsequent business development process constrains the discretion of top managers who may want to change the firm's course of actions in response to the development of technology and the market for a new business.

Escalation (Deescalation) of a Firm's Strategic Commitment

Like several studies on strategic innovation and change (e.g. Kanter 1983; Nonaka 1988), the B–B model emphasizes the role of middle managers as integrators and value creators. Middle managers interpret corporate visions and broker the bottom-up initiatives of front-line managers based on their beliefs and motives, thereby bridging the gap between those with authority to commit corporate resources to strategic proposals and those with direct knowledge of the market and new technology. These middle managers sponsor strategic initiatives of front-line managers, and then strive in obtaining corporate resources and top managers' attention, while putting their organizational reputation for good judgment at stake. This critical role played by middle managers in the resource allocation process helps us understand another striking observation in the study—that is, the impact of early operational results for a new business, particularly their evaluations against planned targets, on the subsequent business development process, resulting in the escalation or deescalation of a firm's strategic commitment to the new business.

The field data reveal that early operational results critically determine whether strategic initiatives of front-line managers would gain support of middle managers in the impetus process. The early successful ('better-than-expected') operations of BMI created excitement among middle managers—initially with Jack Roberts and Duane Ackerman, followed by Charlie Coe, Roger Hale, Sid Boren, and Earl Mauldin—while the poor ('worse-than-expected') operating results of NewVector made a few supportive middle managers such as Bob Runice indecisive. Additionally, the early operational results affect the credibility of middle managers who decide to support the initiatives. This is a proxy which top managers, in making resource allocation judgments concerning strategic proposal, tend to rely on for calibrating the soundness of highly uncertain forecasts of the market and technology incorporated in the proposal. At BellSouth, the early successful results of cellular business enhanced the track record of wireless proponents in the eyes of top managers and made it relatively easy for wireless proposals to get resources, but in comparison, wireless proponents at US WEST lost credibility with the top managers due to the early poor operation results of NewVector.

These two critical links—one between operational results and middle managers' sponsorship and the other between operation results and the credibility of supporting middle managers—seem to provide an explanation for the escalation (or deescalation) of a firm's commitment in new business development through iterations of resource allocation. Early successful results create excitement among middle managers, whose strong support leads to the realization of strategic proposal. The resulting success of subsequent moves, in turn, induces further excitement of middle managers to the new business. At the same time, successful early operational results and the success of subsequent strategic actions increase the batting average of proposing middle managers and enhance their track record in the eyes of top managers, which, in turn, increases the likelihood that their next proposal will be selected in resource allocation. The escalation (deescalation) process observed in this study is similar to the success-bred-success (failure-bred-failure) pattern reported in Burgelman's (1983a) ICV study. BellSouth followed this favorable cycle of business expansion and consequently escalated its strategic commitment to wireless communications businesses over time. US WEST, in contrast, fell into a vicious cycle. Most of its top executives lost confidence in the wireless business and proponents. Jack MacAllister did not overrule the decisions of rejecting cellular acquisition proposals not only due to inertial forces of structural context, but also because his confidence in wireless proponents was somewhat shaken, although to a lesser extent than other corporate executives. Instead, the company allocated resources into nonwireless businesses, in particular, real estate and financial service businesses, and later cable TV business, and consequently developed a weak strategic commitment to wireless. Thus, these observations lead to the following proposition:

> Proposition 2: In the case of a new business development that involves a high degree of uncertainty, the iterations of the resource allocation process generate a pattern of escalation or deescalation of a firm's strategic commitment based on early results from operations that confirm or disconfirm the premises of the first investment and the credibility of the champions.

The Determination of Strategic Context Revisited

The study's observation on the escalation (deescalation) of strategic commitments through iterations of resource allocation allows us to understand better the role of top managers in determining strategic context, i.e. their incremental learning leading to the increasing/decreasing belief in the new business. Top managers learn as a consequence of earlier actions, and this learning changes their beliefs in the business and subsequently reshapes the firm's strategic context. As subsequent rounds of resource allocation proceed, top managers become more actively involved in defining opportunities and further modifying the strategic context. What might first appear as a developing cognitive bias towards a new business that is meeting its forecasts takes clearer shape over time, and eventually develops into a fully expressed commitment to the business. This incremental view of strategy making is consistent with this observation of Quinn (1980: 58): 'The most effective strategies of major enterprises tend to emerge step by step from an iterative process in which the organization probes the future, experiments, and learns from a series of partial (incremental) commitments rather than through global formulations of total strategies.'

What should be reconciled here is the discrepancy between this incremental change in top managers' beliefs in a new business and the seemingly sudden emergence of the official or explicit corporate strategy in the case of successful business development. In the context of this study, BellSouth's top managers did not articulate their strategic commitments to the wireless communications business until the late 1980s, as demonstrated in this comment by one anonymous wireless proponent:

John Clendenin, of all the seven CEOs of the RHCs, was probably the most predisposed to like cellular if it worked well. He always cautioned us. He said, 'You know, I like cellular, but by God, it better pay off, or I am not supporting it.' So it was not that he was supporting it automatically, but once it looked good, he was already saying, 'Yep, I knew that stuff would work.'

The discrepancy exists presumably because top managers may delay the official announcement of a new corporate strategy until the potential of the new business or the need for change in their enterprise's strategic direction become obvious in order to avoid political friction between multiple groups or subunits within the organization. As pointed out by Neustadt (1960), successful leaders, who know that influence for any manager is based on the success of his interventions, are very cautious in their public positions. From this perspective, deferring the announcement of public commitments until learning reduces uncertainty in new business development can be a wise choice for top managers who are concerned to preserve and enhance their 'power' within the organization.[16]

Burgelman's (1983*a*, 1983*b*) conceptualization of the change in corporate strategy as 'retroactive rationalization' of strategic initiatives seems to be based on the observation of this political aspect of the strategic determination process. The top manager's role in determining strategic context is active, not passive, in the sense that they are willing enough to recognize strategically bottom-up initiatives and capitalize on them rather than pass them by. The present study, however, provides more detailed insights into the critical role played by top managers in the strategic context determination. The data of the study strongly suggest that corporate strategy is the outcome of continuous, incremental confidence building made manifest in iterations of resource allocation rather than formal, explicit statements of 'the corporate strategy'. Whereas such public statements are not announced in a timely fashion, the incremental learning of top managers can shift (escalate or deescalate) resource allocation quite readily. BellSouth allocated more resources to wireless projects over time without its official announcement of global/mobile corporate strategy, and so did US WEST to nonwireless projects without an explicit strategy for neither supporting such projects nor rejecting wireless ones. Accordingly:

Proposition 3: In the case of successful business development, continuous, incremental learning of top managers during business development, and the resulting fine tuning of strategic context, shift resource allocation and precede the articulation or change in official statements of the corporate strategy for the new business.

Conclusions

The interfirm comparison of new business development and strategy-making processes using the B–B model highlights intra-organizational dynamics by which managers at multiple levels relate to external and internal forces and deal with cognitive, political, and organizational consequences of their actions. The iterated process model proposed in this chapter capitalizes on the process map of the B–B model to identify seminal elements of strategy making in a complex firm, such as entrepreneurial initiatives of front-line managers, integrating/brokering activities of middle managers, and the corporate context set up by top managers and its subsequent changes. It suggests that the interaction of these elements causes two firms, which are facing similar business opportunities and are endowed with virtually the same marketing and technological capabilities, to respond differently—one with escalating and the other with deescalating strategic commitments to the new businesses. The iterated model therefore contributes to the field of strategy by enriching our understanding of intra-organizational strategy process and elucidating multilevel, simultaneous, interrelated managerial activities which are combined to generate 'emergent' strategy.

The model makes additional contributions to the field by providing a framework that links multilevel managerial activities with organizational learning in the strategy-making process. The findings reveal that overall strategic direction for an enterprise, which reflects top managers' crude strategic intentions, has noticeable impact on the business development at operating levels of a complex firm. This preliminary phrasing of strategic direction, together with the structural context, strongly influences the way managers at responsible operating or business units perceive new business opportunities, and shapes the premises of the concrete and detailed strategic analysis for new businesses. For example, NewVector managers were aware that the US WEST corporate thought cellular to be an 'executive toy'. Cellular was also close to the regulated core business from which it made sense to move away. The message, in effect, was 'don't get excited and invest too much'. In contrast, BMI managers heard that 'cellular is small, but complementary to the core telecommunications business to which we are committed'. This message at least did not preclude BMI managers from developing an innovative approach to cellular and investing in the new business.

These primitive assertions, what we might call 'strategic premises', then serve as aspiration levels (Cyert and March 1963; Levitt and March 1988) for local search by entrepreneurs at lower levels of the organization, and provide the standards of performance that they must meet. Contrasting cellular business plans for BMI and NewVector were tangible manifestations of these standards. Early operating results are measured against the standards and, in this way, determine what is learned about the potential of the new markets. The inability of New-Vector to meet its forecasts taught US WEST corporate executives that cellular was a bad business, while BellSouth executives learned that cellular was more interesting than expected. Middle managers play a key mediating role in interpreting the results and communicating them with the top managers. The iterations of the resource allocation process that then escalate or deescalate a firm's strategic commitments to the new business, therefore, reflect local learning derived from a sequence of tests in which investment outcomes are measured against continuously revised strategic premises.

The strong influence of top managers' crude intentions on strategic assertions for a new business, however, does not rule out the role of entrepreneurial activities by operating managers in the new business development (Burgelman 1983c). Entrepreneurial managers can and actually do develop independent strategic premises based on their visions and intentions regardless of those of top managers. For example, Richard Hohn, Bob Tonsfeldt, and Jack Roberts—the BellSouth's initial cellular champions—rejected the prevailing AMPS mind-set and developed an innovative approach for cellular. While they certainly benefited from the benevolent BellSouth's corporate context, their initiatives are indeed a key driver for the BellSouth's successful wireless business development. On the other hand, the NewVector executives were less innovative although they needed to deal with a more constraining corporate context than their counterparts experienced at BellSouth. Interesting questions to be addressed are: What would have happened if Hohn, Tonsfeldt, and Roberts had worked at US WEST instead? Could they have overcome the constraints posed by the US WEST's corporate context and still initiated the concrete determination process of the strategic context for wireless as they did at BellSouth?[17] Future research should therefore explore the balance between top managers' intents reflected in corporate context and entrepreneurial activities of lower-level managers (Van de Ven 1992) in determining the strategic context.

As discussed by Burgelman (1991, 1994) and reconfirmed by the field data of this study, the direction of companies evolves in response to changing markets in a way that is mediated by the internal contest for corporate resources and top management attention. The interfirm comparative analysis of this study provides strong field-based evidence on how different corporate contexts function as an internal selection environment to generate a varied resource allocation pattern and to shape different evolutionary dynamics among competing multiple businesses. By identifying the role of top managers and 'strategic levers' available for them to intervene (i.e. the design of corporate context), demonstrating the sources of inertia (e.g. stability of structural context), and highlighting the feedback mechanism through learning by multilevel managers and their interplay, the iterated model of resource allocation extends Burgelman's intra-organizational ecology perspective and contributes to further develop an evolutionary perspective on strategy.

The model and propositions presented in this chapter are obviously tentative. They are based on an interesting but very limited sample in a unique industrial situation. Further field studies in different settings as well as large sample studies are required to validate the model and test the propositions. This study demonstrates that firm-level, comparative longitudinal studies are a very effective approach although they are certainly not easy to execute. It is hoped that this study will spur interests of strategy researchers in the iterative approach and move the field of strategy closer to the establishment of a formal process theory of strategy making.

Acknowledgements

This research is part of the doctoral dissertation of this chapter's first author. Financial support from the Doctoral Programs of the Harvard Business School is gratefully acknowledged. The authors would like to thank William Barnett, Robert Burgelman, John Roberts, and two anonymous *SMJ* reviewers for their insightful comments and suggestions on earlier drafts of this chapter.

Endnotes

1. In setting up the rules for competition, the Federal Communications Commission divided the nation into 734 cellular service areas, issued two licenses for each of these areas, one for wireline telephone companies such as the RHCs and other independent telephone companies (the wireline license) and one for nontelephone companies (the nonwireline license).

2. Because of legal and regulatory requirements, both adopted a similar multihierarchical holding company structure, with strict separation between regulated telephone operating companies and new unregulated subsidiaries, and with the corporate office focusing primarily on policy matters such as strategic planning, financial management, resource allocation, and regulatory relations. Resource allocation was centralized: 100 percent of net income of business units, including telephone operating companies, was passed up to the corporate office as dividends and then reallocated down to business units to accomplish financial and strategic objectives. Performance measurement and evaluation also were similar: both based almost exclusively on net income.

3. These penetration rates are calculated by using the 1980 Census data and the company's estimated ownership in each local cellular market.

4. Bill Dixon commented on NewVector's attitudes at that time. 'We knew that those markets [Minneapolis, Denver, Seattle and all those within the region] were not Los Angeles and Chicago. So, we said to ourselves very consciously that we would not be able to survive long term in this business with the markets we have. We have to go build presence in other places. We have to make ourselves bigger. We believed that from the very beginning. We said any time that we can find an opportunity on the outside that looks as though it's going to be a winner, we have to add that to our portfolio.'

5. The nation's total subscribers increased from 340,000 at the end of 1985 to 682,000 by 1986 and to 1,231,000 by 1987. Cellular license prices, which used to be \$7–10 per POP in 1984, skyrocketed from \$40–60 per POP in mid-1986 to more than \$300 per POP in 1989.

6. NewVector's total cellular subscribers in those local markets at the end of 1986 remained at 32,700, which represented 0.32 per cent service penetration, compared to BMI's 80,000 subscribers (0.69% penetration) in fifteen within-region local markets.

7. Part of the reason for this poor performance was that NewVector faced rising competitive challenges in major local markets, eventually was forced to switch from cream-skimming to a growth/market share strategy to win customers, and consequently got 'stuck in the middle' (Porter 1980). It is also fair to note here that NewVector was more unfortunate than BMI because the former faced duopoly competition in its major local markets relatively earlier than the latter did.

8. It will be possible and necessary to theoretically distinguish between two aspects of confidence building—the cognitive (i.e. confidence in the business) and the sociopsychological or organizational (i.e. confidence in the individuals who promote the business), although top managers often mix them up in actual behavior. In the B–B model, the former is related to strategic context determination and the latter to the impetus process.

9. The nation's cellular subscribers exceeded 3.5 million by the end of 1989.

10. The following comment of Bill McCoy is illustrative: '[In the domestic wireless business] we always did better than we thought we would. The same thing happened internationally. About that time, various countries began to talk about issuing licenses, and so we decided to start putting all of our efforts right there. And we entered into the Argentine market at a time when a lot of people were concerned about [the country's economics.] We introduced the service there in 1989. We had to lease equipment instead of selling it because nobody had any money. But, it has just gone gang busters. We've grown that business about as fast as we can get the equipment down there to do it. So we've been making a profit there for a good while. Then, we bid for the Venezuela license. That [cellular] business has been fantastic. In the US, we're averaging about 150 minutes of use per customer per month, and that number is coming down a little bit. In Argentina and Venezuela, we're running about 425 minutes a month, and it's going up...Then, we went to Guadalajara, Mexico, Uruguay, and Chile.'

11. The pursuit of international opportunities was driven by an idea somewhat similar to what BellSouth found in Buenos Aires: a wireless communications business as a successful substitute for wired telephone service in developing countries with an inadequate telecommunications infrastructure. It was also a result of acquiescing to pressures from the corporate structural context. Because of the very early phase of industry development, acquiring cellular licenses overseas cost much less than in the USA. These international investments with smaller earning dilution were therefore more congruent to US WEST's heavy net income focus.

12. BellSouth's domestic cellular subscribers continued to increase, from 498,000 (1.63% penetration) in 1990 to 774,000 (2.14%) in 1991, to more than 1,118,000 in 1992 (2.92%), and to 1,559,000 (4.01%) in 1993, whereas the number of NewVector's cellular subscribers was 180,000 (1.30% penetration) in 1990, 259,500 (1.75%) in 1991, 358,000 (2.32%) in 1992, and 408,000 (3.30%) in 1993.

13. He became more specific in the 1991 *Annual Report*, 2–3: 'We aggressively grew our cellular operations worldwide last year—with acquisitions, through partnerships, and internally through marketing...We strengthened the foundation for long-term growth in promising new wireless markets. We enhanced our position in key areas, both geographically and from a marketing standpoint. Now we can offer our customers almost anything on the wireless continuum—from tone-only paging to fully featured cellular. In between are numeric and alphanumeric paging, mobile data, and innovative personal communications services—and BellSouth is moving assertively in all these markets. Geographically, we now have as many cellular POPs, or potential customers, outside the US— some 36 million in nine countries—as we do in the 54 metropolitan markets we serve in this country...BellSouth's wireless operations con-

tributed significantly to our financial results in 1991 . . . While cellular is now well established in the US, it also is still clearly a growth market here.'

14. The consensus paved the way for US WEST's strategic alliance with Time Warner in May 1993 to develop a 'Full Service Network' across the nation as well as in some other advanced countries. US WEST emerged with a new mission to be 'a leading provider of integrated communications, entertainment, and information services over wired broadband and wireless networks in selected local markets worldwide' (1993 US WEST *Annual Report*, 2).

15. US WEST's failure to exploit cellular opportunities is not an 'unintended' outcome, but an 'unanticipated' consequence. When Jack MacAllister initially designed the corporate context, he intended to move away from regulated businesses (including cellular). He did not anticipate at that time that cellular would be an important business for the company.

16. While this discussion is most relevant to the case of successful business development (i.e. BellSouth), it can also be applied to the unsuccessful case (i.e. US WEST). For example, it was not until the end of the 1980s when the potential of cellular became obvious to almost everyone and the uncertainty in the business development was significantly reduced, that MacAllister started to take steps to support cellular initiatives. It may also be possible that MacAllister hesitated to overrule the decisions of rejecting cellular proposals because he was correctly aware that his early interventions would incur risks of damaging his power base within the organization.

17. The investigation on this balance, however, may face some 'chicken and egg' problems because business-unit managers are chosen by top managers and the selection of business-unit managers reflects top manager's intents. For example, at BellSouth, it was John Clendenin who recruited Bob Tonsfeldt to head BMI with his emphasis on telecommunications and personal interest in cellular. Tonsfeldt was intimately familiar with cellular as a result of his work at AT&T, and it was he who chose Richard Hohn, the man who turned out to be a critical driver for wireless.

References

Ackerman, R. W. (1970). 'Influence of Integration and Diversity on the Investment Process', *Administrative Science Quarterly* 15: 341–52.

Aldrich, H. E. (1979). *Organizations and Environments*. Englewood Cliffs, NJ: Prentice-Hall.

Allison, G. T. (1971). *The Essence of Decision: Explaining the Cuban Missile Crisis*. Boston, Mass.: Little, Brown.

Andrews, K. R. (1971). *The Concept of Corporate Strategy*. Homewood, Ill.: Dow-Jones Irwin.

Ansoff, H. I. (1965). *Corporate Strategy: An Analytical Approach to Business Policy for Growth and Expansion*. New York: McGraw-Hill.

Barnard, C. I. (1938). *The Function of the Executive*. Cambridge, Mass.: Harvard University Press.

Bower, J. L. (1970). *Managing the Resource Allocation Process: A Study of Corporate Planning and Investment*. Boston, Mass.: Harvard Business School Press.

——and Doz, Y. (1979). 'Strategy Formulation: A Social and Political Process', in D. E. Schendel and C. W. Hofer (eds.), *Strategic Management: A New View of Business Policy and Planning*. Boston, Mass.: Little, Brown, 152–66.

Burgelman, R. A. (1983*a*). 'A Process Model of Internal Corporate Venturing in the Diversified Major Firm', *Administrative Science Quarterly* 28: 223–44.

——(1983*b*). 'A Model of the Interaction of Strategic Behavior, Corporate Context, and the Concept of Strategy', *Academy of Management Review* 8/1: 61–70.

——(1983*c*). 'Corporate Entrepreneurship and Strategic Management: Insights from a Process Study', *Management Science* 29/12: 1349–64.

——(1991). 'Intraorganizational Ecology of Strategy Making and Organizational Adaptation: Theory and Field Research', *Organization Science* 2: 239–62.

——(1994). 'Fading Memories: A Process Theory of Strategic Business Exit in Dynamic Environments', *Administrative Science Quarterly*, 39: 24–56.

Campbell, D. T. (1969). 'Variation and Selective Retention in Sociocultural Evolution', *General Systems* 14: 69–85.

Chakravarthy, B. S., and Lorange, P. (1991). *Managing the Strategy Process: A Framework for Multibusiness Firms*. Englewood Cliffs, NJ: Prentice-Hall.

Chandler, A. D. (1962). *Strategy and Structure*. Cambridge, Mass.: MIT Press.

Child, J. (1972). 'Organization Structures, Environment, and Performance: The Role of Strategic Choice', *Sociology* 6: 1–22.

Crozier, M. (1964). *The Bureaucratic Phenomenon*. London: Tavistock Publications.

Cyert, R. M., and March, J. G. (1963). *A Behavioral Theory of the Firm*. Englewood Cliffs, NJ: Prentice-Hall.

Eisenhardt, K. M. (1989). 'Building Theories from Case Study Research', *Academy of Management Review* 14/4: 532–50.

Gersick, C. J. G. (1991). 'Revolutionary Change Theories: A Multilevel Exploration of the Punctuated Equilibrium Paradigm', *Academy of Management Review* 16/1: 10–36.

Glaser, B. G., and Strauss, A. L. (1967). *The Discovery of Grounded Theory*. Hawthorne, NY: Aldine de Gruyter.

Hamermesh, R. (1986). *Making Strategy Work*. New York: Wiley.

Hannan, M. T., and Freeman, J. (1984). 'Structural Inertia and Organizational Change', *American Sociological Review* 49: 149–64.

Hannan, M. T., and Freeman, J. (1989). *Organizational Ecology*. Cambridge, Mass.: Harvard University Press.

Haspeslagh, P. C. (1983). 'Portfolio Planning Approaches and the Strategic Management Process in Diversified Industrial Companies'. Unpublished doctoral dissertation, Graduate School of Business Administration, Harvard University.

Jensen, M. C., and Meckling, W. H. (1992). 'Knowledge, Control and Organizational Structure', in L. Werin and H. Wijkander (eds.), *Contract Economics*. Oxford: Blackwell, 251–74.

Kanter, R. M. (1983). *The Change Masters*. New York: Simon & Schuster.

Learned, E. P., Christensen, C. R., Andrews, K. R., and Guth, W. D. (1965). *Business Policy: Text and Cases*. Homewood, Ill: Irwin.

Leonard-Barton, D. (1990). 'A Dual Methodology for Case Studies: Synergistic Use of a Longitudinal Single Site with Replicated Multiple Sites', *Organization Science* 1/3: 248–66.

Levitt, B., and March, J. G. (1988). 'Organization Learning', *Annual Review of Sociology* 14: 319–40.

Lindbloom, C. E. (1959). 'The Science of "Muddling Through"', *Public Administration Review* 19: 79–88.

March, J., and Simon, H. A. (1965). *Organizations*. New York: Wiley.

Miles, R. H. (1982). *Coffin Nails and Corporate Strategies*. Englewood Cliffs, NJ: Prentice-Hall.

Miller, D., and Friesen, P. (1984). *Organizations: A Quantum View*. Englewood Cliffs, NJ: Prentice-Hall.

Mintzberg, H. (1978). 'Patterns in Strategy Formation', *Management Science* 24: 934–48.

—— and McHugh, A. (1985). 'Strategy Formulation in an Adhocracy', *Administrative Science Quarterly* 30: 160–97.

—— and Waters, J. A. (1985). 'Of Strategies, Deliberate and Emergent', *Strategic Management Journal* 6/3: 257–72.

Nelson, R., and Winter, S. (1982). *An Evolutionary Theory of Economic Change*. Cambridge, Mass.: Harvard University Press.

Neustadt, R. (1960). *Presidential Power*. New York: Wiley.

Noda, T. (1996). 'Intraorganizational Strategy Process and the Evolution of Intra-Industry Firm Diversity'. Unpublished doctoral dissertation, Graduate School of Business Administration, Harvard University.

Nonaka, I. (1988). 'Toward Middle-Up-Down Management: Accelerating Information Creation', *Sloan Management Review* 29/3: 9–18.

Pascale, R. T. (1984). 'Perspectives on Strategy: The Real Story Behind Honda's Success', *California Management Review* (Spring), 47–72.

Pettigrew, A. M. (1990). 'Longitudinal Field Research on Change: Theory and Practice', *Organization Science* 1/3: 267–92.

Pfeffer, J., and Salancik, G. R. (1978). *The External Control of Organizations: A Resource Dependence Perspective*. New York: Harper & Row.

Porter, M. E. (1980). *Competitive Strategy*. New York: Free Press.

Porter, M. E. (1990). *The Competitive Advantage of Nations*. New York: Free Press.

—— (1994). 'Toward a Dynamic Theory of Strategy', in R. P. Rumelt, D. E. Schendel, and D. J. Teece (eds.), *Fundamental Issues in Strategy*. Boston, Mass.: Harvard Business School Press, 423–61.

Quinn, J. B. (1980). *Strategies for Change: Logical Incrementalism*. Homewood, Ill.: Irwin.

Schumpeter, J. A. (1934). *The Theory of Economic Development*. Cambridge, Mass.: Harvard University Press.

Simon, H. A. (1945). *Administrative Behavior*. New York: Macmillan.

Strauss, A., and Corbin, J. (1994). 'Grounded Theory Methodology: An Overview', in N. K. Denzin and Y. S. Lincoln (eds.), *Handbook of Qualitative Research*. Thousand Oaks, Calif.: Sage, 273–85.

Thompson, J. D. (1967). *Organizations in Action*. New York: McGraw-Hill.

Tushman, M., and Romanelli, E. (1985). 'Organization Evolution: A Metamorphosis Model of Convergence and Reorientation', in L. L. Cummings and B. M. Staw (eds.), *Research in Organizational Behavior*, Greenwich, Conn.: JAI, vii. 171–222.

Van de Ven, A. H. (1992). 'Suggestions for Studying Strategy Process: A Research Note', *Strategic Management Journal*, Summer Special Issue 13: 169–88.

Vaughan, D. (1992). 'Theory Elaboration: The Heuristics of Case Analysis', in H. Becker and C. Ragin (eds.), *What Is a Case?* New York: Cambridge University Press, 173–202.

Weick, K. E. (1979). *The Social Psychology of Organizing*. Reading, Mass.: Addison-Wesley.

Wrapp, H. E. (Sept.–Oct. 1967). 'Good Managers Don't Make Policy Decisions', *Harvard Business Review*, 91–9.

Yin, R. K. (1989). *Case Study Research: Design and Methods*. Newbury Park, Calif.: Sage.

Appendix

The past decade witnessed a spectacular growth of wireless communications businesses. AT&T, who invented cellular technology and prepared for its commercialization, originally predicted 900,000 cellular subscribers in the nation by the year 2000, but the number reached approximately 16 million by the end of 1993. As the market rapidly grew, acquisition of cellular licenses for local service areas boomed, and prices sky-rocketed. With technological advances, paging has evolved from a one-way, tone-only beeper to a two-way, alphanumerical device, and new wireless services such as personal communications and mobile data service have also emerged. Such success in the USA encouraged many foreign governments to introduce wireless communications services, affording American companies opportunities to leverage their expertise.

Strategic responses of BellSouth and US WEST to the new opportunities differed widely. BellSouth was one of the first Bell regional holding companies that moved to acquire out-of-region cellular licenses. In mid-1985 it formed a cellular joint venture with Mobile Communications Corporation of America (MCCA), a paging and cellular operator based in Jackson, Mississippi. Since then, BellSouth continued to explore domestic cellular opportunities. It acquired the remaining share of MCCA in early 1988 and battled with McCaw Cellular Communications in the acquisition of Lin Broadcasting in late 1989. Although the company eventually withdrew from the Lin deal, it subsequently acquired Graphic Scanning, a paging and cellular provider, at the end of 1990, and acquired cellular properties from GTE and McCaw in early 1991 to develop a larger cluster of domestic cellular operations. It added paging operations within the region in early 1986 and, since then, consistently expanded the business beyond its franchised region through the acquisition of paging propertics of MCCA and Graphic Scanning and the purchase of one of three nationwide paging licenses in 1990. More important, BellSouth has been increasingly aggressive in pursuing international wireless opportunities. Early activities centered around the acquisition of paging operators such as Air Call in the UK and Link Telecommunications in Australia. It then led the consortium that was awarded a cellular license for Buenos Aires, Argentina in 1988. As the 'global/mobile' strategy emerged as an articulated corporate strategy for wireless communications businesses, it accelerated expansion of international wireless operations by conquering the Latin American cellular markets, including Uruguay, Venezuela, and Chile, and successfully entered Australia, New Zealand, and some European countries, such as France, Denmark, and Germany. In late 1990, BellSouth announced the formation of a major joint venture with Ram Broadcasting to build and operate mobile data networks worldwide.

At the beginning, US WEST was as aggressive as, or perhaps more aggressive than, BellSouth in exploring new wireless communications opportunities. Immediately after the official break-up, even long before its introduction of cellular operations in four major markets within its franchised region, it had announced its intention to explore out-of-region wireless opportunities, such as a cellular venture serving the Gulf of Mexico and entry into cellular operations in Costa Rica, although these ventures did not materialize. Observing a few RHCs, including BellSouth, acquiring nonwireline cellular licenses in mid-1985, US WEST followed suit and announced the acquisition of the San Diego (out-of-region) nonwireline license at the end of 1985, and a small share of the Omaha (within-region) nonwireline license in mid-1986. Although it participated in several subsequent cellular deals, the company became increasingly inactive in exploring domestic cellular opportunities during the second half of the 1980s. Like BellSouth, US WEST added a paging business in 1986, but its paging operations remained small, mostly limited within the franchised region. In the late 1980s, the company became active in exploring international wireless opportunities. It led the consortium that was awarded a license for a personal communications network—new wireless communications service—in the UK in late 1989. It then entered into cellular operations in East European countries, such as Hungary, the Czech Republic, Slovakia, and Russia. With its emerging interests in broadband and multimedia opportunities, however, US WEST placed less strategic focus on its wireless communications businesses. It announced the sale of its paging business in 1993 and agreed to turn its domestic cellular operations into a 30/70 joint venture with AirTouch Communications, a spin-off of Pacific Telesis, another RHC, in mid-1994.

11

Beyond Resource Allocation: How Definition and Impetus Interact to Shape Strategic Outcomes

Clark G. Gilbert

Introduction

Up to now, most of the chapters in this book have focused on whether firms will or will not allocate resources to a given project. Burgelman asks whether Intel will invest in microprocessors, Christensen looks at commitments to new disk-drive technologies, Sull tries to explain why Firestone will not divest old tire technologies, and Noda compares the expansion and contraction of investment in cellular telephony. That emphasis is appropriate, given the book's premise that these resource commitments shape strategic outcomes.

But what happens when the process building impetus behind an investment impacts the definition of plans that use those resources? This chapter will examine a resource allocation failure—commitment to disruptive technology—and show how overcoming the resource allocation problem can actually lead to problems with strategic definition.

Although technological shifts can take many forms, the particular challenge of disruptive change has proved extremely problematic for incumbent firms (Christensen 1997). Disruption occurs not when new technologies attack established markets head-on, but when the initial attributes of the emerging technologies cause them to be valued only in emerging markets, prior to invading established markets (Christensen and Bower 1996; Foster 1986). This type of market shift has led to the decline of established leaders and the rise of new entrants across a range of industries, including: disk drives, computers, transportation systems, excavation equipment, accounting software, and retail distribution (Christensen and Rosenbloom 1995; Christensen 1997; Cooper and Schendel 1976). Previous research described the challenge of incumbent firms as a problem of resource commitment. Christensen and Bower explain: 'The inability of some successful firms to *allocate sufficient resources* [italics added] to technologies that initially cannot find application in mainstream markets, but later invade them, lies at the root of the failure of many once-successful firms' (1996: 198). Because firms commit resources to the needs of the mainstream markets, resource allocation mechanisms act to starve disruptive innovation of the resources required to generate sufficient response.

More recently, we have begun to see a number of firms recognize the threat of disruptive technology and aggressively commit resources to new technologies. Does overcoming the problem of commitment imply effective incumbent response? The initial response of Kodak to digital imaging is worth consideration. As with other disruptive technologies, the early products built around digital imaging initially did not meet the performance criteria demanded by Kodak's mainstream customers in their established chemical film markets. Previous findings suggest that Kodak might starve the new imaging technology of the resources required for its development (Christensen 1997; Christensen and Bower 1996). However, unlike the previously observed cases of firm response, Kodak *aggressively* allocated resources to the new technology. Between 1996 and 1998, Kodak spent over $2 billion on digital imaging, nearly half of its budgeted R&D resources. Unfortunately, rather than finding markets that would value the unique attributes of the new technology, Kodak's response was to force the product into its existing markets, installing over 2,000 digital kiosks through its established retail network. Kodak chose to focus on its established market despite the fact that new entrants were rapidly developing applications for an emerging market around home usage and file management. Kodak had recognized the threat of disruption and overcame the problem of resource commitment, only to aggressively cram the new technology into its established markets.

This chapter is motivated by three research questions that relate to this response phenomenon. First, what allows firms to overcome the challenges of resource commitment in response to disruptive change? Second, how does this affect the process of strategic definition? Third, what implications does this response have for our more general understanding of the resource allocation process itself? The phenomenological nature of these questions motivated the inductive study outlined in this chapter.

The setting for the research is the newspaper industry and firm response to digital publishing. Like other disruptive innovations studied previously, the established markets of newspaper companies initially undervalued digital publishing. But unlike the previous research on disruptive technology, the industry responded quite aggressively. Unfortunately, despite intense commitment, many firms forced the new technology into existing market models at the expense of innovating around a new market segment.

The data will show that the challenges of resource commitment described previously in the literature do exist and, uninterrupted, will act to starve the new business of the necessary resources for development. And yet, we will also show that a strong sense of threat to the core organization can act as a catalyst to motivate resources that otherwise would be denied. Unfortunately, the same threat-motivated mechanism required to trigger resources also leads to aggressive rigidity around the established market and product. This finding is supported in the subset of social psychology literature called 'threat rigidity' (Dutton and Jackson 1987; Staw, Sandelands, and Dutton 1981).

The broader implication of this phenomenon relates to our overall understanding of the resource allocation process itself. In the following section, I will use the data on threat-framed response to show how the cognitive framing of managers can shape the bottom-up processes of resource allocation. Subsequently, I will use the response of newspapers to new media to illustrate that strategic response is more than just committing resources. All the firms in this study were able to commit resources to a disruptive technology, but they failed to adapt the substance of their strategic plans to the changes underway in their markets. The next section presents the research methods used to study this phenomenon. Those that follow present the data and discuss their implication for our research on resource allocation.

Research Methodology

Using a multicase design, I follow a 'replication logic' where a set of cases is treated as a series of experiments, each case serving to confirm or disconfirm inferences from another (Yin 1994). The current study provided an opportunity to observe and analyze a phenomenon previously inaccessible to scientific investigation (Yin 1994). There are numerous examples where organizational phenomena have been examined productively using inductive case study research (Burgelman

1983*a*; Eisenhardt and Bourgeois 1998; Gersick 1988). The following research employs a Type IV embedded, multicase design (Yin 1994). The primary unit of analysis is the new venture, and the embedded units are the sponsoring division and the corporation itself. In total, eight new ventures launched in response to a new technology were examined across eight different newspapers and four different corporate settings. The eight newspapers are presented in Table 11.1 with relevant descriptive statistics. Because of the sensitivity of the data, the names of these newspapers and their parent organizations have been disguised.

Digital publishing was a productive research setting for several reasons. First, the response of firms in the newspaper industry was anomalous to previous research findings (Christensen and Bower 1996). Firms did respond quite aggressively to the new technology, despite its initial lack of application in their mainstream markets. The second reason I selected a single industry was more methodological— selecting a single industry allowed me to have a controlled sample (Eisenhardt 1989*a*). I selected specific case sites based on a theoretical sampling (Glaser and Strauss 1967; Yin 1994) using polar types that were likely to replicate or extend the emerging theory (Pettigrew 1988; Eisenhardt 1989*a*).

Data sources

Four main sources of data were collected: (1) open-ended interviews, (2) archival documents, (3) direct observations, and (4) public documents. Yin suggests: 'With triangulation, the potential problems of *construct validity* also can be addressed because the multiple sources of evidence essentially provide multiple measures of the same phenomenon' (1994: 92). Following the embedded nature of the study, data were collected at the corporate level, the newspaper level, and the online venture level across each of the sources of data (see Table 11.2).

Interviews   In total, fifty-one in-depth, one- to two-hour interviews were conducted. These interviews included the senior executive at each level of the analysis: corporate, the newspaper, and the online venture. Where possible, functional managers at the newspaper and online-venture level also were interviewed. At each level, semi-structured interview templates were designed around issues such as: what motivated the manager to commit to the digital media, how that commitment had evolved over time, the relationship between the print and online

Table 11.1 *Description of the eight newspapers studied*

Newspaper	Parent organization	Local paper daily print circulation	Online launch date	Number of online employees (2000)
The Beacon A	The Beacon Company	250,000	1994	45
The Beacon B	The Beacon Company	200,000	1995	20
The Press A	The Press Company	>500,000	1994	~100
The Press B	The Press Company	400,000	1995	60
The Expositor A	The Expositor Company	>500,000	1995	~100
The Expositor B	The Expositor Company	200,000	1996	32
The Morning News A	The Morning News Company	>500,000	1994	~100
The Morning News B	The Morning News Company	300,000	1996	41

Table 11.2 *Summary of data collection*

Newspaper	Interviews				Archival Documents		Direct Observations	
	Corporate	Newspapers	Venture	Total	No.	Examples	No.	Examples
The Beacon A	2	2	3	7	7	Business plan, customer list, internal memo, strategic plan, sales collateral	5	Planning meeting, sales calls
The Beacon B	1	2	2	5	5	Business plan, internal memo	N/A	N/A
The Press A	2	2	3	7	5	Business plan, customer list, internal memo, sales collateral	5	Content development meetings, budgeting meetings
The Press B	2	2	3	7	6	Business plan, customer list, strategic plan, sales collateral	4	Sales calls, newsroom planning meetings
The Expositor A	2	2	3	7	2	Business plan, internal memo	N/A	Budgeting meetings, planning meetings
The Expositor B	1	2	3	6	6	Business plan, customer lists, internal memo	5	N/A
The Morning News A	2	2	3	7	2	Business plan, customer lists, internal memo	5	Budgeting meetings, planning meetings, sales calls
The Morning News B	1	2	2	5	N/A	N/A	N/A	N/A
TOTAL	13	16	22	51	33	N/A	24	N/A

efforts, etc. (see Table 11.2). Where possible, efforts were made to triangulate across multiple sources of information, using multiple informants and cross-checking against other sources of data to avoid retrospective bias in the interviews. Nearly all the interviews were recorded and transcribed prior to their entry into a comprehensive case study database.

Archival Documents   One of the most useful sources of cross-checking against informant recall was archival documents. Over thirty different internal archival documents were collected across seven of the eight sites. Documents included online business plans, strategy proposals, internal memos, annual strategic planning documents, customer lists, and various historical sales of collateral materials. Most helpful were the various business plans, starting as early as 1990, that discussed arguments over whether or not to fund the online ventures.

Direct Observations   Direct observations served as another source of triangulation, though they were used almost entirely as a means of observing real-time processes. Because of the timing of the study, this could reveal processes post-funding only. During a one-and-a-half year period, 2000–1, I directly observed the following types of organizational events: reporting meetings between the online venture and newspaper/corporate executives, planning meetings for the online venture, the process of story creation for the newspaper and website, sales calls for both the newspaper and online products, and other planning meetings. In total, I observed twenty-four discrete field events and recorded them into the case study database.

Public Documents   Finally, I analyzed over 150 public documents, including press releases, annual reports, analyst research reports, and industry articles. These external sources of data were useful in the triangulation effort to cross-validate other sources of data. The public data also served as a useful source of identifying new entrants into the digital information and publishing market and as a useful source of comparisons to what was being observed in the newspaper online ventures.

Analysis of the Data

Inductive theory development from case data is a highly iterative process. Beginning with data collection (Eisenhardt 1989a), the research builds from a cycle of comparison of data and theory. In the extreme, researchers are told to enter the field with no theoretical lens whatsoever (Glaser and Strauss 1967). However, while efforts should be made not to direct toward a given theory, using existing theory can help sharpen a line of inquiry and specify a set of constructs examined in the field (Eisenhardt 1989*a*). In the current research, I drew on the resource allocation literature and threat rigidity literature to help specify the focal constructs and their measurement. However, I considered other constructs also, including power (Pfeffer and Salancik 1974).

Propositions then took form initially from early case analysis. The preliminary analysis came from a set of matched pair, polar cases at *The Beacon A* and *The Expositor A*. I induced an initial set of propositions by analyzing the case data and enfolding a set of relevant literatures using methods for inductive theory development advocated by Eisenhardt (1989*a*) and Glaser and Strauss (1967). After developing an initial set of propositions, I then returned to the case data from subsequent case sites to see if the emerging relationships were confirmed or disconfirmed through a process of analytical replication (Yin 1994). Eisenhardt points out the difference between this process and more traditional deductive hypothesis training:

> The key difference is that each hypothesis is examined for each case, not for the aggregate cases. Thus, the underlying logic is replication, that is, the logic of treating a series of cases as a series of experiments with each case serving to confirm or disconfirm the hypotheses. Each case is analogous to an experiment, and multiple cases are analogous to multiple experiments. This contrasts with the sampling logic of traditional, within-experiment, hypothesis-testing research.   (1989*a*: 542)

To test whether the relationships identified in each proposition were confirmed or disconfirmed, data were arrayed following techniques for cross-case pattern sequencing (Eisenhardt 1989*b*) and tabular displays (Miles and Huberman 1984). Similar to deductive hypothesis testing, the propositions presented here fit well with the evidence, though they did not always conform perfectly (Sutton and Callahan 1987; Eisenhardt 1989*a*).

Existing Customer Demand Constrains Impetus

The resource allocation process articulated by Bower, Burgelman, and their colleagues (Bower 1970; Burgelman 1983*a*, 1983*b*; Noda and Bower 1996) is a model designed to map the way in which organizations decide to commit resources to a given proposal. An important feature of the model is the process of building *impetus*, which Bower describes as the 'force that moves a project forward' (1970: 67). Another way of understanding this force is to examine the set of considerations that a manager considers when he or she decides to sponsor or commit to a new project. Considerations might include career risk, likelihood of success, and external pressures, such as capital markets and existing customer demand.

By identifying what has been described as disruptive technology, Christensen and Bower (1996) added new insight to research on corporate innovation. Disruption occurs not when new technologies attack established markets head-on, but when the initial attributes of the emerging technologies cause them to be valued only in emerging markets, prior to invading established markets. The insight came largely from making linkages between resource dependency theory (Pfeffer and Salancik 1978) and resource allocation research (Bower 1970; Burgelman 1983*a*, 1983*b*). The linkage demonstrated that the customers in an organization's mainstream markets largely determine the *impetus* required to motivate resources. 'When the initial price/ performance characteristics of emerging technologies render them competitive only in emerging market segments, and not with current customers, resource allocation mechanisms typically deny resources to such technologies' (Christensen and Bower 1996: 198).

I found a considerable amount of evidence initially confirming this earlier research. However, one subtle change from earlier findings is the emphasis on the source of the impetus in building toward commitment. When impetus is built around a company's leading customers and established markets, we would expect to see results similar to earlier findings. This is consistent with the results of Christensen and Bower (1996), but constrains the impetus link- age to resource dependency theory (Pfeffer and Salancik 1978). Formally stated:

Proposition 1. When the impetus for commitment is built predom- inantly around the demands of customers in a firm's established markets, resource allocation mechanisms will deny resources to disruptive technology.

Table 11.3 summarizes the evidence from the field data for this proposition. In nearly every case examined, business plans for online newspaper sites spent over two years in the project proposal process. Since it was unclear early on how to make money in digital media

Table 11.3 *Existing customer demand constrains impetus*

Newspaper	Evidence[a]	Years in proposal	Reason for financial commitment	Date of launch	Challenges to operating commitment[b]	Examples: financial and operation
The Beacon A	I, A, O, P	2	Publisher sponsorship	1994	N, S, B	Newsroom: 'Get the hell out of here, I've got a *real* newspaper to get out.' (Newspaper editor)
The Beacon B	I, A	2	Forecast profitability	1995	N, S, B	Sales: Staff provided training, but then dropped program multiple times due to lack of client interest.
The Press A	I, A, O, P	2	Forecast profitability	1994	N, S	Sales: 'I occasionally sell a bundled print and online package … it is hard to really know what print advertisers would want.' (Sales rep)
The Press B	I, A, P	2	CEO sponsorship	1995	N, S, B	Newsroom: Editors call online content 'low brow' for using radio feeds for breaking news, personals, and unedited user posted content (Newspaper editor)

The Expositor A	I, P	3	CEO sponsorship	1995	N, S, B	Budgeting: 'And in the end, the only real value is cash and cash creation. You can't build a business just on potential or hope.' (CEO)
The Expositor B	I, A, O, P	2	Forecast profitability	1996	N, S, B	Budgeting: 'Look. When we roll these up into our budgets, we miss our targets.' (VP product development)
The Morning News A	I, P	1	Publisher sponsorship	1994	N, S	Newsroom: 'I will be god damned if some online reporter is going to call my sources and say they are from our paper.' (Publisher)
The Morning News B	I, P	2	Forecast profitability	1996	N, S, B	Sales: 'We bundled print and online, but there were clients who wanted online only. These were less interesting to sales reps, and the organization wasn't ready to deal with that reality.' (VP marketing)

[a] I = Interviews, A = Archival documents, O = Direct observation, P = Public documents

[b] N = Newsroom, S = Sales, B = Budgeting

and these ventures did not appear as attractive when measured against the dominant models used for the core newspaper business, these proposals stalled in the formal budgeting process. The chairman and CEO of The Expositor Company explained his thinking: 'My training is in finance. And in the end, the only real value is cash and cash creation. You can't build a business just on potential or hope.' The vice president of Product Development at *The Expositor B* explained how that philosophy spilled over into the resource allocation metrics:

We had operating targets we had to meet...Even in business development, these units were expected to be profitable from day one...We proposed it to finance and they said, 'Look. When we roll these up into our budgets we miss our targets.' What that means is that most greenfield businesses don't get invested in—unless they are very small, and the Internet is not very small.

When projects did receive funding, it was because their budgeted forecasts promised to generate the types of return that would fit the resource allocation requirements of the firm. The CFO at *The Expositor B* describes how proposals she reviewed frequently hid costs:

I remember being the CFO and the first proposal came to me saying we will make money, and I sent it back to them because I knew it would not. People were trying to figure out what they had to do to get it approved. The goal was to get a modest loss...You almost had to hide its costs so that it didn't look as bad as it was.

At the Beacon Company, newspaper publishers actually did approve funding for their new media businesses, but did so only once the forecasts showed these ventures breaking even in short time horizons and returning EBITDA margins exactly in-line with the targets already set for the core business.

Unfortunately, resource allocation mechanisms can reach far more broadly than just the financial budgeting process. Resource allocation also includes the commitment of time- and attention-based resources at the operating levels of the organization (Ocasio 1997). Because the new business did not fit the operating decision rules and priorities of the functional print organization, managers consistently prioritized time elsewhere. For example, the sales organization found that their leading customers in the established newspaper advertising markets were not interested initially in online media advertising.

An online sales rep at *The Beacon A* recalled the challenges print reps had selling the online product, saying: 'Print reps could sell the online product, but with varying degrees of success. Their margins were higher on other products that were easier for them to sell. Online was really just a novelty to them.' A print rep at *The Press A* described his efforts: 'I occasionally sell a bundled print and online package. There is no standard package, and it is hard to really know what the print advertisers would want.' Data were gathered on five of the research sites concerning the customer overlap between print and online. Managers were asked to estimate how many of their top twenty-five advertisers online were in the top twenty-five advertisers in the news-paper. Of a possible customer overlap of 125, there were only seven. The net effect of these customer differences was that print reps concluded that the Internet ad was a small, difficult, and unprofitable product to try to sell.

Similar challenges occurred in the newsroom. Online users were often very different from print readers, as was the way they engaged with the product. Consequently, print editors often viewed online content as low-quality journalism. An experience reported by the publisher at *The Beacon A* is indicative of the challenge online managers faced getting commitment from the editorial staff of the newspaper:

I had trumpeted the new business to everyone and asked for their cooperation with the online group. One day I asked an online staff member how things were going and if the newspaper staff was helping out. He told me that he had recently asked for some help, and the response was, 'Get the hell out of here, I've got a *real* newspaper to get out.'

Thus, when the impetus for commitment was built around customer demands in the existing organization's market, resources were denied to the disruptive business. I found evidence for this at nearly every site in the sample. Even when websites were launched, both financial and attention-based resources were scarce.

Threat Unlocks Impetus

Though the initial stages of the resource allocation process appeared likely to deny resources to the venture, a new source of impetus began to emerge that differed from previous findings in Christensen and Bowers' research (1996). Online media were now perceived as a threat to the institution's survival. The sense of crisis provided a new kind of impetus. The difference in impetus also was accompanied by very different behavior patterns. Previously, management scholars identified the role threat framing can play in creating action around a desired response (Kotter 1996). Hurst found that creating a sense of crisis can serve as a catalyst for action (Hurst 1995). Psychologists also have noted that response in the domains of loss leads to an increased willingness to commit resources (Mittal and Ross 1998; Kahneman and Tversky 1979). The data in my research showed evidence that a sense of threat to the core organization can motivate commitment of resources, creating the impetus necessary to break the cycle of resource dependency articulated by Christensen and Bower (1996). Stated formally:

> *Proposition 2.* When the impetus for commitment is built around a strong perception of threat to the core organization, resource allocation mechanisms will aggressively commit resources to disruptive technology.

I considered threat as a construct prior to coming to the field and was largely informed by measurement of that construct. While no technique to collapse multiple indicators into a single measure was used because of the complex nature of the field data (Eisenhardt 1989*a*), the investigation was informed by three common characteristics associated with threat perception. Research in the social psychology literature recognizes threat perception as displaying a *negative focus, emphasis on loss,* and *lack of control* (Jackson and Dutton 1988; Dutton and Jackson 1987). Evidence supporting the relationship between threat perception, the process of building impetus, and a subsequent intensified commitment is summarized in Table 11.4. The data show that a perception of threat to the newspaper increased both financial and organizational commitment to disruptive technology. In some instances, the concern developed around losing the classified products, including employment, real estate, and auto listings. In other cases, the concern was placed around the entire business itself, as managers perceived a threat to the fundamental readership and advertising market for a printed newspaper.

The source of increased perception of threat often came from external analysts. For example, a 1997 report by a leading news media analyst argued that the Internet would drive many newspaper organizations to extinction. The cover of the article featured the image of a fossilized set of dinosaur bones. A 1998 research report entitled 'Goodbye to Classifieds' predicted a \$4.7 billion dollar annual displacement by 2003. The director of marketing at *The Morning News B* described how this emerged:

Table 11.4 *Threat unlocks impetus*

Newspaper	Primary stated concerns	Impetus of threat motivation	Evidence[a]	Examples	Expenditure expansion[b]	Employee expansion[b]
The Beacon A	Readership, display advertising, classified advertising	Publisher → corporate level	I, A, P	*Lack of Control:* 'What if we do every damn thing we can think of and execute flawlessly and we still don't make it? We can slow it down, but we can't stop it.' (Publisher)	1996–8 400%	1996–8 15 → 40
The Beacon B	Classified advertising	Corporate level → publisher	I, A	*Focus on Loss:* 1997 Internal estimates of 15–20% loss of classified share by 2001 (1997 Strategic Plan)	1997–9 300%	1997–9 5 → 18
The Press A	Readership, classified advertising	Publisher → corporate level	I, A, P	*Focus on Loss:* 'There were people who thought we would lose half of our circulation.' (CEO, Internet group)	1997–9 300%	1997–9 50 → 100+

(Continues)

Table 11.4 (Continued)

Newspaper	Primary stated concerns	Impetus of threat motivation	Evidence[a]	Examples	Expenditure expansion[b]	Employee expansion[b]
The Press B	Readership, display advertising, classified advertising	Simultaneous impetus from both corporate level and NP publisher	I, A, P	*Negative Focus:* 'People were telling us that newspapers were heading to the graveyard and we were beginning to believe them.' (Publisher)	1997–9 250%	1997–9 30 → 50
The Expositor A	Stock price, classified advertising	Operating → publisher, blocked to corporate until stock price concerns	I, P	*Focus on Loss:* 'We were worried about classifieds primarily. These new firms were set to come in and take our most profitable piece of business.' (Early online president)	1997–9 300%	1997–9 50 → 100+
The Expositor B	Readership, display advertising, classified advertising	Operating → publisher	I, A, P	*Negative Focus:* 'We [middle managers] had been concerned for a while, but … the reason we finally got into the market was that our CEO was taking heat from Wall Street.' (VP product development)	1998–2000: 250%	1998–2000 15 → 31

					1997-9
				1997-9:	60 → 100 +
The Morning News A	Threat not primary motivation,	Threat not primary motivation	I, P	*Not Threat:* 'Eighty per cent of my costs are production and distribution. Now all of a sudden I have a solution. It is not a content play, but a major cost reducer and product expander.' (Publisher)	200%
The Morning News B	Classified advertising	Publisher → Corporate	I, P	*Negative Focus:* 'You felt like Chicken Little screaming 'the sky is falling', but after a while people started listening.' (VP marketing)	1998–2000: 400% · 1998–2000 5 → 40

[a] I = Interviews, A = Archival documents, O = Direct observation, P = Public documents

[b] Period based on relevant expansion of threat perception based on process analysis across each site—see Table 11.2.

You felt like Chicken Little screaming 'the sky is falling', but after a while people started listening when they saw what the other competitors were doing. We made watch lists for TV, radio, vertical start-ups, telephone companies, and Citysearch. Citysearch was poaching people. . . . The publisher was unlike some in that he saw the threat.

In all the primary research sites but one, threat was the primary motivator toward action. In each of these cases, various manifestations of threat perception were consistent with the construct as described in the social psychology literature. For example, the CEO of The Press Company's Internet group described how his organization was motivated out of fear of loss:

McKinsey had come in and had done a rather startling analysis of the classified business . . . They predicted that 20 to 30 percent of our classified revenue would disappear by 1998. That raised enormous alarm bells in some people. I think the notion that people would start reading their newspapers on the screen was also quite prevalent . . . There were people who thought we would lose half of our circulation.

There was also a general concern that the future of this media was largely out of the newspaper companies' control. The publisher of *The Beacon A* expressed this fear: 'What if we do every damn thing we can think of and execute flawlessly and we still don't make it? We can slow it down, but we can't stop it.' The potential for opportunity was not completely absent, but the overall tone was generally defensive and negative.

In seven of the cases where threat became the impetus for commitment, there was an increase in the financial and organizational resources provided. Financial expenditures expanded by as much as 400 per cent during the years that threat perceptions were building (see Table 11.4). Sites also expanded their dedicated online employees, many increasing their numbers to over 100 individuals. However, commitment of resources was not limited to dollars and personnel. There was also an expanded commitment at the operating levels. As one sales manager at *The Beacon A* commented, 'Look, it didn't make any sense for us to try to sell this stuff, but we began to feel that if we didn't work on it, it might come back to haunt us.'

Evidence for the linkage between expanded threat perception and expanded commitment came not only from interview data and informant recollections, but also from triangulation with independent archival data. For example, of the five business plans obtained during the period of most rapid expansion, all five stated categorically the threat of inaction. A 1997 business plan at *The Beacon B* suggested they would lose 15–20 per cent of their print classified revenues if they did not respond aggressively. Several documents from other newspapers pointed out that if the newspapers did not cannibalize themselves, someone else would. Unlike earlier proposals that had emphasized financial returns and new market opportunities, arguments for increased funding were now focused on the potential downside to the print business. This expansion came despite increasing losses, typically greater than 100 per cent of revenues.

The notable exception to threat as impetus was *The Morning News A*. Nevertheless, the pattern exception was consistent for theoretically consistent reasons (Yin 1994). In *The Morning News A*, the Internet created a new distribution opportunity and therefore needed less threat motivation to generate response. Note that *The Morning News A* was the only pure nationally distributed newspaper in the sample. In this sense, the Internet offered some unique operational benefits that sustained the existing business. The president and publisher described the benefits:

This was a wonderful opportunity from the start. If you are a national newspaper with a three percent penetration, all of a sudden you have an opportunity for virtually no cost to distribute the product . . . The Internet creates huge opportunities to deliver product in areas that were uneconomical before . . . Eighty percent of my costs are production and distribution. Now all of a sudden I have a solution. It is not a content play, but a major cost reducer and product expander.

The newspaper also had a limited classified advertising product and was not strapped by the fear of cannibalization like the other sites in the sample.

Threat Constrains Strategic Definition

Unfortunately, the data from the research show that the same threat-based mechanism required to motivate resources also leads to a rigid definition of the market, product, and business model. In fact, despite solving the problem of building impetus, firms faced a new set of strategic problems. The new-found resources were being deployed in very rigid ways. Consistent with research in social psychology, threat-motivated response had increased commitment levels, but led to an increased rigidity in the underlying nature of that commitment (Staw, Sandelands, and Dutton 1981; Dutton and Jackson 1987). In this sense, we see that strategic outcomes move 'Beyond Resource Allocation' or beyond the actual commitment of resources and must include the definition process itself. Solving the problem of resource commitment does not necessarily solve the strategy problem—which is a function of both impetus and definition. This shows up in the third formal proposition:

> *Proposition* 3. When the definition process is built around a strong perception of threat to the core organization, strategic plans will be rigidly defined.

Table 11.5 presents evidence for this proposition. Seven of the eight research sites relied on the printed newspaper as the source of their website content. In these sites, greater than 75 per cent of the product came directly from the newspaper. As the publisher of *The Beacon A* described: 'We learned [from early involvement with new media] that there wasn't very much appetite for an "electronic" newspaper ... But that is exactly what we did with the new Internet.' The newspapers failed to include features that were common for other content sites such as Yahoo, Monster.com, and Citysearch. These included electronic bulletin boards and site searching tools. The Chairman and CEO of The Beacon Company described the problem:

Where I think we missed the boat is that we saw it as an extension of the newspaper. In other words, something richer and deeper than the newspaper ... But here was the real mistake. When the search companies came along in 1995, we didn't really pick up on the fact that this was really a way of getting all kinds of information. So when they were starting up search, we never really jumped on the bandwagon and our internet operations were really run by people who came out of the newsroom, so they were editors who tended to look at this more as a newspaper.

In most of these sites, the product looked and functioned exactly like the printed newspaper. The CEO who was hired to run *The Press A* business recalled, 'Remember that I had said to the CEO at the time that it made absolutely no sense to replicate the newspaper on the internet. Then I saw the product and it was just that.'

Threat also led managers to define narrowly the business model used to pursue the venture. Using a panel set of five entrant competing firms, I compared the income statement of the sites in the research sample. This revealed six new categories of revenue that were different from the revenue model of the newspaper business. And even though other online companies were able to develop five or more new categories of revenue, most of the newspaper sites in the sample developed only one (see Table 11.5). The CEO of The Expositor Company complained, 'We couldn't see any models that we were familiar with, nor any we knew how to make money with.'

Definition and Impetus Interact

Part of the reason strategic definition became so rigid is that the pace of resource commitment affected the interaction of impetus and definition. Recall that threat led to expenditure increases of more than 100 per cent per year from 1996 to 1998, despite repeat market failure and slow customer adoption. Whereas traditional learning models suggest that failure leads to adaptive behavior, threat motivation led to an intense replication of the same behavior (March 1991). If initial behavior is similar to traditional response patterns, even if only because that was the point of origin, then aggressive resource commitment may only reinforce and harden commitments around those previously applied patterns.

The other way threat-motivated response caused impetus to interact with definition came from the way threat led to a contraction of authority by senior management. This response is consistent with research on threat rigidity. For example, Staw, Sandelands, and Dutton found that threat situations were associated with 'increased centralization of authority, more extensive formalization, and standardization of procedures' (1981: 513). Hermann also observed a contraction of authority associated with crisis situations (1963). This contraction of authority can block the traditional bottom-up process of resource allocation. At nearly every research site, threat led to corporate level executives defining the plans for the new ventures. For example the vice president of technology and operations at *The Beacon Company* described the general development process: 'It was very centralized in the beginning, which was very uncharacteristic, because the culture is very much to let these guys run their own businesses. We had a basic business model for every site. We gave them money, we told them they could hire people, but we told them exactly how to do it.'

It is interesting to note that the one site where the strategic definition process remained somewhat flexible was where managers structurally decoupled the new venture from the parent organization. Management at *The Press B* decided very early to structure the venture as a separate, wholly owned subsidiary and hired outside management. They developed a separate brand name, separate sales force, and moved out of the newspaper offices. This had a direct impact on the way managers

Table 11.5 *Threat constrains strategic definition*

Newspaper	Early product	Percentage of product from print newspaper by 1998[a]	Number of new categories revenue by 1998[b]	Examples
The Beacon A	Extension of newspaper	>75	1	'We learned … that there wasn't very much of an appetite for an "electronic" newspaper … But that's exactly what we did with the Internet.' (Publisher)
The Beacon B	Extension of newspaper	>85	1	'Where I think we missed the boat is that we saw it as an extension of the newspaper. In other words something richer and deeper than the newspaper.' (CEO)
The Press A	Extension of newspaper	>85	3	'Remember that I had said to the CEO at the time that it made absolutely no sense to replicate the newspaper on the Internet. Then I saw the product and it was just that.' (CEO, Internet group)
The Press B	New international media site	<50	3	'We are really becoming a separate company from the newspaper. I came from there. I love the paper, but we

				are now a different group with a very different way of working.' (Online editor)
The Expositor A	Extension of newspaper	>85	1	'We couldn't see any models that we were familiar with, nor any we knew how to make money with.' (CEO)
The Expositor B	Extension of newspaper	>85	1	'We failed to recognize the importance of tools such as search, but rather presented this in the layout of a printed newspaper.' (VP, product development)
The Morning News A	Extension of newspaper	>90	1	'Where we made our mistake was we missed the next wave of opportunity. We could have said we want to be a national classified source. We could have become different content verticals. But we have done very little on content verticals.' (Publisher)
The Morning News B	Extension of newspaper	>80	1	'I don't see this as that different than what the newspapers currently do, it is just another channel.' (VP marketing)

[a] Based on internal estimates and income statement analysis at each site.

[b] Based on comparisons of print newspaper income statement analysis and pure-play entrant income statement analysis. Six categories of revenue were identified as being 'new' relative to a print newspaper: (1) fee-based archival access, (2) e-mail marketing, (3) e-mail list rental, (4) data analysis fees, (5) behavioral targeting, and (6) demographic targeting.

defined their business. Rather than replicating the newspaper, the site evolved to become a regional source of news and information with significant differences from the newspaper. One online editor described the evolution: 'Page views from the newspaper are now barely more than one third of the available pages on our site. We are really becoming a separate company from the newspaper. I came from there. I love the paper, but we are now a different group with a very different way of working.' And even though the business model did not adapt to become exactly like new entrant competitors, it was considerably more innovative than most of the other sites in the newspaper sample (see Table 11.5).

Discussion

The observations in this study have direct implications that contribute to our understanding of the resource allocation process. The first contribution relates to the forces that shape the bottom–up processes of definition and impetus. Previous research by Christensen and Bower suggest that the problem of disruptive technology is one of allocating sufficient resources to new technologies. 'When the initial price/performance characteristics of emerging technologies render them competitive only in emerging market segments, and not with current customers, resource allocation mechanisms typically deny resources to such technologies' (Christensen and Bower 1996: 198). And yet, the data in the newspaper study reveal resource allocation mechanisms repeatedly able to provide significant resources, even in the absence of current customer demand.

The phenomenon responsible for this behavior is threat perception. The data in the study show that varying this cognitive perception can significantly change the response that Christensen and Bower observed. More generally, this also reveals the importance of cognition as a separate force affecting resource allocation. Previous studies had suggested that managers could drive significant change in bottom–up resource allocation by varying either the strategic context (Burgelman 1983*a*, 1983*b*; Noda and Bower 1996) or the structural context (Bower 1970; Christensen 1997). In the current study, there were significant changes in observed behavior, despite relatively stable structural and strategic contexts. The observed variance was tied to changes in cognitive framing. Thus, the study not only expands research on disruptive technology, but helps reveal another force that is fundamental to shaping resource allocation.

The second key contribution of the study to our understanding of the resource allocation model comes in highlighting the definition process and its interaction within the impetus. Perhaps the core premise of this book is that the pattern of resource allocation leads to realized strategy. Surprisingly, the importance of definition in this process often can be overlooked because of the model's emphasis on the actual allocation of resources. Recall that the previous research presented in this volume reveals that almost every study is trying to predict whether resources will or will not be allocated to a given proposal. Whether it was microprocessors, disruptive technology, cellular telephony, cable companies, or radial tires, most of the previous studies focused on the actual allocation of resources.

The current study highlights the fact that even if you allocate resources to a new business, you have not solved the strategy problem—especially if the process required to secure those resources impacts the pattern of strategic definition. Resource allocation still affects strategy, but through the interaction of impetus and definition. Previous research by Christensen (1997) suggested that the structural autonomy was important because it solved the problem of building impetus behind disruptive technologies. But in the current study, threat perception solved the impetus problem without structural autonomy. Preliminary data would seem to indicate that at least some of the benefits of structural autonomy appear linked to de-coupling the definition process of the parent from the definition process of the new venture. This further reinforces the idea that realized strategy has to be the result of both definition and impetus—you cannot solve one without considering the other.

Conclusion

This chapter highlighted two developments in our understanding of the resource allocation model. First we observed that cognitive framing shapes the bottom-up process of resource allocation in ways that are similar to other forces previously identified (e.g. structural and strategic context, customers, and capital markets). Second, we reinforced the idea that realized strategy (not just investment) is the key outcome variable in the resource allocation model. Thus, resource allocation affects strategy through both definition and impetus. Interventions by corporate management that seek to restore bottom-up processes by simply allocating resources to a problem without considering the impact those resources will have on strategic definition are likely to struggle. Part III of the book has considered how changes to structural context, strategic context, or cognitive framing can restore bottom-up process. When these are ineffective, the role of the corporate office may significantly expand. This idea is considered in Part IV of the book.

References

Bower, J. L. 1970. *Managing the Resource Allocation Process*. Boston, Mass.: Harvard Business School Press.

Burgelman, R. (1983*a*). 'A Model of the Interaction of Strategic Behavior, Corporate Context, and the Concept of Strategy'. *Academy of Management Review* 3/1: 61–9.

——(1983*b*). 'A Process Model of Internal Corporate Venturing in the Diversified Major Firm'. *Administrative Science Quarterly* 28: 223–44.

Christensen, C. M. (1997). *The Innovator's Dilemma: When New Technologies Cause Great Firms to Fail*. Boston, Mass.: Harvard Business School Press.

——and Bower, J. L. (1996). 'Customer Power, Strategic Investment, and the Failure of Leading Firms'. *Strategic Management Journal* 17: 197–218.

——and Rosenbloom, R. S. (1995). 'Explaining the Attacker's Advantage: Technological Paradigms, Organizational Dynamics and the Value Network'. *Research Policy* 24: 233–57.

Cooper, A., and Schendel, D. (1976). 'Strategic Responses to Technological Threats'. *Business Horizons* 19: 61–9.

Dutton, J., and Jackson, S. (1987). 'Categorizing Strategic Issues: Links to Organizational Action'. *Academy of Management Review* 12: 76–90.

Eisenhardt, K. M. (1989*a*). 'Building Theories from Case Study Research'. *Academy of Management Review* 14/4: 532–50.

——(1989*b*). 'Making Fast Strategic Decisions in High-Velocity Environments'. *Academy of Management Journal* 32/3: 543–76.

——and Bourgeois, J. L. (1988). 'Politics of Strategic Decision Making in High Velocity Environments: Toward a Mid-Range Theory'. *Academy of Management Journal* 31: 737–70.

Foster, R. J. (1986). *Innovation: The Attacker's Advantage*. New York: Summit Books.

Gersick, C. (1988). 'Time and Transition in Work Teams: Toward a News Model of Group Development'. *Academy of Management Journal* 31: 9–41.

Glaser, B., and Strauss, A. L. (1967). *The Discovery of Grounded Theory*. Chicago, Ill.: Aldine.

Hermann, C. F. (1963). 'Some Consequences of Crisis Which Limit the Viability of Organization'. *Administrative Science Quarterly* 8: 61–82.

Hurst, D. K. (1995). *Crisis and Renewal*. Boston, Mass.: Harvard Business School Press.

Jackson, S. E., and Dutton, J. E. (1988). 'Discerning Threats and Opportunities'. *Administrative Science Quarterly* 33/3: 370–87.

Kahneman, D., and Tversky, A. (1979). 'Prospect Theory: Analysis of Decision Under Risk'. *Econometrica* 47: 263–91.

Kotter, J. P. (1996). *Leading Change*. Boston, Mass.: Harvard Business School Press.

March, J. G. (1991). 'Exploration and Exploitation in Organizational Learning'. *Organization Science* 2: 71–87.

Miles, M., and Huberman, A. M. (1984). *Qualitative Data Analysis*. Beverly Hills: Sage.

Mintzberg, H., Raisinghani, D., and Theoret, A. (1976). 'The Structure of "Unstructured" Decision Processes'. *Administrative Science Quarterly* 21: 246–75.

Mittal, V., and Ross, W. T. (1998). 'The Impact of Positive and Negative Affect and Issue Framing on Issue Interpretation and Risk Taking'. *Organizational Behavior and Human Development* 76/3: 298–324.

Noda, T., and Bower, J. L. (1996). 'Strategy Making as Iterated Processes of Resource Allocation'. *Strategic Management Journal* 17: 169–92.

Ocasio, W. (1997). 'Toward an Attention-Based Theory of the Firm'. *Strategic Management Journal* 18 (Summer): 187–206.

Pettigrew, A. (1988). 'Longitudinal Field Research on Change: Theory and Practice'. *National Science Foundation Conference on Longitudinal Research Methods in Organization*: Austin, Tex.

Pfeffer, J., and Salancik, G. R. (1974). 'Organizational Decision Making as a Political Process'. *Administrative Science Quarterly* 19: 135–51.

————(1978). *The External Control of Organizations*. New York: Harper & Row.

Staw, B. M., Sandelands, L., and Dutton, J. (1981). 'Threat Rigidity Effects in Organizational Behavior'. *Administrative Science Quarterly* 26: 501–24.

Sutton, R. I., and Callahan, A. (1987). 'The Stigma of Bankruptcy: Spoiled Organizational Image and Its Management'. *Academy of Management Journal* 30: 405–36.

Yin, R. K. (1994). *Case Study Research: Design and Methods*, 2nd edn. Thousand Oaks, Calif.: Sage.

Part IV

The Need for Top-down Intervention

12

Corporate Intervention in Resource Allocation

Thomas R. Eisenmann

In Part III, we discussed how senior executives manage traditional, 'bottom-up' resource allocation processes to shape strategy. In Part IV, we now consider circumstances in which corporate executives bypass bottom-up processes altogether and assume responsibility for defining investment plans.

Part IV explores two interrelated issues regarding the role of the corporate office within large, complex, diversified companies. First, when should a CEO play the primary role in defining unit-level strategies, rather than simply reviewing and ratifying proposals advanced by lower-level executives? Second, when should a diversified corporation reduce its equity ownership in certain business units below 100 per cent, thereby relaxing corporate control over strategic resource allocation processes within these units?

In Part II, two contingencies that might encourage CEO activism and partial equity ownership were described. Christensen and Bower argue that bottom-up processes could lead firms to underfund disruptive innovations, relative to sustaining innovations. Divisional executives will favor sustaining innovations because they tend to yield higher, more predictable near-term returns (consistent with structural context requirements) and appeal to core customers (consistent with strategic context requirements). Micropolis, for example, relied on the active intervention of its CEO to fund disruptive innovation within its mainstream organization. All others who successfully managed disruptive innovations did so by establishing independent organizations. Based on these results, Christensen (1997: 199–200) prescribed spinning off 'an independent company whose stock is largely owned by the corporation' to manage disruptive technology.

Also in Part II, Sull discusses a second contingency under which CEO activism and partial equity ownership may yield strategies that maximize long-term value. Disinvestment proved problematic for the tire manufacturers Sull studied. Functional managers were disinclined to suggest plant closures that could lead to their own dismissal. Furthermore, senior executives were reluctant to shut down redundant facilities in communities where they had strong social ties. In the face of mounting capital market pressure, Firestone eventually replaced its long-tenured CEO with an outsider who circumvented the firm's resource allocation processes and personally led a top-down effort to reduce production capacity. In similar circumstances, spinning off a business unit as a separate, partially owned entity could amplify capital market pressures and shelter the unit from forces within the parent company that discourage disinvestment.

Two of the chapters here in Part IV point to a third contingency under which top-down intervention by corporate management and partial ownership of business units' equity may benefit a diversified company. Traditional resource allocation processes may be dysfunctional when diversified companies confront decisions about large, up-front investments in turbulent new markets. Traditional processes are *slow*, because participants at multiple levels of the organization consume time in testing the political viability of new proposals and building consensus. Delays can be costly in new markets when first-mover advantages are salient. Traditional processes also yield *incremental* proposals, because division presidents propose initiatives only at a scale commensurate with their authority. Division presidents are unlikely to sponsor projects that require a large share of the corporation's, or perhaps even their division's, capital budget. Under these conditions, a top-down management approach speeds decision making and shifts career risk for big bets away from division presidents to the executive best able to bear the risk: the CEO.

Eisenmann and Bower suggest that bottom-up processes may fail irreparably under these conditions. Their case study of Viacom shows how and why a bottom-up resource allocation process broke down, and how the corporate office subsequently intervened to promote strategic integration, that is, new business initiatives that crossed divisional boundaries (Burgelman and Doz 2001). Eisenmann and Bower use the term 'entrepreneurial M-form' to describe diversified firms that rely on corporate intervention to promote strategic integration requiring huge resource commitments in the face of high levels of environmental uncertainty.

Raynor's case study of BCE also examines decisions about major capital expenditures in a turbulent environment. As boundaries eroded between previously separate telecommunications markets, the ramifications of investment decisions for various BCE business units were inherently uncertain. Raynor shows how a 'real options' approach to resource allocation preserved BCE's flexibility to exploit future strategic integration opportunities without over-investing. Just as at Viacom, BCE's corporate executives bypassed the traditional resource allocation process to define and build impetus for investments that business unit managers otherwise might have neglected. However, these investments were structured as minority equity stakes in stand-alone businesses. When strategic integration opportunities came to fruition, BCE exercised the option to boost its equity stake and assumed full control over strategy. When integration opportunities failed to materialize, BCE abandoned the option by divesting its stake or accepting dilution as the business raised new equity.

In the final chapter of Part IV, Doz investigates a fourth context in which managers may not be able to rely on traditional, bottom-up RAP to shape strategy—that of the multinational corporation (MNC). MNCs have complex nonlinear organizational structures that span various geographies, product lines, and functions. In such organizations, distinctions between 'bottom-up' and 'top-down' are not always clear or meaningful. Furthermore, MNCs often target new markets through alliances, joint ventures, and consortia—all of which entail partial equity ownership. When an MNC cooperates with other firms in this manner, it cannot reliably transfer its own structural and strategic context to the resulting entity. Within nonlinear hierarchies and multifirm ventures, traditional approaches to managing resource allocation processes are less feasible. Consequently, Doz observes that more frequent and more direct intervention by an MNC's corporate office may be required.

Directions for Future Research

The chapters in Part IV suggest several directions for future research on corporate intervention in strategic resource allocation processes within large, diversified firms.

The Prevalence and Performance of Entrepreneurial M-Forms

Eisenmann and Bower suggest that CEO intervention may facilitate strategic integration requiring large resource commitments in the face of high levels of environmental turbulence. However, we lack empirical research on the propensity of diversified firms that operate in this 'high commitment/high turbulence' context to structure themselves as entrepreneurial M-forms. Also, we lack an understanding of the financial performance impact of the top-down strategic management processes employed within entrepreneurial M-forms, relative to traditional resource allocation processes. These issues seem well suited for the research design employed in studies of strategic resource allocation by Christensen (1992), Noda (1996), Sull (1996), Eisenmann (1997), and Gilbert (2001). Those studies all analyzed the behavior of the full set of firms within a single industry, to control for common environmental pressures, then employed field interviews within a few firms to examine more closely relationships between organizational structure, resource allocation processes, and strategy outcomes.

Managing the Risks of Corporate Intervention

In smaller companies or firms focused on a single line of business, CEOs personally can serve as the architects of strategy. The situations they face are simple enough to allow CEOs to track internal and external developments closely. In large, complex, diversified firms, however, it is unusual for a CEO to have sufficient grasp of the issues facing multiple business units to manage division-level strategies in a top-down manner (Mintzberg and Waters 1982; Ghoshal and Bartlett 1994). When top-down processes are employed in such firms, they tend to suffer from two limitations:

- *Bounded rationality.* As explained by March and Simon (1958), there are natural limitations on a single human's ability to collect and process information, especially when there are many competing demands for the individual's attention—the situation confronting the CEOs of large, diversified corporations.
- *Groupthink.* Janis (1982) observed that organizations, when faced with threats, often rally around a strong leader, offering uncritical support of the leader's policies.

Bounded rationality and groupthink can have devastating consequences when the CEOs of diversified firms personally define 'bet-the-company' strategies, such as those described by Eisenmann and Bower. Firms that rely on activist CEOs confront a potential trade-off between decision-making *efficiency*—that is, speed—and *effectiveness*, which implies rigorous and objective evaluation of a comprehensive set of alternatives. Actions that guard against groupthink—for example, increasing the flow of information to key decision makers—may exacerbate bounded rationality.

Seminal work by Eisenhardt and her colleagues suggests a set of actions that managers in high-velocity environments can take to increase simultaneously the efficiency and effectiveness of their decision-making processes (Bourgeois and Eisenhardt 1988; Eisenhardt 1989; Eisenhardt, Kahwajy, and Bourgeois 1997). However, this work does not explicitly address the challenges confronting large, diversified firms in a high commitment/high turbulence context. Eisenhardt's studies were conducted in turbulent industries, but they included small firms operating in a single line of business, and they did not focus exclusively on large, irrevocable resource commitments. More research is needed to understand whether actions previously observed to increase simultaneously decision-making efficiency and effectiveness are valid in the settings described in this part.

The Moderating Influence of CEO Equity Ownership

Researchers who study the effect of the entrepreneurial M-form structure on financial performance outcomes should consider the moderating influence of CEO equity ownership. Eisenmann's analysis of the cable industry (2000, 2002) indicates that owner-managers, confident that they would not be terminated for sponsoring a failed strategy, were more likely to support big, risky investments than agent CEOs. However, Eisenmann did not evaluate the performance consequences of owner-managers' risk-taking behavior. If the payoff from big, risky bets depends in part on persistence, and owner-managers are better positioned to see their strategies through to completion, then we might expect entrepreneurial M-forms run by owner-managers to outperform those run by agents. In agent-led firms, shareholders may lose patience with a bold strategy that is slow to produce promised results, terminate the CEO, and scuttle the strategy prematurely. This hypothesis remains to be tested. For two reasons, global media firms would be suitable subjects for a future study of the relationships between reliance on top-down strategic management, CEO equity ownership, and financial performance. First, they are organized as entrepreneurial M-forms (Eisenmann and Bower 2000). Second, the set of the largest global firms includes some that are owner-managed (Viacom, News Corp.) and others that are agent-led (Disney, Time Warner, Bertelsmann, GE's NBC/Universal). With the hypothesis above, it is interesting to note that three agent CEOs were terminated in 2002 after their aggressive expansion strategies suffered severe setbacks: Levin at AOL-Time Warner, Messier at Vivendi Universal, and Middelhoff at Bertelsmann. By contrast, owner-managers Redstone at Viacom and Murdoch at News Corp. retained their positions, even though both firms' stock prices declined steeply in response to their respective growth plans. Time will tell whether continuity of strategy yields a performance advantage for Viacom and News Corp., relative to agent-led rivals. A skeptic might expect these owner-managed entrepreneurial M-forms to perform poorly over the long term, because their entrenched CEOs are more likely to ignore feedback from outside investors.

Research on Partial Equity Ownership

As Raynor points out in Ch. 14, not much research has been conducted by scholars of strategic management on when and why diversified firms choose to own less than 100 per cent of their business units' equity. Raynor suggests that the creation and preservation of real options might be one motive for partial equity ownership. Eisenmann's case study of TCI (1997, ch. 7; 1999) suggests other possible motives, including the exploitation of what management perceives to be asset mispricing by external investors.

Consistent with Raynor's findings, Eisenmann observed that TCI's heavy reliance on partial equity ownership exacerbated internal conflict over transfer pricing and strategic integration opportunities. At each business unit in which TCI held a partial equity stake, managers had a fiduciary responsibility to their separate shareholders as well as powerful personal financial incentives (through equity and option holdings) to improve their unit's stock price.

Unlike BCE, however, TCI did not boost its equity ownership to mitigate internal conflict when it 'exercised' real options. In Raynor's study, when previously speculative integration opportunities were realized, BCE managers increased the company's equity stake to 100 per cent, so they could avoid fiduciary conflicts and address cross-unit quarrels within a traditional hierarchy. In contrast, TCI relied on its corporate CEO, John Malone, to adjudicate quarrels—he held the chairman's position in multiple publicly traded companies—even though Malone's multiple roles could potentially create what lawyers call a 'cognizable conflict' over fiduciary duties. Future research should explore the circumstance under which BCE's approach to strategic integration (i.e. eliminate fiduciary conflict by boosting equity stake to 100%) yields better results than TCI's (i.e. conserve capital and accept higher levels of cross-unit conflict).

Scholars might also explore regional differences in the propensity to use partial equity ownership. The heavy reliance on this organizational form by TCI and BCE is unusual among Anglo-American corporations. Only a handful of other US-based examples come to mind, including Barry Diller's InterActiveCorp and Craig McCaw's collection of telecommunications companies during the late 1990s. In continental Europe and Asia, by contrast, it is quite common for large, diversified companies to hold partial equity stakes in their business units. This difference probably can be explained by institutional factors such as the prevalence of ownership by banks and extended families (e.g. the Rothschilds). Researchers might explore whether these continental European and Asian firms have tailored governance and resource allocation processes to manage units in which they hold a partial equity stake, and consider whether such processes could be successfully adapted to an Anglo-American context.

References

Bourgeois, L., and Eisenhardt, K. (1988). 'Strategic Decision Processes in High Velocity Environments: Four Cases in the Microcomputer Industry'. *Management Science* 34: 816–35.

Burgelman, R., and Doz, Y. (2001). 'The Power of Strategic Integration'. *Sloan Management Review* 42/3: 28–39.

Christensen, C. (1992). 'The Innovator's Challenge: Understanding the Influence of Market Environment on Processes of Technological Development in the Rigid Disk Drive Industry'. Unpublished doctoral dissertation, Harvard Business School.

—— (1997). *The Innovator's Dilemma: When New Technologies Cause Great Firms to Fail.* Boston, Mass.: Harvard Business School Press.

Eisenhardt, K. (1989). 'Making Fast Strategic Decisions in High-Velocity Environments'. *Academy of Management Journal* 32: 543–76.

—— Kahwajy, J., and Bourgeois, L. (1997). 'How Management Teams Can Have a Good Fight'. *Harvard Business Review* 75/4: 77–86.

Eisenmann, T. (1997). 'Structure and Strategy: Explaining Consolidation Patterns in the U.S. Cable Television Industry'. Unpublished doctoral dissertation, Harvard Business School.

—— (1999). *Tele-Communications, Inc. (A): Cascading Miracles.* Harvard Business School case 899–215.

—— (Spring 2000). 'The U.S. Cable Television Industry, 1948–1995: Managerial Capitalism in Eclipse'. *Business History Review* 74: 1–40.

—— (2002). 'The Effects of CEO Equity Ownership and Firm Diversification on Risk Taking'. *Strategic Management Journal* 23: 513–34.

Eisenmann, T., and Bower, J. (2000). 'The Entrepreneurial M-Form: Strategic Integration in Global Media Firms'. *Organization Science* 11: 348–55.

Ghoshal, S., and Bartlett, C. (1994). 'Linking Organizational Context and Managerial Action: The Dimensions of Quality of Management'. *Strategic Management Journal* 15: 91–112.

Gilbert, C. (2001). 'A Dilemma in Response: Examining the Newspaper Industry's Response to the Internet'. Unpublished doctoral dissertation, Harvard Business School.

Janis, I. (1982). *Groupthink*. Boston, Mass.: Houghton Mifflin.

March, J., and Simon, H. (1958). *Organizations*. New York: Wiley & Sons.

Mintzberg, H., and Waters, J. (1982). 'Tracking Strategy in an Entrepreneurial Firm'. *Academy of Management Journal* 25: 465–99.

Noda, T. (1996). 'Intraorganizational Strategy Process and the Evolution of Intra-Industry Firm Diversity'. Unpublished doctoral dissertation, Harvard Business School.

Sull, D. (1996). 'Organizational Inertia and Adaptation in a Declining Market: A Study of the U.S. Tire Industry'. Unpublished doctoral dissertation, Harvard Business School.

13

The Entrepreneurial M-Form: A Case Study of Strategic Integration in a Global Media Company

Thomas R. Eisenmann and Joseph L. Bower

The 'pyramid' headed by the single, all-powerful individual has become a symbol of complex organizations, but through historical and misleading accident. The all-powerful chief can maintain such control only to the extent that he is not dependent on others within his organization; and this is a situation of *modest complexity*, not one of a high degree of complexity.

(James Thompson, *Organizations in Action*, 1967: 132)

I think Sumner ends up with the biggest pyramid in the desert.

(John Malone, CEO of TCI, referring to Sumner Redstone, Chairman and dominant shareholder of Viacom Inc.[1])

Introduction

Organizational researchers contend that in large, complex, diversified corporations, the CEO cannot possibly have enough specific knowledge of the threats and opportunities facing individual business units personally to develop their strategies. This argument was advanced by Thompson (1967; see the epigraph above) and by Mintzberg and Waters (1982), who noted in their case study of the Steinberg grocery chain:

As long as the strategy maker knew the firm's operations intimately, the entrepreneurial mode was effective. It was when the operations spread beyond the comprehension of one man—first to diversify geographically to regions outside of its leader's personal knowledge, and then horizontally to new kinds of retailing—that a shift in the mode of strategy making became inevitable.

Echoing this view, Ghoshal and Bartlett (1994: 108) assert that a model that assigns to top management 'the superhuman role of being the designers of strategy, the architects of structure and the builders of systems . . . is no longer interesting to strategy researchers even as the "straw man".' Instead, the CEO is seen as orchestrating a 'bottom-up' process whereby division-level managers advance for corporate-level evaluation proposals that typically will be consistent with strategies previously reviewed and endorsed by corporate management (Bower 1970; Burgelman 1983).

Notwithstanding the skepticism of some scholars, 'superhuman' CEOs seem to be alive and well in the media and entertainment industries, at least according to the business press. In the past, such entrepreneurs as William Randolph Hearst, William Paley at CBS, and Henry Luce at Time Inc. built vast media empires, managing strategy in a top-down manner (Swanberg 1984; Smith 1990; Baughman 1987). Today, careful journalists report that executives such as Rupert Murdoch, Ted Turner, and John Malone of TCI, the largest US cable company, manage their firms in much the same way (Auletta 1997). Although some researchers may dismiss these accounts as being sensationalist and simplistic, we disagree. We argue below that cultural industries are rich with expansion opportunities that require large resource commitments in relation to an industry participant's asset base. Furthermore, these opportunities can be exploited most effectively when diversified media firms move decisively to capture first mover advantages, and in doing so, coordinate the activities of multiple existing business units engaged in film and television program production and distribution. In this environmental context, firms can derive significant benefits when they rely on their CEOs to define and direct personally their expansion efforts. Top-down approaches typically yield faster decisions than bottom-up resource allocation processes (RAP), especially when efforts to coordinate the strategies of multiple divisions engender internal conflict. Likewise, top-down approaches are more likely to yield ambitious expansion plans; by contrast, in a bottom-up process, risk-averse division managers may be reluctant to sponsor 'bet-the-company' strategies.

The next two sections summarize past research on the conditions that favor an activist role for the CEO in developing strategy within large, complex, diversified firms and describe how the structural characteristics of cultural industries are consistent with those conditions. In the subsequent section, the rationale for choosing a single case study to investigate when and why diversified media firms choose to rely on an activist CEO is discussed, along with the reasons for choosing Viacom Inc. as a research site, and our data collection methods. Central to the case, which comprises the next section, is a cross-divisional debate that delayed a major strategy decision at Viacom and thereby encouraged the company's executive team to adopt a top-down approach to strategic management. The final section summarizes our findings, speculates on whether they can be generalized to other industries, and discusses areas for future research.

Theoretical Background

Following Chandler (1962), Williamson (1975) saw the delegation of operating decisions to divisions as crucial to the success of the multi-divisional organizational form (M-form). Such delegation freed corporate managers to focus on the strategic processes of performance appraisal, resource allocation, and long-range planning. Williamson distinguished 'pure' M-forms, which delegated operating decisions to division managers, from 'corrupted' M-forms, in which corporate managers became extensively involved in operating decisions. He held that such involvement would divert corporate managers from critical strategic processes, and as corporate managers invested their reputations in operating decisions, diminish their objectivity in determining whether to allocate resources to divisions.

Extending Williamson's analysis, researchers have suggested that 'pure' M-form management practices are best suited to the pursuit of *governance economies* by firms engaged in *unrelated diversification* (Dundas and Richardson 1980; Pitts 1980; Hill and Hoskisson 1987; Hill 1988; Hill, Hitt, and Hoskisson 1992). Governance economies are available when senior corporate managers are better able to dislodge information impacted within divisions than external capital providers, and thus can avoid problems of moral hazard and allocate capital more efficiently through an internal capital market (Williamson 1975). According to these researchers, realizing *economies of scope* from *related diversification* requires fundamentally different management practices from those used to exploit governance economies. Specifically, to ensure resource sharing and skill transfer among divisions, some degree of central coordination typically is necessary. Empirical research indicates that firms engaged in related diversification are more profitable when they: (1) delegate less operating authority to division managers,

(2) rely more on subjective and firm-wide measures in structuring incentive compensation for division managers, and (3) employ mechanisms to promote cross-unit cooperation, such as project managers and task forces (Gupta and Govindarajan 1986; Hill 1988; Hill, Hitt, and Hoskisson 1992; Argyres 1993).

Whether and how the corporate office adds value in a firm engaged in related diversification seems to depend on the basis for economies of scope. In describing value-creation opportunities that result from cross-unit cooperation, Burgelman and Doz (1997: 2) distinguished between *operational integration*, which involves 'routinely interdependent activities' such as joint procurement or sharing a sales force, and *strategic integration*, which involves the combination of resources from different units to create new businesses. By their nature, routinely interdependent activities can be coordinated through mechanisms such as matrix reporting structures. Corporate managers typically play a role in designing such mechanisms, but otherwise, operational integration should not require frequent head office intervention. By contrast, it is difficult to design standard operating procedures that promote strategic integration, which by definition involves nonroutine activity. The corporate center may need to play an active role in identifying strategic integration opportunities and in encouraging cross-unit cooperation to bring them to fruition (see e.g. Bower 1995). The alternative, relying only on divisional management to define and provide impetus for such opportunities (Bower 1970), is problematic for two reasons. First, concerned that a failed strategy could damage their career prospects, division managers may be reluctant to sponsor risky ventures that require major investments by the corporation. Second, division managers may not monitor remote markets where strategic integration opportunities emerge, especially when such opportunities 'stretch' the corporation into the 'white spaces' between divisions, or into fundamentally new product-market domains (Hamel and Prahalad 1993; Itami and Roehl 1991).

When the corporate office promotes strategic integration, it must choose between two means of intervention. The first relies on an *activist corporate staff* to identify opportunities for cross-unit cooperation and help coordinate their implementation. The second relies on an *activist CEO* to drive strategy in a top-down manner, with more limited staff support. 'Top-down' implies that the CEO is substantively engaged in the development of strategy initiatives, not just their review and ratification. We call the second approach the Entrepreneurial M-form, following from the original meaning of 'entrepreneur' as one who 'takes' (*prendre*, in French) from 'between' (*entre*). CEO-led strategic integration is consistent with Schumpeter's view of the entrepreneurship as combining previously separate factors of production in a novel manner (Schumpeter 1912; Burt 1992: 274).

When is reliance on an activist CEO more likely to result in successful strategic integration efforts than reliance on an activist corporate staff? First, we can speculate that the scale of the integration effort, relative to the corporation's total asset base, may be a significant issue. Corporate planners, like division managers, reasonably may be concerned that sponsoring large-scale integration proposals could put their reputations at risk: their careers could suffer if the proposals were rejected, or worse, were implemented but turned out to be expensive failures. CEOs are likely to be more willing to bear such risks. Second, we can speculate that the level of environmental turbulence confronting a firm may influence its propensity to favor an activist CEO instead of an activist corporate staff. Corporate planning often is slow and bureaucratic (Mintzberg 1994); when the environment is changing rapidly, formal planning processes are likely to produce obsolete strategies. By contrast, when a CEO takes responsibility for both initiating and approving strategies, a company can move more quickly to capture strategic integration opportunities. So, we might expect the Entrepreneurial M-form to be more prevalent in industries that are subject to high levels of environmental turbulence and are rich with strategic integration opportunities that tend to be resource-intensive, relative to the total assets of the companies pursuing them. In the next section, we argue that cultural industries closely fit these criteria.

Strategic Integration in Global Media Firms

Companies that produce and distribute theatrical films and television programming (referred to here as 'content') tend to be linked in a vertical chain and tend to compete globally. Content production is 'hit-driven': only a small share of films and TV programs are commercially successful. Consequently, Hollywood studios spend heavily trying to increase the odds of producing a 'blockbuster'. To spread fixed production costs, which averaged $40 million per film in 1996, studios must secure global distribution.[2] In seeking to maximize global revenue, studios must contend with content distributors who often play a 'gateway' role, potentially extracting a large share of the economic rent generated by films and TV programs.

The distribution of television programming through terrestrial broadcasting stations, cable systems, or direct-to-home satellite broadcasting services typically is subject to technological and regulatory entry barriers, for example, limited broadcast spectrum and cable channel capacity constraints. Shielded by these entry barriers, successful distributors can earn high returns. However, technology and regulation evolved rapidly during the 1980s and 1990s, and established distributors periodically faced the threat of substitution. For example, beginning in the late 1970s in the United States, programming delivered by cable systems captured audience share from terrestrial broadcasters. By the mid 1990s, however, US cable systems encountered competition from direct-to-home satellite broadcasters and from telephone companies able to use their plant to deliver video programming.

Because the payoff from establishing a new distribution gateway can be large, and because first-mover advantages in distribution frequently are significant, competitors often exhibit 'racing' behavior when technological or regulatory change opens a market opportunity. To succeed, new content distributors usually must build infrastructure in advance of demand, often using unproved technology. They also must secure proprietary programming to build audience demand, which involves bidding against incumbent distributors. Upfront spending on infrastructure and programming implies high fixed costs, which in turn yields high operating leverage for new distribution businesses. Hence, like content production, content distribution is a business of big, risky bets. Given these financial dynamics, content production and distribution companies tend to limit operating risk by integrating vertically, especially to facilitate the start-up of new distribution channels. Integration ensures a content producer access to a new channel that might otherwise be blocked, and at the same time, provides proprietary programming for the content distributor, serving to foreclose competition.

In summary, global media firms have faced an unusually rich set of strategic integration opportunities since the 1950s, when the film and television industries began to converge. Convergence, which accelerated with the rise of cable, satellite, and videocassette technologies, is likely to continue well into this century with the advent of 'streaming video' on the Internet. Pursuing strategic integration opportunities requires global media firms to coordinate the strategies of multiple divisions, which can engender internal conflict for three reasons. First, when new businesses require resources resident within established divisions, debates can emerge over transfer prices and whether divisions should be required to release the resources in the first place. Second, in an integrated company, one unit's customer sometimes is another unit's competitor, so conflict can arise over the need for a corporate-wide 'diplomatic' posture toward other global media companies. Third, launching new businesses can cannibalize established divisions. Intervention by the CEO often is required to manage cross-divisional conflict over strategic integration efforts, thus encouraging the adoption of the Entrepreneurial M-Form.

Research Methods

In contrast to operational integration, Burgelman and Doz (1997: 3) asserted that strategic integration 'has received only scant attention' from management scholars. Our investigation of the organizational forms that facilitate strategic integration in global media companies thus fits the criteria proposed by Yin (1994) for employing a single case study. Yin suggested that studying a single case is appropriate when the research objective is to develop theory about a contemporary phenomenon that previously has been inaccessible to researchers. We selected Viacom Inc., one of the world's largest media and entertainment companies, with $12 billion of revenue in 1996, as our research site. Viacom recently had acquired Paramount Pictures, a leading producer and distributor of motion pictures and television programs, and Viacom's managers faced decisions about whether to adapt their existing organizational form and processes to meet the strategic integration challenges that followed from this acquisition.

Our interviews at Viacom were conducted over an eight-month period beginning in August 1995. We studied, in real time, a specific strategy decision requiring the coordination of three divisions' business development activities in Europe. Tracking a decision that still was being debated helped minimize interviewees' problems with recalling past events and attitudes and with the ego-defensive retrospective rationalization of their choices (Huber and Power 1985). Consistent with the assumption that strategy making is a complex cognitive, social, and political process that unfolds simultaneously across multiple levels of the organization (Bower and Doz 1979; Burgelman 1996), we conducted sixteen interviews with ten executives at different hierarchical levels, both in Viacom's corporate office and within the three business units (see Table 13.1).

We took several steps to safeguard reliability in collecting interview data. First, to ensure accuracy and to encourage candor, we gave each interviewee the opportunity to review and approve views and comments we attributed to them. During a review, executives sometimes

Table 13.1 *Interviewees*

Name	Position	Date(s) Interviewed
Frank Biondi	President and CEO	25 Aug. 1995 16 Nov. 1995
Nicole Buss	VP—Strategy and Planning, MTV Europe	30 Nov. 1995
Jonathan Dolgen	CEO, Paramount Pictures	17 Nov. 1995
Thomas Dooley	Corporate EVP—Finance, Corporate Development, and Communications	2 Oct. 1995 3 Oct. 1995 23 Oct. 1995* 12 Mar. 1996*
Jeffrey Dunn	EVP—Strategy and Business Operations, Nickelodeon	3 Nov. 1995
Thomas Freston	CEO, MTV Networks	2 Oct. 1995 18 Dec. 1995
Anthony Garland	EVP—MTV International	30 Nov. 1995
Geraldine Laybourne	CEO, Nickelodeon	3 Oct. 1995
Gregory Ricca	EVP—MTV Networks	18 Dec. 1995
Sumner Redstone	Chairman	14 Mar. 1996 18 Feb. 1999

*Telephone interview

expanded or qualified their remarks (usually to protect themselves or others from embarrassment). However, any changes invariably could be made in a way that preserved their original points. Second, we employed a consistent, semi-structured interview guide, asking each executive for: (1) their views on the merits and drawbacks of different strategy options from their business unit's perspective, (2) a description of the process being used to choose between the options, and (3) their opinions regarding the strengths and weaknesses of that process. We tape recorded and transcribed all the discussions, except for two telephone interviews.

Strategic Management at Viacom

In late 1995, Viacom's management team was reassessing its organizational form. The company long had been run as 'pure' M-form (Williamson 1975). Viacom had prospered in the United States with a highly decentralized management approach, relying on aggressive financial targets and high-powered incentives for divisional managers. As Viacom's divisions expanded overseas, however, they increasingly were being challenged by competitors that were organized as Entrepreneurial M-forms—notably Rupert Murdoch's News Corporation. In the face of this competition, Viacom's corporate managers had to decide whether to continue to allow the divisions a high level of operating autonomy or whether to adopt the Entrepreneurial M-form and pursue international opportunities as a single, integrated corporation.[3]

Background

In 1987, Sumner Redstone, the owner-manager of National Amusements, a movie theater chain, launched a hostile takeover bid for Viacom. A diversified media company, Viacom then owned TV and radio stations; cable television systems; a unit that produced and distributed television programs; and several cable programming services, including MTV, which aired rock music videos, and Nickelodeon, which exhibited programs for children. Redstone paid $3.4 billion for Viacom and financed the acquisition with $2 billion in debt. He assumed the role of Chairman and hired Frank Biondi, an entertainment industry veteran, as Viacom's President and CEO. Biondi and Redstone replaced most of Viacom's senior executives and focused the new team on increasing cash flow to service Viacom's debt.

Viacom's cash-flow growth was strong, and by 1993, the company's balance sheet had improved to the point where Redstone and Biondi could consider options for aggressive strategic expansion. In September 1993, they announced plans to acquire Paramount Pictures, the only Hollywood studio then available for purchase. The announcement set off an auction for Paramount, which Viacom won in February 1994 with a bid of $9.9 billion. However, investors were alarmed by the acquisition price and by the additional debt required to fund the deal: the value of Viacom's stock had declined by 64 per cent, or $3 billion, from the date that plans to acquire Paramount were first disclosed.

After the acquisition of Paramount, international expansion became a strategic priority for Viacom. The opportunities in international markets seemed potentially enormous, but so did the risks. Even by the standards of the fast-paced US media and entertainment industry, the velocity of events in international markets was remarkable. Strategic decisions often had to be made quickly and with fairly sketchy information. In many markets, this led to over-investment, relative to rapidly growing but still modest revenues. In late 1995, Biondi described these dynamics and Viacom's international strategy:

We are putting a lot of bets down, in the People's Republic, in Japan, all over the place. We are going to be building everything including theaters, satellite television networks, video stores, and conventional broadcasting networks, wherever we can get regulatory approval. The vision is shared by all our divisions and by all our senior management. I think to a certain degree we are moving earlier and faster than we would in an ideal world. But everybody else is rushing overseas in a big way. Look at satellite TV in China. At one point we were talking about a joint venture to distribute children's programming there. Someone asked, 'How big is the advertising market?' Dead silence. There *was* no children's advertising in China, outside of Taiwan.

The challenge is whether you have all the facts you need. It's very different than in domestic markets, where you probably have too many facts. In international markets you have to have faith that growth in these markets will bail you out for any logistical errors you make. The biggest mistake would be to do nothing at all. It's a very different mindset. It's pervasive now among all the competitors.

In late 1995, Biondi and other senior executives at Viacom were reevaluating their international strategies. They also were questioning whether their management processes, developed for a smaller company operating largely in domestic markets, would continue to work well for a company with greater scale and scope.

Management Processes

When he was hired as Viacom's CEO, Biondi had prior experience in three of Viacom's industry segments—television program production and syndication, cable programming networks, and cable TV systems. Given his industry experience and the urgent need to manage Viacom for cash flow, it would have been straightforward for Biondi to adopt a top-down management style. However, he resisted this impulse, noting:

Moving from Time Inc. [where Biondi had been CEO of HBO, a leading US cable programming service] to Coca-Cola [where Biondi became the CEO of Columbia Picture's television operations, then owned by Coca-Cola] really changed my views on how to run a company quite dramatically. When I moved to Coke, it was a $4 or 5 billion enterprise, far-flung in terms of its geographic reach. As opposed to asking you to go through months of strategic planning, Coke's CEO would say, 'I want three pieces of paper. I want your budget for next year, your three-year plan, and your strategic issues. We'll spend as much time talking about this as you want.'

At Time Inc., it was pretty clear that the CEO reserved the right to make the final decision on almost anything of significance. It was a pyramid structure, very hierarchical. But at Coke, you couldn't talk to the guy running Australia every day. Coke's top management was incredibly effective, despite this. They pushed down responsibility, and they were very clear on goals.

Leveraging his experience at Coca-Cola, Biondi introduced decentralized management to Viacom. He described the basic elements of this approach: 'Our rules are very simple. You can do anything within your budget. If you want to do something outside your budget, you are going to have to come back and ask.' Tom Freston, the Chairman and President of MTV Networks (which included MTV and Nickelodeon), confirmed that Viacom's operating managers had a high degree of autonomy, and cited this freedom as a critical factor in his division's success. He said, 'It's very informal. There's immediate access. They basically manage us through financial measurements. And we've been called upon to deliver pretty healthy growth rates since '87—about 30 percent a year in terms of operating income.'

Viacom's compensation plans provided strong incentives for divisional managers to achieve their performance targets. A senior division manager's annual and long-term incentive compensation (excluding the value of stock options) could equal four times salary, assuming performance targets were met. About 85 per cent of this payment was directly linked to divisional (as opposed to corporate) financial results.

Several managers noted that Viacom's decentralized management approach, particularly its high performance culture and its practice of linking compensation to divisional financial results, made it more difficult to pursue interdivisional initiatives. Geraldine Laybourne, Nickelodeon's CEO, said:

Synergy is hard, because we are high performance units who are used to a lot of independence, and we're used to tough negotiations. When you put the ad sales guy from MTV and the guy who buys ads for Paramount together in a room, it's hard for them not to strive to get the best possible deal for their division. Sometimes Corporate has to step in to break the ties.

Opportunities in Continental Europe

In the fall of 1995, the Kirch Group, CLT, Bertelsmann, News Corp. and other media companies were vying to establish the next generation of satellite programming platforms in continental Europe. Platforms encompassed a suite of satellite-delivered programming services, along with the equipment that consumers used to access the services. The suite typically was anchored by a movie service offering recent theatrical films. Usually, it included services dedicated to sports, news, children's programming, and music videos. Consumers accessed programming platforms either through cable TV systems or through direct-to-home satellite broadcasting systems. Strategies for ensuring a platform's dominance varied by market, but a common element was a capital intensive and often risky investment in physical assets. For example, this might involve launching satellites, acquiring cable systems, or investing in TV set-top converters that employed proprietary decryption technology. Experience in the United States and other industrialized countries suggested that between one-third and two-thirds of homes would pay roughly $30 per month for access to such a suite of satellite-delivered programming services. Thus, huge revenues were at stake for companies seeking to establish platforms.

As had been the case in the United Kingdom and other markets, the most vigorous competition between potential platform providers was over the exhibition rights for recent Hollywood films. In mid-1995, CLT licensed rights from Warner Brothers, a leading Hollywood studio, severing a decades-long relationship between that studio and the Kirch Group. In response, the Kirch Group offered Paramount more than $1 billion for an exclusive multiyear supply contract. While considering that offer, Paramount continued to negotiate with other companies, some of whom had suggested that Viacom might become an equity partner in their new satellite programming platforms.

After considerable debate, managers at Paramount decided they wanted to pursue the long-term supply contract with the Kirch Group. Whereas the potential upside from owning equity in a platform was large, they reasoned, so were the downside risks, given the scale of investments required and the likelihood of competing platforms. Anxious to meet their budget targets, executives at Paramount also felt that revenues from the Kirch Group would help offset escalating talent and marketing costs for the studio's theatrical films.

In the meantime, managers at Nickelodeon and MTV believed that to guarantee distribution for their services in continental Europe, Viacom should pursue equity partnerships with companies seeking to launch new satellite programming platforms, instead of a supply contract with Kirch. Nickelodeon's managers had determined that international expansion would require locally tailored channels to match the high levels of brand identification the service had achieved in the

United States and to accommodate the limited foreign language proficiency of younger children. Likewise, MTV Europe, which reached 59 million homes across Europe through a single satellite channel, was facing increasing competition from services that operated in a single country, programming 'chart-oriented' music in the local language. It seemed likely that as a competitive response, MTV Europe would need to localize its programming in Germany, France, and other European countries. Jeff Dunn, Executive Vice President of Strategy and Business Operations for Nickelodeon, explained why some managers at Nickelodeon and MTV were concerned that their access to European markets might be foreclosed:

In a nutshell, people have seen what MTV Networks, both MTV and Nickelodeon, have done in the United States, and have determined not to let it happen again. They have learned the power of branded television, one. Two, the people that we have historically bought shows from, who have giant libraries, say, 'Why shouldn't I capture that revenue, why do I need to pass that off to Nickelodeon? I guess I'll get into this business, it doesn't look that hard.' So, our suppliers are vertically integrating. Last, you have distribution issues. And this is the really classic problem for us, because the people who control distribution are also thinking about integrating forward into our business, and they have become real gatekeepers. You have Murdoch in every region of the world we care about, attempting to play this gatekeeper role. He has Fox Kids, and he has clearly stated that he plans to distribute the Fox Kids programming globally on his satellite platforms.

Moving toward Strategic Integration

Beyond the strategic issues under debate, the decision regarding continental Europe raised questions about whether Viacom's existing organizational structure and management systems were well suited to the challenges of global expansion. Dunn noted that competing as a decentralized company against a large, integrated player such as News Corp. posed problems:

In terms of Viacom Corporate, they've been very hands off. Gerry Laybourne believes that this is all good news. She thinks the strength of Nickelodeon has been that the people running it were really allowed to run it and come up with great ideas. You know, 'Just give me the number, and I'll hit the number'—that kind of management, which is really how Frank and Sumner operate.

But internationally, we compete against people who aren't acting in a decentralized way. Murdoch has a global vision, and he's leveraging his entire company against the individual divisions of our company.

Dunn and some other managers called for a much more activist role for their CEO in integrating strategies across Viacom's divisions. Murdoch's News Corp., which was run as an Entrepreneurial M-form, was held out by these managers as the model for organizational change.[4] Murdoch moved instinctively and decisively: he personally developed most of News Corp.'s strategy initiatives with help from a handful of senior operating executives, but with little staff support. As Peter Chernin, News Corp.'s Chief Operating Officer said, 'We don't buy the idea of having a huge corporate phalanx of MBAs who have to go analyze everything before you can make a move.'[5] Recalling one of News Corp.'s most successful episodes of strategic integration, the mid-1980s launch of the Fox Network, which leveraged the resources of News Corp.'s recently acquired Fox studio and Metromedia TV stations to create a fourth US broadcasting network, Jamie Kellner, the network's first President, said: 'The most amazing thing to me . . . was they had done no study whatsoever to see whether or not it was possible to build a fourth network. There was no business plan, no model, just guts.'[6]

In formulating the strategies of News Corp.'s diverse businesses, Murdoch avoided information overload through selective intervention. He often would focus 100 per cent of his attention on a particular division for a period of weeks or months, as he did in 1990 when he assumed responsibility for the day-to-day management of Sky Television, a UK-based satellite programming platform.[7] When focused in this manner on one division's issues, Murdoch tracked the performance of other units by reviewing a one-page weekly report of their performance against their operating budget.

Tom Dooley, Viacom's Executive Vice President in charge of finance and corporate strategy, acknowledged that among Viacom's competitors, News Corp. was exceptional, but doubted whether Murdoch's top-down management style could be successful at Viacom:

You have a formidable competitor in Rupert Murdoch, who lives on a jet, traveling around the world. He knows the markets; he knows what he's trying to accomplish; and he's cutting deals while the rest of us are trying to analyze things and figure out where to go next.

But I don't think Rupert's strategy would work at Viacom. He directs people very firmly. It's, 'Here's the strategy. Get on board, or get out.' At Viacom there's much more of a collegial process.

Rupert rolls the dice. He takes big chances, goes to the brink, and then pulls it back. It's a very different formula than most other people use. But as an individual with a clear vision and total control over the situation [through his ownership of shares controlling a majority of shareholder votes], he can do those sorts of things. In a company like Viacom, where there's more of a collective judgment of management at work, I don't think we can go that far, that fast, and take that kind of risk. We have a much more measured risk approach.

Biondi was more reserved in his praise of Murdoch, and questioned whether he had a grand strategy: 'There is probably more a fear than a conviction that he sees something the rest of us don't. You can do some pretty dramatic things, sometimes stupid, reacting to beliefs like that. But he may just be opportunistic. His strategy may be evolving on the fly.'

In addition to debating the merits of emulating Murdoch's management style, Viacom's management considered whether a change in organizational structure could allow the company better to exploit its scale and scope in a coordinated manner in international markets. Early in 1995, Biondi and Dooley hired a management consulting firm to study this issue. Options evaluated by the consultants included strengthening coordinating mechanisms (e.g. by creating a formal and permanent cross-divisional committee to review international strategy issues, or by using ad-hoc task forces to address specific questions), and substantially increasing incentive compensation payments for cross-unit cooperation. A more extreme option involved creating a new senior position to head all Viacom's international operations. Not surprisingly, this option was rejected by divisional managers. Freston explained:

You can't just say, 'This guy's the new head of International for Viacom'. That's not going to work, because Blockbuster, Paramount, Nickelodeon, they all see themselves as global brands. So, it's going to be a question of coordination, information flow, and agreement on general strategy. There has to be a forum for this to take place. Right now, we've self-generated our own system. There are two or three people in each division who are at the epicenter of these international activities, and they talk to the other guys, and we've got a couple of deals under our belt now. People are beginning to know each other, becoming friendly. We also rely on Tom Dooley and Phillipe Dauman, our corporate general counsel, to act as clearinghouses. The system, as it works now, is pretty good, and it's improving.

Internal debate over a coordinated strategy for leveraging Viacom's assets in continental Europe began in the spring of 1995 and continued until the end of the year. By summer, the interested parties had agreed that Paramount should lead the negotiations with European media companies, because it was clear that the financial stakes were greatest for the studio; that Paramount managers had the strongest relationships with prospective partners; and that the demand for Paramount's programming gave the studio leverage to negotiate concessions for other Viacom units. Managers from MTV Networks were to brief their counterparts at Paramount on their strategic priorities, and if necessary, participate in the negotiations to ensure that their interests were represented. Despite agreement on their respective roles, it took many months for managers at Paramount and MTV Networks to resolve their differences over strategy. Debate centered on which European media companies should be targeted as prospective partners and what concessions Paramount might seek on behalf of MTV Networks. For example, in exchange for exclusive exhibition rights for its programming, Paramount might be able to secure an agreement from a partner that MTV and Nickelodeon would be guaranteed carriage on the partner's satellite. However, the terms of carriage could range from granting MTV and Nickelodeon 'most favored nation' status vis-à-vis competing music video and children's programming services (i.e. comparable revenue sharing arrangements) to awarding MTV and Nickelodeon outright exclusivity that would cut out competitors. Paramount's managers had to determine whether bargaining demands made on behalf of MTV Networks would reduce the value the studio would realize from a deal, or even be perceived as so extreme that prospective partners might walk away from the table.

Consistent with his preference for decentralized management, Biondi endorsed the idea that Paramount should lead the negotiations, with input from MTV Networks. Biondi did not involve himself personally in discussions with prospective partners, nor did he intervene to ensure that Paramount and MTV Networks reached agreement on their negotiating strategy. Internal debate over Viacom's European strategy continued into the fall of 1995 and became increasingly politicized. Under these circumstances, Paramount's managers were reluctant to close the deal; they felt obliged to seek solutions that were acceptable company-wide. In October, all the interested parties attended a meeting in New York to exchange information and to ensure that each division's priorities were clearly understood. Then Dooley and Dauman completed a fact-finding mission to Europe. By late fall, managers at Paramount had become increasingly concerned that their bargaining leverage had been weakened by the delays, because the Kirch Group was now negotiating with another studio.

In January 1996, Redstone fired Biondi and assumed the title of CEO at Viacom, a move greeted with some skepticism on Wall Street, where Biondi was highly regarded. The day after the announcement, the company's stock declined by 5 per cent. Redstone explained that

Biondi's decentralized management style would not enable Viacom to address problems and opportunities quickly in a rapidly changing environment. Redstone said: 'The Murdoch style is better for this company. If there's a problem in China you don't wait three months to fix it, you get on a plane tomorrow with a go-for-it, seize-the-day attitude. I would have preferred that Frank go out and fix it, but he's not confrontational, not hands-on.'[8]

In April 1996, Viacom announced a contract with the Kirch Group, reported to be worth $1.7 billion.[9] The deal would give the Kirch Group the German television rights to all Paramount's programming for a ten-year period and would secure carriage for MTV and Nickelodeon on Kirch's new satellite platform. A few weeks before the deal was formally announced, Redstone cited Biondi's failure to resolve international strategy issues as one reason for his dismissal:

We [Redstone, Dooley, Dauman, and Kerry McCluggage, Paramount's head of TV operations] went to Europe in February. That was probably a trip that would not have been taken had it not been for the management changes. We accomplished more than we could have anticipated, by meeting with principals of several major media companies there. I would say the value of our European deal has increased substantially as a direct result of that trip.

There's a certain amount of leeway that your managers should have. But it's clear to me that this company did not know what it should have known as to what was happening in Europe. And I want to tell you, that trip wasn't taken any too early. You can't send somebody else over and say, 'Tell me what happened'. You have to go yourself.

During the next three years after he assumed the CEO's position at Viacom, Redstone managed Viacom as an Entrepreneurial M-form, intervening regularly to address the company's strategy issues.[10] However, it is difficult to ascertain whether Viacom's performance improved as a consequence. During 1996 and 1997, the company experienced serious performance problems, and its stock price slid from about $40 at the time of Biondi's departure to a low of $25 in 1997. Redstone was criticized sharply by the business press and by investors. For example, *Business Week* (3 March 1997: 68) reported that Redstone's 'hands-on approach and involvement in comparatively minor decisions has imposed a troublesome management gridlock at the company'. By early 1999, however, Viacom's stock price had reached $90, due largely to Redstone-led efforts to turn around its Blockbuster Video unit and to sell assets and thereby reduce the company's debt.

Discussion

Prior to its 1994 acquisition of Paramount, Viacom employed a structure resembling the 'pure' M-form with superior results. M-form organizational arrangements—including the decentralizing operating decisions, reallocating cash flows between competing divisional claims, centralizing control systems built around divisional profit budgets, and using incentive compensation tied to division profit performance—promoted growth in cash flow that was urgently needed in the wake of Redstone's 1987 leveraged buyout. With few strategic interrelationships between its business units prior to 1994, Viacom could avoid head office involvement in operating decisions.[11]

The acquisition of Paramount considerably increased the level of strategic interdependence between Viacom's divisions and presented management challenges common to other global media companies. Global media companies face an unusually demanding strategic management task when they seek to expand by coordinating the efforts of multiple divisions. First, such expansion efforts confront a high level of environmental turbulence. This is true almost by definition, because expansion opportunities typically follow some discontinuity in technology or regulation. Second, expansion often involves large, irreversible investments. For example, Murdoch literally 'bet the company' in 1986 when he launched the Fox Network, and again in 1990 when he pursued the market for direct-to-home satellite broadcasting in the United Kingdom. Formulating strategy under such 'high commitment, high turbulence' conditions is exceptionally difficult: decisions regarding large investments call for long-range forecasts. However, it is likely that such forecasts will be rendered obsolete in an environment characterized by rapid, discontinuous, and unpredictable change. Pursuing an adaptive strategy instead could lead to over-investment in pursuit of ever-shifting markets and technologies. Finally, delaying investments in order to resolve uncertainties risks forfeiting first-mover advantages (Lieberman and Montgomery 1988).

Given these challenges, the benefits of a top-down approach for managing strategic integration in a high commitment, high turbulence context seem apparent. First, a top-down approach can exploit first-mover advantages by avoiding delays that may be created when decisions are based on extensive staff analysis (Starbuck and Milliken 1988) or are negotiated through a political process (Bower 1970; Haspeslagh 1983; Eisenhardt 1989). Second, compared to division managers who may perceive significant career risk from sponsoring an ambitious integration strategy, a CEO should be more willing to bear the personal risks that follow from 'bet-the-company' investments (Bower 1986).

Extending this logic, the organizational form best suited for managing strategic integration appears to be contingent on: (1) the scale of resource commitments implicit in the integration opportunity, in relation to the corporation's total asset base; and (2) the level of environmental turbulence that new businesses are expected to encounter. Further research is needed to test this contingency theory. First, research should establish whether firms pursuing strategic integration opportunities are in fact more likely to adopt the Entrepreneurial M-form when they must make large capital commitments in the face of high levels of environmental turbulence. In addition to the media and entertainment business, other industries that share these characteristics may warrant further study, including telecommunications, energy, and high technology. Anecdotal evidence suggests a high incidence of top-down strategy making in these industries.

Second, the contingency theory implies a performance hypothesis that remains untested, because it is not possible to draw inferences from the single case study of Viacom. According to the theory, under 'high commitment, high turbulence' conditions, companies that adopt the Entrepreneurial M-form should outperform others that do not, in terms of profit and shareholder value growth. Furthermore, the source of the performance advantage for Entrepreneurial M-form companies should be related to their strategic integration efforts. Large sample analysis is required to test these propositions.

The Entrepreneurial M-form facilitates rapid decision making. Rapid decision making however, seems to be necessary, but not sufficient, for maximizing value in a commitment-intensive, turbulent environment. Decision makers also must engage in *rigorous* decision making, which requires a thorough search for information relevant to a comprehensive set of alternatives, and the close appraisal of those alternatives (Janis 1989). Scholars who have studied strategic decision making in turbulent environments (e.g. Bourgeois and Eisenhardt 1988; Eisenhardt 1989; Burgelman and Grove 1996, Eisenhardt, Kahwajy, and Bourgeois 1997), suggest that organizations can encourage decision making that is both rapid and rigorous by promoting constructive conflict (Anderson 1983; Burgelman and Grove 1996; Eisenhardt, Kahwajy, and Bourgeois 1997), and by selecting CEOs with backgrounds and management styles well suited for top-down strategy making (George 1980). Further empirical work—ideally conducted in a context where companies are pursuing strategic integration—is required to validate the prescriptive view that emerges from this research.

Endnotes

1. Quoted in Ken Auletta, 'Redstone's Secret Weapon', *The New Yorker*, 16 January 1995. Malone, owner-manager of the largest cable television system group in the United States, was responding to speculation that Viacom would surpass Time Warner as the world's largest media company.
2. For descriptions of the economics of theatrical film and television program production and distribution, see Vogel (1998). Data on film production costs are from the Motion Picture Association of America.
3. This section draws on a teaching case published by the authors, which describes Viacom's management processes and its European expansion strategy in greater detail. See Eisenmann and Bower (1996).
4. The following discussion of Murdoch's management style is based on: (1) discussions with Viacom managers who had contact with Murdoch and other executives at News Corp., and, in the case of Jonathan Dolgen, CEO of Paramount Pictures, who had worked at News Corp.; and (2) a review of published sources on Murdoch's career, most notably Auletta (1997) and Shawcross (1997). Other useful sources included Neil (1997) and Evans (1994), memoirs written by senior executives who had resigned from News Corp.
5. *Los Angeles Times Magazine*, 1 January 1999: 10.
6. *Fortune*, 26 Oct. 1998: 92.
7. See George (1980: 50) for an account of Franklin D. Roosevelt's similar use of selective intervention.
8. *The Wall Street Journal*, 1996: January 19 B1.
9. *The New York Times*, 9 April 1996: D1.
10. Based on a review of business periodicals and on an interview we conducted with Redstone in February 1999, he was actively involved with three types of strategy issue. First, Redstone led strategy formulation efforts within divisions experiencing performance problems. For example, after the division president of Viacom's struggling Blockbuster Video unit resigned, Redstone assumed direct responsibility for leading the division's turnaround effort. Second, he engaged in 'top-to-top' diplomacy with the CEOs of other global media companies to protect and advance Viacom's interests. For example, when TCI dropped MTV from some of its cable systems, Redstone persuaded TCI's CEO to reverse the decision, citing promises made in the wake of antitrust litigation between the companies. Finally, Redstone encouraged strategic integration efforts. For example, when Paramount and Nickelodeon managers disagreed over the amount of money to be spent making Nickelodeon's animated series, 'Rugrats', into a Paramount theatrical film, Redstone resolved the dispute.
11. Prior to 1994, the major points of interdependence between Viacom's divisions involved: (1) the coordination of cable system affiliate relation-

ships between Viacom's various cable programming networks; (2) the need to establish transfer pricing between Viacom's television program production and distribution (i.e. syndication) business and the company's TV stations, which purchased syndicated programs, and likewise between Viacom's cable programming networks and its own cable systems; and (3) the need for decisions about carriage commitments for Viacom's new syndicated programs from company-owned TV stations, and likewise for new cable networks from the company's cable systems. Note that in these last instances, Viacom did not own enough TV stations or cable systems to provide its syndication unit or cable programming networks with a significant strategic advantage in launching new ventures.

References

Anderson, P. (1983). 'Decision Making by Objection and the Cuban Missile Crisis'. *Administrative Science Quarterly* 28: 201–22.

Argyres, N. (1993). 'Technology Strategy, Governance Structure and Inter-divisional Coordination'. *Journal of Economic Behavior and Organization* 28: 337–58.

Auletta, K. (1997). *The Highwaymen: Warriors of the Information Superhighway*. New York: Random House.

Baughman, J. (1987). *Henry R. Luce and the Rise of the American News Media*. New York: Twayne.

Bourgeois, L., and Eisenhardt, K. (1988). 'Strategic Decision Processes in High Velocity Environments: Four Cases in the Microcomputer Industry'. *Management Science* 34: 816–35.

Bower, J. (1970; 1986 edn.). *Managing the Resource Allocation Process*. Boston, Mass.: Harvard Business School Press.

——(1986). *When Markets Quake*. Boston, Mass.: Harvard Business School Press.

——(1995). *WPP: Integrating Icons*. Harvard Business School case 396-249.

——and Doz, Y. (1979). 'Strategy Formulation: A Social and Political Process', in D. Schendel and C. Hofer (eds.), *Strategic Management: A New View of Business and Planning*. Boston, Mass.: Little, Brown.

Burgelman, R. (1983). 'A Model of the Interaction of Strategic Behavior, Corporate Context, and the Concept of Strategy'. *Academy of Management Review* 3/1: 61–9.

——(1996). 'A Process Model of Strategic Business Exit: Implications for an Evolutionary Perspective on Strategy'. *Strategic Management Journal* 17: 193–214.

——and Doz, Y. (1997). 'Complex Strategic Integration in the Lean Multi-business Corporation'. *INSEAD Working Paper*, 97/03/SM.

——and Grove, A. (1996). 'Strategic Dissonance'. *California Management Review* 38/2: 8–28.

Burt, R. (1992). *Structural Holes: The Social Structure of Competition*. Cambridge, Mass.: Harvard University Press.

Chandler, A. (1962). *Strategy and Structure: Chapters in the History of the American Industrial Enterprise*. Cambridge, Mass.: MIT.

Dundas, K., and Richardson, P. (1980). 'Corporate Strategy and the Concept of Market Failure'. *Strategic Management Journal* 1: 177–88.

Eisenhardt, K. (1989). 'Making Fast Strategic Decisions in High-Velocity Environments'. *Academy of Management Journal* 32/3: 543–76.

—— Kahwajy, J., and Bourgeois, L. (1997). 'How Management Teams Can Have a Good Fight'. *Harvard Business Review*, 75/4: 77–86.

Eisenmann, T., and Bower, J. (1996). *Viacom Inc.: Carpe Diem*. Harvard Business School case 9-396-250.

Evans, H. (1994). *Good Times, Bad Times*. London: Phoenix.

George, A. (1980). *Presidential Decisionmaking in Foreign Policy: The Effective Use of Information and Advice*. Boulder: Westview.

Ghoshal, S., and Bartlett, C. (1994). 'Linking Organizational Context and Managerial Action: The Dimensions of Quality of Management'. *Strategic Management Journal* 15: 91–112.

Gupta, A., and Govindarajan, V. (1986). 'Resource Sharing Among SBUs: Strategic Antecedents and Administrative Implications'. *Academy of Management Journal* 29/4: 695–714.

Hamel, G., and Prahalad, C. (1993). 'Strategy as Stretch and Leverage'. *Harvard Business Review* 71/2: 75–84.

Haspeslagh, P. (1983). 'Portfolio Planning Approaches and the Strategic Management Process in Diversified Industrial Companies'. Unpublished doctoral dissertation, Harvard Business School.

Hill, C. (1988). 'Internal Capital Market Controls and Financial Performance in Multidivisional Firms'. *Journal of Industrial Economics* 37/1: 67–83.

—— Hitt, M., and Hoskisson, R. (1992). 'Cooperative Versus Competitive Structures in Related and Unrelated Diversified Firms'. *Organization Science* 3/4: 501–21.

—— and Hoskisson, R. (1987). 'Strategy and Structure in the Multiproduct Firm'. *Academy of Management Review* 12/2: 331–41.

Huber, G., and Power, D. (1985). 'Retrospective Reports of Strategic-level Managers: Guidelines for Increasing their Accuracy'. *Strategic Management Journal* 6: 171–80.

Itami, H., and Roehl, T. (1991). *Mobilizing Invisible Assets*. Cambridge, Mass.: Harvard University Press.

Janis, I. L. (1989). *Crucial Decisions: Leadership in Policymaking and Crisis Management*. New York: Free Press.

Lieberman, M., and Montgomery, D. (1988). 'First-Mover Advantages'. *Strategic Management Journal* 9: 41–58.

Mintzberg, H. (1994). *The Rise and Fall of Strategic Planning*. New York: Free Press.

—— and Waters, J. (1982). 'Tracking Strategy in an Entrepreneurial Firm'. *Academy of Management Journal* 25/3: 465–500.

Neil, A. (1997). *Full Disclosure*. London: Pan.

Pitts, R. (1980). 'Toward a Contingency Theory of Multibusiness Organization Design'. *Academy of Management Review* 5/2: 203–10.

Schumpeter, J. (1912; 1961 edn.). *The Theory of Economic Development*. Cambridge, Mass.: Harvard University Press.

Shawcross, W. (1997). *Murdoch: The Making of a Media Empire*. New York: Touchstone.

Smith, S. (1990). *In All His Glory: The Life of William S. Paley*. New York: Simon & Schuster.

Starbuck, W., and Milliken, F. (1988). 'Executives' Perceptual Filters: What They Notice and How They Make Sense', in D. Hambrick (ed.), *The Executive Effect: Concepts and Methods for Studying Top Managers*. Greenwich: JAI.

Swanberg, W. (1984). *Citizen Hearst: A Biography of William Randolph Hearst*. New York: Scribner.

Thompson, J. (1967). *Organizations in Action*. New York: McGraw-Hill.

Vogel, H. (1998, 4th edn.). *Entertainment Industry Economics: A Guide for Financial Analysis*. Cambridge: Cambridge University Press.

Williamson, O. (1975). *Markets and Hierarchies*. New York: Free Press.

Yin, R. (1994, 2nd edn.). *Case Study Research: Design and Methods*. Thousand Oaks, Calif.: Sage.

14

Strategic Flexibility: Corporate-level Real Options as a Response to Uncertainty in the Pursuit of Strategic Integration

Michael E. Raynor

Introduction

Contemporary diversified corporations are justified almost exclusively in terms of the increased competitiveness of their operating divisions when compared with stand-alone analogs (Porter 1987). That is, the current orthodoxy holds that an operating division in a diversified corporation must be better off than an otherwise similar independent entity, or the corporation should divest that division.[1]

The competitive advantage gained by divisions as a result of corporate ownership is most often conceptualized in terms of interdivisional synergies: the sharing or transferring of resources, processes, or knowledge between divisions more effectively or efficiently than they can be contracted for between companies transacting in a market (Teece 1980, 1982). This notion of synergy is typified by, for example, divisions that make different products for a common customer base sharing a sales force.

A type of interdivisional synergy that has been formally articulated only recently is 'strategic integration'. More than simply sharing or transferring resources between established operating divisions, strategic integration consists of recombining resources from two or more established divisions in order to pursue product market opportunities that lie beyond the capability of any single division (Burgelman and Doz 1998). For example, STMicroelectronics found great success in a particular segment of the microprocessor market—its 'system on a chip' products—by combining capabilities from many different and largely autonomous operating divisions.

How best to achieve effective strategic integration is the subject of considerable debate. Not surprisingly, the central issue is the appropriate balance between divisional autonomy and corporate direction. Some argue that the corporate office should adopt a largely hands-off approach and focus on facilitating the identification of opportunities for strategic integration—and indeed any type of synergy (Goold and Campbell 1998). The assumption is that valuable synergies will appear valuable to the relevant divisions, and so divisional managers need little in the way of additional corporate intervention in order to do what is best for the corporation as a whole.

Others suggest that a more activist corporate role is appropriate (Eisenmann and Bower 1998). Drawing on Bower's RAP model (Bower 1970), recent case studies (Eisenmann and Bower 2000), and concepts of risk aversion (Eisenmann 2002), the argument is made that senior executives must be willing to override established resource allocation processes in order successfully to pursue valuable strategic integration opportunities.

Based on a clinical analysis of case studies at a diversified corporation for which strategic integration is a critical part of its corporate strategy, this chapter suggests an important contingency that colors the corporate center's approach to strategic integration and identifies key managerial behaviors that make it possible to pursue—or not pursue—a given opportunity.

Specifically, when companies face particularly high degrees of uncertainty surrounding industry boundaries and structure—so-called 'industry convergence'—what types of strategic integration are valuable also will be unclear (Chakravarthy 1997). Yet, despite this uncertainty, competitive pressure often calls for commitment to specific courses of action (Ghemawat 1991). Consequently, executives face a potentially paralyzing combination of a need to act in the face of material uncertainty surrounding what actions to take. Should a company make a given acquisition? Should it sell a given division? Should it restructure around an emerging marketplace? Not acting can allow competitors to lock up the best opportunities, or establish a valuable beachhead (Lieberman and Montgomery 1988). Yet, committing to the wrong path can result in catastrophe, as evidenced by wrenching changes at Vivendi in the wake of Jean Marie Messier's ouster, triggered by his failed attempts to remake the French water company into a worldwide media conglomerate.

The next section discusses why senior management involvement is critical to the pursuit of strategic integration opportunities, and shows that this is especially true in the face of competitive uncertainty. The third section, a preamble to the case studies, serves to establish the telecommunications industry as an appropriate setting for examining the challenges of pursuing strategic integration in the face of uncertainty. The fourth section describes four examples of how the executive team at one company actually responded to these challenges, and the fifth section suggests a framework for understanding what these actions accomplished and the value they created. A final section offers prescriptive advice on how better to pursue strategic integration in high uncertainty, high commitment environments.

RAP and Strategic Integration

It is beyond the scope of this chapter to rehearse the RAP model in its entirety (see Chs. 1 and 2 for a more complete explanation of RAP). For present purposes, it is sufficient to recall that investment initiatives take shape within a set of financial and product market parameters established by the group or corporate level in a hierarchy (structural and strategic context).

Stereotypically, corporate executives set the financial targets that operating managers use to prioritize investment opportunities. In addition, the determination of the structure of the organization—that is, how resources are collected together into operating divisions and the reward systems that motivate the managers working within those divisions—is decided largely by the corporate office. These activities constitute the corporate phases of the definition and context-setting processes respectively.

Both specific investment initiatives and an articulation of a need to change the structural context spring out of discrepancies as observed by the operating levels of the hierarchy. For example, capacity shortages or quality deficiencies are observed first by operating managers, and investment proposals are framed and justified in terms of resolving such issues. These activities constitute the initiating phase of the definition process. Structural context is determined in a similar way. Sufficiently debilitating stresses and strains arising from attempting to serve a given product market within an existing structural context are manifested at the operating level, which initiates the process of creating a new structural context.

In each case, an initial set of constraints is put in place by the corporate office within which operating managers operate and to which operating managers propose changes when those constraints prove binding in inappropriate ways.

Strategic integration initiatives are unlikely to find traction within such a framework for action. Opportunities for strategic integration can be expected frequently to go beyond the established product market scope of organizational units as defined by the preexisting structural context. In addition, the reward systems—especially high-powered, division-specific reward systems typically in place in multidivisional companies—are usually designed to reward primarily performance at the divisional level. This results in a number of barriers to successful strategic integration, if pursued solely within the confines of the traditional model.

First, boundedly rational managers will necessarily find those potential solutions to product market difficulties (the trigger to the initiating phase of the definition process) that lie within their operating divisions more salient than those that might lie beyond those boundaries. Second, high-powered reward systems that are necessarily geared to capturing the effect of divisional management's decisions on their own divisions will skew management's assessment of the relative attractiveness of strategic integration opportunities that do not benefit the divisions for which they are responsible, even if the overall effect on the corporation is positive.

This familiar 'local versus global' optimum is compounded by psychological considerations that suggest that managers prefer those initiatives that improve their relative standing with reference to their perceived peer group—most likely their organizational peer group—over other alternatives. Specifically, even if pursuing strategic integration provides greater absolute benefit to them or their division than independent action, if behaving independently results in higher relative standing among their peers, managers will, at the margin, choose independent action over cooperating in the interests of strategic integration.

These impediments are magnified by any uncertainty that might surround the attractiveness of any specific opportunity, because uncertain outcomes will reduce the expected value of strategic integration. There are at least two types of such risk.

The first type is execution risk. Because managers can be expected to have relatively less experience evaluating opportunities for strategic integration than opportunities that fall within the existing structural context, strategic integration opportunities can be expected typically to be seen as, and be, more uncertain, and hence riskier and so less attractive, than initiatives that fall entirely within the purview of a single division. Consequently, managers are likely to see greater risk associated with strategic integration because there is more risk, and they are likely to magnify this greater level of risk. Much of the current research agenda around strategic integration deals with ways of mitigating this execution risk.

Second, in at least some circumstances, which resources should be recombined, in what ways, and when, can be subject to material uncertainty. In other words, there can be 'strategic' uncertainty surrounding the specifics of strategic integration.

The greater level of risk associated with strategic integration undermines the willingness of operating or divisional managers to find such opportunities attractive. This is because projects that fall within the existing structural context but fail can at least in part be chalked up to the fact there are no guarantees; not every proposal that is approved ultimately succeeds. But those that go beyond the structural context require managers involved in the integrating phase of the impetus process (typically division-level management) to invest much more of their 'political capital' in a project in order to win senior management approval. In other words, they must stake much more of their reputation for good judgment on strategic integration initiatives than on those that fall within the established structural context.

There is therefore a 'perfect storm' of structural impediments to the pursuit of strategic integration within the archetypal resource allocation process in multidivisional companies. The managers who define or sponsor investment projects that require strategic integration are

- unlikely to have as much information for such initiatives compared with more conventional investment opportunities due to bounded rationality and the salience of local solutions;
- not motivated to pursue opportunities for strategic integration, due to a structural context that necessarily emphasizes local versus global optima, and psychological considerations that place relative advantage above absolute gains;
- likely to see strategic integration initiatives as much riskier and costlier, in reputational terms, to pursue due to unavoidable execution risk; and
- at least in some cases, facing 'strategic risk', i.e. situations in which the very need for strategic integration is open to doubt because of uncertainty surrounding either or both of two critical

considerations: whether the requisite marketplace conditions will emerge, and when the answer will be known.

It is as a consequence of these forces that the successful pursuit of strategic integration is seen as necessarily involving a much more activist corporate office. Specifically, within the RAP framework, very senior executives—most often the CEO—must become deeply involved in the initiating and integrating phases of both the definition and impetus processes. Only senior corporate executives are positioned to overcome the divisional-level impediments to identifying and sponsoring opportunities for strategic integration, and for three reasons.

First, senior executives have access to a greater range of information, both internally and externally. This difference mitigates the salience of division-level responses to product market opportunities. Second, the CEO's structural context is by definition corporate-wide. There is no explicit trade-off between local and global optima, because the CEO's local optimum is expected to be, perforce, the global optimum for the organization.

With a better vantage point and better aligned incentive systems, the CEO can largely escape two of the four impediments to defining and lending impetus to strategic integration. But what about operational and strategic risk?

At the operational level, the CEO's position is structurally advantaged versus lower-level managers. The CEO, like other managers, will be relatively inexperienced with strategic integration initiatives compared to traditional investment proposals. However, as the highest ranking manager in the company, the CEO is responsible for creating the structural context. Consequently, the third structural advantage enjoyed by corporate executives lies in lower levels of political risk associated with going beyond whatever the current structural context might be, and relatively less benefit to remaining within it.

Strategic risk is another matter. Better information and better aligned incentives make it possible for CEOs more effectively to integrate strategically divisional resources when the nature of the advantages to be pursued is clear. But there does not seem to be a structural answer to how best to cope with strategic uncertainty. A response would seem to have to lie in the ways in which CEOs seek the benefits of strategic integration rather than in the forces that impinge on their assessment of the associated costs and benefits. The direct observation of executives grappling with this problem is perhaps the best way to inform the development of a theory that can guide action.

In the next section, a case will be made for the telecommunications industry as an appropriate setting to pursue such observation.

Opportunities for Strategic Integration in Telecommunications

In every country, the structure of the telecommunications industry is a consequence of the interplay of changing technology and shifting political exigencies. For much of the industry's history, these two forces have been more or less aligned, serving primarily to prevent dominant players from exploiting their size and consequent market power to make incursions into other markets. In the main, regulatory policy largely has mirrored technological divisions. For example, when telephony technology was first invented, there were real differences in the requirements for delivering 'local' versus 'long distance' services. Consequently, the regulator took the view that there were two industries, and each was (and largely still is) regulated differently. Similarly, at its inception, wireless telephony was a very weak substitute for established wireline-based voice services due to its initially very different performance profile. And so it, too, was seen as a separate industry and regulated accordingly. Ranging still further afield, cable television services are delivered using a network technology that initially could not carry voice signals, and so cable television and telecommunications were seen as separate industries, with, predictably, very different regulatory environments as a result.

In the early 1990s, these once clear industry boundaries began to crumble, due largely to technological change. Rapidly falling costs for signal transmission, thanks to advances in fiber optics, meant that differences between local and long-distance services were obsolete; it now costs no more to send a signal across the ocean than across the street. Improvements in wireless technology meant that it became increasingly viable as a substitute for wireline services. And advances in Internet protocol technology meant that cable television service providers could credibly claim to be able to offer voice services over their existing infrastructure. Whatever their promise, however, such advances remain largely harbingers of an almost assuredly different but still uncertain future. Precisely what shape converged communications services will take, and when they will arrive, remains unclear.

But the bricks have long been crumbling faster than the mortar. The regulatory framework within which these increasingly substitutable services operate continues to impose technologically nearly irrelevant distinctions. A large part of the problem lies in the fact that the difficulties facing regulators and legislators are fundamentally different than the challenges they faced in the past. Rather than having simply to regulate a new technology, they are struggling with the collision of regulatory frameworks due to the convergence of the underlying technologies. In addition to the typical political battles over the driving principles of legislation, the uncertainty surrounding the technologies themselves exacerbates the difficulties associated with taking decisive action. Regulatory change long has appeared imminent in many jurisdictions, but in the face of such uncertainty surrounding precisely what is to be regulated, ultimately inaction has proved the safest thing to (not) do.

Caught between the Scylla and Charybdis of technology and regulatory uncertainty, traditional, wireline-centric telecommunications carriers were unclear about how they should respond through the late 1990s, and in many respects remain uncertain to this day. Even if the proximate pressures somewhat abated due to economic recession in 2001–2, the underlying tectonic shifts are still under way. Will it become technologically and commercially viable to connect phone numbers to people rather than phones, and, if so, when? Will services combining video and voice services become technologically and commercially viable, and, if so, when? Can long distance and local services be bundled, and if so, how? What are the implications of Internet access to both wireline and wireless telephony services—and when will this become clear? And, to the extent new technologies render their precursors obsolete, how long will it take for governments to modify their policies accordingly?

In the 1990s (and still today), for a telecommunications company to answer these and many other related questions meant facing up to a strategic challenge of the first order: what business were they in? What capabilities did they need to compete and—more pressingly—what resources would they need to control in order to be able to compete in the future? When would the technological and regulatory changes that appeared imminent manifest themselves in ways that required a decisive and committed change of direction?

The challenges associated with these uncertainties were intensified by the seemingly irreducible magnitude of the investments required to remain a viable player in almost any sector of the industry. Acquiring or establishing assets such as a viable wireless business, new video services, or restructuring long-established organizations around new value propositions (e.g. service bundles) are all typically difficult, time-consuming, and expensive. Yet, in a competitive environment where alacrity seemed at a premium, hoping to wait out the storm before choosing a tack did not seem a viable choice.

Just about every incumbent telecommunications firm of any size faced the same dilemma as a result of this industry-level convergence coupled with unsettled technological and regulatory landscapes: they needed to do something—but what and when? The senior management of any major telecommunications firm was therefore forced to grapple with strategic integration that required large-scale commitments despite unavoidable and material uncertainty.

One such firm, Montreal-based BCE Incorporated, served as the field site for a study of how top management faced up to this challenge.

Strategic Integration at BCE

The largest telecommunications services provider in Canada, BCE, began as the Bell Telephone Company of Canada, formed by an act of the Canadian parliament in 1880. The company's first wave of diversification began over a century later, in 1983, when then-CEO A. Jean de Grandpré restructured the company, creating 'Bell Canada Enterprises' (BCE), a holding company, so that management could pursue growth opportunities outside the boundaries defined by the original act. Only Bell Canada, the division responsible for the legacy 'phone company' operations, continued to be bound by those obligations.

Between 1983 and 1990, BCE undertook a series of initiatives that turned out to be a failed exercise in 'unrelated' diversification. The company launched a wireless telephony business (the only putatively 'related' new division) and acquired full ownership of an oil and gas pipelines company, a trust company, a real estate developer, and a commercial printer. Between 1990 and 1993, poor results and pressure from investors forced the company to shed all these assets, save the wireless telephony business.

Beginning in 1995, BCE embarked on a second wave of diversification very different from the first. Highlights of this push include the 1995 purchase of a 20 per cent stake in CGI, a network consulting and IT outsourcing firm, a 1998 joint venture offering direct-to-home satellite television services called ExpressVu, a 65 per cent stake in an e-commerce services provider taken in 1998 and renamed BCE Emergis, and the 1999 C$1.6 billion buy-out of the minority shareholders in BCE Mobile, the wireless telephony company initially launched in 1984.

There were at least two important differences between this diversification initiative and de Grandpré's. First, although each of these investments was operationally separate from the core telephony business, the potential for meaningful synergies at some point in the future featured prominently in the company's stated strategy. Second, each investment took the form of a partial ownership stake rather than outright acquisition.

To provide a context for interpreting the case studies and foreshadow the analysis of the next section, the framework that emerges has the following outline. Faced with uncertainty surrounding which operating assets needed to be combined in what ways, BCE's corporate office, primarily in the person of CEO Jean Monty, acquired strategic control (versus operational control or outright ownership) of a range of potentially important companies through partial equity stakes. This strategic control enabled BCE to ensure that these companies remained viable integration partners in the face of temptations to pursue strategies that might have rendered the realization of future synergies with Bell Canada unlikely. The timing and nature of subsequent investments in integration or divestiture were also driven by the corporate office. In sum, the initial investment stake can be seen as an 'option' on future investments in integration 'preserved' by the corporate office's judicious use of its position of strategic control, and then 'exercised' or 'abandoned' as key uncertainties were resolved.

The case studies that follow provide the raw data that motivated the development of this framework.

Wireline–Wireless Integration

In 1984, BCE Mobile (Mobile) was launched as part of the BCE's first diversification push, and was a wholly owned subsidiary. Given the novelty of wireless telecommunications at the time, entering the wireless telephony industry via acquisition was not feasible, and so the creation of this division is an example of organic growth.

In 1987, BCE sold 35 per cent of the company to outside shareholders. This financing strategy had at least two purposes. First, it allowed BCE to accommodate the very different risk and return profiles of its established wireline and comparatively nascent wireless business. The capital necessary to underwrite the network roll-out and customer acquisition costs associated with the rapid uptake of services could well have been supported by Bell Canada. By selling equity to outside shareholders in order to fund this roll-out, BCE management protected the dividend and risk profile of the wireline division, thereby responding to differences in investor tastes. Second,

Mobile's public float gave BCE a valuable tool for motivating Mobile's executive team.

In the ensuing decade (1987–97) the two companies—Bell and Mobile—operated entirely independently of each other, and with good reason: the wireless and wireline businesses had different technological infrastructures, cost models, and market and competitive dynamics, and were in very different places in their respective life cycles.

In recent years, technological and market convergence have been rapidly eroding these differences. Wireless services, which have become a mass market offering, are no longer the high margin service of the late 1980s. Consequently, everyone who was a potential customer for wireline services was now also a potential customer for wireless services. Service features (e.g. call waiting, call forwarding, etc.), call quality, and call reliability were not yet entirely comparable, and so most consumers still relied on wireless services mostly for mobility. Nevertheless, rapidly falling costs and prices coupled with continued technological improvements meant that the spectre of 'wireless substitution' was very real. Finally, both wireline and wireless services had become competitive markets in their own rights, with wireline resellers eating into Bell's market share, and facilities-based wireless carriers competing aggressively in all Mobile's markets.

These changes in industry dynamics created new opportunities for cooperation between Bell and Mobile. Each could offer the other a key complementary service that could provide for its own competitive health. From the corporate perspective, managing the collaboration between the two divisions provided a way to cope with the potential of the disappearance of distinct wireline and wireless markets and transition of the company to more solutions-focused structure.

One of the first opportunities for synergy—rather than full-blooded strategic integration—was in retail distribution. Until 1999, Bell maintained a chain of Teleboutiques, retail locations that sold only Bell products: branded phone equipment, telecommunications services, etc. A chain of Phone Centers served the same purpose for Mobile. The integration opportunity, according to BCE's CEO Jean Monty, was to develop a single retail presence that would sell not only Bell and Mobile products but everything else in the BCE arsenal as well, especially Sympatico (Bell's internet access offering) and ExpressVu (the satellite television service).

The problem was that, as an independent company with minority shareholders, Mobile's participation could be secured only through an extensive negotiating process designed to ensure that minority shareholders' interests were protected. It wasn't enough that the overall effect of combining retailing strategies would be strongly positive; that benefit needed to be allocated back to Mobile and to Bell in precisely specified and legally binding terms.

This proved enormously difficult to accomplish. Such decisions essentially had to be made twice: once by each organization's management team and board of directors. Despite the fact that BCE executives and even Bell and Mobile executives were convinced of the value of the synergies to be gained in the short run and the opportunities for strategic integration in the future, it was structurally all but impossible to take any substantive action. Fiduciary responsibilities demanded that each party to cooperative efforts have explicit agreements regarding what the benefits of cooperation would be; and when dealing with synergies, such agreements are very difficult to codify between two essentially independent entities.

In order to pursue these opportunities, BCE bought back the outstanding equity in Mobile for C$1.6 billion, a 31 per cent premium to BCE Mobile's market price one month prior to the deal. The company was renamed Bell Mobility and made an operating subsidiary of Bell.

Taking a full ownership position in Mobile obviated the protracted and generally fruitless negotiations between Bell and Mobile that generally focused on allocating wealth rather than simply creating it. With common ownership, interests were now much better aligned, and the allocation of benefits between divisions had become a managerial decision rather than a fiduciary responsibility. This greatly facilitated more rapid and decisive action. Randy Reynolds, formerly CEO of Mobile and President of Mobility in 1999, explains:

one of the governance issues we had [when pursuing synergies] before [the buy-back] was if you took a 10% cut across the top for all those bundled services, who takes the cut? And where [are] the provision economies that make the bundle more profitable to us? And when you've got minority shareholders in individual companies, that's a somewhat tricky decision.

As a combined entity, it's still tricky, but now it's only a battle between Guy Marier, John Sheridan, and me over who gets what slice of the revenue. But for the shareholder it doesn't matter any more. So it's a relatively unimportant decision, one that can get made in an afternoon between the three of us, instead of having to get made through the development of business plans, me cranking up my machinery, them doing the same, it going to both boards, and all that run-around. Now, if we think it makes sense for the overall company, we can go ahead and act. That's the benefit.

Removing the need to quantify the benefits of integration for minority shareholders was only part of the benefit, however. Within the Bell and Mobility organizations was also considerable resistance from relatively senior management to even preliminary efforts to pursue strategic integration, rather than merely synergies. For example, Simply One was a product launched in 1999 that gave residence customers a single phone number that forwarded incoming calls to multiple devices (e.g. a series of mobile telephone numbers) until either the subscriber answers or all previously identified numbers have been tried, in which case the caller can leave a message.

Bernard Courtois, Chief Strategy Officer for Bell, explains the tensions surrounding the launch of Simply One:

The drive [for Simply One] came from Bell, not from Bell Mobility. Bell Mobility viewed that as a threat. As far as they were concerned, they owned the mobile business. When Bell started selling a service that included mobility, Bell was sort of encroaching on their turf and taking something away. So they actually resisted it.

What got it pushed through, though, was a strong view from the top that bundles are the future of our industry. But I have to say the resistance worked for almost more than a year, and it came from both sides. Not only did some folks in Mobility feel threatened, but as Simply One got developed we found that there were people in Bell who had to be disturbed in the way they did things and they didn't want to do it anymore.

Resolving these tensions required persistent pressure from the corporate office that the benefits of such integrated services outweighed the division-specific costs. In a world where such benefits would have had to have been quantified in detail by managers who were predisposed to view such initiatives negatively, it is all but a sure thing that products such as Simply One would never have been launched.

In brief, the Mobility buy-back and subsequent drives for developing integrated products and services were precipitated by a belief on the part of senior executives that the 'time was right'. The ability to do this, however, was created by a portfolio play over ten years earlier that put in place the raw materials for such integration—raw materials that would have been much more expensive and difficult to integrate had BCE been forced to acquire a wireless player of sufficient scale only after management had reached the conclusion that wireless–wireline integration was viable. In addition, although the ownership structure greatly facilitated this integration, actually making anything happen still required significant senior management intervention to override divisional parochialism.

E-Commerce Solutions

The Electronic Data Interchange (EDI) market was born in the late 1970s and experienced rapid growth through the 1980s. EDI promised increased efficiency by automating the generation, transmission, and processing of routine paper documents using software and telecommunications networks. Instead of paper-based purchase orders or invoices, everything would be done electronically, with minimal human involvement. EDI was, in a very real sense, an early example of e-commerce.

A key factor limiting EDI's growth was its reliance on expensive and proprietary software and networking technologies. Only the most costly processes could take advantage of what EDI offered, and then only between commercial enterprises: connecting with consumers electronically was hardly imaginable, let alone feasible.

The advent of the Internet as a general-purpose electronic network relaxed this constraint. It suddenly seemed possible to connect all businesses and all consumers using standardized software interfaces. What was needed to facilitate this shift was a new set of software services that exploited these common building blocks to create customized solutions for a given business's products, processes, and customers.

A key component of these so-called 'e-business solutions' was the provision of the network services required to deliver them, primarily connectivity geared to the demands of Internet protocol (IP) traffic and bandwidth sufficient to cope with a mass-market offering. Elements within Bell's network services group were uniquely positioned to provide these components in virtue of Bell's dominant, incumbent position.

It was with this complementarity in mind that Bell Emergis was launched in 1997 under Bell's then-CEO John McLennan. A wholly owned subsidiary of Bell, the new business is an example of organic growth, much like the initial launch of BCE Mobile. And, as with BCE Mobile, Bell Emergis's position within the larger Bell organization compromised its ability to pursue growth opportunities.

Operating as a division within Bell created a number of difficulties. The strategic imperative given to Bell Emergis was to pursue a broad range of emerging businesses—from unified messaging to consumer Internet access services, to e-commerce solutions. (It was this 'emerging business' element of the division's strategic mandate that inspired the name *Emergis*.) As a result, although significant resources were devoted to Bell Emergis, they were thinly spread across many different ventures. Consequently, no single initiative ever became big enough to 'matter', and in fact there was a desire on the part of operating managers within Emergis to stay small, to fly 'under the radar' and avoid what they perceived to be the heavy hand of senior Bell management that would surely be felt if their venture grew to any significant size.

In particular, according to BCE executives, a large part of what drove the need to 'stay small' was that BCE was valued largely on a multiple of its EBITDA and new ventures, because they were typically unprofitable in their start-up phase, consumed EBITDA, and drove down the market value of the larger organization. Any individual new venture that got big enough to lose enough money to matter was sure to come under intense scrutiny, which only increased the likelihood of being shut down.

This perverse incentive structure (start new ventures, but not big ones) also manifested itself in the seemingly perpetually tentative involvement of Bell Emergis's e-commerce solutions group with Mpact Immedia (Mpact), a Montreal-based company competing in the same space. Brian Edwards, CEO of Mpact at the time, recalls the nature of his negotiations with Bell to buy his company:

We generally would call the guy running the electronic commerce or the electronic messaging division of Bell. They might want 19% so it doesn't show on their balance sheet... and although we had lots of discussions, I would say it never really went anywhere. What we wanted them to think about was a small piece of their overall business, and it had a really hard time getting any attention up the ladder. Those kinds of discussions had gone on for about two years.

Persistent losses over two years at Bell Emergis are attributed by informed observers—mostly consultants to the BCE and Bell at the time—to a pattern of significant, but insufficient, investment in a broad array of initiatives. No single undertaking was big enough to command senior management attention—a corollary of which was that no single undertaking was big enough to succeed. Yet, middle management within Bell Emergis was hesitant to undertake initiatives that would command senior management attention, because their new ventures would then be subject to the performance criteria of the established businesses.

At the prompting of another BCE executive, Serge Godin of CGI (see below), Edwards contacted Monty, by then CEO of BCE, and within weeks a deal was struck whereby Bell Emergis and Mpact Immedia were merged, creating a new publicly traded company, BCE Emergis (Emergis), that was 65 per cent owned by BCE with Edwards at the helm.

In the wake of the acquisition, Emergis's scope of operations was significantly restructured. Mpact Immedia had built a significant consumer Internet service provider (ISP), TotalNet, but as BCE Emergis, the company was pointed firmly at commercial markets and e-commerce. With Monty serving as chairman of the board at Emergis, there was significant pressure to divest TotalNet.

BCE's consumer market ISP, Sympatico, was Canada's largest, and, *prima facie*, it would seem to have made sense to transfer TotalNet to Sympatico. Such a transfer might have been a good opportunity to demonstrate synergies. However, the minority shareholder interests precluded such an asset transfer: the Emergis board was obliged to maximize shareholder wealth in the sale of an asset for which there was an active market. Serge Fortin, who led negotiations for Sympatico, explains why Sympatico did not buy TotalNet:

It looked like Emergis was going to get about $30 million for TotalNet [from another buyer]. That works out to $600 per customer; taking into account BCE's 65% ownership of Emergis, it's still $200 per customer. My per customer acquisition cost is $65. And they're better customers: less churn, primarily. So I just didn't think it made sense.

In addition to this seemingly free hand with respect to the tactical details of a strategic divestiture, there have not been any synergies exploited and certainly no strategic integration between Bell and Emergis. However, Emergis did not enjoy strategic or operating autonomy, despite the lack of linkages. Instead, BCE's ownership of Emergis has imposed constraints on Emergis, primarily with respect to Emergis's options for growing through acquisitions. Brian Edwards explains:

Suppose we could buy a $5 million company with a $5 billion market cap with our shares. We would dilute the hell out of them and they would probably be unlikely to want to spend $3 billion or $4 billion on that kind of a deal. So I think we do have a constraint that we didn't have before because they have to use real money in a world that trades cash at a discount.

In other words, were it not for BCE's ownership position, Emergis would likely pursue, if not a different strategy, at least different ways of implementing the same strategy. These constraints were not offset by any benefits from synergies or strategic integration with Bell. Rather, the explicit objective was to build Emergis into a 'growth engine' that would, in time, reinvigorate the existing organization in as-yet undetermined ways. Jean Monty:

The strategy is not, at least at this stage and under my leadership, to build them up and spin them off. It's to look at the concept of Bell being an anchor, and the other units being growth elements of the total business, including Bell. [Emergis is] a growth engine ... [a]nd in time probably my successor will be successful in bringing those companies to 100% ownership.

In May 2004, BCE sold its stake in Emergis. In press releases, senior management said that the company was no longer core to BCE's operations. Even if Emergis remained a viable and successful business in its own right, in the absence of any meaningful probability of future strategic integration, management concluded that the assets tied up in Emergis were better deployed elsewhere.

Systems Integration Consulting and IT Outsourcing

In addition to e-commerce, another potential growth engine for Bell lay in systems integration and IT outsourcing. As Bell's large corporate customers increased their reliance on technological infrastructure and network connectivity, competing as a service provider seemed to demand a broader range of services (Raynor and Christensen 2001). It was no longer always sufficient to offer network provisioning and rudimentary network management services. Instead, Bell's marquee customers—the financial institutions, natural resource companies, and professional services firms in particular—were exploring more integrated IT/network solutions. Service providers offering these integrated solutions often ended up hosting and managing the IT infrastructure associated with them as well, typically as a result of their superior expertise which was itself a function of being able to offer an integrated solution (Raynor and Littmann 2003).

As with the Emergis deal, it was Monty's decisiveness that ultimately got a deal done. Monty explains how BCE came to invest in CGI, a Montreal-based systems integration company:

This was my third attempt to get into network consulting. I tried in 1991 when I was with Bell, and the target was [SHL] Systemhouse in Canada. The second time, I was at Nortel [as CEO] and I tried to do the same thing with CSC Index, at the time, number three after IBM and EDS.

Come back to Bell and BCE. Turns out Bell already had 20% of CGI. They did a contract sharing on a distribution channel, and Bell put money into it, about $10 million or $15, I forget the amount, and they ended up with 20% of the company.

I said, 'What are you doing with this? Why don't we go for control?' 'Well, we don't know,' they said.

What the hell do you think? This is the perfect opportunity and I missed twice before. This time I'm not going to miss.

Part of the resistance to doing a deal with CGI was that, as with the Emergis deal, it involved combining an organically grown, but not particularly successful, business unit offering similar services with an outside firm. In this case, it was Bell Sygma that was merged with CGI. Sygma's assets and an additional cash infusion gave BCE a 42 per cent stake in the new entity.

Bill Anderson, then CFO of BCE, explains that this initiative, although characteristic of Monty, was not consistent either with the approach taken by other Bell senior managers, or the previous executive team:

With Monty in as chairman and CEO of BCE and Chairman and CEO of Bell, there's a stronger drive from the top. With the CGI acquisition, for example, that required moving faster and making a bigger commitment than would have been likely with the previous management team. You see, since the days he was at Bell and before he went to Nortel, Jean had always felt strongly that this kind of systems integration capability was important. The way he drove through the decision did cause a little bit of friction. But without that kind of a person to drive that decision, it probably wouldn't have happened.

Interestingly, at the previous level of ownership, at just under the 20 per cent threshold that would have triggered a balance sheet consolidation, attempts to identify and exploit integration opportunities seemed half-hearted and were not effective. Andre Nadeau, then-EVP of Strategy at CGI, explains:

We had an initial strategic alliance with Bell that began with an infusion of capital and two Bell seats on the CGI board in 1995. The idea was to try and find opportunities to sell combined IT/telecoms services. Bell didn't do much, formally, with their influence, and the arrangements were rather soft. We did have an alliance manager who worked with the Bell account reps and the industry sector leaders. His role was to tell them about our services, and respond to opportunities, to try to connect our office organizations and professionals in the field with the appropriate Bell representatives where there were joint opportunities. And although we had identified some broad objectives for these cooperative efforts, they weren't even factored into our budget. There was no real recognition of these efforts because we felt that these were additional opportunities and we already had strong growth and profitability. It worked somewhat. But certainly not to the extent that either party hoped.

However, as the market has matured, and BCE has increased its stake, Nadeau reports that the Bell/CGI relationship has improved, even if the originally intended scope has been somewhat reduced:

The convergence of IT and telecoms is still more a technological convergence than a marketplace convergence. Clients still do tend to want to make those business decisions distinctly. And when they're looking for advice about IT broadly speaking, they'll naturally go an IT play, not a telco. At CGI, we're looking for clients that have large IT budgets and are transforming their organizations. A telco is looking for high telecom expenditures, which means networks. It doesn't necessarily mean that there's a lot of IT behind it. Where there's convergence is when you have the opportunity for both, and that's where we are today. We've narrowed down the relationship to more of a pursuit of the bigger opportunities and made the relationship harder, with better metrics, and important parts of our operating budgets devoted to those initiatives.

A commitment to exploring strategic integration creates its own problems, however. For example, prior to the CGI acquisition, Bell Canada had long-term agreements with a major IT services organization (here disguised as InfoTech) that compelled each organization to present joint networking/IT services bids only with each other. In addition, InfoTech was also a major corporate customer for Bell.

The complications associated with this arrangement came to the fore when a major financial services organization (here disguised as InvestCo) released a request-for-proposal (RFP) for an integrated outsourcing solution worth over $7 billion over ten years. Bell could not submit an integrated bid with CGI; and even if it were not encumbered by the previously existing contract with InfoTech, pursuing such a significant deal without InfoTech might well have had adverse consequences on its client relationship with that organization.

As a consequence, Bell senior management sought to convince InvestCo to split their RFP into networking and systems integration/outsourcing components. The private hope was that Bell and CGI would each win their respective bids, and then the two companies would explore ways in which they might integrate their offering to greater advantage, both for the client and for BCE.

In addition to these difficulties, CGI faced the same kinds of growth constraints as Emergis. Nadeau:

What BCE has to decide is if it wants to stay in the IT business as it grows. The Nortel model was a good one, in that Nortel was a strong, world class, public company that has a currency that it can use to make the important acquisitions and drive itself forward. When the Bay [Networks] acquisition came along, I'm not sure it wouldn't have been a good idea to think about selling something else off to stay in control of Nortel, to reinvent BCE along that new trajectory. Because if we continue to grow the way we think we will, they'll be a tough choice to make on CGI that could look an awful lot like what they went through with Nortel.[2]

Since 2000, BCE has allowed its stake in CGI to be diluted through various acquisitions CGI has made as it has grown, primarily in the US market. Well-placed company analysts—primarily equity analysts—report that the originally sought-after integration opportunities never materialized, in large part because CGI's most attractive growth opportunities lay in the United States, where Bell is unable to provide facilities-based network services. Because equity markets have fallen considerably since BCE increased its stake from 19 to 42 per cent, an outright sale of CGI would amount to 'selling low'. Consequently, the most reasonable exit strategy is a gradual dilution as CGI grows, selling only if equity values recover to the point that a large-scale sale becomes financially attractive again.

As of late 2003, BCE's stake in CGI had fallen to 29.9 per cent, largely as a result of BCE's non-participation in twenty acquisitions between September 2000 and January 2003. Organizationally, CGI no longer reports to the CEO's office, but instead is clustered with other so-called 'orphan' businesses, including various international investments that soured but proved difficult to divest. As CGI's stock price has recovered, there is increasing talk and enthusiasm both in the investment community and among BCE senior management for a full divestiture.

Satellite Television Services

A key uncertainty coloring the strategy of most telecommunications services providers was the nature and extent of the challenge cable companies might mount to both their core voice offering and potential new growth markets, especially residential data services (Internet access). Technological advances opened up the possibility of cable companies one day offering 'VoIP'—voice over internet protocol—at much lower cost than incumbent telecoms firms could provide voice services over their copper networks (or even VoIP over their copper networks). However, telcos were working on invasion plans as well. In their laboratories, they were experimenting with a technology platform known as VDSL (video digital subscriber loop), which showed promise as a means of delivering video services over telco networks. Although each posed only a nascent threat to the other, the magnitude of the potential challenge was enough to command senior management attention in both industries.

In addition, both cable companies and telcos were beginning to see the promise of high-speed Internet access, a new market for both industries. Dial-up access had created limited growth for telecoms firms as some households purchased a second or third line for dedicated computer use, but in the mid-1990s the industry was not a growth opportunity for network service providers as much as for the ISPs directly, such as AOL. High-speed access, however, promised to be a facilities-based battle that offered significant growth potential. The cable firms had a relatively inexpensive offering that exploited the DOCSIS standard, whereas telcos had a higher-cost DSL (digital subscriber loop) service that offered some performance advantages (e.g. security).

Out of this tumult emerged the notion of a 'triple play' bundle: video, data, and voice services all provided by the same provider over the same technological infrastructure. The industry view was that such a service would be enormously 'sticky', and that customers would be very reluctant to change providers. Consequently, whichever services provider—telcos or cable—was able to offer combined services first would create an almost insurmountable marketplace advantage.

For Bell, the competitive dynamic being played out against the dominant cable provider in its territories—Rogers Communications—was complicated by the fact that Rogers was also the second-largest (after Bell Mobility) mobile services provider in Canada, with a strong presence in Bell's markets. A 'home run' bundle would include not only wireline voice, but mobile voice and data as well.

The technological difficulties attendant to providing VoIP services were dwarfed by the challenges of delivering VDSL cost effectively. Consequently, Bell saw itself as potentially at a competitive disadvantage. What if Rogers, which could offer a 'video-centric' bundle, was first to market? Even if Rogers's voice offering was comparatively weak (e.g. low quality, unpowered lines) or relied largely on wireless substitution, consumers might be effectively locked up. By the time VDSL was viable, it would be too late ever to recoup the investment costs. Without some way to put pressure on cable's core business (video) and create at least an interim video offering, the game could be over before it started.

It was for this reason that in 1996 BCE entered into a joint venture with three other investors to explore the viability of direct-to-home satellite television services. Although BCE had the wherewithal to enter the business on its own, there were too many uncertainties surrounding satellite-based services and the nature of the relationship between such services and the rest of BCE's divisions to warrant such a commitment. Anderson, BCE's CFO at the time, explains:

There were a lot of unanswered questions at the time: what satellite will you use, what kind of capacity will you have, when will it be digital, will the customers buy it? At the same time, whether a phone company might offer a video signal over its copper wire went from, 'Yeah, it's going to be great', to 'No, it's not going to work at all', to 'Well, it may be possible but not for five or six years'. Meanwhile, the cable companies were figuring out how to compete with the phone companies with high-speed Internet access and VoIP. BCE ultimately purchased full control of ExpressVu, but not for the purposes of capitalizing on opportunities for strategy integration. Instead, ExpressVu's value emerged as an offensive weapon in the battle against cable. Monty explains:

To me the issue is how can Bell spin off for its growth reasons other entities that it can nurture for growth? ExpressVu is a great example. Can we grow a DBS [Direct Broadcast Satellite] service in Canada, bundle it with our services, and will that be a different approach to what the cable companies will do? Obviously, yes. It's a different approach and less expensive for a company our size than going six megs to the residence on ADSL.[3] We prefer the model where for $1 billion we reach 11 million homes in the country, which is the whole of Canada, including Innuvik[4] and even the snowbirds going to the U.S., to Arizona and Florida.[5]

So you take that approach and you say, 'Can I build value rather than be the distributor of DirecTV in Canada?' I'm going to own my DirecTV, then I'll bundle it with my services and use it to serve my strategic goals, rather than just trying to defend myself against the cable guys.

In other words, if satellite television services were purely a defensive play, BCE could have become the Canadian distributor of a successful US-based service, DirecTV. However, Monty's comments come against the backdrop of disappointing developments regarding the cost structure of wireline-based video offerings: it was by then known that VDSL would be far more expensive than satellite and offer no material performance advantage. Yet, a nonfacilities-based bundle was seen as potentially viable, obviating the single-provider/single-pipe model. That is, the thinking was that ExpressVu could be more than merely a stop-gap—it could become a key component in future service bundles that included a video offering.

The first of these offerings took the form of the 'ComboBox', a specially designed version of the terminal required to receive satellite television services that integrated high-speed DSL Internet access functionality. In addition, it acted as an Internet hub connecting computers in the home via DSL service. Finally, an integral element of the ComboBox was 'Personal Video Recorder' (PVR) technology of the type pioneered by TiVo, a US-based start-up that acts as an 'intelligent hard drive' that stores video programming digitally for later viewing. Taken together, the ComboBox was the first offering in the Canadian market that constituted a 'double play' bundle (video and data) and, ironically for a phone company, one that was essentially video-centric.

Peter Nicholson, then SVP of Strategy for BCE, explains how the ComboBox product was created and introduced as BCE's first major 'convergence' consumer product:

The notion of convergence was in the air; it had become part of the ethos at Bell and BCE as a result of all the portfolio activity—Emergis, CGI, ExpressVu, and the like. Network and device technologists were playing around with the art of the possible, from a technology point of view, and this was one of the ideas that surfaced inside Bell. But it had no hope of going anywhere from inside Bell: their success depends on cutting cost, and the ComboBox promised to cost money, a lot of it, and the upsides were enormously uncertain.

What they [the technologists] had developed in terms of a value proposition to the customers and in terms of a feasible business case was totally inappropriate. Over the course of a couple of weeks, my staff and I essentially created the concept and the business case in the course of crafting the press release announcing the product. I'm in constant communication with Jean [Monty], and he was enthusiastic about it because it provided tangible evidence of making the convergence strategy a reality. And so what began as a technological 'gee-whiz' in the bowels of Bell became a highly visible element of corporate strategy.

By late 2003, the ComboBox had proved a disappointment, even though its PVR functionality was well received in the marketplace. As a result, ExpressVu now sells PVRs embedded in their decoder boxes. 'Simple' bundles exist between various Bell products and ExpressVu services, wherein customers receive a discount for buying some combination of services (local, long distance, DSL service, and satellite services) from Bell, but bundles of the kind presaged by the Combo-Box, i.e. bundles requiring true strategic integration, have not yet materialized. Nevertheless, BCE still owns 100 per cent of ExpressVu, and there is no indication of any desire to divest any or all of the division.

Future opportunities for integration might yet emerge. Specifically, as network architectures generally migrate to an IP structure, fully featured and fully integrated voice, data, and video services become increasingly viable. Under such circumstances, the benefits of ExpressVu could well lie more in the experience and expertise it has given BCE in managing the content side of video services rather than the physical satellite network, which lacks the interactivity that future successful services are likely to require.

A Real Options Model for Managing Strategic Integration

Perhaps the most salient aspect of these case studies is the fractional and varying ownership stake that BCE took in each of Wireless, Emergis, CGI, and ExpressVu. In each case, BCE avoided a commitment, in the form of outright acquisition, to these companies. Instead, a partial ownership position was taken that then either increased or decreased depending on the nature and value of the opportunities for strategic integration with the mainstream business.

Staging its investments in this way served at least four strategic objectives. First, it effectively locked up potentially valuable resources, precluding the possibility of being boxed out of attractive markets by nimbler competitors. Second, as a partial ownership stake, this foothold was secured at much lower cost than outright acquisition would have entailed. In particular, Emergis, CGI, and Mobility all had publicly traded shares, making BCE's stake especially easy to value and highly liquid compared to wholly owned subsidiaries. Consequently, not only was the absolute amount of money invested lower, it was subject to much lower investment risk.

Third, these early stage investments created the ability to gain privileged access to company information: BCE's stakes often brought with them key board or management positions. From these vantage points, BCE—namely, Jean Monty and his corporate staff—were especially well situated to evaluate the potential for meaningful integration, strategic or otherwise, between these divisions and Bell Canada. Should additional investment be required to maintain a given ownership stake, or certain key interventions prove necessary to prevent precluding future integration, BCE's corporate management could make such decisions on the basis of first-hand knowledge.

Fourth and finally, the structure of these ownership positions typically provided a clear migration path to full ownership of each company. This is critical to viewing these investments as vehicles for strategic integration: recall, a key premise of strategic integration is that recombination of assets across divisions in the pursuit of certain opportunities happens more effectively within firm boundaries than across them. Consequently, when BCE executives decided that certain strategic integration opportunities were worth pursuing, they needed a mechanism by which to gain full ownership so that they could focus on creating wealth for shareholders rather than allocating wealth between parties to a transaction.

Seen in this light, BCE's investment strategy in pursuit of strategic integration has all the hallmarks of a 'real options' approach to strategy.

Real options are investments in operating assets that create the right, but not the obligation, to make further investments at a future date at a specified price (Trigeorgis 1995). By taking partial stakes in companies that might generate opportunities for valuable strategic integration, BCE created the right, but not the obligation, to invest the additional funds required to capture the benefits of strategic integration at a future time.

The price of these additional investments was sometimes left to be determined in ad-hoc negotiations, as with Mobility. In that instance, BCE had to strike a deal with then-BCE Mobile's shareholders. In other cases, as with ExpressVu, CGI, and Emergis, BCE held explicit call options on additional equity, most often priced at a specified premium above the trading average over a specified time interval (e.g. 10% above the previous sixty-days' average closing price).

The four case studies above suggest a three-phase model for BCE's real options investment strategy. First, the initial investments served to *create* the option on future strategic integration. Second, subsequent actions, either by way of additional investment or intervention in key strategic decisions allowed BCE to *preserve* the option value of its investments. Third, when ownership was acquired and strategic integration pursued, or, alternatively, the company began to dilute its ownership because integration opportunities were not emerging as expected, the company could *exercise* or *abandon* its options. The case studies presented here offer varying degrees of insight into each phase.

Wireline–Wireless Integration: Create, Exercise

Although Bell Canada initially created its mobile telephony division as a wholly owned subsidiary, it soon sold off 35 per cent of the equity to the public markets. This sale reduced BCE's investment in mobile telephony, but the remaining stake was significant enough to ensure board representation and an ability to influence future decisions in appropriate ways.

Preservation of the option was not really an issue in this case. No strategic issues emerged that were attractive to Mobility that would have undermined subsequent integration with Bell. Consequently, there was no need for BCE to intervene in Mobility's strategic decision making.

The exercise of this option occurred when BCE acquired the outstanding equity in the face of intractable difficulties surrounding integration attempts with Mobility. The challenges of ensuring minority shareholders were protected when combining resources in novel ways was making the integration itself impossible. However, with full ownership, the only challenge was ensuring that shareholders overall were better off; parceling out between the divisions the value created by the integration was largely obviated.

BCE's evolution with respect to the strategic integration of wireline and wireless operating units is unique. Other major telecommunications firms appear to have followed far less strategically flexible paths. Verizon, for example, has always been the sole owner of its wireless arm.[6] This approach provided greater control than BCE enjoyed during its minority ownership period; but as a consequence, it had more capital tied up and less ability to abandon wireless, should it have proved unprofitable.

At the other end of the spectrum, USWEST (now Qwest) sold off its wireless division, and now finds itself a wireless services reseller, and comparatively handicapped in providing wireless/wireline bundles.

SBC and BellSouth appear to have the worst of both worlds with their 55/45 joint venture in Cingular. Neither company is able to optimize Cingular's investment decisions around its own opportunities for strategic integration opportunities, so Cingular is run essentially as an independent entity. Yet, ironically, Cingular is likely to have largely the same value to both parties: strategically important in the event integration opportunities became valuable, and conversely of little strategic value should integration prove unimportant. Consequently, either both parties would be motivated to buy or sell at the same time, making it difficult to either buy out or sell out.

In BCE's case, floating 65 per cent of the equity in public markets granted a ready valuation of the division and created both an exit strategy—simply sell the rest—and a migration strategy to full ownership: simply buy the rest. The value of any synergies or opportunities for strategic integration between wireline and wireless would be unavailable to the shareholders of BCE Mobility, providing a buyer's surplus to draw from in offering a control premium.

Sprint is the one telecommunications firm that has pursued a similar option-like structure in its wireless–wireline integration strategy. Originally entering the wireless space in 1992 with the acquisition of Centel, Sprint divested the division in favor of a joint venture with two cable firms to launch a PCS network in 1994. In 1998, Sprint bought out its joint venture partners through issuance of a PCS tracking stock. In 2004, Sprint folded the PCS tracking stock into its 'primary' FON stock, effectively reintegrating the control structures of the two divisions—which had become increasingly operationally integrated as well: wireless–wireline integration is a cornerstone of Sprint's differentiation strategy in the highly competitive US wireless telephony services market.

The effect on BCE's performance versus these alternative structures is all but impossible to determine with so many other variables to control for. From an operational perspective, however, BCE seems to be at least as far along with respect to wireline–wireless integration, if not farther, than Verizon and other telecoms companies that owned their wireless divisions from the start, although it has endured structurally less risk. It is clearly ahead of those that do not enjoy a control position today and find it more difficult to integrate effectively.

E-Commerce Solutions: Create, Preserve, Abandon

The merging of Bell Emergis with Mpact Immedia to create BCE Emergis, with 65 per cent owned by BCE and 35 per cent publicly traded, created an option on integration between Emergis and Bell. As was the case with Mobility, the public float provided a way to value BCE's holding on an ongoing basis and important liquidity with respect to either increasing or decreasing BCE's holding as strategic considerations dictated.

Given the markets in which Emergis competed and the pressure to use stock for acquisitions, the need for BCE to preserve Emergis's option value was especially acute. Had Emergis 'spent' its equity during the so-called dot-com bubble of the late 1990s, BCE would have been unable to maintain its majority ownership position on terms acceptable to BCE shareholders. Consequently, BCE had to use its influence, via its board seats, to constrain Emergis's strategy with respect to which acquisitions were feasible and the structure of those deals.

These actions served to preserve the value of the option, because unconstrained growth by Emergis would likely have both diluted BCE's ownership position to the point that it would no longer have the control necessary to effect strategic integration and changed Emergis's strategy in ways that made integration no longer valuable.

Selling off its stake in Emergis served to abandon the option. In the language of this framework, the option on integration that Emergis represented to BCE had come to be seen as perpetually 'out of the money', and as a result the costs to Emergis and BCE of preserving the option no longer were justified.

Few other telecoms companies pursued similar investments. One possible analog is Sterling Commerce, a provider of Electronic Data Interchange (EDI) and related e-commerce services. Similar to BCE,

SBC has made little material progress in pursuing strategic integration between its e-commerce investment and the mainstream telecoms business, suggesting that BCE's lack of total control has not necessarily been a limiting factor. Rather, it is reasonable to suggest that the root cause of a lack of integration in both cases has been a lack of any compelling argument to do so. And, just as Emergis has suffered sharp declines in value since 2000, SBC's investment in Sterling has suffered in the wake of general market declines. BCE, however, did not bear the full brunt of Emergis's devaluations because it was less than a full owner.

Systems Integration Consulting and IT Outsourcing: Create, Preserve, Abandon

The option created by the partial ownership of CGI is very similar in structure to the Emergis deal. With 40 per cent and powerful board representation, BCE was in a position to gain, at much lower cost than outright acquisition, critical insight into an industry with potentially powerful synergies with Bell. And, as with Emergis, there was a clear structure in place to allow BCE to acquire greater control and, if desired, full ownership at specified premiums to market value within specified time periods.

As with Emergis, there was a need to influence CGI's strategy. In order to assess the viability of integration opportunities, both Bell and CGI had to navigate particularly tricky negotiations with long-time business partners who were suddenly competitors for key accounts. Once again, board representation brought the requisite influence with the appropriate executives at CGI.

It has turned out that the integration opportunities between CGI and Bell were not as lucrative as they might have been nor have they emerged as quickly as might have been hoped. As a result, as CGI has pursued its growth strategy through acquisition, BCE has not participated on a *pro rata* basis. The result is that BCE slowly has diluted its ownership position in CGI, signaling an 'abandoning' of the option on integration with Bell.

Several other telecoms companies made similar significant investments in systems integration. The stories of MCI and Sprint are especially instructive. MCI acquired the Canadian firm SHL Systemhouse outright in 1995; recall that this was the firm that Monty had wanted to acquire in 1991. Despite significant efforts, meaningful synergies proved elusive, and the division was sold, at a profit, in 1999 to EDS.

In 1997, Sprint acquired Paranet, also an IT systems integration consulting firm. After a number of reorganizations, Sprint sold the division in 2002 to Vivare, a telecommunications security and infrastructure consulting firm, which reconstituted the division as Paranet LLC.

In Europe, British Telecom (Syntegra), Telecom Italia (Finsiel), Deutsche Telekom (T-Systems), and COLT Telecom (Fitec) all launched systems integration divisions; none achieved any demonstrable synergy. In COLT's case, Fitec was sold off. All the other telecoms companies are operating their systems integration divisions as independent entities.

BCE's seeming inability to create effective integration opportunities would appear to be a function of unfavorable general conditions, insofar as other major players have made similar attempts, and realized a similar lack of synergy, strategic or otherwise. Unlike the outright acquisitions and subsequent divestitures endured by MCI and Sprint, however, BCE has had much less capital at risk. And unlike its European analogues, BCE is able to exit less painfully from its systems integration investment and avoid selling in a down market by diluting its investment as CGI grows thanks to its share float.

Satellite Television Services: Create

ExpressVu began as a joint venture and consequently had many of the defining characteristics of an option; specifically, it created a lower-cost exposure to an industry with potentially valuable synergies with Bell than would have been possible via outright acquisition.

Interestingly, the short- and medium-term value of ExpressVu has lain not in synergies with Bell, but in the ability to put pressure on cable's core video offering—forestalling the dreaded 'triple play' (voice, data, video) by cable operators. This has required, arguably, a rate of expansion that the satellite business could not have supported on its own, but that was closer to optimal from the perspective of the overall business.

Such competitive interdependence does not constitute strategic integration—but capturing it does appear to have required outright ownership of ExpressVu by BCE. Interestingly, however, because the acquisition of ExpressVu has been justified on its own terms, and not on the basis of strategic integration in the service of a larger convergence strategy, any residual optionality is especially valuable, because it has been acquired essentially 'for free'.

The largely failed ComboBox was an attempt to explore the potential of strategic integration opportunities. As technologies and markets change, there will doubtless be additional opportunities to explore new integrated service offerings. For as long as ExpressVu makes sense as a competitive weapon in the fight against cable, such small-scale explorations of strategic integration will continue to make sense.

The only major telecoms company to offer video services is SBC, which resells Echostar satellite TV. Lacking an ownership position, or even exclusive reselling rights, the ability of SBC to explore opportunities for strategic integration between the two organizations would seem to be severely limited. In addition, it has not had opportunity to master the intricacies of providing video services directly, knowledge that could prove especially valuable as high-bandwidth IP-based network architectures are deployed.

Fig. 14.1 provides a summary of the real options-based approach to strategic integration and the elements of this framework best illuminated by each case study.

Real Options and Strategic Flexibility

In every case above, the corporate office was highly active in defining the nature of the option to be created, in pushing through the appropriate decisions, and in the ongoing process of preserving and eventually either exercising or abandoning the option. This level of activity is entirely consistent with the prescriptions of earlier researchers with respect to the role of top management in the pursuit of strategic integration.

This chapter provides some insight into how these activist senior executives go about pursuing strategic integration opportunities in the face of uncertainty. What the case studies reveal is that, faced with both competitive pressures to decide and significant risk associated with any given decision, senior management adopted a *de facto* real options approach. These options served to secure critical assets and knowledge, yet deferred the high levels of investment needed to actually implement strategic integration between existing operating divisions until new information made action sufficiently less risky.

As is not uncommon in managerial research, the managers themselves did not appear to think of their actions in terms of the model their actions suggest. The explicit justification given by Monty and other BCE executives for their various investments was to find a way to grow BCE beyond the confines of its regulated telephony businesses.

| | Phases of Real-Options-Based Strategic Integration | | |
	Create	Preserve	Exercise/Abandon
Phases defined	• Sufficient control over a potentially useful asset to preclude competitors from acquiring it • Deal structure that permits additional follow-on investment required to effect significant operational changes or liquidation of initial investment	• Guiding strategic and operational choices in order to ensure that future integration opportunities remain viable	• Making additional investments in order to implement strategic integration • Liquidating the initial investment when strategic integration no longer appears valuable or likely to become valuable
Cases Wireline–wireless integration	An option was created out of a commitment when 35% of BCE Mobile was sold	--	The option was exercised when the publicly traded equity was acquired and the strategic integration of BCE Mobile and Bell Canada began
E-commerce	An option was created when Bell Emergis was combined with Mpact Immedia, leaving BCE with 65% of the newly formed BCE Emergis	BCE Emergis's growth strategy was constrained by BCE's need to maintain its controlling interest	As it became clear that meaningful strategic integration was unlikely, the stake in Emergis was sold
Systems integration	An option was created when Bell Sygma was combined with CGI to give BCE 42% of combined entity	Exploring opportunities for strategic integration required constraining CGI's growth strategy with respect to business partners and customer targets	Integration proved unfruitful. BCE has allowed its ownership stake to be diluted as it has removed the constraints on CGI's growth strategy
Satellite television	The option was created through the creation of ExpressVu as a joint venture	--	--

Figure 14.1 The phases of real-options-based strategic integration

The language of synergies was never far beneath the surface, but the various elements of the portfolio were never publicly identified as options on synergy. Indeed, public pronouncements by Monty as late as 2000 were unambiguous: BCE's portfolio of companies was aimed squarely at making 'convergence' a reality.

There is, therefore, a seeming conflict between management's stated intentions and the structure of the benefits their actions actually created. Monty and other BCE executives seem to have articulated a strategy of commitment, yet behaved in a way that suggested a more tentative approach. In light of this dissonance, it is not over-reaching to suggest ways in which a real options strategy might be implemented yet more effectively.

Perhaps one of the most fruitful avenues for further research to emerge from these case studies is the strategic use of partial equity ownership stakes. The existing literature on this topic is sparse, and has tended to view the problem almost exclusively in terms of solving small numbers bargaining problems without having to resort to vertical integration (Dasgupta and Tao 2000). What the case studies reported here reveal is that partial ownership can serve a very different purpose: to secure the control of potentially valuable assets, thereby creating real options with significant strategic value.

From a tactical perspective, when taking a partial ownership stake in a company in order to create options on future strategic integration, a more explicit understanding of what levels of control and access are required to create and preserve an option should inform the degree of ownership taken. Partial equity stakes are a common feature of the investment strategy of many diversified corporations.

What is surprisingly poorly examined is how they choose how much to own. In other words, how much is enough? Certainly the strategic objectives of partial ownership should inform this decision. What the real options framework suggests is one particular strategic objective with specific implications for what degree of ownership is appropriate. In particular, where the creation and preservation of real options is the aim, the requisite degree of control will turn on the extent to which the holder of such an option must understand and guide the strategy of the option-creating investment. Where significant strategic constraints are required, as was the case with Emergis and CGI, a relatively high level of ownership will likely be necessary in order to exert sufficient influence, via the board, on the relevant decisions. Where investment provides little more than access to industry activity, a lower level of ownership will likely suffice.

The exception to this in BCE's case is ExpressVu, where strategic integration still seems at best nascent, yet the firm has taken full ownership control. The motivation here, however, has been to invest more heavily in ExpressVu's growth than its original investors would have in order to create a more effective countervailing threat to cable's entry into local telephony services. What we observe, then, is not partial ownership to create an option on strategic integration, but full ownership in order to drive a very specific strategy based on multipoint competition considerations (Baum and Korn 1999).

Beyond deciding what ownership stakes are required to create an option, deciding which options to create is perhaps the most difficult problem to resolve. Faced with uncertainty at the level of fundamental industry structure, it is likely that even the largest organizations will run out of money before they run out of bets to cover.

It is here that the long-established field of scenario-based planning might be a welcome addition to real options analysis. Scenarios are not predictions of the future, but conceptual 'boundary conditions' of what the future might hold. A set of scenarios could serve as the vertices of a 'possibility space' within which a company's future can be expected to fall.

Strategies keyed to the requirements of each of these vertices can be expected to have idiosyncratic resource requirements. Executives seeking to prepare their organization for multiple possible futures simultaneously could seek to create real options on strategy-specific resources. Such options could be preserved as long as the scenarios in which such resources would be valuable remain plausible, and could be exercised or abandoned as those same scenarios are made manifest or become sufficiently unlikely (Raynor 2004).

The combination of scenario-based planning, a real options investment structure, and a corporate office attuned to the specific requirements of the identification and pursuit of strategic integration promises to create a 'strategically flexible' corporation. The term, used advisedly, is intended to capture the tension between strategy—which is so often conceived in terms of commitments—and the need for flexibility in the face of uncertainty—which tends to eschew commitment. But with scenarios to bound the range of possibilities that must be prepared for, real options to secure valuable assets without committing to specific courses of action, and a corporate office willing to calibrate investment to the changing competitive landscape, it may well become possible to square this particular circle.

Endnotes

1. This might seem self-evident, but at one time, most notably the 1960s in the United States, the combination of high tax rates on dividends versus capital gains and an aggressive interpretation and enforcement of antitrust legislation made the reinvestment of corporate profits in unrelated businesses economically rational from a shareholder wealth perspective, even though the competitive position of any given division was not necessarily enhanced by its corporate owners.

2. Nortel, formerly Northern Telecom and now Nortel Networks, is a network equipment manufacturer that was once a wholly owned subsidiary of BCE. As the capital requirements of growth in that industry outstripped BCE's ability to fund them, Nortel's equity was sold to

minority shareholders in several tranches. With Nortel's acquisition of Bay Networks for $8 billion in 1998, BCE was diluted to less than a controlling stake, and by 2000 BCE had divested itself of Nortel entirely.

3. 'Asynchronous Digital Subscriber Loop', a form of VDSL technology.

4. Innuvik is a settlement of 3,800 people at the mouth of the McKenzie River in Canada's Northwest Territories on the coast of the Beaufort Sea.

5. Canadians that winter in Florida are generally referred to as 'snowbirds', an expression made particularly popular by number-one-selling 1970 pop song *Snowbird*, by Anne Murray, a Canadian singer from Nova Scotia.

6. European wireline operators such as British Telecom, France Telecom, and Deutsche Telekom pursued similar strategies.

References

Baum, J. A. C., and Korn, H. J. (1999). 'Dynamics of Dyadic Competitive Interaction'. *Strategic Management Journal* 20/3: 251–78.

Bower, J. L. (1970). *Managing the Resource Allocation Process*. Boston, Mass.: Harvard Business School Press.

Burgelman, R. A., and Doz, Y. A. (1998). *Complex Strategic Integration in the Lean Corporation*. Stanford, Calif.: Stanford Business School Press.

Chakravarthy, B. (Winter 1997). 'A New Strategy Framework for Coping with Turbulence'. *Sloan Management Review*, 69–82.

Dasgupta, S., and Tao, Z. (2000). 'Bargaining, Bonding, and Partial Owner-ship'. *International Economic Review* 41/3: 609–36.

Eisenmann, T. R. (2002). 'The Effects of CEO Equity Ownership and Firm Diversification on Risk Taking'. *Strategic Management Journal* 23: 513–34.

—— and Bower, J. L. (1998). 'The Entrepreneurial M-Form: A Case Study of Strategic Integration in a Global Media Company'. *Harvard Business School Working Paper*.

—————— (2000). 'The Entrepreneurial M-Form: Strategic Integration in Global Media Firms'. *Organization Science* (Special Issue on Cultural Industries) 11/3: 348–55.

Ghemawat, P. (1991). *Commitment: The Dynamic of Strategy*. New York: Free Press.

Goold, M., and Campbell, A. (1998). 'Desperately Seeking Synergy'. *Harvard Business Review* (Sept.–Oct.): 131–43.

Lieberman, M. B., and Montgomery, D. B. (1988). 'First-Mover Advan-tages'. *Strategic Management Journal* 9: 41–58.

Porter, M. E. (1987). 'From Competitive Advantage to Corporate Strategy'. *Harvard Business Review* 65/3: 43–59.

Raynor, M. E. (2004). 'Strategic Flexibility: Taking the Fork in the Road'. *Competitive Intelligence* 7/1: 6–13.

—— and Christensen, C. M. (2001). *Integrate to Innovate: The Determinants of Success in Developing and Deploying New Services in the Telecommunica-tions Industry*. New York: Deloitte.

—— and Littmann, D. (2003). 'Outsource IT, Not Value'. *Optimize*.

Teece, D. J. (1980). 'Economics of Scope and the Scope of the Enterprise'. *Journal of Economic Behavior and Organization*, 1: 223–47.

—— (1982). 'Toward an Economic Theory of the Multiproduct Firm'. *Journal of Economic Behavior and Organization* 3: 39–63.

Trigeorgis, L. (ed.) (1995). *Real Options in Capital Investment: Models, Strategies, and Applications*. Westport, Conn.: Praeger.

15

Resource Allocation Processes in Multidimensional Organizations: MNCs and Alliances

Yves L. Doz

In large complex firms, research on resource allocation often has been premised on three critical assumptions:

1. Resource allocation takes place in the context of a single and unidimensional hierarchy of functions, product lines, business units, and business groups or sectors, typified by the 'M-Form' organizational structure.
2. Resource allocation takes place in a simple governance structure consisting of one owner and one set of decision rights competing for customers against similar corporate entities in an open market.
3. Resources are capital allocated through a process largely distributed in a centrally designed structural context.

The multinational company differs from these assumed conditions in significant ways. To begin with, multinational companies (MNCs) relatively early developed multidimensional structures, with at least a geographic and a product/business perspective intersecting in some matrix form of organization to deal with increasing product and geographic diversity (Fouraker and Stopford 1968; Stopford and Wells 1972). Over time, further dimensions have been added, such as global accounts, 'horizontal' technology platforms, and 'route to market' supply chains targeted at specific 'vertical' market segments. Although many of today's companies build complex systems that cope with multiple strategic and governance demands, multinationals have been the forerunners in developing complex structures and systems. Second, global competition increasingly takes place between alliance constellations of multiple partners, among which resource allocation decisions need to be coordinated and integrated into a coherent whole, although each partner retains its strategic decision-making autonomy. Resource allocation has to take place in a timely, consistent, and well-integrated fashion among firms in which each firm retains autonomous governance and decision rights. MNCs first faced this challenge in the guise of market access joint-ventures (JVs). JVs are still problematic for MNCs, in particular when they are part of an increasingly global integrated supply system. Perhaps more critically today, complex alliances also compete globally against each other and have the potential for resource allocation difficulties and conflicts among alliance partners. The assumption of a simple, single hierarchy and ownership structure does not correspond with the reality.

Third, although like any other big corporation the MNC allocates funds among priorities and subunits, this is probably not where its strategic advantage resides. Researchers have noted that MNCs are privileged conduits for sharing knowledge, in particular complex process knowledge not easily captured by clear-cut intellectual property rights across distance and national contexts (Dunning 1981, 1988; Kogut and Zander 1993). Earlier than other firms, MNCs have been concerned with the peculiarity of knowledge, as compared to capital, as a strategic resource.

This chapter explores what we can learn from these three critical differences between the conditions usually assumed by RAP models and the reality first faced by MNCs. The goal is to test the limits of the RAP framework and extend our understanding of resource allocation processes insofar as corporate management roles are concerned.

1. Multidimensional Hierarchies

MNCs face complex trade-offs under conditions of imperfect, or 'semi' globalization. In the 1950s and 1960s, the issues were first identified as potential conflicts between the rising role of MNCs (particularly of US MNCs) and the territorial sovereignty of national governments (Vernon 1971). More recently (e.g. Ghemawat 2003), similar points have been made to justify continued scholarly interest in MNCs. Multiple and differently configured stakeholders affect MNCs and are impacted by their activities, including stakeholders, some territorial (local communities, states, unions), and some global (key customers, increasingly investors, and other global competitors and complementors). Beyond the choice of structural forms (e.g. geographic structures versus global product decisions), this array of differently configured stakeholders means management must consider multiple demands and priorities in resource allocation.

Prahalad (1975) and Doz (1976) were the first to discuss these problems from a resource allocation process research perspective. Prahalad's work considered how a major chemical company realigned resource allocation processes over time from a geographic (what Porter (1986) would later call 'multi-domestic') to a global business unit perspective. Doz (1976, 1979) considered companies and industries where the resource allocation process had to carefully balance, integrate, and transcend economic and technological pressures forcing global integration with political demands calling for a national response. This problem was characteristic of technology and scale-intensive companies selling to (then) national state-owned industries, such as producers of electrical power and telecom equipment.

Although the dimensions of the problem to be managed may have expanded since these pioneering studies, the underlying dilemmas, now widely called in the international business academic community the 'integration/responsiveness' challenge (or in short-hand the 'IR grid') have remained essentially the same, and spawned a whole stream of empirical research at various levels of aggregation, from the cognitive perspective of individual managers (Murtha, Lenway, *et al.* 1998) to that of industry structures or even the world economy.[1] Two particularly noteworthy contributions shifted the perspective of researchers. Bartlett and Ghoshal (1989) studied the challenges of learning and innovation, and Birkinshaw (1997) adopted a more fluid perspective of subsidiary entrepreneurship.

Based on this brief summary of recent research in MNCs, what can we conclude about the features of an effective resource allocation process in a multidimensional organization?

The Need for Multiple Perspectives

Complex trade-offs can be made only if the various perspectives and stakeholders' interests in the MNC are effectively represented in the decision process for resource allocation.

Perhaps the simplest way to represent multiple interests is with separate organizational hierarchies, each aligned with a different perspective and each providing elements of organizational context sustaining attention, commitment, and focus along that particular dimension. Managers at the lower cross-over points of this organization find themselves having to fit within a context differentiated along each dimension, and they have to respond to these various demands (Bartlett and Ghoshal 1989).

In principle, this approach provides strategic agility. Rather than the stability and the weight of a single hierarchical pyramid, these intertwined and matrixed hierarchies provide a more complex force field for operating unit managers. In the same way as modern fighter planes are designed to be directionally unstable, their instability being controlled permanently by flight control computers, a matrix organization is organizationally unstable (hence, the widely used metaphor of 'tilting the matrix') and controlled by softer and more discriminating features of the organizational context than structure. For instance, as described by Bartlett and Ghoshal (1989) and many other case studies of matrix organizations, operating and financial priorities may be embedded into a geographic context and strategic and market development priorities in a global business unit with different long-term objectives. Where the contexts intersect, for instance, in establishing reward criteria for subunit managers, life gets very complicated. Bonuses might, for instance, be based on financial results and the award of stock options on strategic ones. Secondary dimensions can be reflected in additional structural overlays, such as incentives for key account and project teams or vertical market and industry communities of practice. The reflection in compensation of additional corporate overlay groups organized around issues such as sustainable development and environmental protection would further complicate the determination of compensation.

This multidimensional approach has been seen as both an answer to the multiplicity of demands faced by MNCs and as a major source of difficulties as well. The advantages, beyond the ability to reflect multiple dimensions and potential agility, are many.

Because they are unstable, multidimensional organizations can be quite responsive. Their internal selection environments[2] can flexibly reflect changes in the external environment. At a particular point in time, the dimensions along which the most critical contingencies for the organization develop gain in influence. For instance, in his early work on the tension between economic and political imperatives, Doz (1979, 1986) showed that the internal distribution of management power and the influence over resource allocation ebbed and flowed as a function of the location and demands of major markets and of specific contracts. Rather than running the risk of embodying and reflecting past sources of contingencies and influence, the internal selection environment for strategic initiatives adapted quickly to external conditions, solving the potential rigidity in selection patterns identified by Burgelman (1988).

Because they are adaptive and fluid, multidimensional structures simultaneously provide for market/customer responsiveness, entrepreneurship, and resource interdependence across units. Rather than becoming imprisoned in one particular type of subunit—e.g. business units in M-form organizations, or national subsidiaries in multidomestic MNCs—resources can be allocated more fluidly along multiple dimensions as the need and the opportunity arise.

Multiple hierarchies structured along different dimensions also submit key resource allocation decisions to scrutiny from multiple angles, allowing greater efficiency and cost discipline in sharing scarce resources. Put differently, resources flow more freely, although subject to a greater number of controls—a combination that arguably should result in better resource allocation.

In a well managed situation, penalties for repeated escalation of conflict to top management and the need to establish consensus among multiple hierarchies also encourages faster lateral conflict resolution and favorable conditions for cooperation at a lower level— 'closer to the action', closer to where detailed knowledge resides. In other words, multidimensional organizations have the potential to allow leadership from operating levels of the corporation closer to customers, potentially in a 'pull from market' mode of management. This, in turn, should contribute to more responsive self-adjusting organizations.

Some researchers, in particular Hedlund (1986, 1996), pushed further the logic of a multidimensional organization led by operating levels close to the action. Hedlund espouses the concept of 'nearly recomposable systems'. The central idea is that the MNC is a collection of decentralized and autonomous subunits, each imprinted with common cultural traits that reproduce the essential elements of context from one unit to another in a 'holographic' process (Hedlund 1993). In fact, some recently evolving modes of MNC organization appear to be based on mobility and reproducibility. Business infrastructure and support functions in professional service firms, or in the latest interactions in companies such as Nokia, can be seen as attempts to put variants of this MNC concept into practice.

In fact, in a slightly schizophrenic mindset, managers in MNCs have professed a great desire for simplification and streamlining of structures (and sometimes taken a reductionist approach toward the 'truly global company') while at the same time putting in place increasingly complex forms of organizational context. Growing complexity and a desire for simplicity go hand in hand, which perhaps contributes to the growing frustration felt toward matrix organizations within the ranks of multinational managers.

Matrix Pathologies and Possible Cures

Reality is often a far cry from the ideal situation hypothesized by some researchers. In many companies, 'matrix' became a 'four-letter word' rather quickly. Why did reality fall so far short of potential?

The flipside of flexibility and reactivity, as we suggested earlier, is instability and a lack of central guidance. For resource allocation in multidimensional organizations, this raises several difficult and thorny issues.

1. *The 'crazy quilt' syndrome.* The practice of allowing decentralized decisions at the lower cross-over points of the multidimensional organization may tempt executives with inherently varied perspectives to resolve complex problems by seeking areas of easiest agreement and of safest delivery of predictable performance. A classic case in a typical product-geography matrix organization is that of the largest country organizations (because they serve large national markets and/or enjoy high market shares) agreeing easily with managers of the leading product divisions on high targets for key products, and achieving them. While consistently delivering financial performance, such an approach may lead, over the long term, to strategic dead-ends. Shifts in market location, channels, or technologies and product functionality are not addressed. Rather than deliver strategic momentum, this approach leads to inertia. Resource allocation choices for tomorrow reflect yesterday's patterns of success. The presence of the company is reinforced in locations and product lines where it is already strong, but new opportunities are ignored and gaping holes are left to the competition. Rather than reflect a coherent and competitive strategic future, the pattern of activities becomes a 'crazy quilt' deployed around the world in no particular order.

Matrix organizations may, therefore, require specific top management intervention to counteract this tendency. Some may be structural and contextual adjustments, for example, a 'headquarters' region' reporting directly to the CEO, made of a combination of high-growth markets where the company is not already strong, no matter where these are located around the world. Key account teams may be set up in the same way. In the absence of some form of central corporate guidance, a multidimensional organization is likely to be reactionary rather than responsive in a proactive fashion. This may not matter too much in large project organizations (for instance, major construction and engineering companies) where what can be done is dependent on a handful of customers, or in consulting and other professional services companies where responsiveness to client needs can be more critical than proactive strategizing. This may be deadly, however, in industry sectors such as fast-moving consumer goods where market guidance is not as strong or clear-cut.

2. *Matrix paralysis.* Dealing with multidimensional and often conflicting goals is both a source of innovation and creativity for some and of paralysis for others. Matrix organizations require entrepreneurial behavior from managers of business units and country organizations to mobilize support and resources on multiple dimensions at critical intersections. Clearly, this puts more pressure and more demand on relatively junior operating level managers than hypothesized in a traditional M-Form organization where the delegation of decision rights is clear-cut and integration lines clear. In a multidimensional organization, several executives play the RAP model's integrator's role, each with individual priorities, bringing a whole series of particular perspectives, or framings, of the decision at hand.

This may lead to a desire to delegate upwards, i.e. to escalate to the upper cross-over point of the matrix or to the lateral negotiations between integrators, all difficult decisions. This, in turn, can result in a slow down, or even breakdown of decision making. The balance between corporate 'push-back' for decentralized entrepreneurship and lateral integration, in routine situations, and corporate involvement, in strategic development situations that matrix processes might not handle successfully is hard to set and to maintain.

A very successful and experienced CEO of a multidimensional organization asked by the author how he handled the discrimination between routine and strategic decisions and the possible glut of decisions to be made at the corporate level with insufficient information answered: 'When in doubt, I always help the weak, provided they call for help loudly enough.' Although hardly an analytically satisfactory heuristic, this approach, over a wide range and a large number of decisions, did maintain the integrity of the matrix organization.

The dilemma here is that corporate intervention is both selectively needed and dangerous. The anticipation of corporate intervention may lead to dysfunctional behavior on the part of middle management.

3. *A tournament culture.* Managers at operating levels of a matrix organization may seek to anticipate and influence top management intervention through all kinds of political means, such as coalition building on specific issues, reciprocal side deals for mutual support, or mutual avoidance. Rather than genuine dialogue, or even more

debate based on fact-based positions, the management process can become a ritualized set of posturing presentations, never meant to allow a transparent data-based exploration of an issue, but always intended to ensure that corporate intervention will go 'our way'. This leads to resource allocation process breakdowns such as Gerstner found upon his arrival at IBM (Gerstner 2002).

Behind the dangers of falling into a tournament culture lies a deeper problem. As argued earlier in this chapter, corporate leaders typically resort to a multidimensional organization in order to ensure that multiple perspectives are effectively represented in resource allocation processes. For this to work, managers must identify cognitively and often emotionally with their assigned perspective and associated priorities. For example, a key account manager who does not have the importance of the account at heart is unlikely to be effective. But in their identification with a particular perspective, each manager becomes a champion of that perspective. Putting managers in a box so they have a perspective may ensure an organization full of parochial managers. Reconciling those different perspectives, and their holders, may not be easy, and yet the strength of identification to each of these commitments is required for the system to function.

Reconciliation cannot be achieved by regular direct top management substantive arbitration (the dangers of which are too clear) or by simple permanent context adjustments. These approaches will produce chaos in short order. Temporary contexts, such as issue-based continuous planning (which Nokia, among others, practices routinely), task teams, or ad-hoc groups may provide an answer, so far as they are led through some form of adaptive leadership (Heifetz 1994; Heifetz and Laurie 2001). But this must allow initially conflicting individual positions to be transcended. Adaptive leadership allows collective insight development around particular issues, and influence in outcomes to be rooted in contribution to that insight, not in sheer resource dependence or strength of personal charisma. Developing shared insight over time also allows one to learn how to be a champion of a perspective without running an excessive risk of over-relying on partisan analysis, or confusing strength of conviction for fact-based argument in the resource allocation process. Corporate intervention takes the form of setting up temporary multidimensional decision contexts and exercising the kind of adaptive leadership that makes them productive.[3]

Adaptive leadership does not equate with democracy or consensus, however. Ensuring 'fair process' in decisions, as seen by all involved is essential to sustaining the commitment of the 'losers' on a particular decision, or stream of decisions (Rawl 1971; Kim and Mauborgne 2003).

This discussion of the evolution in management of the MNC from pure multidomestic or global logics toward subtle multidimensional perspectives, structures, and processes indicates that the MNC may well have pioneered a more agile, more responsive, form of organization, one that is much harder to structure and to run, one that requires more fragile capabilities but one that is in the end more discriminating and effective for strategic resource allocation.

Corporate Intervention in the Multidimensional Organization

A multidimensional (matrix) organization creates a multidirectional force field for subunit managers who have to be concerned with strategic integration along those multiple dimensions. In principle, a multidirectional force field allows greater flexibility and creates an internal selection environment for strategic initiatives and resource allocation proposals that is more closely, and swiftly, responsive to the external environment. In practice, as argued above, this approach is fraught with difficulties, largely because it is much more demanding of middle managers than traditional hierarchical approaches. Self-efficacious entrepreneurial-minded managers are likely to flourish in fluid multidimensional contexts; but less entrepreneurial managers may be paralyzed or engage in endless negotiations in search of consensus and support. Corporate intervention plays a critical role, not so much in direct arbitration between the various dimensions—an approach or a temptation which has a strong toxic side effect—but in setting the process conditions, i.e. in providing features of context that reflect the particular needs and opportunities of multidimensional integration.

The multidimensional organization can be conceived of as a selection environment for strategic initiatives and the resources they require. The effectiveness of that decision environment in allocating resources can be gauged on three dimensions:

1. *The strength of external orientation.* This approach requires managers able to adopt the appropriate market perspective associated with their business location and stakeholders, who can develop grounded understanding and insight and represent particular contexts and priorities, with both analysis and advocacy. Typically, these managers,

also part of different professional and social networks, enrich the social capital available to the firms.

2. *The quality of internal decision making.* Advocacy from internal units grounded in multiple perspectives is intrinsically divisive, unless carried out in a real dialogue among holders of the different perspectives. Sustaining the quality and speed of this dialogue is difficult. That difficulty lies at the heart of why 'matrix organizations' have such a bad reputation among MNC managers. Differentiation and integration processes are key. They must legitimize fact-based analytically grounded dissent. The power structures must be fluid to permit alignment with shifting external contingencies. But adaptive leadership must provide a disciplined and fair decision process in order to foster the mutual understanding and tolerance that permits participants to transcend rather than become fixated on differentiated starting positions.

3. *The balance between delegation and self-adjustment on one side and corporate intervention on the other.* Matrix organizations left to their own volition tend either to be static—the best products going to the strongest markets—or to lose balance, erring either on the side of fragmentation (multidomestic companies where local managers ally with local stakeholders to keep 'corporate' at bay) or on central integration ('global' businesses that lose sensitiveness to external contexts and contingencies). Corporate management needs to intervene constantly to maintain a balance and to foster entrepreneurship and new business development in new markets and new products, in both cases systematically helping today's weakest who can be tomorrow's growth opportunities.

These three dimensions—a way to gauge the effectiveness of the resource allocation process—are all the more critical as the MNC's superiority over market and arm's length transactions is noted in its ability to access and process complex knowledge and other less fungible strategic resources—intangible assets such as relationship and reputation—better than arm's length transactions. The interesting issue here, though, is that such strategic resources need to be mobilized, i.e. cannot be allocated from the top, but need to be contributed from the bottom, in ways that conform neither with an induced resource allocation process nor with an emergent one.

2. From Resource Allocation to Resource Mobilization

As the organizational form of MNCs matured, both the practice of managers and the attention of researchers shifted from 'either/or' forms of organization (e.g. global, local, or transnational) to a richer, more complex approach. Here, the MNC can be seen as a network of differentiated sources of competencies and capabilities, each invested in the particular learning opportunities offered by their local environment, and brought together for specific projects focused on new products and market development, sometimes at the initiative of subsidiary managers in relatively peripheral locations. Research on so-called 'metanational' companies has analyzed this evolution and its implication for companies, geographies, and the global economy (Doz, Santos, and Williamson 2001; Doz, Wilson, and Williamson, forthcoming).

The story reported in these studies illustrates the theme of this chapter. The further one moves away from the single corporate hierarchy perspective toward the MNC as a network of differentiated contributing nodes, the more lateral global knowledge mobilization becomes important relative to straightforward hierarchical allocation of capital. What managerial activity is essential to the lateral mobilization of knowledge?

Complementarity is key. Effective collaboration results from complementarity not similarity. Consistent with the view that resource allocation within a common ownership structure succeeds where markets fail, complementarity across units is most important where each unit brings differentiated resources. Almost necessarily, differentiated resources are knowledge-based.[4]

Extending the resource allocation process perspective from capital to other strategic resources allows one to test the limits of the framework and to highlight how it must change in order to deal with these new circumstances. Beginning with the most fundamental difference, knowledge is a public good; i.e. using knowledge does not consume it. The more knowledge is used, the better honed and the more useful it becomes. In principle, knowledge is redeployable at no cost. The most strategically valuable knowledge is collective, tacit, situated know-how and therefore 'sticky' and hard to move and redeploy (Teece 1977; Kogut and Zander 1993; Nonaka and Takeuchi 1995; Szulanski 1996). In today's world, knowledge cannot be allocated; it can be only acquired or contributed by the knowledge holder. By failing to recognize that it must be solicited and absorbed, rather than transferred and allocated, many companies fail to exploit fully the knowledge available to them, or even to recognize the existence or relevance of that knowledge, particularly when it is distributed across geography, units, and domains (Doz, Santos, and Williamson 2001). The temptation to equate, or at least approximate, knowledge with information, and the legacy, in MNCs, of the 'technology transfer' model, as well as the excessive faith often put in information technology platforms, lead to the disillusionment with 'knowledge management' approaches described by so many MNC managers.

To use knowledge as a strategic resource, corporate management first must understand the underlying challenges to effective knowledge mobilization. *Foremost among these is what I call 'imprisoned knowledge'.*

Most MNCs consider local, peripheral knowledge developed in far-flung subsidiaries as only relevant locally, at best, and thus tolerated but legitimately ignored from the center. Further, knowledge that may be useful more widely is often not shared, because geographic subunit managers are not encouraged or rewarded for contributing knowledge. A few years ago, for instance, Glaxo Wellcome acquired Medikredit, a prescription reimbursement and health plan management operation in South Africa, with the view to running a low-cost experiment to develop competencies in managed healthcare and to use patient databases better to target the marketing of new drugs. Although very valuable learning was accumulated locally, the lack of 'knowledge pull' from the center, and the fact that the local subsidiary manager was measured and incentivized on local financial performance prevented the sharing of knowledge within the firm. The opportunity to have the knowledge from South Africa contribute to global learning was lost.

More generally, we observed in our research that various forces combined to imprison knowledge. First, relevant knowledge is often localized and invisible and thus not recognized as useful. Sharing knowledge is serendipitous or accidental—fortuitous circumstances arising by coincidence. Unilever was able to create a very successful low-end detergent business in Brazil because, by coincidence, a young Brazilian manager posted temporarily in Pakistan became aware of Hindustan Lever's successful response to the emergence in the Indian market of Nirma, a low-cost local Indian producer, and thought a similar opportunity might exist in the poor areas of Brazil.

Second, as we saw with the Glaxo Wellcome South Africa example, the organizational context of major MNCs often discourages knowledge sharing.

Third, and perhaps most critically, management assumptions inherited from capital allocation, and the rivalry they trigger, may lead to knowledge hoarding and protecting rather than knowledge sharing. Managers in large companies develop careers based on resource owning and controlling, rather than resource accessing and leveraging.

Knowledge mobilization faces tremendous difficulties in most mature MNCs. Fostering such mobilization requires a deep transformation of organizational contexts from multi-domestic fragmentation of knowledge ownership to global teamwork for knowledge mobilization.

Freeing up Knowledge

To understand how global knowledge sharing gets started in a MNC, it is helpful to consider the case example provided by Alfa Laval Agri, one of many 'old' multinational companies in which a multidomestic approach made global knowledge sharing impossible.

Alfa Laval Agri (Agri) was built in the nineteenth century on the strength of the cream separator innovation, allowing farmers to separate cream from milk easily. It then branched into milking equipment and milk storage tanks. Following a buoyant period after World War II, the imposition of milk production quotas in the EEC in 1984 cut its sales by nearly half. The importance of local distribution, sales, engineering, and installation for milking systems sold to dispersed farmers had led Agri, over many years, to build strong 'market companies' in a growing number of countries. Most of these companies engineered their own systems, using components supplied in part from Agri's mother company in Sweden and in part purchased locally. In some countries, such as the United States, Agri recruited strong dealers and delegated system engineering installation and maintenance work to them. The home base, in Tumba on the outskirts of Stockholm, was relegated to a role of component developer and supplier. In response to the imposition of milk quotas and the abrupt business downturn that followed, Tumba's staff had been cut drastically. Local product proliferation in the various market companies, combined with the weakening of Tumba's staff for product development, and the lack of respect they elicited from market companies whose local contexts they could not grasp, led to poor product designs that resulted in installations that were not reliable or required inordinate maintenance. These installations did not meet market needs well, nor did they secure dealer loyalty. Costs of complexity burgeoned out of control, warranty costs surged, and customer satisfaction plummeted. Although financial results were still good, Alfa Laval's market position became precarious.

These difficulties led Alfa Laval's main shareholders, the Wallenberg family, to sell Alfa Laval to TetraPak, creating the Tetra Laval Company. In addition to synergies in other businesses, TetraPak's owners saw the potential for Agri to grow into emerging markets and to exploit strategic synergies between milk production and TetraPak's core milk packaging business. The UHT process used by TetraPak called for high-quality milk to be reliably produced, and Agri could contribute to this, particularly in developing countries, which offered the most growth potential. TetraPak appointed a new CEO, Staffan Bohman, who came from Alfa Laval corporate where he was group controller with an earlier experience at Agri, to run Agri. He quickly took several key steps to build global teamwork.

Giving Voice to the Periphery

Bohman replaced several staff heads in Tumba with managers drawn from the far-flung country organizations. This was a strong signal about bringing market knowledge to the center and non-Swedes to top management.

Defining Global Success

Bohman stressed a 'growth and quality' crisis and developed a strategic vision that provided a framework he would use over the years. He worked to ensure that Agri would not be content with 'satisfactory' local performance. The core message was growth and profitability, a focus on product development, quality, and global performance. Although very simple, this message provided common ground for both market companies and central staff. Both had to contribute.

Building Interdependence

The organization of product development and product management by product centers in Tumba focused the dialogue with market companies. Previously, an increasingly wider product range and proliferation of locally engineered systems taxed the capability of functionally organized central staff to add value to market company activities. This product-center organization also enabled the country organizations and Tumba to share knowledge. It also showed that though mere cross-functional cross-geography teams focused on individual product lines lacked decision-making power, their work could bring value to country organizations by giving them a voice in influencing central product policies and an opportunity to develop mutual understanding.

In a symmetrical move to the creation of product organization at home, country organizations were clustered into regional groups, a move that allowed more focused dialogue with them (their sheer number, growing to fifty-five with entry into new emerging markets and all reporting directly to the CEO, made dialogue impossible). Heads of major country organizations were given regional leadership roles (something the Swedish national market company already did for the Nordic area) and made part of a Group Management Committee, a way to co-opt them into a corporate role and identity. Agri previously had failed to pursue, develop and share 'best practices' across its country organizations. Each region was given responsibility to spearhead and support entry into new emerging markets. The US affiliate, for instance, was given responsibility for Latin America, the Nordic region for the Baltic States and Poland, and the Western European region for other newly opened markets in Central and Eastern Europe.

Between a limited number of product lines and a limited number of regions, a sharper dialogue, more detailed and substantive and less hostage to individual functional perspectives, could lead to mutual understanding and common ground.

Keeping Score and Increasing Efficiency in Operations

A new head of R&D, recruited from Siemens' medical electronics operations, pruned the product development project portfolio. He first focused on improving and simplifying the product assortment and decided not to develop new products without the commitment from market companies in 'pilot countries' to test market, refine, and shepherd the diffusion of the new product to other market companies. Second, he started to focus on products that could really make a difference, marketwise and competitively, and resisted pressures for more product proliferation. Third, he moved from developing components to developing standardized modules that would facilitate installation and decrease the diversity of systems to be maintained locally. This effort led, in particular, to accelerating the development of an automated milking system that promised to take nearly all labor costs out of dairy farming in midsize farms in Europe (still Agri's 'heartland' market) where labor was a major cost.

To measure results by product area, new accounting and control systems paved the way for subsequent transformation of product centers into full-blown business units. These systems allowed a better understanding of the overall contribution of each product, system, and installation, and also allowed joint optimization of activities and new business development between business units and market companies. A subsequent accounting exercise showed the high costs and negative contributions of locally designed products and systems, and provided a strong incentive for country organizations to rely on common products and modules rather than develop their own installations. Their managers were now sufficiently convinced that central business units could contribute valuable solutions that met their needs and were sufficiently aware of the opportunity costs of not drawing upon their work. Accordingly, they were increasingly willing to rely on the center.

In turn, this beginning of mutual confidence and shared understanding led the country organization managers to engage jointly with business units in a major product range integration and simplification exercise. In short, the driving idea was to build centrally a series of preassembled standardized modules, with some but limited variety, to be combined and assembled locally into systems. Sales persons, both in market companies and at dealers, would be equipped with a laptop-based solution design expert system that would help them configure the best possible solution for individual farmers based on predefined modules. Not only would this cut sales, installation, and maintenance costs drastically, it also would greatly simplify the manufacturing and logistics of components and modules and allow focused factories to operate efficiently.

Table 15.1 summarizes the key steps in the transformation of Alfa Laval Agri from a fragmented multidomestic company that was fast losing competitiveness to a metanational company able to capitalize both on central capabilities and widespread market learning. It also shows the steps that had particular effect on the leveraging of knowledge and on the operations of Agri and that relate directly with the local global dilemma.

As the multidomestic company applies policies to exploit its locally entrapped knowledge in its many subsidiaries around the world, it must not forget its own particular advantage: that of being plugged in locally in many different national economies. The movement toward a metanational model (and perhaps also a more global or transnational strategy) must preserve the quality of local sensing; if the local subsidiaries become too interdependent and connected with the rest of the company, they may actually decrease the quality and intensity of their external connectivity to their local milieu. That result would be detrimental.

Complex Knowledge   Managers unused to accessing and melding knowledge from differentiated and distant sources may not recognize that colocation makes sharing complex knowledge uneventful, but that distance and differentiation singularly complicate that sharing process. Knowledge that is tacit, collective, embedded in patterns of interaction,

Table 15.1 *Key steps in transforming Alpha Laval Agri into a metanational company*

Action	Meaning/Logic
Appoint local market company managers to head central functions	Strongly signals a value of market/customer interface experience/expertise
	Signals will to restore dialogue with market companies and their primacy over central staff
Stress 'growth + quality' crisis	Challenges 'status quo', complacency and denial of difficulties
Strategic vision: growth, quality, profitability, product development	Provides a shared contact/framework within which to place dialogue between market companies and central units and functions
	Signals shared problem and shared action agenda
Organize product development & product policy by product centres	Focuses dialogue between market companies and staff functions on specific product lines, overcomes functional specialization
Create cross-function/cross-geography product teams	Shows value of joint knowledge sharing and constraints of lack of joint decision making
Cluster market companies into a few regions, give regions leadership roles for new market development and for best practice sharing	Co-opts heads of major market companies by giving them a corporate role
	Emphasizes knowledge, intensive learning and sharing processes
	Focuses product × geography dialogue into a limited number of 'points' at the intersection of matrix dimensions
Focus and simplify product assortment	Reduces costs of complexity
Develop products only with 'pilot countries' commitment	Signals value of market expertise and market company commitment
Focus on key product development projects	Restores credibility/technical leadership of center, builds competitive advantage

(*Continues*)

Table 15.1 (*Continued*)

Action	Meaning/Logic
Develop VMS	Emphasizes breakthrough innovations that market companies could not achieve on their own
Install new accounting systems	Understands total contribution of each product
	Gives product centers the tools to assess and steer overall product policy
	Moves to real business units
	Allows joint optimization of product policy and marketing decisions between center and market companies
ABC analysis of product profitability	Shows high costs and poor performance of locally developed systems and opportunity costs of not drawing on central solutions
Push to reduce, standardize, and modularize product range	Reduces sales, installation, and maintenance costs, putting the burden of cost reduction and resource redeployment back to market companies
Expert system 'solution design' software made available to sales forces	Reduces required expertise (and thus influence) of sales forces and dealers

and dependent on local social, cultural, and semantic contexts for interpretation often is ignored.

For example, most of the literature examining the innovation process either assumes or recommends colocation and ignores the additional complexities distance and differentiation create. In situations of resource and capacity colocation, much of the difficulty stemming from knowledge architecture goes unnoticed, because colocation provides the intensity and speed of interaction and feedback that allows these difficulties to be resolved quickly and informally. Where knowledge needs to be mobilized across distance, defining consistent knowledge architecture and trying to align knowledge modules with project or product work packages, and with knowledge sites (so each module/ package can benefit from colocation), becomes paramount.

To alleviate, if not eliminate the problems of knowledge sharing at a distance, top management can act in several dimensions:

1. Determining the configuration of activities to minimize the distance problem. Novartis relocated most of its US research activities from several sites in New Jersey to one site in Cambridge (Mass.) next to MIT. The main logic for this decision was to locate a critical mass of its researchers in close enough proximity to MIT scientists to allow ongoing informal intellectual and social interactions, in particular around new areas of medical and biological innovation where knowledge remains more complex than in traditional chemistry-based pharmaceutical research. In other words, most complex knowledge was colocated, and distant links were used only to access peripheral centers (such as a satellite lab in La Jolla close to the Scribbs Institute).

2. The configuration of individual projects also can be managed. Although top management usually would not determine individual project configurations, it might intervene to avoid configurations that ignored the complex distribution of knowledge in a particular area. Put differently, a context for effectively accessing and sharing complex knowledge—rules of good practice for knowledge sharing—needs to be created.

3. Top management also may intervene to ensure that complex knowledge is not inadvertently destroyed by benign neglect, for instance by the inadvertent relocation of activities and closure of sites holding complex knowledge, or from inappropriate retirement or promotion policies that break up vital centers of development. The opposite of benign neglect might be building a 'people's' context for knowledge sharing through fair process and norms of generalized reciprocity. This is a more subtle form of context-development, a context that drives people to share knowledge. The work of Sir Martin Sorrell to leverage the capabilities of dozens of strong subsidiaries provides a good example of a context that encourages the sharing of knowledge (Bartlett and Ghoshal 1993; Bower and Hout 1996; Raynor and Bower 2001).

My purpose in this chapter is not to provide a full treatment of the challenges faced by management in mobilizing knowledge as a strategic resource. Rather, it is to show that the resource allocation process modeled in this book is taxed as one moves from capital investment to mobilization of other types of resources, in particular those that present the paradox of positive externalities and high stickiness, as does complex knowledge.

As one extends the range of strategic resources, the nature of the process has to shift from resource allocation to resource mobilization.

Both the type of organizational context to be created and the specific corporate interventions required shift accordingly, and therefore the processes of resource mobilization are contingent on the resources being used.

A useful first cut to understand these contingencies is to recognize that resources differ fundamentally on two dimensions: whether they are public or private goods and their respective stickiness or fungibility. Figure 15.1 displays the way various types of strategic resource are likely to differ on these dimensions.

Strategic alliances are a good example of the complexity considered above. They combine both the challenges discussed in the first two sections. They are used by partners not just to coinvest, but often to share more complex types of strategic resources, and resource commitments are subject to multiple hierarchies.

3. Strategic Alliances as Overlapping Contexts for Resource Allocation

As opposed to multidimensional multinational organizations, where contexts are intertwined and purposefully differentiated, alliances often have parallel but unintended differentiated contexts.

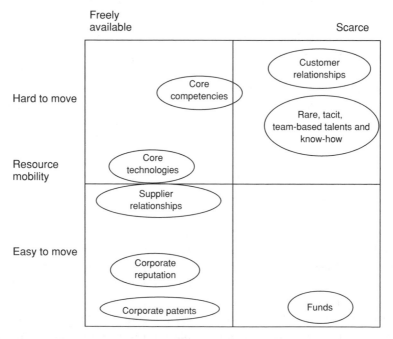

Figure 15.1 Differences in various types of strategic resources

Strategic Contexts

An alliance naturally straddles the context of its various partners, and in most cases these contexts are structurally different. Even before recognizing structural contextual differences, it is necessary to consider the strategic importance of a given alliance to its partners and the way it relates to their respective strategic contexts. For example, in a small innovative start-up, an alliance with a large distributor may be a lifeline fundamental to its success and survival. To a larger partner of the entrepreneurial start-up, the same alliance may represent one of many bets that will be subjected to the vagaries of wider resource allocation choices. Texas Instruments, for instance, was among a handful of partners to collaborate with French start-up PixTech to develop a flat-screen display technology that could provide an alternative to LCDs. The integrated circuit division of TI was the interface, but TI's involvement made sense mainly for their PC business. Unknown to either the integrated circuit or PC groups, at precisely that time, the corporate office of TI was in the process of selling the PC business to Acer.

More generally, the continuity of resource commitments in an alliance is subject to the vagaries of resource allocation processes in each partner, each of whom has a very different range of investment options and a different strategic and financial predicament. Although one would expect more instability to result, the opposite also may be true, each partner wanting to spare itself the embarrassment of having been the first to 'pull the plug'. What became one of the most successful alliances ever—in jet engines between General Electric and French engine maker SNECMA—was saved in its early days before sales took off because each feared it would be the first to give up! In strategic alliances characterized by separate strategic decision-making centers and ownership and resource allocation processes, where partners have different opportunity sets, the strategic context within which resource allocation decisions take place may be quite incoherent. The fragility of process and the fragmented pattern of outcomes that result are consequences of the temporary and constantly questioned alignment of strategic interests between the 'partnering' firms.

Structural Contexts

Beyond strategic contexts, structural contexts are likely to be deeply different among partners. Paradoxically, this may be particularly true between alliance partners for two very different reasons. Value-creating alliances are logically more likely between very different partners, partners bringing together different competencies, access to different markets, and different backgrounds. Alliances also take place in industries where regulatory restrictions may limit acquisitions, and, in particular, among firms where state influence and ownership still may be significant (e.g. energy, transportation, armament) and where privatization, deregulation, and market liberalization proceed at a different pace in different countries.

This means that the scope and nature of organizational contexts are likely to be very different among the partners. In negotiations, each partner also may selectively highlight or obfuscate parts of their own resource allocation contexts. This action serves the partner's negotiation tactics and strategy. The partner who has the more 'transparent' and/or self-contained resource allocation context has fewer opportunities to play this bargaining game and, conversely, the partner who can keep its contexts opaque and its boundaries unclear has a strong advantage to exploit. In military equipment alliances in Europe, for instance, the Italian partners typically enjoyed this advantage. They had less visible and less explicit resource allocation processes than their partners, in particular, the German members of the partnerships once part of the Daimler group (which had very clear-cut resource allocation rules and procedures). The opacity of one's structural context becomes a strategic asset in the negotiations among partners.

Under these circumstances, an alliance itself may become a mere pawn in a wider game. For state-owned enterprises in the course of privatization, an alliance with a major multinational partner may be both a source of fiscal discipline—in particular, over politicians who have a stake in the future of the company (i.e. a constraint on the domestic political game) and a ploy to extract from a partner the resources the state once provided. In its failed alliance network building efforts, Swissair was confronted with these issues in a way that became costly enough to lead Swissair to bankruptcy (Doz and Hunter 2004).

When an alliance takes the form of an equity joint-venture, it also may be positioned very differently in each partner's context. An alliance partner that grants more autonomy to organizational subunits and relies to a greater extent on emergent resource allocation processes will naturally grant more autonomy to a joint venture. A partner's relative size also plays a role. Larger companies may assign to negotiations or to the governance process of an alliance, middle managers whose resource allocation authority is limited or non-existent, to interface with the CEO of a smaller company who can make decisions independently.

Even between firms of relatively similar sizes and complexity, the quality of the resource allocation process may differ considerably in its speed, comprehensiveness, strength of integration, and internal quality of strategic dialogue—in particular when it comes to strategic integration. Strategic integration ambition, scope, and reach also may vary dramatically across firms (Burgelman and Doz 2001).

National cultures and institutional contexts, in addition to corporate contexts, also play a role. Some cultures are more context-rich, some are less (Hofstede 1980). Some cultures more explicitly define and assume delegation of authority, others favor an informal process of lateral consensus seeking and gaining support from one's hierarchy before commitments are defined. In other words, both the definition and the impetus processes may be deeply different between partner firms. Forms of alliance that bring them into close meshing (like joint ventures, often a form of 'localized' subunit merger) suffer from the inability to create a common organizational context for the alliance or to reconcile differences among the partners' context. For instance, an alliance between an Italian state-owned firm and a British multinational resulted in the creation of a coordination center in Brussels plagued by these cultural differences. Over time, the partners came to rely increasingly on external hires for the joint venture to staff it and to recall their own—culturally incompatible—secondees. On each side, they had been too strongly 'imprinted' by the contexts of their respective parent company to work effectively together in the joint venture.

Reconciling contextual differences between partners in a strategic alliance calls for various types of corporate intervention.

Explicating and Sharing Strategic Logic

Although strategic logic in alliances keeps evolving over time and is likely to get more strongly defined as the alliance proceeds, clarity and mutual exploration of strategic logic between partners allows strategic contexts to be mutually understood, if not to converge. Some very robust alliances benefit from their partners sharing the same strategic context (e.g. at the broadest level as the GE and SNECMA alliance took shape, both were new entrants experiencing similar challenges in the civilian jet engine market). Compatible, if not similar, strategic contexts are key, and the CEOs or corporate managers or both or the several partners need to ascertain and affirm compatibility.

Mirroring Organizational Contexts

In situations where partners are not using differences in organizational context, scope, and transparency to further their own interests in ongoing bargaining between partners, making their respective organizational contexts more similar over time, with similar structures, similarly defined roles, and aligned measurements and incentives with regard to the alliance facilitates collaboration. GE Aero-engines and SNECMA for instance, came to develop organizational contexts that were mirror images of each other, with in addition a few key executives playing both an alliance role together with their counterpart (in a kind of 'two-in-a-box' model) and a parent company role. This allowed the alliance to 'sit' in a similar way in both partners' respective organizational contexts.

Bridging at Multiple Levels

Substantive dialogue concerning alliance strategy, governance, and quality of relations needs to take place both vertically—across levels—within each partner's organization (following the usual strategic integration of the resource allocation process) and also among partners at each level of their organizations. This permits bridges of lateral integration and mutual understanding between managers playing similar roles in the partners' respective resource allocation process. Of course, some of these bridges may be inclined, titled, and variously oriented to recognize differences between the partners' organizational contexts and resource allocation processes. It is also important that the partners agree on making their processes sufficiently compatible for a useful flow of 'traffic' to cross the bridges. Figure 15.2 sketches top management actions that can help reconcile the strategic and organizational context differences between partners and build integrative processes within each partner's organization.

Improving One's Own Capabilities for Strategic Integration

Strategic alliances are often an 'acid test' for the quality of an organization's strategic integration capabilities. Paradoxically, for instance, we observed strategic integration processes within large bureaucratic partner organizations being performed by smaller and more strategically agile partners (Doz 1988). In sum, collaborative capability is constrained by internal integration capability.

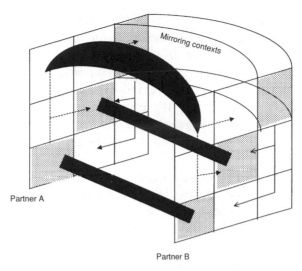

Figure 15.2 Actions that help reconcile differences in strategic and organizational context

Conclusion

By considering the circumstances in which resources are allocated in the context of multidimensional and multi-institutional organizations as well as the challenges posed by categories of strategic resources—such as complex knowledge—that differ from capital investment funds, this chapter has highlighted limits to the descriptive power of a distributed multilevel, multi-process model of resource allocation and the need for different types of corporate intervention. Multidimensional and multi-institutional contexts, as well as more 'sticky' strategic resources (that have to be contributed and mobilized rather than allocated) raise hard challenges for resource allocation, probably first encountered and first observed in multinational companies.

The mechanisms that structure and provide context need to foster high-quality interactions along multiple dimensions. Even more than in classic M-form organizations, top management of complex organizations must provide mutual understanding, interpersonal trust, and shared ambitions and commitments while allowing individual units, subsidiaries, business units, partners, and centers of competences to make differentiated and distinctive contributions. 'Quality of management' (Ghoshal and Bartlett 1994) is more important in these multidimensional organizations—that are inescapably unstable—than in simpler forms of organization.

Equally inescapable is a blurring of the simple distinction between subunit, integrating, and corporate roles in the resource allocation process. The simple elegance of having individual subunit managers responsible for a complete value chain disappears, and strategic integration becomes not simply hierarchical and vertical but multidimensional and complex. Finally, the contribution of 'sticky' strategic resources calls for an energizing context where both autonomy and interdependence are strong—again, something that calls for 'quality of management'.

We have observed CEOs reconfiguring their organizational contexts to cope with these challenges. The Alfa Laval example developed in section 2 is representative of these efforts to weave together a new organizational fabric. We also have observed executives very aware of temptations and perils of direct corporate interventions into resource allocation choices. Perhaps most importantly, we have observed CEOs take advantage of the blurring of roles to build more integrative top management teams that identify more with the total corporation than with their own units.

In conclusion, as more and more firms—multinational or not—adopt complex structures, enter webs of alliances, and gain a deeper appreciation of the range of strategic resources on which advantage may be built, the issues first encountered by MNCs and explored in this chapter will become increasingly relevant to researchers of the resource allocation processes.

Endnotes

1. For a summary perspective, see Doz (2004).
2. Robert Burgelman (1994).
3. In his description of a 'velcro organization', Bower (2004) describes the work that an adaptive leader must carry out in order to drive the mechanisms of a complex contemporary organization.
4. We leave aside the significant differences in regulatory and tax regimes across countries and the mostly temporary differences in labor and other input costs, except for raw materials. From a resource allocation standpoint, they are not so interesting.

References

Bartlett, C. A., and Ghoshal, S. (1989). *Managing Across Borders: The Transnational Solution*. Boston, Mass.: Harvard Business School Press.

——————(Winter Special Issue, 1993). 'Beyond the M-form: Toward a Managerial Theory of the Firm'. *Strategic Management Journal* 14: 23–46.

Birkinshaw J. (1997). 'Entrepreneurship in Multinational Corporations: The Characteristics of Subsidiary Initiatives'. *Strategic Management Journal* 18/3: 207–29.

Bower, J. L., and Hout, S. E. (1996). *WPP: Integrating Icons to Leverage Knowledge*. Harvard Business School case 396-249. Cambridge, Mass.

Burgelman, R. A. (1988). 'Strategy Making as a Social Learning Process: The Case of Internal Corporate Venturing'. *Interfaces* 18/3: 74–85.

—— (1994). 'Fading Memories: A Process Theory of Strategic Business End in Dynamic Environments'. *Administrative Science Quarterly* 39/1: 24–56.

—— and Doz, Y. (Spring, 2001). 'The Power of Strategic Integration'. *Sloan Management Review*, 28–38.

Doz, Y. (1976). 'National Policies and Multinational Management'. Doctoral dissertation, Harvard Business School.

—— (2004). 'Toward a Managerial Theory of the MNC.' *Advances in International Management* 161: 3–30.

—— (1988). 'Technology Partnerships Between Larger and Smaller Firms: Some Critical Issues', in F. J. Contractor and P. Lorange (eds.), *Cooperative Strategies in International Business*. Lexington, Mass.: Lexington Books.

—— (1986). *Strategic Management in Multinational Companies*. New York: Pergamon.

—— (1979). *Government Control and Multinational Management: Power Systems and Telecommunications Equipment*. New York: Praeger Special Studies.

—— and Hunter, M. (2004). 'Swissair and the Qualiflyer Alliance'. INSEAD case study.

—— Santos, J., and Williamson, P. (2001). *From Global to Metanational: How Companies Win in the Knowledge Economy*. Boston, Mass.: Harvard Business School Press.

—— Wilson, K., and Williamson, P. *Managing Global Integration* (forthcoming 2005).

Dunning, J. H. (1981). *International Production and the Multinational Enterprise*. London: George Allen & Unwin.

—— (1988). 'The Electric Paradigm of International Production: A Restatement and Some More Extensions'. *Journal of International Business Studies* 19: 1–31.

Fouraker, Lawrence E., and Stopford, John M. (1968). 'Organizational Structure and the Multinational Strategy'. *Administrative Science Quarterly* 13/1: 47–65.

Gerstner, L. (2002). *Who Says Elephants Can't Dance? Inside IBM's Historic Turnaround*. New York: Harper Business.

Ghemawat, Pankaj (2003). 'Semiglobalization and International Business Strategy'. *Journal of International Business Studies* 34/2: 138–53.

Ghoshal, S., and Bartlett, C. (1994). 'Linking Organizational Context and Managerial Action: The Dimensions of Quality of Management'. *Strategic Management Journal* 15/5: 91–113.

Hedlund, G. (1986). 'The Hypermodern MNC—A Heterarchy?' *Human Resource Management* 25: 9–35.

——(1993). 'Assumption of Hierarchy and Heterarchy, with Applications to the Management of the Multinational Corporation', in S. Ghoshal and D. Eleanor Westley (eds.), *Organization Theory and the Multinational Corporation*. New York: St Martin's Press, 211–36.

——(1996). 'The Intensity and Extensity of Knowledge and the Multinational Corporation as a Nearly Recomposable System'. Stockholm, IIB Working Paper.

Heifetz, R. A. (1994). *Leadership Without Easy Answers*. Cambridge, Mass.: Belknap Press.

——and Laurie, Donald L. (2001). 'The Work of Leadership'. *Harvard Business Review*, 79/11: 131–41.

Hofstede, G. (1980). *Culture's Consequences: International Differences in Work-Related Values*. Beverly Hills: Sage.

Kim, W. Chan, and Mauborgne, Renée (2003). 'Fair Process: Managing in the Knowledge Economy', *Harvard Business Review* 81/1: 127, 136.

Kogut, B., and Zander, U. (1993). 'Knowledge of the Firm and the Evolutionary Theory of the Multinational Corporation'. *Journal of International Business Studies* 24/4: 625–45.

Murtha, T. P., Lenway, S.A., *et al.* (1998). 'Global Mind-sets and Cognitive Shift in a Complex Multinational Corporation'. *Strategic Management Journal* 19/2: 97–114.

Nonaka, I., and Takeuchi, H. (1995). *The Knowledge Creating Company*. New York: Oxford University Press.

Porter, M. E. (ed.) (1986). *Competition in Global Industries*. Boston, Mass.: Harvard Business School Press.

Prahalad, C. K. (1975). *The Strategic Process in a Multinational Corporation*. Boston, Mass.: Harvard Business School Press.

Rawl, J. (1971). *A Theory of Justice*. Cambridge, Mass.: Harvard University Press.

Stopford, J. M., and Wells, L.T. Jr. (1972). *Managing Multinational Enterprise: Organization of the Firm and Ownership of the Subsidiaries*. New York: Basic Books.

Szulanski, G. (Winter Special Issue, 1996). 'Exploring Internal Stickiness: Impediments to the Transfer of Best Practices Inside Firms'. *Strategic Management Journal* 17: 27–44.

Raynor, M. E., and Bower, J. L. (2001). 'Lead from the Center: How to Manage Divisions Dynamically'. *Harvard Business Review* (May–June).

Teece, D. J. (1977). 'Technology Transfer by Multinational Firms'. *International Executive* 19/3: 15–18.

Vernon, R. (1971). *Sovereignty at Bay: The Multinational Spread of U.S. Enterprise*. London: Basic Books.

Part V

Outside Commentaries on the RAP Perspectives

16

Resource Allocation, Strategy, and Organization: An Economist's Thoughts

John Roberts

The chapters in this volume, and the decades of work on which they build, document the complexity and subtlety of the processes that generate firms' resource allocation decisions and, thereby, their strategies. This work raises issues of the extent to which the predictions of standard theories of the capital allocation process are accurate, given that the theoretical models typically do not reflect the documented institutional realities. The studies also clearly reveal the fact that—Chandler's dictum notwithstanding—structure does not necessarily follow strategy. Indeed, it more often may be the case that, as John Browne of British Petroleum has said, 'the organization is the strategy'. The organization of the firm—the people, the architecture, the routines and processes, and the culture (Roberts 2004)—fundamentally shapes behavior within it. Thus, the organizational design choices executives make largely determine the strategic actions employees take. These causal relationships have implications for the study of strategy and organization. In this brief chapter, I will address these two issues: the accuracy of economic models and the implications of the work in the Bower–Burgelman framework and its extensions for the study of strategy and organization, particularly as practiced by economists.

Thirty years after the first publication in this line of research, many standard corporate finance texts (e.g. Van Horne 2001; Ross, Westerfield, and Jaffe 2002) still treat capital allocation essentially as a mechanical decision problem: array the possible projects, rank them by NPV (assuming they are independent), and undertake all those that bring a positive NPV. Any qualifications are around possible lack of independence, difficulty of establishing the dollar amounts and interest rates that go into the NPV calculation, or constraints on the availability of capital. No real attention is paid to the process whereby projects are identified, proposed, refined, and approved—the complex and subtle process first described by Bower (1970).[1] Still, the textbooks do not necessarily represent the latest thinking—or even the state of the current consensus—among scholars. Over the last three decades, in fact, economic research has put much more life into the study of capital allocation and other decisions within firms. This work is largely model-based theory. Although there also has been some empirical evidence developed, I will refer to this work as 'theory'.

By and large, the theory research is consistent with a basic finding in Bower's work: that managers act in accordance with the incentives they face. Bower argues that the front-line people who come up with projects basically are motivated by the need to get their jobs done, and the middle managers who effectively choose among the projects by deciding which ones to support are concerned with their own reputations and career prospects. The recent theorizing universally assumes that managers involved in resource allocation are self-interested. Further, it assumes their interests do not automatically line up with maximizing value creation for the firm. The career concerns that Bower accentuated figure prominently in this work (Holmström and Ricart i Costa 1986), and compensation is almost always a factor, but other matters often are assumed to enter the manager's utility function; for example: maintenance of personal employment (Meyer, Milgrom, and Roberts 1992; Shleifer and Vishny 1989), enjoyment of slack resources (Antle and Eppen 1985), empire-building (Harris and Raviv 1996), and avoidance of effort (Harris, Kriebel, and Raviv 1982; Lambert 1986).

Yet, whereas self-interest figures in both literatures, managers in the theoretical models appear to be more cunningly and systematically self-interested than those in the firms Bower and his colleagues studied. The former display what Williamson called 'opportunistism' or 'self-interest with guile' and a complete lack of concern for the welfare of the organization (except to the extent that it affects their individual well-being). They take full advantage of any opportunity to advance their own narrow interests, and they are remarkably clever about identifying such opportunities and thoroughly amoral about the actions they take in pursuit of them. In contrast, the real managers Bower and his colleagues describe often seem genuinely concerned about the welfare of the organization and about doing a good job (at least as they perceive and define it). The managers Noda describes at US WEST continued to support their proposals because they believed in the future of wireless telephony, despite the skepticism of their CEO (Noda and Bower 1996). The old-line newspaper managers Gilbert observed opposed the on-line news because they believed in the importance of good editing, the sort available only in a 'real newspaper'. This gap presents a question. Is the theory too pessimistic about managers and their motivation, and—since it seems extremely likely that the answer is 'yes'—does this lead the theory into incorrect predictions? Or is the right argument that institutional arrangements aimed at preventing abuse are needed not because everyone is potentially an abuser but because there are apt to be some potential abusers who must be deterred? At the same time, how do we come to understand the actual motives of managers and other members of organizations in a way that allows more descriptively accurate models? Studies in Part IV of this book argue for ad-hoc direct intervention by top management that is difficult to model. How important are such situations to a general theory?

There is a second element of consistency between the theory work and Bower's: both emphasize the informational problems involved in making allocation decisions. Front-line managers and top executives do not share the same information, either in theory or in real firms. In particular, in Bower's work, the front-line manager is much better informed about technology and likely too about supply and demand conditions, whereas senior and top managers are better informed about possible spillovers, capital availability and costs, and strategic intentions.

Christensen's work suggests that mid-level managers may block some new technologies because their information is derived from existing customers. Noda finds corporate managers focused on signals from the capital markets. Both the introduction and summary chapters of the book argue that most resource allocation decisions require both sorts of information: product and capital markets. Therefore, problem-solving across organization levels in the face of informational asymmetries appears to be key.

Meanwhile, the theory typically posits that managers are privately informed about the availability of projects, the likely returns the projects would generate, the effort they exert in developing and implementing projects, the private benefits they would enjoy from their projects' being funded, or other factors relevant to the investment decision. Top executives may have beliefs about the distributions of these variables, but do not know and cannot observe their actual values. These informational asymmetries create incentive problems, because they mean that it may not be possible fully to align the interests of the managers and the firm through the design of the organization (including, in particular, compensation).

The theory focuses on the possible inefficiency of investment decisions and resource allocations that may result from the imperfect incentives that managers face, which result from the informational asymmetries and the lack of inherent alignment between the managers' interests and those of the firm's owners. Managers may seek to get more capital allocated to them than is efficient because they like having empires and slack. This may lead them to distort or withhold information about their own pet projects or to denigrate or sabotage others' proposals. They may push for investments that increase their personal value to the firm and thus increase their individual bargaining power, thereby increasing their job security and incomes. Or, if they are risk averse, they may hide projects that the firm would optimally undertake because they face risks to their reputations if they propose projects that fail.

The theory models then seek to show how explanations of some stylized facts regarding the decision processes used in firms can be seen as attempts to improve efficiency. For example, Holmström and Ricart i Costa (1986) generate the use of internal hurdle rates that exceed the firm's cost of capital; Fama and Jensen (1983) and Athey and Roberts (2001) explain why different parties within the organization are made responsible for initiating, approving, executing, and monitoring projects, although this may not use information most efficiently; Milgrom and Roberts (1990) and Scharfstein and Stein (2000) explain tendencies for multibusiness firms to deviate from NPV maximization towards more 'equitable' allocations of investment across businesses; Meyer, Milgrom, and Roberts (1992) suggest why troubled divisions are more likely to be spun off; Aghion and Tirole (1997) use the need to motivate searching for worthwhile projects to approach hierarchic integration and the boundaries of the firm; Rotemberg and Saloner (1994) show that adopting a narrow business strategy and accepting only projects that are consistent with it can lead to better investment choices; and Rotemberg and Saloner (2000) and Van den Steen (2004) argue that 'managerial vision' can be important in motivating employees to make appropriate investments.

Typically, these models predict that the potential inefficiencies that arise because of the differing interests and informational asymmetries cannot be avoided fully. Thus, the models predict that the allocation of resources inside the firm will be less than the value-maximizing ideal.

Although the source, nature and extent of inefficiency are starkly and unambiguously identified in the theoretical models (even though different models predict different patterns of inefficiency), the field-based work deals with a more complex reality. Establishing that a given decision was not optimal is a much more subtle task. Obviously, there are some investment decisions that did not work: Intel's massive investments in a video-conferencing tool that came to naught are an excellent example (Burgelman 2001). But Andy Grove, a hard-headed, analytic, rational executive if there ever was one, genuinely believed on the basis of the information available to him at the time that the project was a good investment. That is not prima facie evidence of inefficiency. On the other hand, arguably, Lou Hughes created more value than would have been achieved by applying the approved capital budgeting tools and sticking to the mandated location-decision criteria. Still, Bower (1970) argued that there were strong reasons to expect inefficiencies in the processes and decisions he observed. He attributed these to misaligned systems of organization, information, and incentives, exacerbated by the focus on projects rather than businesses. These arguments are, of course, fundamentally in line with the modern theory. Beyond that abstract diagnosis, however, does the field-based work generate any consistent pattern of differences between the investment choices that were actually made and those that the naive finance model would generate?

In fact, there does appear to be one possibly systematic pattern of misallocation. It emerges especially in the work of Burgelman (2001), Christensen (1997), and Sull (1999). It seems that firms may continue to invest in strategies too long after it would be better to switch to something new. Firestone continued to invest in bias tires long after radials had captured the market. Intel arguably invested in DRAMs too long. The generations of disk-drive manufacturers might well have been better off to de-accentuate their existing products and move towards the disruptive upstart technologies. Is this in fact a systematic bias in strategizing and choice? Determining this is tricky, because it is hard to observe and identify cases where a strategy was abandoned too soon. But if this is in fact a systematic pattern, it needs theoretical explanation, and that explanation ought to be consistent with the history documented in the work underlying this volume. Gilbert opens one avenue for research by separating the problem of incentives from the problem of conceptualizing opportunity.

Turn now to some of the implications of this work for the economics of strategy, organization, and management. There is wide acceptance of the idea that performance results from achieving and maintaining a fit between strategy and organization and between them and the firm's environment. If strategy and organization are thought of as being developed in a top-down or centralized fashion, then ideally the two should be developed together holistically, so that they fit with one another and the environment. This may be reasonable in a start-up, where the founders can largely specify the strategy and make the key organizational design choices. As the studies here document, however, in larger, established organizations, no single person makes these choices alone, nor should any executive try to do so.

In an interview done in 2000, Olli-Pekka Kallasvuo, then the CFO of Nokia, made the point nicely when he discussed strategy:

In the paper business, say, you make one or two decisions annually that are extremely important. The CEO says, 'We will invest in this activity', and the rest is implementation. You don't even have to know in the organization why we are making the investment. But we don't make one or two decisions a year. We make thousands of small decisions a year by hundreds of people. We need to ensure that these decisions take place in harmony or are aligned with each other, but we cannot make them. And I really strongly believe that decisions in the organization need to be made where the expertise is greatest.   [Quoted in Doornik and Roberts 2001]

The organization is the means through which the leaders of the firm can hope to ensure that the dispersed decisions that ultimately generate the strategy are aligned. As the environment changes, the dispersed decision makers make new resource allocation decisions to attempt to regain alignment between strategy and the environment. In this they are guided, as Bower has argued, by the incentives provided by the design of the organization. But these same environmental changes also disrupt the alignment of the organization with the environment, and the adjustment of the strategy may well increase the overall misalignment. So the organizational design may need to be adapted too, on an ongoing basis, just as the strategy evolves. Formal incentives may need to be adjusted, lines of communication may need to be redirected, decision authority may need to be moved, jobs may need to be redefined, and so on.

Just as with the strategy, the changes to the organization that together redesign it must be done in a dispersed way by managers close to the problems. But what then ensures that their design decisions are coherent and 'in harmony'?

At Nokia, operating in the turbulent environment of the 1990s' mobile telephony industry, the solution was a combination of a clear strategic intent combined with a persistent and strong corporate culture shared among a carefully selected set of people. Top executives paid a lot of attention to making sure the general strategic direction was well understood—to keeping the values and norms that marked the organization fresh and strong and to ensuring that the rapidly growing membership of the organization shared these values and embraced the norms. Meanwhile, the less inertial elements of the organization—the architecture and the routines and processes—were adjusted continually by managers on the front lines, with intra-organizational boundaries shifting, project teams emerging and disbanding, and new measures and decision criteria being established and amended. These organizational changes were made by the same managers who were making the dispersed strategic decisions, ensuring coherence of the two (Doornik and Roberts 2001).

Is the Nokia example isolated, or does it fit in a general pattern? Would the same approach work in a larger, more bureaucratic company? In one not using a high-commitment employment system? In one operating in a less rapidly changing environment? I believe we do not know the answer to these questions. More generally, we need to understand better the alternative methods of maintaining alignment. What are the benefits and costs of dispersing these decisions? When is this best? How can existing systems be improved? These are real challenges for researchers.

Endnote

1. Brealey and Myers (2003) is an exception here. They briefly describe the process, citing Bower. They also survey some of the modern theory of capital allocation.

References

Aghion, Philippe, and Tirole, Jean (1997). 'Formal and Real Authority in Organizations'. *Journal of Political Economy* 105: 1–29.

Antle, Richard, and Eppen, Gary (1985). 'Capital Rationing and Organizational Slack in Capital Budgeting'. *Management Science* 31: 163–74.

Athey, Susan, and Roberts, John (2001). 'Organizational Design: Decision Rights and Incentive Contracts'. *American Economic Review* 91: 200–5.

Bower, Joseph (1970). *Managing the Resource Allocation Process: A Study of Corporate Planning and Investment*. Boston, Mass.: Harvard Business School Press.

Brealey, Richard A., and Myers, Stewart C. (2003). *Principles of Corporate Finance* (7th edn.). New York: McGraw-Hill Irwin.

Burgelman, Robert (2001). *Strategy Is Destiny: How Strategy-Making Shapes a Company's Future*. New York: Free Press.

Christensen, Clayton (1997). *The Innovator's Dilemma: When New Technologies Cause Great Firms to Fail*. Boston, Mass.: Harvard Business School Press.

Doornik, Katherine, and Roberts, John (2001). 'Nokia Corporation: Innovation and Efficiency in a High-Growth Global Firm'. Stanford, Calif.: Stanford University Graduate School of Business case IB-23.

Fama, Eugene, and Jensen, Michael (1983). 'Separation of Ownership and Control'. *Journal of Law and Economics* 26: 301–26.

Harris, Milton, and Raviv, Artur (1996). 'The Capital Budgeting Process: Incentives and Information'. *Journal of Finance* 52: 1139–74.

——Kriebel, Charles, and Raviv, Artur (1982). 'Asymmetric Information, Incentives and Intrafirm Resource Allocation'. *Management Science* 28: 604–20.

Holmström, Bengt, and Ricart i Costa, Joan (1986). 'Managerial Incentives and Capital Management'. *Quarterly Journal of Economics* 101: 835–60.

Lambert, Richard A. (1986). 'Executive Effort and the Selection of Risky Projects'. *The RAND Journal of Economics* 17: 77–88.

Meyer, Margaret, Milgrom, Paul, and Roberts, John (1992). 'Organizational Prospects, Influence Costs and Ownership Changes'. *Journal of Economics and Management Strategy* 1: 9–36.

Milgrom, Paul, and Roberts, John (1990). 'The Efficiency of Equity in Organizational Decision Processes'. *American Economic Review* (Papers and Proceedings), 80: 154–9.

Noda, Tomoyoshi, and Bower, Joseph (1996). 'Strategy Making as Iterated Processes of Resource Allocation', *Strategic Management Journal* 17: 159–92.

Roberts, John (2004). *The Modern Firm: Organizational Design for Performance and Growth*. Oxford: Oxford University Press.

Ross, Stephen A., Westerfield, Randolph W., and Jaffe, Jeffrey F. (2002). *Corporate Finance* (6th edn.). New York: McGraw-Hill Irwin.

Rotemberg, Julio, and Saloner, Garth (Dec. 1994). 'The Benefits of Narrow Business Strategies'. *American Economic Review* 84: 1330–49.

————(2000). 'Visionaries, Maragers, and Strategic Direction'. *The Rand Journal of Economics* 31/4: 693–716.

Scharfstein, David, and Stein, Jeremy (2000). 'The Dark Side of Internal Capital Markets: Divisional Rent-Seeking and Inefficient Investment'. *Journal of Finance* 55: 2537–64.

Shleifer, Andrei, and Vishny, Robert (1989). 'Managerial Entrenchment: The Case of Manager-Specific Investments'. *Journal of Financial Economics* 25: 123–39.

Sull, D. (1999). 'The Dynamics of Standing Still: Firestone Tire & Rubber and the Radial Revolution'. *Business History Review* 73/3: 430–60.

Van den Steen, Eric (2004). 'Organizational Beliefs and Managerial Vision'. *Journal of Law, Economics, and Organization* (forthcoming).

Van Horne, James C. (2001). *Financial Management and Policy* (13th edn.). Englewood Cliffs, NJ: Prentice-Hall.

17

Comments on the Resource Allocation Process

Daniel A. Levinthal

It is a pleasure and honor to have the opportunity to comment on this impressive body of work. As a graduate student in the early 1980s, I vividly recall my first reading of the resource allocation process (RAP). Here was a work that tackled one of the principal tasks of a firm: allocating scarce financial capital. The problem had been nominally solved by financial economists, but Bower presented it in a way that both brought forth the richness of the phenomena and provided a clear theoretical framework that illuminated the underlying processes at work. The ultimate test of a piece of scholarship is its ability to influence other scholars.[1] By that standard, as illustrated in this collected volume, the RAP framework is a huge success. Not only has it attracted enormous attention (and citations) from scholars pursuing related topics, but it has generated multiple generations of scholars to build upon and enrich the original framework. As the theoretical structure becomes more elaborated, it may be worthwhile to reflect on the core features of the argument. Doing so, I believe, will help researchers outside the immediate RAP 'family' to see the power of the underlying theoretical argument and help embed this literature in the larger literature on organizational decision making and adaptation of which it is a part.

The notion of search is central in the behavioral theory of the firm (March and Simon 1958; Cyert and March 1963). However, the literature tends to emphasize alternative generation—a point powerfully made by Nelson and Winter (1982) in their argument that production sets do not exist a priori, but production techniques must be discovered or invented. Relatively neglected in this literature has been the other facet of search processes—the role of selection. Typically, effective adaptive efforts are thought of as constrained due to the challenge of identifying more desirable alternatives. However, an equally important constraint is the selection process. Even if a 'thousand flowers' are brought to bloom, if they are selected over by a single type of 'lawn-mower', then the variety being generated will have no effect.

It is to this issue of selection that the RAP framework provides much needed insight and contribution. Yes, lower-level actors may define initiatives; but for those initiatives to take hold and have operational effect within the firm, they must receive support—financial resources, use of a firm's on-going operational infrastructure, managerial and technical staff time and talent, and so on. This perspective on selection also casts the role of upper management in a different light than the classic imagery of command and control. Rather, top management exerts influence by its effect on the selection context in which middle- and lower-level management operate. In this manner, top management influences what Burgelman refers to as the internal ecology of the firm.

Intentionally rational lower-level managers will, to an important degree, internalize the selection criteria imposed by upper management and generate initiatives that are reasonably consistent with these criteria and thereby stand a fair chance of being endorsed by middle management and ultimately approved. This is what Burgelman refers to as the 'induced' process of initiative creation. Actors also may generate initiatives outside the strategic context of the organization. However, such 'autonomous' initiatives need not be viewed as random variants. Although not induced by some internalization of corporate objectives, these initiatives still are responding to some set of beliefs about what might constitute a valuable initiative.

I think an important extension of the RAP framework, an extension researched most notably by Clay Christensen, is to recognize the role of the structural and strategic context external to the firm. Firms are not operating in a vacuum—they have customers, their scientists and engineers operate in professional communities, and they operate in a regulatory environment. Whether or not the objectives and concerns of these external constituencies are incorporated into the firm's own strategy and selection criteria, they exist and may be quite salient for a number of actors within the firm and, indeed, in some cases more salient than the firms' own objectives. In this sense, autonomous initiatives are not taking place in a vacuum and are not undirected. They are simply other-directed.

A critical tension in corporate entrepreneurship is that whereas 'other-directed' initiatives may be an important mechanism to keep the ecology of corporate initiatives tethered to a number of distinct and evolving consumer and technical contexts, the firm's own selection environment is likely to be relatively stable across time and is certainly going to be far less heterogeneous than the variegated selection environments of these external contexts (Adner and Levinthal 2002). External selection environments provide niches that both guide and potentially provide resources for internal development.

Even though external contexts may guide the birth and early development of new internal initiatives, ultimately the firm itself must validate and reinforce these efforts. In a dramatic instance, this can take the form of the strategic 'recognition' that Burgelman characterizes in the case of Intel's shift from the memory business to the microprocessor. But in less dramatic fashion, negotiated order between the internal and external selection criteria occurs quite often. The acceptance, or at least tentative acceptance, of a new initiative by the external context becomes an important part of the basis of the internal corporate dialogue and argumentation for further resources. Thus, the basic RAP framework is enacted, but definition is importantly shaped by external forces and, more subtly, impetus may be provided by external reinforcers, such as tentative early success in early stage markets (Adner and Levinthal 2002). Thus, initiatives may be 'induced' both by internal structures, as suggested by the original RAP framework, and by external contexts, as suggested here. Similarly, impetus may take place via a process of internal evaluation as originally suggested, but also may have external elements.

As noted in Eisenmann and Bower's work on the entrepreneurial M-form, top management can not only act as orchestrators of the selection environment, but may also at times define initiatives themselves. Top management in a diversified firm may be uniquely well positioned to identify possibly useful linkages across businesses; it is at the higher level of the organization that the interactions across businesses should be most salient (Gavetti forthcoming). Although top management may be uniquely well positioned to define certain classes of initiatives, there is an inherent risk in such initiatives to the extent that the dual role of alternative generation and alternative evaluation or selection gets carried out by the same set of individuals. The often frustrating, but in many cases useful, tension between the goals and objectives influencing the definition process and the goals and objectives embedded in the structural and strategic context is absent. The net effect should be that a higher proportion of initiatives defined by top management is enacted, but one would expect the distribution of outcomes to be far more variable than initiatives defined at lower levels of the organization. The history of diversification efforts, and merger and acquisitions initiatives, initiatives often defined by top management, seem roughly consistent with this argument. This danger of the joint role of definition and selection also may speak to Gilbert's finding that projects framed as threats rather than opportunities tend to be less successful. Newspaper firms that view the Internet as a threat are more likely to engage in initiative definition by higher-level actors than firms that treated the rise of this technology as an opportunity, an opportunity to which lower-level actors might respond and craft initiatives they would then try to shepherd through the resource allocation process.

The more typical hierarchical nature of the resource allocation process in which lower-level actors define initiatives that mid-level managers subsequently might endorse, all of whom operate in structural context influenced by top management, fits well with the dual imperative of search processes to both explore new bases of action and exploit the intelligence of current knowledge. The potentially vast parallel search effort that lower-level definition permits is ideally suited to exploration. A broad set of initiatives may be defined, each of them potentially speaking to a different facet of the internal or external environment faced by that lower-level actor. The resource commitments associated with each of these initiatives is likely to be relatively modest. Indeed, in many cases, it is likely to consist of time and operational resources unofficially 'borrowed' from existing previously endorsed initiatives. The firm's internal selection environment then slowly shifts through this rich array of initiatives. This process might in part be political and reflect the power and status of different individuals and subunits within the firm; alternatively, it may reflect some degree of external validation, possibly in the form of willing customers for prototype products and services; or it may reflect a more analytical discourse of forecasts of promising outcomes and their possible consistency with broader corporate agendas.

However, it would be a gross mischaracterization to frame such a process as being akin to a real option (see Adner and Levinthal (2004) for a fuller argument regarding the boundaries of the application of real options in characterizing managerial decision making). Although both processes are sequential, a real-options investment reflects a conscious allocation of resources to a particular initiative that may, depending on initial outcomes, receive subsequent resource investments. The large set of parallel initiatives that characterize 'definition' within the resource allocation process are, quite explicitly, not specified by the firm as a whole. They consist of responses of lower-level actors to their particular circumstances. Indeed, from the lower-level actor's point of view, the process of creating a new initiative may have more of the quality of an exploitation effort than being one cog in a broader system of exploration and exploitation (Adner and Levinthal 2002 and 2004). Initiatives are defined by managers, engineers, and salespeople who are trying to achieve some instrumental end; they are unlikely to view themselves as 'experimenting'.

Independent, however, of the mind-set of the lower-level actors, the broad system of the resource allocation process does speak to the need to balance the dual imperatives to explore and exploit. Diversity is generated at lower levels of the organization with relatively modest resource commitments associated with any one such initiative. Based on the initial outcome of these initiatives and the broader evaluation of their intrinsic merit and fit with the overall corporate strategic direction, this population of initiatives is culled, and the subset of initiatives that survives this culling process is provided the resources to scale up and thereby be given a chance to realize its full promise.

As Bower noted in his original research (1970: 67), the work on RAP fits squarely with the efforts of Cyert, March, and Simon in the late 1950s and early 1960s, to develop a view of the firm as a problem-solving entity adapting to its complex and often changing environment. The research on RAP, however, makes important contributions to this intellectual lineage. It provides a refined sense of the importance of the hierarchical nature of these organizational processes—a sensitivity that exists in Simon's early work on *Administrative Behavior*, but one that is often underplayed if not lost. Politics and the contesting of agenda—themes that are beginning to re-emerge within the Carnegie tradition (Occasio 1999)—are issues that have been fully embraced by work on RAP from its beginnings. Furthermore, this body of work has acted as an important counterforce to the focus on variation generation and the relative neglect of selection processes in work on technology management. Whether selection is on- or off-line (Gavetti and Levinthal 2000), it is inherently an organizational phenomenon. Organizations are systems in which the dual process of exploration and exploitation are carried out and the contributors to this volume offer us enormous insight regarding these processes.

Endnote

1. Another criterion could be the influence on practice. Indeed, the issue of multiple-selection criteria is a theme to which I want to return shortly.

References

Adner, R., and Levinthal, D. (2002). 'The Emergence of Emerging Technologies'. *California Management Review* 45: 50–66.

—— (2004). 'What is *Not* a Real Option: Considering Boundaries for the Application of Real Options to Business Strategy'. *Academy of Management Review* 29: 74–85.

Bower, J. (1970). *Managing the Resource Allocation Process*. Boston, Mass.: Harvard Business School Press.

Cyert, R., and March, J. (1963). *The Behavioral Theory of the Firm*. Englewood Cliffs, NJ: Prentice-Hall.

Gavetti, G. (forthcoming). 'Cognition and Hierarchy: Rethinking the Microfoundations of Capabilities' Development'. *Organization Science*.

—— and Levinthal, D. (2000). 'Looking Forward and Looking Backward: Cognitive and Experiential Search'. *Administrative Science Quarterly* 45: 113–37.

March, J., and Simon, H. (1958). *Organizations*. New York: Wiley & Sons.

Nelson, R., and Winter, S. (1982). *An Evolutionary Theory of the Firm*. Cambridge, Mass.: Harvard University Press.

Occasio, W. (1997). 'Towards an Attention-Based View of the Firm'. *Strategic Management Journal* 18: 187–207.

18

Research Complementarities: A Resource-Based View of the Resource Allocation Process Model (and Vice Versa)

Margaret A. Peteraf

The Power of Complementary Combinations

The Resource Allocation Process (RAP) model, as introduced by Bower (1970) and extended by Burgelman (1983), has proven to be among the most enduring contributions to the field of business strategy. It has inspired a rich array of field studies, in settings ranging from large multinational organizations to smaller, focused firms and entrepreneurial start-ups. Taken collectively, these studies provide an impressive base of supporting evidence for RAP applications.

Although the basic model continues to gain empirical support, some of the most promising research has been in the realm of theory building. New research is extending the reach of the model, introducing factors external to the firm, and delineating the boundary conditions of the model. Other studies have begun to explore the limits of the RAP model, questioning the conditions under which the model is likely to be prescriptive as well as descriptive. Eisenmann and Bower's (2000) study of 'top–down' strategic decision making in global media firms is an example. These studies bring new insights, more richness, and greater dimensionality to the model.

Much of this new work is the result of combining the insights of the basic RAP model with those of another theoretical lens. Eisenmann (2002), for example, brings both agency theory (Fama 1980) and transaction costs theory (Williamson 1975) to bear on the question of whether the RAP model correctly predicts strategic response to risk in diversified firms. Similarly, Gilbert (2004) and Gilbert and Bower

(2002) link the literatures on resource allocation, cognitive frames (Kahneman and Tversky 1984), and threat rigidity (Staw, Sandelands, and Dutton 1981) to address the question of why firms' responses to disruptive change are often maladaptive.

Theory development often is spurred by applying a new lens from outside the core theory domain, as these examples suggest. In Ch. 4, Gilbert and Christensen view other disciplines as a means to uncovering anomalies that spur further theory development in the core area.[1] But new lenses play another role in theory development as well. Different lenses may provide complementary perspectives. When they are brought to bear on the same phenomena, the result can be synergistic rather than antagonistic. And when this is the case, the result is likely to take theory in productive new directions, regardless of whether any anomalies are uncovered in the process. Just as product innovation often comes from recombining existing technologies or capabilities, the same may be true of theoretical innovation. By shining multiple lenses on the same phenomenon, new insights and new understandings may emerge that could not be seen with a single lens alone (Kuhn 1962).

This observation has normative implications for theory development. The key to driving the kind of theoretical advance that stems from a synergistic combination of perspectives is to identify complementary research streams. Thus, there is a need for 'complementarity seeking' research that parallels Gilbert and Christensen's call for 'anomaly-seeking' research designs.

An example of a complementary combination of perspectives that already has borne fruit is the melding of Resource Dependence Theory (Pfeffer and Salancik 1978) with RAP theory. Both theories are concerned centrally with the patterns by which firms allocate resources to fundamental activities. Both are concerned with capital investment decisions. But where RAP theory focuses on factors involved at multiple levels inside the firm, Resource Dependence Theory looks outside the firm for explanations. In bringing these complementary perspectives together, a more complete, integrative picture emerges of firms' resource allocation and capital investment processes.[2] Christensen's (1997) highly influential book on the Innovator's Dilemma is one of the products of this combination. Others include Christensen and Bower's (1996) study of customers' influence on resource allocation and Sull's (2002) work on disinvestment.

The Potential and the Challenge of a New Combination

A combination that may prove even more fruitful is that of the Resource-Based View of the Firm (Wernerfelt 1984; Peteraf 1993) and the RAP model. The complementary aspects are strong, but they are particularly evident when one includes various permutations of the resource-based view, such as the Knowledge-Based View of the Firm (Grant 1996), the Dynamic Resource-Based View (Helfat and Peteraf 2003), and the work on 'dynamic capabilities' (Teece, Pisano, and Shuen 1997). Linking these three rich perspectives with a RAP point of view likely will result in a dual payoff, adding new insights to each research stream.[3]

Like the RAP model, the resource-based view (RBV) is concerned with resources and capabilities internal to the firm and their connection to strategic decision making. There is likewise a mutual concern with the commitment effects of 'sunk' investments in strategic assets. But whereas the core RAP model is focused on competitive processes internal to the firm, the RBV directs attention to how a firm's resources affect external competitive processes and outcomes. Thus, just as Resource Dependence Theory forged a connection between the RAP model and the external environment, so the RBV may do the same. What the RBV adds is the element of rivalry among competing firms and the role played by resources internal to the firm in determining competitive outcomes. It draws attention to a resource-based heterogeneity among rivals and to the importance of evaluating a firm's resources in relative terms. It suggests a natural way to tie the RAP model more directly to the performance implications of the processes described in the RAP field studies. One result of this may be to facilitate a better understanding of the normative implications of the RAP model itself.

Numerous points of intersection between the RAP model and the RBV suggest strong complementarities. Both are concerned with sustainability and adaptation in the face of environmental turbulence. Both have an affinity to evolutionary models. Both acknowledge the importance of distributed tacit knowledge in driving strategy. At the same time, the differences between these perspectives are such that it may take time to realize the potential of their synergistic combination.

The impediments to realizing the combinative power of the RAP model and the RBV stem largely from differences in discipline base and field domain. For the most part, the RBV is a theory rooted in economics, whereas the RAP model's disciplinary foundations are more in the realms of sociology and politics. Differences in disciplinary foundation imply differences in associated literatures, knowledge bases, and frames of reference that can impede mutual understanding. The ideological split so often observed between economics and other social sciences may exacerbate this problem.

The RAP model and the RBV are further separated by being on opposite sides of another divide. They address different types of questions, reflecting a division in the domain of the strategy field. In the main, the RBV is oriented toward strategy content and strategy formulation. In contrast, the RAP model is one of strategy process and implementation. Perhaps because of a correlation with underlying disciplinary differences, this division within the strategy field also reflects problematic ideological differences.

Overcoming these barriers is nontrivial. Cross-disciplinary research faces a unique set of challenges, not the least of which is the difficulty in recognizing a synergistic opportunity. In essence, there is a structural hole (Burt 1992) preventing the ready flow of information across the disciplinary, ideological, and domain-based divides separating these two streams of research. What is needed is a bridge to span the structural hole, facilitate the exchange of ideas and information across the divide, and provide access to the untapped realm of productive, mutually beneficial opportunity.

In the spirit of bridging this divide, the main body of this chapter is devoted to suggesting some potentially productive ways to bring the RAP and RBV perspectives together. Appreciating the potential inherent in the underlying complementarities requires some knowledge of both perspectives, however. Accordingly, I begin with a brief description of the Resource-Based View of the Firm for those for whom this theoretical perspective is not familiar.[4]

Understanding the Resource-Based View: An Abbreviated Primer

The Resource-Based View of the Firm sees the firm, at its most elemental level, as a bundle of resources and capabilities (Penrose 1959; Wernerfelt 1984). A key assumption of the RBV is that firms compete on the basis of their resources and capabilities. Differences in the resources and capabilities of rival firms give some firms a competitive advantage over others (Peteraf 1993).

A firm's resources can be classified into three principal types: tangible, intangible, and human resources (Grant 2002). Tangible resources include physical assets such as plant, equipment, and financial resources. Intangible resources include trade secrets, brand equity, and reputation. Human resources include the knowledge base of managers and employees, their collaborative skills, and their social capital.

Capabilities refer to what the firm can do with its resources (Amit and Schoemaker 1993). They are made up of interlocking routines that provide managers with a set of decision options regarding how to deploy the firm's resources (Grant 1991; Winter 2000). Higher-level organizational capabilities, known as 'dynamic capabilities', are of particular interest (Teece, Pisano, and Shuen 1997). Dynamic capabilities are applications that enable the firm to create, extend, or alter other organizational capabilities (Winter 2003).

According to the RBV, strategy is a matter of deploying the firm's resource bundle to meet the needs of the marketplace while blunting the ability of rivals to respond effectively. Thus, resources and capabilities lie at the very heart of business-level strategy. Because valuable resources often can be leveraged across the multiple businesses of a diversified firm, they lie at the heart of corporate-level strategy as well (Collis and Montgomery 1997).

At the business level, researchers have explored the links between resources and sustainable competitive advantage (see e.g. Dierickx and Cool (1989), Barney (1991), and Peteraf (1993)). The focus has been on what makes some resource bundles superior to others and why rivals cannot easily acquire, create, or imitate the better bundles. The answer seems to lie in the characteristics of a subset of resources and capabilities known as 'strategic assets' (Amit and Schoemaker 1993). 'Isolating mechanisms' prevent the ready imitation of these assets by rival firms (Rumelt 1984). Strategic assets, such as a firm's culture, that are socially complex, tacit in nature, and causally ambiguous (ibid.) have attracted particular attention.

At the corporate level, there has also been concern with the question of how strategic assets affect firm performance (Montgomery and Wernerfelt 1988). The effect depends not only on the characteristics of the resources, but also on the firm's coordination and communication mechanisms. These factors enable the firm to leverage its strategic assets across its set of businesses. A firm's performance depends, as well, on the internal consistency among the three elements of its 'corporate strategy triangle'—its resources, its businesses, and its organizational mechanisms, which include its structure, systems, and processes (Collis and Montgomery 1997).

The question of how resources drive and constrain the growth of the firm is another important issue for corporate strategy. Strategic assets, for example, can ease a firm's entry into new markets

(Montgomery and Hariharan 1991). They can provide the direction behind an acquisition strategy as well as guidance regarding internal capital investment decisions.

The growth and continued success of a firm, however, will depend on the development of new resources as well as the exploitation of old ones (Wernerfelt 1984). This is particularly true under changing external conditions. Thus, the RBV also is concerned with issues regarding organizational learning, knowledge accumulation, capability development, and associated evolutionary processes (Helfat 2000). A 'dynamic resource-based view' is emerging that ties together these concerns (Helfat and Peteraf 2003).

As this brief introduction suggests, research that falls under the rubric of the RBV covers a broad swath of terrain. It is applicable to the entire range of strategic decisions that managers face. And while it is oriented primarily to questions regarding strategy content and formulation, there is the potential for much more work to be done on the process side.

In the remainder of this chapter, I provide some suggestions for how the RAP model could be employed to realize some of this potential. Similarly, I show how there could be a reciprocal benefit from importing some of the insights from the RBV into the RAP domain. In combination, each of these research streams stands to gain something of value.

The Resource-Based View and the RAP Model: Signs of Synergies

Managerial Capabilities at Multiple Organizational Levels

One strand of the resource-based view with a synergistic relationship to the RAP model focuses on managerial resources, defined as 'the skills and abilities of managers' (Castanias and Helfat 2001). In brief, this research views the top management of firms as a key resource, critical to a firm in attaining sustainable competitive advantage vis-à-vis its rivals (Castanias and Helfat 1991). It suggests that top managers differ significantly in the quality of their managerial capabilities, including the ability to shepherd firms through periods of change (Adner and Helfat 2003). Those with superior capabilities may generate high financial returns for their firms as well as for themselves.

An insight from the RAP perspective that may enrich the RBV is that the capabilities of middle managers matter as well.[5] Indeed, the RAP model suggests that middle management capabilities may be an even more direct determinant of firm performance. If middle managers drive strategy and initiate strategic change, as the RAP model suggests (Bower 1970; Burgelman 1983), then their influence on firm performance should not be overlooked. By focusing mainly on the top management team, researchers in the RBV tradition may be missing a critical piece of the story regarding how firms achieve and sustain a competitive advantage.

Moreover, the RAP model invites a deeper look at the nature of the skills held by managers at different levels of the firm hierarchy and at the ways in which they differ across levels. Research in the RBV tradition has identified a nested hierarchy of managerial skills (held by top managers) that range in terms of their transferability across firms and industries (Castanias and Helfat 2001). The most transferable are termed 'generic' and comprise those types of high-level general management capabilities applicable to virtually any type of firm in any type of industry setting (Castanias and Helfat 1991). Although all CEOs no doubt have some generic capabilities, those who specialize and excel in generic capability might be best employed as the top managers of unrelated diversified firms or holding companies.

At the other end of the managerial skill spectrum are firm-specific managerial skills. Again, whereas all top managers undoubtedly have some firm-specific skills, some may have a higher quotient of these skills than others. In this case, their skills tie them to their firm, because their skills lose relevance and value outside this setting. The two other categories in the hierarchy, going from least to more transferable, are industry-specific skills and related-industry-specific skills, which are relevant to an entire cluster of industries such as the high-tech cluster (Castanias and Helfat 2001).

By analogy, this type of thinking could be applied to types of skills and the corresponding type of knowledge base held by managers at different levels within the firm. For example, there is likely a similar sort of nested hierarchy of managerial skills to be found at multiple levels within firms. These skills will be associated with different types of knowledge that varies in its level of specificity. They also may be associated with different types of search routines that managers employ in seeking solutions to their problems (Maritan 2001).

The most specific skills and knowledge are found at the operational level, where knowledge regarding a particular technology or set of customers is deepest. Managers at higher organizational levels, in general, have less specific skills and knowledge. Thus, division-specific skills are less specific than operational skills, and business-group-specific skills are even less specific. The corporate skills and knowledge base of the top management team are the least specific of all, relative to that of other types of managers within the firm. This suggests that, within the firm, a nested hierarchy of operational-specific, division-specific, business-group-specific and corporate-specific managerial skills corresponds to the taxonomy of top management skill types referenced above. This new taxonomy, which accords with the work done in the RAP tradition, is suggestive of a possible starting point for jointly inspired research in this area.

Beyond Taxonomies

A resource-based perspective suggests a number of directions for future research that goes well beyond the development of such a taxonomy. For example, the RBV suggests that differences in the quality of managerial skills across firms have implications regarding which firms have winning strategies. If this is so, something similar may operate within the firm as well. That is, managers at the operational and middle level 'compete' to drive strategy—a view consistent with the RAP model (Bower 1970; Burgelman 1983). Those with superior knowledge, skills, and managerial capabilities have an advantage in having their strategies 'selected' internally. A set of questions then emerges about what characterizes 'superior' capabilities at each level of management and how the internal competition process unfolds.

A second set of questions revolves around the specificity of managerial resources and their relative transferability to new domains. Resource-based theory suggests that the more specific a manager's knowledge and skills, the less transferable they are to different domains. Moreover, there may be quasi-rents associated with applying highly specific managerial skills (Castanias and Helfat 1991). What then does this imply about the management of incentive systems and the distribution of rents among the different levels of management? What are the implications for the ability of managers throughout a company to share 'best practices'? What is the best way to generate new strategies in the face of radical change if managerial skills are specific to the old regime? Addressing such RBV-inspired questions in the spirit of the RAP research tradition may yield a new set of insights.

A third set of questions addresses the variations among managerial capabilities at the top. If there is a nested hierarchy of managerial capabilities within firms, as suggested above, then top-level managers may vary in the degree to which they possess more specific types of knowledge and capabilities (Bailey and Helfat 2003). This is a reasonable assumption because many types of career path may lead to the top leadership positions in firms. Moreover, managerial learning is cumulative. Thus, different types of experience and learning opportunities will result in different types of capabilities.

For example, some large diversified firms are run by top-level managers, hired from the outside, who have mainly generic types of managerial capabilities. But others are run by managers who reach their position only after many years of experience within the firm and who bring deep cumulative operational experience to their job. When top-level managers have significant operational and firm-specific experience, they may be able to take a more effective hand in shaping the strategy of a firm—even one that is both large and widely diversified. Thus, a class of firms and managerial types may be quite different from those described by the classic RAP model (Bower 1970; Burgelman 1983). Studying such firms more deeply may provide a new way to extend, enrich, or modify the RAP model in powerful new ways.

Top Management Capabilities Reconsidered: A Case Example

Newell Company, prior to its recent acquisition of Rubbermaid, provides an instructive case example (Collis and Johnson 1994; Montgomery and Gordon 1999). Newell (now known as Newell Rubbermaid) is a diversified manufacturer, distributor, and merchandiser of brand-name staple consumer products, serving the needs of volume purchasers. Despite its significant size (revenues of $3.2 billion prior to its acquisition of Rubbermaid in 1999), Newell was managed for most of its 100-plus year history by a top management team with significant Newell-specific operating knowledge.

How was this possible, given the size and complexity of Newell's operations? The key to this puzzle is that all Newell's lines of business conformed to a common template in terms of their basic nature and the business fundamentals.[6] For example, until recently, all Newell's products involved high-volume, low-cost manufacturing similar enough that three standardized manufacturing systems, developed by Newell, were sufficient to manage them all. Similarly, the products of each of the businesses shared a set of common characteristics, despite superficial differences. As a result of these commonalities, it was possible for Newell to manage the distribution, marketing, and merchandizing of all its products in similar ways, even though separate divisions were responsible for the different types of product lines. Moreover, the products of each of Newell's many businesses were sold to the same set of customers under similar conditions (although, again, under the control of separate divisions).

With respect to the basic RAP model, this is a type of firm that had not yet been observed among RAP-inspired field studies. It suggests an opportunity for additional field study research. The RAP model was developed on the basis of field research conducted within widely diversified firms (Bower 1970; Burgelman 1983). Its elegance stemmed in part from the premise that strategy in such firms cannot be directed from the top, due to a lack of specialized knowledge, and the confirming evidence that strategy is indeed shaped from below by those in command of the specialized knowledge. Even though Bower (1970) and others recognized that the process is likely to differ in functionally integrated firms, Newell is not functionally integrated. It is a multi-division, widely diversified firm that looks not unlike the core RAP field study cases, at least at a superficial level. The Newell case suggests that there are conditions under which top level managers can exhibit higher levels of knowledge specificity, even within large and diversified firms. One task for future research is to explore the nature of and limits to those conditions.

An issue worthy of additional field research, then, is the question of whether the locus and process of strategy-making differs in firms where the top management has significant operating knowledge. However knowledgeable the top management might be, it still will be the case that managers at the operational or business level have even deeper and more specific knowledge. Does this imply that the basic RAP model is still applicable or is some modification required?

Again, the Newell case is instructive. Although the top management at Newell does not have knowledge as specific or as deep as the managers at lower levels in the firm, they have something more—a detailed understanding of how the various businesses in the Newell fold fit together. Indeed, by virtue of their position at the pinnacle of the company, they are the only managers who have the capacity fully to comprehend the nature and extent of these linkages. This knowledge of the cross-linkages is not independent of their operating knowledge. Rather, it is their degree of operating knowledge and their familiarity with the basic nature of each of the businesses within Newell that allow them to comprehend the connections among them.

Whereas this type of knowledge might not be best suited for the origination of strategy at the *business level*, it is very much suited to the determination of *corporate level* strategy. Indeed, competing on the bases of the linkages among a set of businesses is the essence of resource-based corporate strategy (Collis and Montgomery 1997). Thus, at Newell, the top management team is very much engaged in the determination of strategy, but only at the corporate level. Strategy at the business level within Newell is likely still the purview of business-level managers. The basic insight of the RAP model, that strategy originates with those having the most appropriate knowledge base, still holds.

What reconciles the Newell case example with the RAP model is the recognition that different levels of strategy require different types of knowledge. Resource-based *corporate-level* strategy requires knowledge that only comes with a view from the top. Middle-level managers, no matter how talented, are myopic by virtue of the position they occupy within the firm. Their limited view of other parts of the firm and how they fit together restricts their ability to craft a coherent corporate-level strategy. On the other hand, the deep operations-specific and business-specific knowledge of middle managers may make them best suited for crafting a resource-based *business-level* strategy.

The *caveat* is simply that strategy at the business level should remain consistent with the corporate-level strategy for the firm to continue to thrive (Collis and Montgomery 1997). Corporate coherence is an important aspect of corporate strategy. This suggests another role for top management—that of strategic oversight—to ensure that the business- and corporate-level strategies remain aligned.[7] Thus, at Newell, top management does not allow a business unit to redefine itself or to make acquisitions that might change the direction of the business (Collis and Johnson 1994).

In diversified companies like Newell, there is a role for top managers in strategy-making that they are uniquely qualified to play. A resource-based view of corporate strategy makes this clear (Collis and Montgomery 1997.) But is there no such role for the top management of more focused firms? Although the answer is unclear, the resource-based view may provide some guidance.

The Case of Focused Firms

The resource-based view of business-level strategy argues that firms compete on the basis of their resources and capabilities (Wernerfelt 1984). Those with superior resources have a competitive advantage in terms of their ability to create more value than rivals (Peteraf and Barney 2003). But none of this can be realized without a strategy to guide the process.

There are unanswered questions about whether a resource-based strategy can emerge without guidance from the top. An assessment of the value of a firm's resources requires intimate knowledge of the competitive landscape and of the capabilities of the firms' rivals. It requires knowledge of the customers and their demands. It requires an appreciation of the firms' own capabilities, but even more importantly, it requires the wisdom to know the limits of these capabilities. This kind of wisdom and the willingness to follow a well-defined strategy rather than a series of emerging opportunities may be qualities found only at the top levels of firm management. They suggest a reason why top managers play an important role in the determination of strategy in more focused firms.[8]

The Edward Jones Company provides an example (Porter and Bond 1999). Edward Jones is a privately held provider of retail brokerage products and services. Relative to other providers of retail financial services, its strategy is narrow and well-defined, reflecting the distinctive nature of its geographic, knowledge-based, and reputational resources. The close fit between Edward Jones's resources and strategy gives it a unique competitive position in the brokerage industry that has proven to be both profitable for Edward Jones and hard for other firms to imitate.

This strategy is a reflection of the discipline provided by the top management of this firm. In the 1970s, the managing partner of Edward Jones made a conscious decision to offer a limited range of products to a single type of customer, rather than be an all-purpose provider (Bachmann 2002). This strategy was soon codified and helped the firm 'to align its resources to serve one customer one way' (ibid. 62). It provided guidance regarding what the firm should do and, even more critically, what it should not do (Porter 1996).

As this example suggests, top management, even in focused firms, may be best positioned to set the limits to a firm's strategy. Managers at lower levels of the organization may be too prone to see all opportunities as attractive. A study of the focused industry of radio station firms shows that firms face intense pressures to change when strategic shifts occur by others in the industry (Greve and Taylor 2000). Maintaining a focused strategy becomes difficult when competing in dynamic environments. Under these conditions, top managers may be better positioned to make difficult choices wisely. To the extent that a firm's strategy is based on the fit between its resources and a select set of environmental requirements, this may be important (Porter 1996).

Like the Newell case, this case poses some challenges for the RAP model. Although Bower (1970) acknowledged early on that intervention by higher-level managers is key to making sense out of bottom-up initiatives, the role of top managers in initiating and guiding resource-based strategies remains unclear. This case, then, presents some opportunities for additional research to plumb the combinative power of the RAP and RBV perspectives. Field-based studies of the processes deep within such companies as Newell and Edward Jones would be particularly revealing.

Organizational Dynamics and Evolutionary Processes

There are numerous other points of intersection between the RAP model and the RBV that may inspire future research. Research in the RAP and RBV traditions, for example, share a common interest in evolutionary processes. Although RAP takes its inspiration from the work on organizational ecology (Aldrich 1979; Hannan and Freeman 1984), and the RBV is more closely aligned with evolutionary economics (Nelson and Winter 1982), there are more similarities than differences in the underlying models. Accordingly, within both research traditions, there is concern with organizational dynamics and adaptation to a changing environment. Both view variation, selection, retention, and competition as key processes. Both recognize the importance of routines and the role of aspirations in driving change.

The branch of resource-based research that is most concerned with such issues is known as Dynamic Resource-Based Theory (Helfat and Peteraf 2003) and includes work on dynamic capabilities (Teece, Pisano, and Shuen 1997; Winter 2000). Paradoxically, despite its attention to organizational dynamics, work in this area remains oriented more toward the 'content' side of strategy than the 'process' side. What remains insufficiently explored is the nature and development of the very processes at the heart of the theory. Based on field work, this is particularly true with respect to filling in the details at the microprocess level. This presents an opportunity for researchers in the RAP tradition to bring an unprecedented level of richness and detail to the work within RBV. At the same time, it presents an opportunity for resource-based thinking to inform RAP theory regarding the role of critical resources and capabilities (Wernerfelt 1989) in the resource allocation process and in determining strategy.

For example, work by Helfat and Peteraf (2003) posits the existence of capability life cycles, similar to the life cycles observed for products and industries (Kotler 1980; Klepper 1997). This work suggests that the evolution of capabilities follows a strongly path-dependent process that reflects prior experience, an initial starting point, and managerial choice regarding available alternatives. It articulates a general path of capability development that then branches off into one of a several possible directions in response to an internal or external selection event.

Although this work describes a general pattern of events along the capability life cycle, the work is conceptual rather than empirical. Moreover, there are unanswered questions about the nature of the processes themselves. This is where work in the RAP tradition provides a ready complement. Helfat and Peteraf (2003) suggest that internal and external selection events may lead to capability transformation along one of six possible paths. But how do the various types of selection processes affect the determination of the subsequent path? What is the role of different levels of managers in this process? Are there interaction effects between managerial capabilities and the evolutionary trajectory of the capability under study?

These questions and others may be addressed best by in-depth field studies of the sort exemplified by the RAP research stream. There is a need for empirical research at each stage of the capability life cycle. Research observing the entire life-cycle pattern, using a method similar to Burgelman's (1983) study of internal corporate ventures under different stages of development, would make an invaluable contribution. Indeed, Burgelman's (1994) study of the influence of the internal selection environment on the evolution of firm-level sources of distinctive competence is strongly suggestive of the power of this type of approach.

There is also a need for more research that connects the internal processes of firms to external consequences. One example is Taylor's (2004) field study of competing new product development efforts within firms. The results of this study suggest, intriguingly, that resource competition among a firm's middle managers may shift the firm's evolutionary trajectory.

Conclusion

These examples provide only a small sample of the many ways in which the RBV and RAP perspectives can be combined profitably. They illustrate numerous areas of overlapping interest. More significantly, they point to differences that are complementary in nature, suggesting the potential for a synergistic combination. The RAP model's attention to middle management, for example, combined with the RBV's concern with how managerial capabilities affect firm performance suggest that a firm's management development programs may be one of its most important strategic assets. A key role for the top management team, then, is to develop middle-level managerial resources—particularly in firms where middle managers are the ultimate architects of a firm's strategy. Research into the management development process that draws on both the RBV and RAP perspectives would be a worthwhile endeavor. Similarly, a firm's resource-allocation process may itself prove to be a key resource. The very characteristics of such processes—as socially complex, internal to the firm, involving tacit distributed knowledge—are suggestive of isolating mechanisms and a potential source of competitive advantage.

Undoubtedly, in the course of combining RBV with the RAP model, some anomalies will be revealed. Anomaly-seeking research, however, adds value only by exposing the limits to a theory. Complementarity-seeking research adds value by extending a theory's reach. By augmenting the insights, revealing interconnections, and providing missing components, a complementarity-seeking approach to theory development provides a path to more complete, more satisfying theories.

Acknowledgements

For helpful comments, I am indebted to Jake Birnberg, Joe Bower, Robert Burgelman, Clark Gilbert, Connie Helfat, Cathy Maritan, and Alva Taylor.

Endnotes

1. See also Christensen and Raynor (2003).
2. Although, as Gilbert and Christensen point out in Ch. 4, anomalies have been unveiled as well.
3. Maritan's (2001) study of capital investment as a means to maintain, upgrade, or acquire capabilities suggests the power of such a combination.
4. Because this volume is dedicated to the RAP perspective, I assume that no further summary of this research is required in this chapter.
5. Castanias and Helfat (2001) make this general point and suggest that their model of managerial rents can be applied to all levels of management. Work on middle-level managerial capabilities, however, remains an undeveloped area of RBV-inspired research.
6. This was true of Newell for most of its history and was a key part of its strategy. It is no longer true to the same extent, as its more recent acquisitions suggest (Montgomery and Gordon 1999).
7. This is consistent with both Bower's (1970) and Burgelman's (1983) view of the role of top management.

8. This is consistent with Bower's (1970) observation that the resource allocation process is likely to differ in functionally integrated firms from the types of processes that he observed at 'National Products'. Indeed, he suggests that all phases of the resource allocation process are likely to be performed at the top of the hierarchy in such firms.

References

Adner, R., and Helfat, C. (2003). 'Corporate Effects and Dynamic Managerial Capabilities'. *Strategic Management Journal* 24/10: 1011–25.

Aldrich, H. (1979). *Organizations and Environments*. Englewood Cliffs, NJ: Prentice-Hall.

Amit, R., and Schoemaker, P. (1993). 'Strategic Assets and Organizational Rent'. *Strategic Management Journal* 14: 33–46.

Bachmann, J. (2002). 'Competitive Strategy: It's OK to be Different'. *Academy of Management Executive* 16: 61–5.

Bailey, E. E., and Helfat, C. E. (2003). 'External Management Succession, Human Capital, and Firm Performance: An Integrative Analysis'. *Managerial and Decision Economics* 24: 347–69.

Barney, J. B. (1991). 'Firm Resources and Sustained Competitive Advantage'. *Journal of Management* 17: 99–120.

Bower, J. (1970). *Managing the Resource Allocation Process: A Study of Corporate Planning and Investment*. Boston, Mass.: Harvard Business School Press.

Burgelman, R. (1983). 'A Process Model of Internal Corporate Venturing in the Diversified Major Firm'. *Administrative Science Quarterly* 28: 223–44.

—— (1994). 'Fading Memories: A Process Theory of Strategic Business Exit in Dynamic Environments'. *Administrative Science Quarterly* 39: 24–56.

Burt, R. (1992). *Structural Holes: The Social Structure of Competition*. Cambridge, Mass.: Harvard University Press.

Castanias, R., and Helfat, C. (1991). 'Managerial Resources and Rents'. *Journal of Management* 17: 155–71.

—————— (2001). 'The Managerial Rents Model: Theory and Empirical Analysis'. *Journal of Management* 27: 661–78.

Christensen, C. (1997). *The Innovator's Dilemma: When New Technologies Cause Great Firms to Fail*. Boston, Mass.: Harvard Business School Press.

—— and Bower, J. (1996). 'Customer Power, Strategic Investment, and the Failure of Leading Firms'. *Strategic Management Journal* 17: 197–218.

—— and Raynor, M. (September 2003). 'Why Hard-nosed Executives Should Care About Management Theory'. *Harvard Business Review* 81: 66–74.

Collis, D., and Johnson, E. (1994). 'Newell Company: Acquisition Strategy'. Harvard Business School case no. 794-066.

—— and Montgomery, C. (1997). *Corporate Strategy: Resources and the Scope of the Firm*. Boston, Mass.: Irwin.

Dierickx, I., and Cool, K. (1989). 'Asset Stock Accumulation and Sustainability of Competitive Advantage'. *Management Science* 35: 1504–11.

Eisenmann, T. (2002). 'The Effects of CEO Equity Ownership and Diversification on Risk Taking'. *Strategic Management Journal* 23: 513–34.

—— and Bower, J. (2000). 'The Entrepreneurial M-Form: Strategic Integration in Global Media Firms'. *Organization Science* 11: 348–55.

Fama, E. (1980). 'Agency Problems and the Theory of the Firm'. *Journal of Political Economy* 88: 288–307.

Gilbert, C. (2004). 'Change in the Presence of Residual Fit: Competing Frames and the Structure of Dynamic Capabilities'. Harvard Business School Working Paper.

—— and Bower, J. (May 2002). 'Disruptive Change: When Trying Harder is Part of the Problem'. *Harvard Business Review*, 95–101.

Grant, R. (1991). 'The Resource-Based Theory of Competitive Advantage: Implications for Strategy Formulation'. *California Management Review* 33: 114–35.

—— (1996). 'Toward a Knowledge-Based Theory of the Firm'. *Strategic Management Journal* 17: 109–22.

—— (2002). *Contemporary Strategy Analysis* (4th edn). Malden, Mass.: Blackwell.

Greve, H., and Taylor, A. (2000). 'Innovations as Catalysts for Organizational Change: Shifts in Organizational Cognition and Search'. *Administrative Science Quarterly* 45: 54–80.

Hannan, M., and Freeman, J. (1984). *Organizational Ecology*. Cambridge, Mass.: Harvard University Press.

Helfat, C. (2000). 'Guest Editor's Introduction to the Special Issue: The Evolution of Firm Capabilities'. *Strategic Management Journal* 21: 955–9.

—— and Peteraf, M. (2003). 'The Dynamic Resource-Based View: Capability Lifecycles'. *Strategic Management Journal* 24: 997–1010.

Kahneman, D., and Tversky, A. (1984). 'Choice, Values, and Frames'. *American Psychologist* 39: 341–50.

Klepper. S. (1997). 'Industry Life Cycles'. *Industrial and Corporate Change* 6: 145–82.

Kotler, P. (1980). *Principles of Marketing* (3rd edn.). Englewood Cliffs, NJ: Prentice-Hall.

Kuhn, T. (1962). *The Structure of Scientific Revolutions*. Chicago, Ill.: University of Chicago Press.

Maritan, C. A. (2001). 'Capital Investment as Investing in Organizational Capabilities: An Empirically-Grounded Process Model'. *Academy of Management Journal* 44: 513–31.

Montgomery, C., and Gordon, E. (1999). 'Newell Company: Corporate Strategy'. Harvard Business School case no. 799-139.

—— and Hariharan, S. (January 1991). 'Diversified Expansion in Large Established Firms'. *Journal of Economic Behavior and Organization* 71–89.

Montgomery, C., and Wernerfelt, B. (1988). 'Diversification, Ricardian Rents, and Tobin's *q*'. *RAND Journal of Economics* 19: 623–32.

Nelson, R., and Winter, S. (1982). *An Evolutionary Theory of Economic Change*. Cambridge, Mass.: Harvard University Press.

Penrose, E. (1959). *The Theory of the Growth of the Firm*. New York: John Wiley & Sons.

Peteraf, M. (1993). 'The Cornerstones of Competitive Advantage'. *Strategic Management Journal* 14: 179–91.

—— and Barney, J. (2003). 'Unraveling the Resource-Based Tangle'. *Managerial and Decision Economics* 24: 309–24.

Pfeffer, J., and Salancik, G. (1978). *The External Control of Organizations: A Resource Dependence Perspective*. New York: Harper & Row.

Porter, M. (1996). 'What is Strategy?' *Harvard Business Review* (Nov.–Dec.), 74: 61–78.

—— and Bond, G. (1999). 'Edward Jones'. Harvard Business School case no. 700-009.

Rumelt, R. (1984). 'Towards a Strategic Theory of the Firm', in R. Lamb, (ed.), *Competitive Strategic Management*. Englewood Cliffs, NJ: Prentice-Hall, 556–70.

Staw, B., Sandelands, S., and Dutton, J. (1981). 'Threat Rigidity Effects in Organizational Behavior'. *Administrative Science Quarterly* 26: 501–24.

Sull, D. (2002). 'No Exit: Disinvestment and the Failure of the Resource Allocation Process'. Harvard Business School Working Paper.

Taylor, A. (2004). 'Innovation Through Internal Competition: Catabolic Learning in New Product Development'. Working Paper, Tuck School of Business at Dartmouth.

Teece, D., Pisano, G., and Schuen, A. (1997). 'Dynamic Capabilities and Strategic Management'. *Strategic Management Journal* 18: 509–33.

Wernerfelt, B. (1984). 'A Resource-Based View of the Firm'. *Strategic Management Journal* 5: 171–80.

—— (1989). 'From Critical Resources to Corporate Strategy'. *Journal of General Management* 14: 4–12.

Williamson, O. (1975). *Markets and Hierarchies*. New York: Free Press.

Winter, S. (2000). 'The Satisficing Principle in Capability Learning'. *Strategic Management Journal* 21: 981–6.

Winter, S. (2003). 'Understanding Dynamic Capabilities'. *Strategic Management Journal* 24: 991–5.

19

CEO as Change Agent?

Joel M. Podolny

When considered from the vantage of organizational sociology, one of the most intriguing aspects of the Resource Allocation Process (RAP) model is the role it ascribes to the CEO in the initiation of strategic change. In this emergent model of the strategy process, strategic change does not originate with the CEO, but instead percolates up from middle-level managers who are in closer contact with the market than the corporate office. We see this clearly in the case study of GM in Germany in Ch. 1. Louis R. Hughes, chairman of the Opel Vorstand in Germany, recognizes that corporate directives are actually an impediment to the competitive success of GM's Opel brand in Germany. He ignores those directives to pursue a new path, and then gradually persuades the 'higher-ups' through not just logic but emotion that this new path is in fact the correct one.

In the study of Intel in Ch. 3, the initial impetus for strategic change comes from the 'autonomous strategy process', which senior management later 'ratifies'. Granted, this process of ratifying need not be a passive one; ratification implies the alignment of organizational elements behind the newly emerged direction, as when Andy Grove sought to 'vectorize' Intel during Epoch II. Nonetheless, Burgleman appropriates March's (1991) term 'organizational exploitation' to characterize Grove's vectorization of Intel as organizational exploitation, indicating that the initiatives emanating from the CEO are incremental attempts at improved alignment behind a strategic direction toward which the firm is already oriented.[1]

By implication, the CEO's vision and agenda for the firm is an inherently conservative force; it is not the origin of transformational change efforts, but a rationalization of that transformation once it is already recognized as transformational.[2] By further implication, the

CEO should strive to be the symbol of the organization rather than the shepherd of the organization.

Such a view obviously stands in stark contrast to the popular view of a visionary CEO as a guiding agent of change. This view, of course, finds support in the writing of management scholars. For example, Kotter (1990, 1999) sees the successful orchestration of the change process as the defining element of senior leadership. This view also finds support in the biographical treatises of many CEOs, such as Jack Welch at GE or Lou Gerstner at IBM, who came to be regarded as the primary agents of change within their own organizations.

In assigning the CEO a less-than-heroic role in adaptation and change, the RAP model certainly resonates with the sociological literature's long-standing skepticism of the CEO's importance as the impetus behind long-run performance improvements. For example, several decades ago, Stanley Lieberson and James O'Connor (1972) sought to assess how changes in CEO leadership related to performance variation across large corporations. They found that changes in CEO leadership had a small effect compared to environmental changes or variation across industries. Similarly, organizational ecology (Hannan and Freeman 1989; Carroll and Hannan 1999), one of the major paradigms in organizational sociology, always has been extremely skeptical of a senior manager's ability to guide the strategic change process. Finally, within the neo-institutional tradition, Khurana (2002) questions the assumption that a charismatic outsider can be the source of transformational change that will result in significantly enhanced corporate performance.

According to the proponents of the emergent view of the strategy process, the reason that the CEO cannot be the primary driver behind the strategic change process is that the CEO occupies a *structural position* that undercuts the CEO's ability to take a more proactive role. So, in Ch. 1, the CEO of General Motors is not close enough to events in Germany to be able to perceive the opportunities of which Hughes is aware. Moreover, if the CEO chooses to drive a significant change effort based on what is believed to be superior information about new opportunities, the actions of the CEO will not be subject to the same level of scrutiny during the selection process in which good ideas are weeded out from the bad. The backing of the CEO is too powerful an organizational force. Although the fact of change becomes a *fait accompli* when initiated by the CEO, the structural position of the CEO implies that the wisdom and the thoroughness of the change effort are likely to be quite limited.

Though such a view may possess a high degree of theoretical resonance with the sociological literature, it does nonetheless present a dilemma for the CEO who is aware of the need for change and wishes to be an initiator of the change effort. Is it a necessary implication of the RAP model that the CEO must be an inherently conservative force, fostering alignment around an emerged strategy but never being a source for a new strategy's emergence?

In Part III of this book, Noda and Gilbert show the CEO intervening by changing the context of the emergent process. And in Part IV, Eisenmann, Raynor, and Doz describe strategic contingencies that would appear to require direct intervention in substance by the CEO.

Motivated by similar observations of my own, I will answer my question by asserting 'no', the CEO is not inevitably a constraining role, and will sketch a role for the CEO in initiating a strategic change effort that leverages the CEO's network of relations beyond the boundaries of the firm. And I will take the word *sketch* quite seriously. What follows is not a theory but a suggestion that will require future empirical work to either validate, or refine, or reject.

Because of the status granted by the position, the CEO is uniquely able to develop a vast network of relationships beyond the boundary of the organization. The CEO will be sought out by those in the broader environment in a way that others simply will not be. Those in the broader environment may seek out the CEO because they believe the CEO has control over resources or information to which they would like access. They also may seek out the CEO simply because they believe their own stature will be enhanced through affiliation with the CEO. The CEO will be granted entrée to gatherings, meetings, and events that simply are not accessible by others in the organization. Moreover, it seems safe to assume that even before occupying a position atop the formal organizational hierarchy, the CEO will have developed a reasonably expansive contact network. A broad network is critical to the mobility of individuals within the firm, especially as they reach the higher levels of the organization (Burt 1992, 1997).

An illustrative, albeit extreme, example of the reach of a CEO's network is afforded by David Rockefeller when he was head of the Chase Manhattan Bank in the 1970s. As Rockefeller traveled around the world, he developed a wide array of contacts. He and his staff kept a record of these contacts in 'black books', which listed the names of the contacts as well as any important information about those contacts. There were 50,000 names in those black books. In preparation for both meetings and social engagements, Rockefeller's staff would distill a list of individuals who were to be at the upcoming event so that Rockefeller could memorize the relevant names as well as any pertinent information to maintaining the relationships.[3] Obviously not all CEOs have networks that rival Rockefeller's, but the example is illustrative of the scope that a broad network can have. Even if a CEO's network were one-tenth the size of Rockefeller's, such a network would no doubt contain ideas, insights, and information that could be of tremendous value for the direction of the firm.

More systematic information on the size of a typical CEO's network is increasingly easy to obtain because of the prevalence of the electronic address books associated with e-mail programs or on-line social networking software. For example, Fig. 19.1 presents the number of contacts for 240 CEOs who are members of the *Spoke Software* open network.[4] The information is based on the number of unique contacts that can be extracted from each CEO's e-mail. Because the CEO is likely to have a number of contacts with whom he or she does not exchange e-mail, these numbers are clearly conservative estimates of network size. As Fig. 19.1 demonstrates, the size distribution follows an exponential curve. The median size is 2,021, the mean size is 3,795,

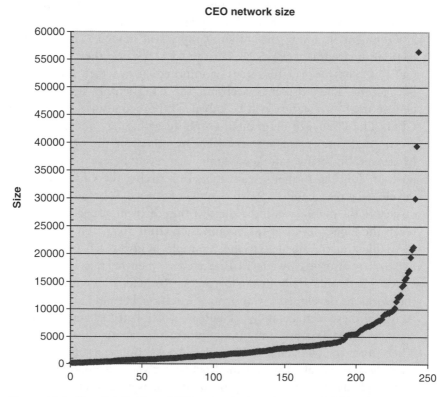

Figure 19.1 Size distribution of CEO networks based on e-mail addresses
Source: Spoke Software (www.spoke.com) network as of 9 February 2004.

and one individual in the database has a network size of 56,381—slightly larger than the reported size of Rockefeller's. The conservative nature of these numbers is underscored by the fact that twelve of the CEOs in the database have e-mail networks of less than 250; no doubt their personal networks are much larger. Moreover, if one realizes that the thousands of individuals in a typical CEO's network have their own networks on which they can draw for information and resources, then the CEO's direct and indirect reach is obviously quite considerable.

On first consideration, the existence of an expansive network would seem to challenge the claim that the CEO lacks the knowledge to initiate a new strategic direction for the firm. A broad array of contacts would seem to present the CEO with a breadth of information, yielding insight regarding new directions. However, the obvious problem is that breadth like that revealed in Rockefeller's network necessarily comes at the expense of depth. The time required to maintain a vast network almost necessarily interferes with a thorough screening of good ideas from the bad. Moreover, when the formal authority of the CEO is enacted through assigning people and rewards to positions, those within the organization will have a strong incentive to provide the CEO with 'good news' and a disincentive to provide the CEO with 'bad news', further inhibiting the CEO's ability to decide whether the organization has the capability to act in a timely fashion on an apparently promising strategic direction. Thus, if we consider the CEO in isolation, the existence of such ties seems to present the CEO with a 'Catch-22'. Although the CEO is uniquely positioned to receive the information that could help to pave the way for future strategic directions for the firm, the CEO is unable to discriminate among the information received.

The solution to this Catch-22 requires that one not consider the CEO in isolation, but in the context of variation-selection-retention processes that are at the heart of organizational learning. If we conceive of the CEO's network as a source of variation and not selection, then there is a way out of this Catch-22. Rather than viewing the network as a source of information allowing the CEO to engage in the selection process, the CEO can view the network as a source of variation providing input for those further down in the organization to discriminate among opportunities. In playing broker between those outside and inside the organization, the CEO needs to be careful not to imply the endorsement of any particular relationship. Were the CEO to do otherwise, the CEO would necessarily be involved in selection among alternative change initiatives rather than in the generation of variation.

To illustrate the point more clearly, consider the example of Sir John Browne, CEO of British Petroleum. Shortly after becoming CEO of

British Petroleum, Browne was offered a position on the board of Intel. By virtue of being on this board, Browne was able to observe an organization that, like BP, was in a commodity business and yet was in a much more volatile and competitive environment. Anticipating that the oil industry could face similar volatility in the future, Browne figured that his position on the board would yield information on how a firm in a commodity business could deal most effectively with volatility. There are two ways in which Browne could respond to the information. On the one hand, he could start to make internal resource commitments based on his own evaluation of the lessons that Intel's experience provides for BP. On the other hand, he could develop an awareness of and relationships with those individuals who could provide others in his organization with information they might find useful.[5]

Before concluding this brief sketch, it is worth reflecting on the differences between the way in which the CEO and the way in which a middle manager such as Hughes ought to use his or her network in the context of strategic change. The network of the middle manager has political as well as informational significance for the change effort. Not only does the middle manager rely on a network for information about opportunities, the middle manager must rely on this network to build an internal coalition to drive the change efforts considered appropriate. In contrast, the structural position of the CEO necessitates a downplaying of the political facet of the network. To the extent that the CEO comes from within the organization suggests that an important challenge for the CEO is the 'depoliticization' of the network. In effect, the network needs to evolve as the CEO's position within the organization changes.

What does depoliticization of a network mean? The sociological literature seems to provide some guidance here. A diverse array of work (Burt 1992; Padgett and Ansell 1993; Fernandez and Gould 1999) points to the fact that an individual has a more multifaceted and therefore less politicized identity when his or her network spans across otherwise disconnected individuals and groups. Thus, unlike the middle manager, whose political strength typically depends on knitting together a coalition in pursuit of a particular objective, the CEO should seek to develop a network that spans across disconnected individuals, group, and organizational boundaries. Figure 19.2 depicts the structural difference with a highly stylized example of the distinction to which I am referring. On the left is the network of a CEO, who is the central node of what would otherwise be disconnected groups. Significantly, the CEO is not more strongly tied to one clique than another. Such a network

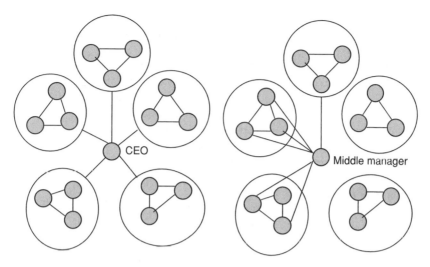

Figure 19.2 Stylized examples of networks

position contrasts with that of the middle manager on the right side of Fig. 19.2, who has much stronger ties into some cliques and a lack of ties to others. Depoliticization thus implies not simply a shift in one's demeanor; it implies a change in the pattern of one's network.

Even though these thoughts obviously require further development, they suggest a way in which a network perspective on organizations can be integrated with an emergent view of the strategy process to make sense of the role of the CEO in initiating strategic change. Additional research is clearly needed to assess whether such integration does indeed advance our understanding of the resource allocation process within organizations.

Endnotes

1. Although I follow others and refer to the emergent model of the strategy process as the RAP model, it is worth acknowledging some differences in the way that Bower and Burgelman approach the role of the CEO. Bower assigns the CEO with some responsibility at least to set a context in which strategic change is a possibility. For example, in the General Motors case, Bower draws attention to such organizational details as the fact that Jack Smith asked Hughes: 'What are you going to do about East Germany?' One could point to similar details in the Intel case, most notably Gordon Moore's blessing of Ted Hoff's decision to buy back the rights to the microprocessor. However, whereas such acts engendered the context for strategic change, they can hardly be said to imply the vision or agenda for

change. Thus, there are some differences; both Bower and Burgelman clearly adopt an emergent view, in which the content of the change is bottom-up.

2. This view of the CEO in guiding strategic change harks back to a quote of a former dean at the Stanford Graduate School of Business. When asked how one leads the faculty, he replied: 'I look at the way the faculty is headed, and then I run really hard to get out in front.' Although such an image is obviously not reflective of the discipline or effort necessary to promote the alignment of organizational elements, it does nonetheless seem to convey the sense in which the CEO is not the driving force behind strategic change efforts, but is a ratifier of a change effort that has moved through the organization.

3. This information was reported on the PBS series *Bill Moyers' Journal* in an episode entitled 'The World of David Rockefeller', which aired on 7 February 1980.

4. Spoke Software (www.spoke.com) is one of a number of emerging social networking companies that use information from an individual's e-mail address book to provide the individual with information about his or her network.

5. See *British Petroleum (B): Focus on Learning* (Case IB16B), available from Harvard Business School Press, for more information on learning at British Petroleum.

References

Burt, R. S. (1992). *Structural Holes: The Social Structure of Competition*. Cambridge, Mass.: Harvard University Press.

——(1997). 'The Contingent Value of Social Capital'. *Administrative Science Quarterly* 42/2: 339–65.

Carroll, G. R., and Hannan, M. T. (1999). *The Demography of Corporations and Industries*. Princeton, NJ: Princeton University Press.

Fernandez, R. M., and Gould, R. V. (1999). 'A Dilemma of State Power: Brokerage and Influence in the National Health Policy Domain'. *American Journal of Sociology* 99/6: 1455–91.

Hannan, M. T., and Freeman, J. (1989). *Organizational Ecology*. Cambridge, Mass.: Harvard University Press.

Khurana, R. (2002). *Searching for a Corporate Savior: The Irrational Quest for Charismatic CEOs*. Princeton, NJ: Princeton University Press.

Kotter, J. P. (1990). *A Force For Change: How Leadership Differs from Management*. New York: Free Press.

——(1999). *What Leaders Really Do*. Boston, Mass.: Harvard Business School Press.

Liebersen, S., and O'Connor, J. F. (1972). 'Leadership and Organizational Performance: A Study of Large Corporations'. *American Journal of Sociology* 37/2: 117–30.

March, J. G. (1991). 'Exploration and Exploitation in Organizational Learning'. *Organization Science* 2/1: 71–87.

Padgett, J. F., and Ansell, C. (1993). 'Robust Action and the Rise of the Medici'. *American Journal of Sociology* 98: 1259–319.

Part VI

Conclusion

20

A Revised Model of the Resource Allocation Process

Joseph L. Bower and Clark G. Gilbert

Introduction

In the thirty-five years since the first field research was conducted at
National Products, we have learned a great deal about how companies
allocate scarce resources to craft corporate strategy. We have presented
and discussed many important contemporary contributions to our
understanding of the resource allocation process (RAP) by authors
who have built upon the RAP model. The working theory that continues to bind this collective research remains consistent: the way
resources are allocated in the firm shapes the realized strategy of the
firm. The fundamental implication of this theory is that understanding
RAP is at the heart of understanding how strategy is made and how to
craft better strategy.

In this final chapter, we discuss the evolution of RAP research and
relevant questions that remain to be considered. We also discuss
important connections to other research streams and the contributions
of the commenting authors. Two broad conclusions can be drawn from
this collective work: first, the processes that lead to strategic outcomes
are remarkably stable even as environments shift. A wide range of
identified forces lends a conservative bias to the way an organization
uses its resources in the face of external changes. Second, despite
remarkable complexity, many of these forces can be managed if they
are understood. Later in the chapter, we revisit the structure of the
RAP model itself. The process of reviewing more than thirty-five years
of work has led us to conclude that it is possible to simplify and advance
the model by replacing the Bower–Burgelman models with a model
consisting of two related processes that are affected by a wide range of

forces—some under the direct control of management and some external to the firm.[1] Finally, we reflect on a new set of questions suggested by the observations reported in the foregoing chapters. We close this chapter and the book with our thoughts about how those questions might be explored in future research.

The Broad Conclusions

The Persistence of Process   In order to understand the observed conservative bias in the resource allocation process, it helps to recognize the inertia that builds up in the bottom-up process. Consider, for example, the original observations described in Bower's 1970 study. At that time, internal cash flow funded most of the capital spending by large corporations. For such companies, the aggregate consequence of their commitment of internal cash flows was their strategy. For those companies whose systems drove capital towards projects with high forecasted NPV, bottom-up forces shaped strategy to a startling degree.

For some time, however, companies have been aware that spreading resources in some formulaic fashion across all divisions was poor corporate strategy. To achieve strategic dominance in a particular line of business, focus was necessary, but one could not focus everywhere at once. This led companies to develop systems for allocating resources to businesses rather than projects. Despite improved conceptualization of the management challenge, viewed in retrospect and with important exceptions, efforts to upgrade the role of the corporate office remained remarkably bureaucratic. Burgelman's original study, conducted more than a decade after Bower's, still emphasized the power of bottom-up forces. Indeed, his most important later insight was that the structural and strategic contexts were so powerful that they may be viewed as an ecological selection process. In his chapter in this book, that process is complemented by an external selection process, but the metaphor is still ecological selection—slow and powerful.

Later research revealed that structural and strategic context are not the only forces that direct the bottom-up dynamics of resource allocation. In Ch. 4, Gilbert and Christensen map the way successive scholars have used the observation of anomalies in the resource allocation process to identify other sources of influence—some external, some internal. Christensen and Bower show how powerful customers can effectively capture the resource allocation process. Noda and Bower, as well as Sull, describe the powerful impact of the capital markets. Gilbert's research indicates that even when structural and

Table 20.1 *Forces that shape the bottom-up process*

Internal forces	External forces
Structural context	Customers
Strategic context	Capital markets
Cognitive frames	

strategic context remains unchanged, different cognitive frames can lead to very different definition and selection processes. The internal and external forces that shape the bottom-up process in RAP are summarized in Table 20.1.

Despite Christensen and Noda documenting the way customers and capital markets shaped resource allocation in the early 1990s, only recently have we begun to model these forces as separate influences that shape definition and impetus. How to conceptualize this influence is the subject of the next section of this chapter. For now, we conclude by noting that structural and strategic context, as well as cognitive frames, customers, and capital markets, can produce a strong conservative bias on the types of project that are defined and selected in the firm.

Overcoming the Persistence of Process   Although much of the research discussed in this book suggests that a persistence of process produces a deep conservative bias, a considerable amount of work also indicates that managers drive change by modifying internal forces that shape the bottom-up processes of definition and impetus. Beginning with his RAP research, Bower recognized that definition and impetus could be managed directly. By changing the structural context—the organization, information systems, and incentives—changes in these bottom-up processes could be effected. Burgelman, Noda, and Gilbert each can be interpreted as showing how changes in the strategic context and cognitive framing produce changes in the bottom-up aspects of definition and impetus.

Recent research also indicates how managers can harness the influence of external forces in order to drive change in the bottom-up process. This is accomplished by modifying the structural and strategic context to change selectively the effect of customers and capital markets on operating management. Christensen, for example, suggests that the capture of impetus by important customers can be mitigated if top management separates the unit dealing with disruptive technology from the structural context of the parent organization. Gilbert confirms that separation can alter patterns of resource commitment, but also shows how it can reshape the definition process itself. Sull showed how Firestone's CEO used capital market pressure to prevent the bottom-up processes from blocking divestment.

Most of these studies describe efforts where senior managers guide bottom-up processes by managing the internal and external forces that shape definition and impetus. There are, however, cases where senior management must override the bottom-up process altogether. Eisenmann's research suggests structural and strategic context sometimes have such a tight grip on the bottom-up process that senior management is forced to circumvent the existing system altogether. In situations such as this, managing context or cognitive frames is not enough to drive the needed change.

In citing research from the 1990s, we do not imply that these studies discovered a new entrepreneurial energy among corporate leaders eager to respond quickly to the need for innovation. Indeed, in 1976 Burgelman studied new venture divisions, and two of Bower's 1967 case studies described as new ventures. What is different today is the sophistication in thinking that contemporary efforts represent and the development of information and control systems that facilitate flatter organizations and improved strategic discussion. In contemporary well-managed companies, it is likely that business unit managers will discuss their strategy with the chief executive and his team with some frequency. Both groups of managers know that, if they are to survive, some initiatives have to be funded and measured as *ventures*.[2] These venture businesses will not satisfy short-term routine performance metrics when considered in competition with well-established businesses. Nonetheless sometimes only projects that meet the metrics of the existing business are funded. But when this is the case, it is often with explicit management recognition that this pattern of resource allocation is shortsighted, even if apparently necessitated by powerful forces in the market for the company's shares. Noda's description of US West is a good example of how this kind of decision making plays out over time.

A Revised Model

In reviewing the research as it has evolved, we propose that the simplest picture of resource allocation that captures the reported behavior is one in which two distinct processes work in parallel—sometimes interacting, sometimes not. One process is focused on the content of strategic thinking from the very broad to the very concrete. In the

Bower and Burgelman models, this process is called *definition*. The other process is focused on the choice of projects and business plans to propose, to sponsor, and to approve funding. Called impetus by Bower, *selection* is probably more intuitive, although it risks confusion because Burgelman uses the phrase more comprehensively than is our intent.

It is important to understand how this conceptualization differs from the original RAP model and Burgelman's modification. As presented in Ch. 2, and shown below, Bower presented a model in which there were three processes: definition, impetus, and structural context. Structural context was discussed as the primary force shaping the content of projects and the provision of impetus leading to commitment. The aggregate of commitments was the revealed strategy. Burgelman then focused much of his attention on the way in which business units could have an autonomous effect on corporate strategic thought that in turn affected definition and impetus. To articulate his observation graphically, Burgelman added a fourth column to the matrix called *strategic context*. RAP was influenced by both structural and strategic context (see Fig. 20.1).

As noted earlier, subsequent research identified other distinct forces that affected the bottom-up processes within RAP (see Table 20.1). Some of these forces were internal and under the direct control of managers. Other forces were external, not under direct management control; but if understood, they could be harnessed by manipulating the structural and strategic context or by exploiting them directly. Our conclusion is that when modeling RAP, it is most helpful to identify these sets of influencing forces as separate from the processes they influence. Initial efforts in this direction can be seen in the research of Sull and Gilbert.

In our simplified model there are two core activities in RAP, definition and selection. Activity can occur across multiple levels of management and can develop in either a bottom-up or top-down manner. The internal and external forces that influence definition and selection are then presented as separate from rather than parallel to the processes

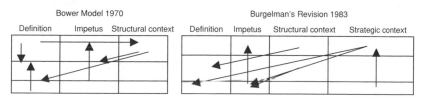

Figure 20.1 Bower model (1970) compared to Burgelman's revision (1983)

they shape. Graphically they are placed in a box outside of definition and selection, but the essence is to think of them as exogenous to the model. Repeated iterations of definition and selection result in the realized strategy of the firm. The revised model is presented in Fig. 20.2.

The revised model retains the attributes of the original models in that the process remains multilevel, simultaneous, and dynamic. Similarly, definition and selection processes continue to comprise the central components of resource allocation. There are, however, four key revisions. First, we have formally identified the set of forces that influence definition and selection as separate from the processes they shape. Second, we have included forces beyond Bower and Burgelman's structural and strategic context. For some time, scholars have struggled to fit these forces into the structure of the original model. Like the increasing use of epicycles to rationalize a heliocentric model of the universe, efforts to expand the RAP model to include customers, capital markets, and cognitive frames without modeling them as separate from the processes they shaped have led to increasingly complicated models. Though less dramatic than a Copernican breakthrough, these revisions not only simplified the model, they improved our understanding of how the entire process works.

The third key revision is the formal inclusion of a firm-level outcome: the resource allocation process leads to the realized strategy of the firm. Although a high-level vision of realized strategy was recognized in Bower's 1970 research, subsequent studies often focused on resource commitment as the dependent variable. The model was used

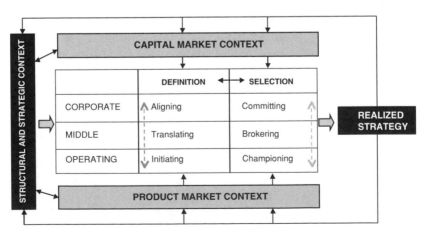

Figure 20.2 A revised model of resource allocation

to predict or explain whether resources would or would not be committed to a venture, existing business, or acquisition. Certainly, the selection process is concerned with resource commitment. But the outcome of the resource allocation process (which includes definition, selection, and the forces that shape these sub-processes) is *realized strategy*. That link is now acknowledged explicitly.

Finally, the revised model acknowledges important interactions not originally included in the modeling process, but reflected in key observations from recent work. The most visible interaction is the feedback loop from realized strategy back on the forces that shape definition and selection as well as the sub-processes themselves. This captures the iterative nature of RAP first described by Noda and Bower. In their study, they tried to model iteration by using the model to map organizational observations presented over sequential time periods. Other interactions are also recognized in the revised model, including: the interaction between structural and strategic context described by Burgelman; the observation in Christensen and Bower that structural and strategic context can shape how an organization responds to customers and capital markets; and Gilbert's observation that cognitive frames can be embedded in the structural and strategic context. Recognizing these interactions explicitly provides a more accurate picture of the complexity involved.

Although each of the four revisions reflects a significant addition to the model, note also that the sub-processes of definition and selection remain fairly robust. Because of their importance to the model, we conclude by reviewing these two critical sub-processes in an effort to clarify their relationship to realized strategy.

Definition. The process of definition originates from a basic problem-solving requirement in the firm. The beginning of projects or plans starts with a discrepancy—perhaps more complicated than that envisaged by Cyert and March (1963) but still a gap between where the business or the corporation is positioned and where its leadership believes it needs to be. At the operating level, these gaps can be very crude: sales exceed capacity; best practice surveys reveal that costs exceed industry standard; intimate customer relations reveal that a competitor will soon have remarkably superior quality. At the corporate level, the gap can take the form of harsh criticism of financial performance from the board of directors or powerful discomfort based on careful study of technology or industry trends. Each phase of the process of definition can occur at any of the levels of management in the firm. A plan must be initiated by exploring the technical, financial, and market characteristics in detail. The plan then is translated to other levels of the organization. Sometimes this is upward to middle management, but it also can be downward if the plan was initiated at the corporate level. Finally, the plan or project must be adjusted to align with the corporate strategy, or that strategy must evolve to fit with the plan.

Interestingly, in the new formulation, the definition process takes on new importance, reflecting the attention paid in recent studies to the content of strategy. Once Gilbert showed the interaction between framing and resource commitment, this balanced approach was an obvious consequence. As noted above, almost every study presented in this volume tries to explain why resources were or were not allocated to a specific proposal. Burgelman explains how resources moved from DRAMs to microprocessors at Intel. Christensen, Noda, and Eisenmann use the model to explain why resources were denied to certain businesses. Sull uses the model to explain why continued allocation of resources blocks exit from a business. Following Bower's original focus, these studies take the allocation of resources to be the key outcome variable.

And yet, a careful review of the research reveals that RAP is more than just the allocation of resources. Because it results in the realized strategy of the firm, RAP also includes the way plans are defined and the manner in which resources are actually deployed. The mechanisms by which definition and impetus interact were subjected to detailed study in Gilbert's analysis of newspaper organizations' response to the emergence of digital media. Previous research by Christensen and Bower concluded that the power of existing customers would act to block resources to the new technology (selection). Gilbert's research revealed that a perception of a threat could help overcome the pull of existing customers, thus enabling aggressive resource commitment even in the absence of current customer demand. Unfortunately, the realized strategy was still problematic as the new-found resources were deployed using product concepts and business models that were developed in the established newspaper business (definition). Despite solving the resource commitment problem, the strategy problem still persisted.

The observed anomaly helps reveal the significance of the definition process in shaping the realized strategy of the firm. Because previous studies were so focused on the actual allocation of resources, they often failed to isolate the unique importance of definition. Gilbert's study made clear that realized strategy is the result of both selection *and* definition. His research also highlights an interesting aspect in the way definition and selection interact. In some of the newspaper companies studied, the definition process that allowed a flexible strategy did not provide adequate resources and selection failed. And yet, a definition process that enabled selection to proceed produced a very rigid strategy.

The same interaction of definition and selection can be observed in other research. For example, Noda showed how definition continues to shape selection long after the initial commitments are made. Future research that explores carefully the interaction of definition and selection should yield valuable insight and new research opportunities.

Selection. In even the most contemporary research, the phases of selection are not described very differently from the original 1970 model. Despite revolutions in organizations and systems, three essential steps appear quite stable. To begin, someone has to be willing to announce and promote 'a good idea'. The more original or innovative an idea, the more important it is for it to have an energetic champion. Championing capacity expansion when sales needs are unmet or lowering costs when R&D has demonstrated that they can be lowered may seem easy if vital. But champions must assemble effective arguments as they seek support from the general managers in the middle who are responsible for the large chunks of business into which major corporations are organized. These managers function as the company's internal merchant bankers, carefully assessing the prospects of proposed investments for profitability and risk and backing those they bless in whatever forums—finance committee, board, or otherwise—the company uses to commit strategic resources: capital, expenses, key talent. The process of committing large sums or key resources inevitably requires at least formal corporate approval whether or not the commitment is already a reality.

Like the process of definition, selection is also a multilevel process, and its activities can develop at each level of the firm. The level in the organization at which a company deals with a type of issue can vary greatly (even within the same company) depending on how it is perceived by management. If a challenge is widely perceived in the company as within the capabilities and charter of a successful operating business unit, the leaders of that unit usually will frame and select the plan for meeting that challenge. In contrast, if the unit is thought to be poorly managed or the challenge is considered quite foreign, top management may well become involved in definition as well as selection.

For example, championing the outsourcing of an historically core function of the company takes great skill and inevitably means enlisting the support of one of the key leaders of the company. Intel's exit from the semiconductor memory business is a classic example. Intervention by the two most senior managers of the company was required to reallocate virtually one-third of the company's R&D budget away from memory even after operating units were deriving 96 per cent of revenues from other lines of business. Identifying and implementing the acquisition of a new line of business or a new geographic market position or turning a disruptive technology into a new business are tasks that test the skills of the best top managements. Usually, the selection processes of multibusiness firms reject these changes. This is why it is so important to recognize that the selection process occurs at all levels of the organization, even the operating levels. The research presented in this book presents numerous examples where operating managers have held significant power over the selection process. In this sense, realized strategy can be determined by selection processes deep in the operating levels of the firm. Christensen's and Gilbert's reports of lower-level managers denying operating time and attention to new projects are representative of this general phenomenon.

Using the Model to Explore Strategic Change

We can illustrate the model's form by using it to consider what is involved when a management team seeks to drive strategic change. The ability to manage ongoing operations with competitive vigor while simultaneously driving innovation that undermines those same operations is rare. It is hard enough to meet the demands of existing customers who seek improved products and lower prices. One's employees are never exactly what one would wish; the economic environment shifts in unanticipated ways; and then there are shocks like the collapse of the Soviet empire. It takes enormous effort and concentration to compete. And it is exactly that concentration that makes it hard to take a detached look at new opportunities or threats.

Michael Tushman calls organizations that can handle both the problems of extension and renewal 'ambidextrous' (Tushman and O'Reilly 1996). Richard Foster and Sarah Kaplan (2001) speak of creative destruction, Schumpeter's term (1934), because successful innovation by a company necessarily requires destruction of business activity thought by its management to be successful and essential. Burgelman speaks of Blue and Green activity at Intel. Helfat and Peteraf (2003) describe the 'capability to develop capabilities'. Our two-process model helps us understand in more detail what kind of management activity is actually required. The story of the Aurora project at Teradyne will help to make the model clear:

In 1998, Teradyne was a leading manufacturer of semiconductor test equipment. Their products made it possible for chip producers such as Intel to test the performance of each of the millions of microprocessors made before they were sold. This required test equipment that operated at higher speeds and with more reliability than the microprocessors themselves. The Teradyne equipment relied on special chips that would not change performance as high-speed functions raised their temperature. They also used proprietary UNIX software. Teradyne's CEO noted that changes in material technology and software made it likely that much cheaper chips and Windows NT software would permit the development of far cheaper, if initially inferior, testers. In a series of strategic discussions over a period of two years, the CEO and his division heads agreed that this was potentially a serious opportunity, but nothing was done. The divisions were preoccupied with the challenge of competing for leadership in the next generation of equipment and capturing the business of the leading customers in the market.

Finally, when the CEO met an engineer who understood the new technology, he hired him as a consultant to Teradyne to develop a prototype chip. When it appeared that the project would be successful and his division heads still would not pick up the new idea, he set up an independent venture called Aurora led by an engineer that had been working for him in another capacity. Aurora reported directly to a board made up of two top corporate officers, the key division officer who had passed on the opportunity and the venture's leader and top engineer. A business plan was written calling for the penetration of two markets where Teradyne was not active, micro-controllers and ASICs. It was approved, but its funding was cut by a third.

Board discussions involved constant requests by the CEO and the vice-chair that the Aurora team focus on one market and devote resources to understand customer needs in that market. Later, when sales of test equipment slowed, headcount was frozen across the company including the Aurora venture. With staffing below levels in the plan, venture management finally found it necessary to focus. For that purpose, further discussion with key potential customers revealed that the micro-controller market offered a better chance of success. This enabled product design to gain traction and eventually spectacular success.

In another instance, the CEO found that despite the choice to use Windows NT, the Aurora team continued to rely on routines appropriate to a UNIX environment. He subsequently sent the venture management to a software start-up that was acclimated to operating in Windows environments. The team discovered that off-the-shelf catalogue-sourced software was available and that they could buy Aurora's key calculating engine for some $300 (far below the cost of an in-house development). This discovery was one of several key steps in developing a cost structure for the product that fit the requirements of potential microprocessor customers.

In still another corporate intervention, the team was required to present its technical progress monthly to Teradyne's main technical community. When after six months it became apparent that the project would succeed, the main operating divisions began to work with the new developments to meet needs of their markets. Eventually, Aurora was a huge success and its technology widely adopted by the other divisions.

Why did the CEO have to create Aurora when the operating divisions acknowledged the importance of the project? Why did the CEO have to limit Aurora's resources in order to get its management to focus? Why did the CEO have to get them to visit a start-up to get them to use Windows NT differently from UNIX?

Notice that the first part of the story is all about selection. The division officers could acknowledge that the new chip technology might be important, but it was not important enough to their specific business to warrant a reallocation of their best talent. Their perception of priority was shaped by their customers' needs exactly as Christensen describes. They wanted more high-end performance, not low cost. It was the CEO who took very seriously the risk to the enterprise if the new technology would become viable. This framing of the problem was reinforced by structural context—budgeting and incentive systems focused on making money in a highly cyclical, high-fixed-cost business. It was the CEO who used scarce resources to recruit a technical consultant and assign a key engineer from his staff to lead Aurora.

But, as observed in Gilbert's research, solving the selection challenge does not preclude recurring problems in the definition process. This is true especially as the resource allocation process iterates over time. Note that when the Aurora team went to work on software, they did it with routines inherited from management of UNIX projects. It was the CEO who knew from his network that NT could be handled differently.[3] His intervention led to a redefinition.

Most interesting is the challenge of getting the team to focus. When he visits our classes at the Harvard Business School, students often ask Teradyne's CEO, 'Why didn't you just tell them to focus. Why deny them resources'? His answer is always 'then they could blame me. This way, *they* had to figure out how to meet the needs of a new customer.'

Aurora's manager explained that he initially saw the problem as meeting the objectives laid out in his business plan. That meant serving a market of a fairly large size. Limiting his resources forced him to choose and, in the process, required him to learn more about customer-specific needs, which in turn shaped the detailed definition of the product specifications.

Note that in this instance, the corporate leaders were committed to using funds to explore a disruptive strategic threat, but they used the selection process to drive different outcomes in the definition process.[4] The power of the selection process drove redefinition in a way that they were unable to achieve through numerous discussions. Scarce resources made it impossible to follow routines that new customers, new suppliers, and the start-up they visited eventually taught them were inappropriate.

Though the case is presented here very briefly, it dramatically illustrates the powerful interaction of definition and selection. The traditional emphasis on selection focuses the role of senior management on the allocation of funds. In the language of economists, the top executives manage the internal market for capital. Their knowledge and experience are somehow not part of the detail of definition except as interference, or as the source of corporate strategy. But as the Teradyne case illustrates, and as Podolny argues in Ch. 19, top management has access to substantive strategic content that may be of high value to the process of definition. And, that knowledge can be expressed through selection as well as through the corporate phase of definition.

The Road Ahead

One of the major goals of this book was to step back from over thirty-five years of research on the resource allocation process and assess where we have come and how the work fits together. Throughout, there is considerable evidence to support the original theory that the way resources are allocated determines a firm's revealed strategy. We also saw recurring evidence that the resource allocation process shows signs of conservative bias, shaped by forces both internal and external to the firm. Absent skillful intervention by management, these forces can become almost deterministic. Intervention can be used to drive changes in the bottom-up process, or circumvent the entire system altogether. But whether it is reframing context or directly intervening in the definition and selection process, change is not likely to occur without active management.

We hope these findings will have impact on three sets of readers. First, future scholars studying the resource allocation process can benefit from the integrative learning presented in this book and can use the revised model for future inquiry. At a certain level, there is a contribution simply in the effort to consider the collective work and build toward a common language set and integrative model. We also have shown how anomaly-seeking research has led to new insights captured in the revised model. This process has led to a series of emerging research questions that offer new opportunities for future RAP scholars. We list four briefly:

• *Interaction between definition and selection.* It is only recently that research has illuminated the interaction between the processes of definition and selection. Efforts to explore and specify the interactions with more detail should present opportunities for understanding the management of strategy content when markets or technologies remain ambiguous. Teradyne is a useful example of how corporate managers can use selection processes to drive definition outcomes that are not immediately obvious.

• *Contingencies for corporate intervention.* Another area of high potential for future research is the development of a contingent model of corporate intervention—when to restore bottom-up processes through manipulation of the structural and strategic context, when to seize the definition or selection process in a top-down effort. One interesting set of contingencies is provided by Eisenmann's work on the effects of high environmental turbulence and quantum investments. A broader contingent model could be very valuable.

• *Considering Different Types of Resource Decisions.* A third consideration is whether all types of resource allocation decisions fit the model. We saw in Sull's research the need for top-down intervention in divestment decisions. Eisenmann's research produced similar findings for extremely large investments in turbulent markets. When should the process be captured more or less completely by top management? One might ask other questions: Is the task of managing the allocation of talent different than that of the allocation of financial resources? Are other resources such as time and attention always consistent with the model? And, in what way are operating budgets different from capital budgets?

• *Performance Studies.* A fourth area that is emerging in the more recent research is the linking of RAP outcomes to performance. As the RAP paradigm has developed, our ability to measure elements of the process has improved. This has allowed the research to move beyond the description of phenomena and become increasingly predictive. In some studies, we have seen these predictive elements emerge in large sample research designs (Eisenmann 2002; Gilbert 2001). More studies of this nature are needed.

We also hope a second set of scholars outside of the RAP research tradition will be influenced by this work. For scholars who have not considered the implications of strategic process, we hope that this book yielded insight into the 'black box' of strategy making. Reported here are details from dozens of firms involved in more than ten in-depth, field-based studies of how a firm's strategy develops. Understanding this process is key for studying the work of general managers no matter which discipline is applied. Understanding RAP also provides a common context for collaboration across disciplines. For example, recognizing the multilevel nature of resource allocation has important implications for other research traditions. Peteraf points out that because decision making occurs at multiple levels, RBV models should include the integrative role of middle management and the initiating role of operating managers in their analysis of competitive advantage. Similarly, Levinthal points out the frequent failure of strategy researchers to consider that many strategic decisions are made deep at the operating levels of the firm and that the role of corporate leadership is often to create the right 'selection context' for decisions, rather than making the decisions directly.

An analysis of the resource allocation process also sheds light on the origins of strategy. This understanding can do much to bridge the gap between the research on strategy content and research on strategy process. Strategies do not develop in a vacuum and are not designed through analysis that is independent of its context and organizational setting. This has led to Mintzberg's critique that strategy research too often ignores the emergent aspects in its emphasis on deliberate design (Mintzberg and Waters 1985). A RAP perspective also opens up opportunities for behavioral studies to have a more general effect on strategy research. We hope an understanding of RAP will expand the growing bridge between these behavioral perspectives and research on strategy by demonstrating how psychology, group decision making, and social networks connect to definition and selection processes across multiple levels of an organization.

Finally, we have always intended the study of resource allocation to be more than a purely academic exercise. An understanding of the resource allocation process should help the thoughtful manager trying to direct strategy in his or her firm. Changing the substance of strategy is not like downloading software to a computer and turning it on. The existing strategy represents a series of resource commitments that have been rationalized by managers at several levels of the company over many years. Those commitments and the forces that led to them are almost certainly still in place. Even if selection processes allow resource commitment patterns to change, the process of definition has proved to be extremely resilient. Asking the following questions can be particularly revealing for a management embarked on a new course: Will the existing structural context allow this change? How will the reporting structure and incentive systems shape the initiative as it develops? What options will I be offered for approval? How will these forces shape the willingness of operating managers to work on a given strategy, day in and day out? Will managers' existing cognitive frames allow for changes in the definition process? How will pressures from existing capital markets and leading customers influence the plans that develop and the willingness to commit time and resources to new initiatives? Providing insight into the structure and functioning of the 'black box' is just as important to managers as it is to academics and explains much of the appeal this work has had with practicing managers.

In conclusion, we hope that thirty-five years of development in resource allocation theory has helped develop useful understanding for a wide range of researchers and managers. We hope that future studies on resource allocation and strategy will use this work and continue to challenge and develop our collective thinking. We hope that our colleagues in other disciplines can use the research to ground their own thinking and that collaboration will continue to develop. Finally, we believe that managers can apply these insights to make their intended strategy a more powerful source of direction in their firm. Ultimately, understanding how the resource allocation process works and how to manage its direction is not only at the heart of firm strategy, but fundamental to the leadership of sustainable and successful firms.

Endnotes

1. The writing of this book began with a series of workshops in the summers of 2000, 2001, and 2002. Many of the ideas presented here were first aired in those sessions. We are grateful to the all of the scholars who participated and provided us feedback, including: Robert Burgelman, Clayton Christensen, Yves Doz, Tom Eisenmann, Charles Galunic, David Garvin, Borsi Groysberg, Dan Levinthal, Ashish Nanda, Quy Nguyen-Huy, Tomo

Noda, Margaret Peteraf, Joel Podolny, Don Sull, Alva Taylor, Mary Tripsas, Michael Raynor, and Michael Roberto.

2. This does not mean that managers are free from the necessity of meeting operating budgets; far from it. But in many companies, strategic resource allocation is recognized as a separate and vital process (Christensen 1997).

3. The use of Podolny's term 'network' is an intentional reference to the ideas laid out in Ch. 19.

4. This is the same phenomenon described by Noda. A commitment to fund the Bakerfield project at Bell South forced a reconsideration of the attractiveness of the business.

References

Christensen, C. M. (1997). *The Innovator's Dilemma: When New Technologies Cause Great Firms to Fail*. Boston, Mass.: Harvard Business School Press.

Cyert, R. M., and March, J. G. (1963). *A Behavioral Theory of the Firm*. New York: Prentice-Hall.

Eisenmann, T. R. (2002). 'The Effects of CEO Equity Ownership and Diversification on Risk Taking'. *Strategic Management Journal* 23: 513–34.

Foster, D., and Kaplan, S. (2001). *Creative Destruction: Why Some Companies that are Built to Last Underperform the Market—and How to Successfully Transform Them*. New York: Currency.

Gilbert, C. G. (2001). 'A Dilemma in Response: Examining the Newspaper Industry's Response to the Internet'. *The Academy of Management Best Paper Proceedings Series*.

Helfat, C., and Peteraf, M. (2003). 'The Dynamic Resource-Based View: Capabilities Lifecycles'. *Strategic Management Journal* 24: 997–1010.

Mintzberg, H., and Waters, J. (1985). 'Of Strategies, Deliberate and Emergent'. *Strategic Management Journal* 6: 257–72.

Schumpeter, J. A. (1934). *The Theory of Economic Development*. Cambridge, Mass.: Harvard University Press.

Tushman, M. L., and O'Reilly, C. (Summer 1996). 'Ambidextrous Organizations: Managing Evolutionary and Revolutionary Change'. *California Management Review* 38/4: 8–30.

Index